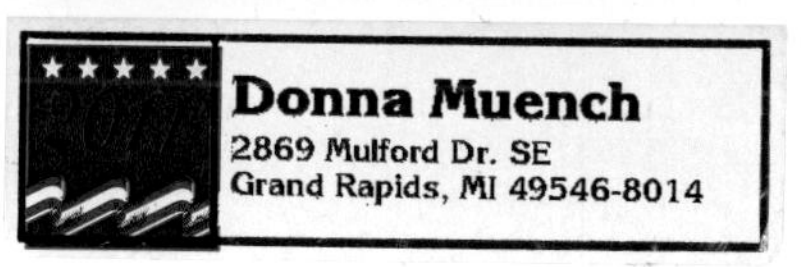

PISSARRO: CREATING THE IMPRESSIONIST LANDSCAPE

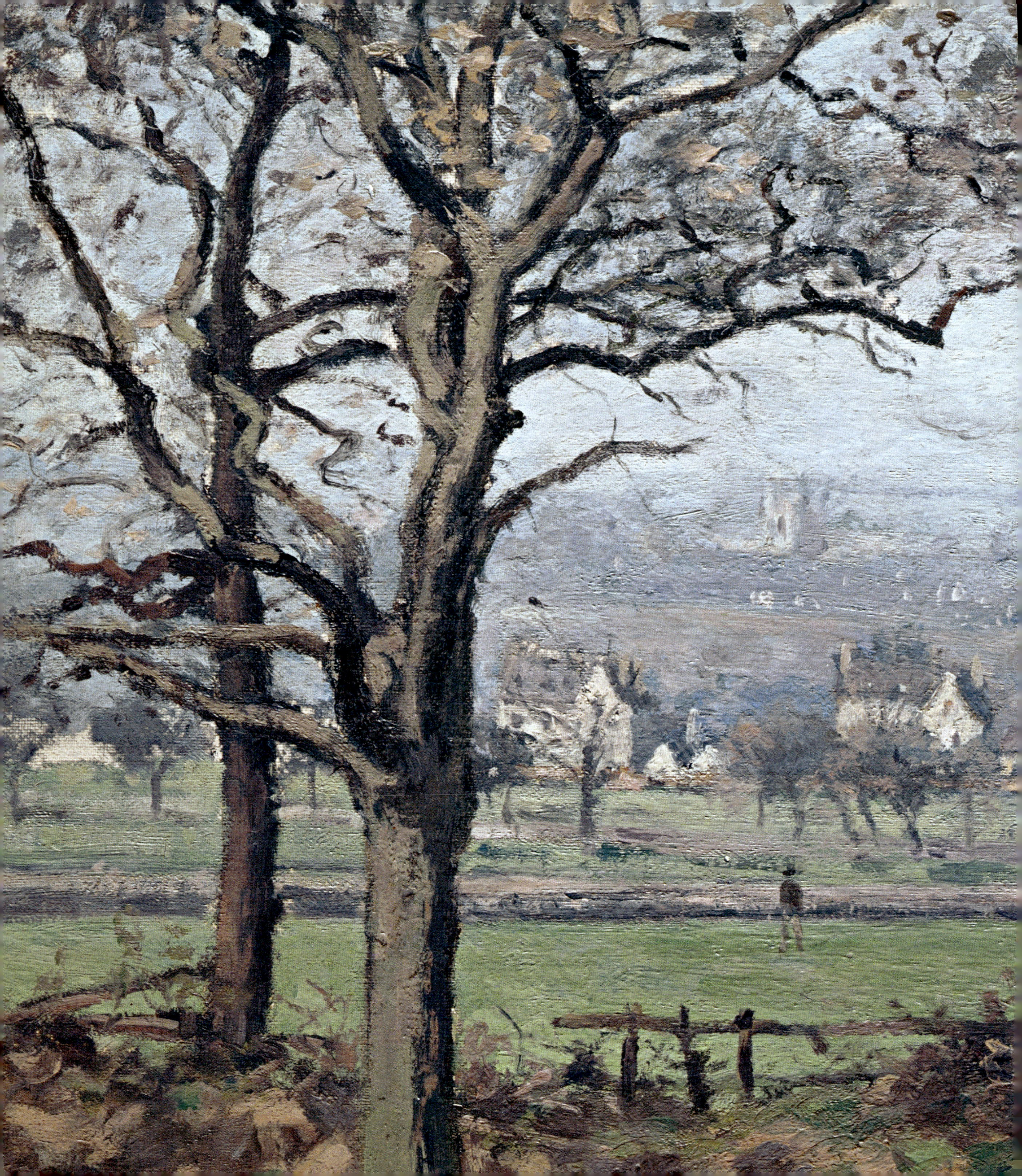

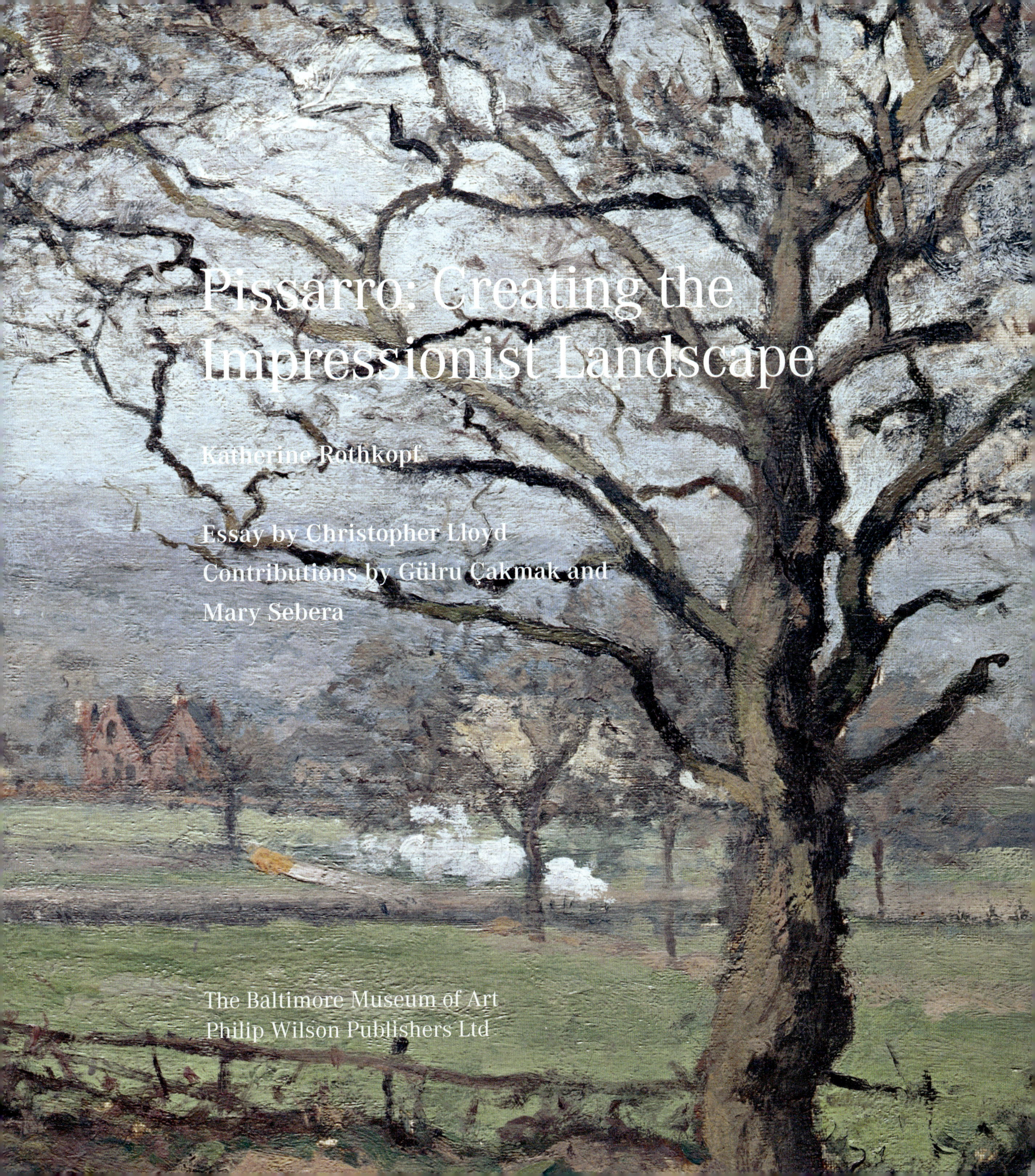

Pissarro: Creating the Impressionist Landscape

Katherine Rothkopf

Essay by Christopher Lloyd
Contributions by Gülru Çakmak and
Mary Sebera

The Baltimore Museum of Art
Philip Wilson Publishers Ltd

This volume has been published in conjunction with the exhibition *Pissarro: Creating the Impressionist Landscape*, organized by The Baltimore Museum of Art, Baltimore, Maryland, and held at:

The Baltimore Museum of Art
February 11, 2007–May 13, 2007

Milwaukee Art Museum
June 10, 2007–September 9, 2007

Memphis Brooks Museum of Art
October 7, 2007–January 6, 2008

The exhibition is generously supported by the Florence Gould Foundation and The Alvin and Fanny Blaustein Thalheimer Exhibition Endowment Fund.

Citigroup is the corporate sponsor of the exhibition.

Additional support for the exhibition catalogue is provided by the Andrew W. Mellon Foundation Publication Endowment Fund.

The exhibition is supported by an indemnity from the Federal Council on the Arts and the Humanities.

Published by Philip Wilson Publishers Ltd, 109 The Timber Yard,
7-27 Drysdale Street, London N1 6ND
Second printing

Library of Congress Control Number: 2006928933

ISBN (softcover edition) 0-85667-632-2
EAN 978-0-8566-7832-1
ISBN (hardcover edition) 0-85667-630-6
EAN 978-0-566-7630-7

Designed by Anikst Design Ltd
Printed in Italy by Printer Trento

Distributed in the United States and Canada by Palgrave Macmillan, 175 Fifth Avenue, New York, NY 10010

Distributed in the UK and the rest of the world by I. B. Tauris & Co. Ltd, 6 Salem Road, London W2 4BU

Front cover: Camille Pissarro, *Strollers on a Country Road, La Varenne-Saint-Hilaire*, detail (cat. 3)

Back cover: Camille Pissarro, *Landscape, Bright Sunlight, Pontoise*, detail (cat. 48)

Title page: Camille Pissarro, *View of Alleyn Park, West Dulwich*, detail (cat. 23)

Catalogue section: Camille Pissarro, *Banks of the Oise at Saint-Ouen-l'Aumône*, detail (cat. 8)

The Salon Years, 1864–1868: Camille Pissarro, *Côte des Jalais, Pontoise*, detail (cat. 10)

Louveciennes and the First Forays into Impressionism, 1869–1870: Camille Pissarro, *The Corner of the Route de Versailles and the Chemin de l'Aqueduc, Louveciennes*, detail (cat. 12)

London, 1870–1871: Camille Pissarro, *South Norwood, Study*, detail (cat. 22)
Camille Pissarro, *Lordship Lane Station, East Dulwich*, detail (cat. 21)

Return to Louveciennes, 1871–1872: Camille Pissarro, *Banks of the Seine at Bougival*, detail (cat. 26)

Return to Pontoise and the First Impressionist Exhibition, 1872–1874: Camille Pissarro, *Factory on the Banks of the Oise, Saint-Ouen-l'Aumône*, detail (cat. 37)

Appendixes: Camille Pissarro, *Banks of the Marne in Winter*, detail (cat. 5)

Contents

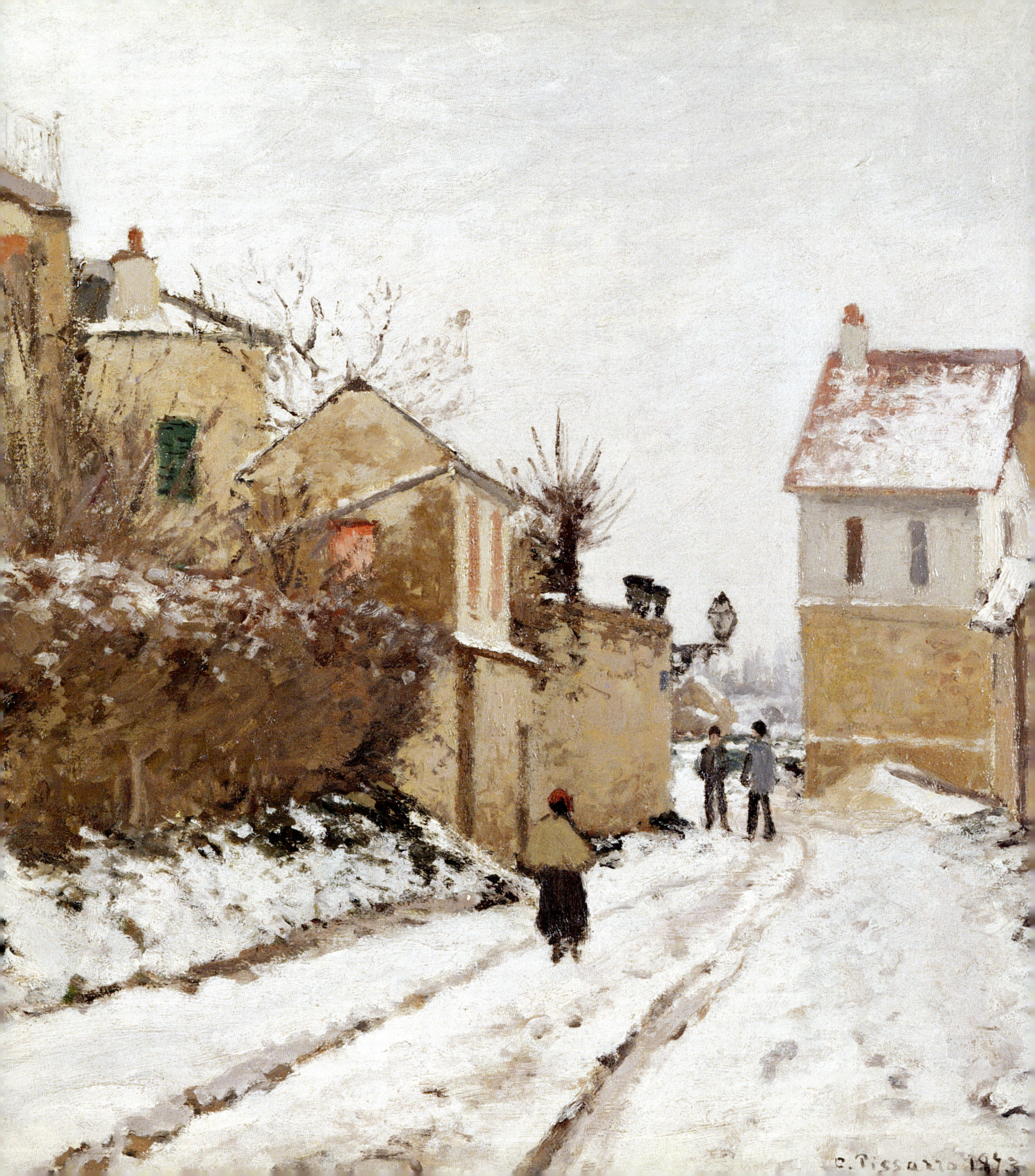
C. Pissarro

Foreword

Pissarro: Creating the Impressionist Landscape is the first exhibition to focus on the early landscape paintings by this leader of the Impressionist movement. A remarkable transformation takes place in Camille Pissarro's work during the intense decade of 1864–1874 that culminates with the first Impressionist exhibition, when he broke free of the French landscape tradition and produced his own modern and compelling views of the world around him.

This exhibition reflects the artistic focus of The Baltimore Museum of Art—the modern era—from the nineteenth century to the present day. It also underscores the BMA's strong representation of nineteenth-century French art in the collection of George A. Lucas (1824–1909), a Baltimore expatriate whose holdings are among the most comprehensive of this material in America. In 1996 the Lucas Collection of twenty thousand objects was acquired by the BMA, where it had been on loan for more than sixty years, with five additional pieces entering the collection of the Walters Art Museum.

Two of Pissarro's early works from the Lucas Collection—*Strollers on a Country Road, La Varenne-Saint-Hilaire*, now in the BMA's collection, and *The Corner of the Route de Versailles and the Chemin de l'Aqueduc, Louveciennes*, now at the Walters Art Museum—were purchased by Lucas in Paris soon after they were painted. Both have been on view in Baltimore for the last seventy years, yet when the first complete catalogue of Pissarro's oeuvre was published in Paris in 1939, neither painting was included, as they were apparently unknown by the authors. Happily, these two marvelous pictures are featured not only in the current exhibition but also in the new catalogue raisonné recently published by The Wildenstein Institute in Paris. This scholarly endeavor, which adds more than two hundred paintings, some previously unknown, to Pissarro's life's work, has greatly expanded our understanding of the artist. *Pissarro: Creating the Impressionist Landscape* will display some of the Institute's fresh discoveries from this period in his career, in which Pissarro produced many of his most beautiful and innovative canvases.

BMA Curator of European Painting and Sculpture, Katherine Rothkopf—the scholar who conceived this show—was intrigued by the BMA's *Strollers on a Country Road, La Varenne-Saint-Hilaire* when she arrived here seven years ago. She had already written about the artist and his Impressionist colleagues but, like others, was less familiar with the formative period that immediately preceded Pissarro's breakthrough as one of the founders of Impressionism. Ms. Rothkopf soon uncovered other examples from this phase of the artist's career, many of which have not been seen together for decades. Her thoughtful survey of his early career—the result of her original research and perceptive connoisseurship—reveals that the artist was producing experimental compositions much earlier than previously assumed and establishes him as one of the most innovative of the Impressionist painters. Her dedication to all matters large and small has made this carefully conceived exhibition a reality.

Camille Pissarro,
Rue de la Citadelle, Pontoise, detail
(cat. 34)

We are also indebted to Christopher Lloyd, former Surveyor of The Queen's Pictures in Great Britain, who, over the past twenty-five years, has explored Pissarro's extraordinary career. Mr. Lloyd advised Ms. Rothkopf on the contents of the exhibition and also contributed a fascinating essay on how the artist's sense of place affected his style and choice of subject. Mary Sebera, The Stockman Family Foundation Senior Conservator of Paintings at the BMA, has undertaken a technical study of Pissarro's approach to painting in the 1860s; her examination of X-rays of four early paintings provides new insights concerning the artist's working methods. Finally, Gülru Çakmak, doctoral candidate in the Department of Art History and the Humanities Center at The Johns Hopkins University and recipient of the BMA/JHU Curatorial Fellowship, contributed many insightful catalogue entries.

At the BMA, as exhibitions move from idea to actuality, they become a highly collaborative effort. I would like to thank all those who made this particular exhibition the experience we will share in the galleries: dedicated educators who advocate for our audience; design and installation staff, whose imaginative minds always find a unique way to present each exhibition; and the unseen efforts of literally dozens of BMA staffers—those who raise the funds that support Museum programs, those who promote and market the exhibition, those who pack, ship, and preserve the art, and, of course, those who protect the artworks every day.

We also express gratitude to those who have so generously offered financial support for this exhibition and publication: the Florence Gould Foundation; The Alvin and Fanny Blaustein Thalheimer Exhibition Endowment Fund; and the corporate sponsor of the exhibition, Citigroup. Additional support for the exhibition catalogue is provided by the Andrew W. Mellon Foundation Publication Endowment Fund. The exhibition is supported by an indemnity from the Federal Council on the Arts and the Humanities.

We are delighted that *Pissarro: Creating the Impressionist Landscape* will reach a national audience through its presentation at the Milwaukee Art Museum and the Memphis Brooks Museum of Art and thank the distinguished colleagues at these institutions as partners in our undertaking.

Finally, the experience of an exhibition requires the assembly of a critical group of artworks to tell a story, and, of course, that means that these treasures are missed in other institutions and sometimes in homes. To each of the lenders to this exhibition, we offer our profound thanks for their willingness to relinquish these magnificent pictures for a tour that will acquaint our audiences with a new view of Camille Pissarro.

Doreen Bolger, Director
The Baltimore Museum of Art

Lenders to the Exhibition

The Art Institute of Chicago
The Baltimore Museum of Art
Kunsthalle Bremen–Der Kunstverein in Bremen, Germany
Carnegie Museum of Art, Pittsburgh
The Sterling and Francine Clark Art Institute, Williamstown, Massachusetts
Courtauld Institute of Art Gallery, London
Ruth and Bruce Dayton
Denver Art Museum
Ann and Gordon Getty
The J. Paul Getty Museum, Los Angeles
High Museum of Art, Atlanta
Indianapolis Museum of Art
Ipswich Borough Council Museums and Galleries, England
The Israel Museum, Jerusalem
Kimbell Art Museum, Fort Worth
Manchester City Galleries, England
Jacqueline J. McMullen
Memphis Brooks Museum of Art, Tennessee
The Metropolitan Museum of Art, New York
Dr. and Mrs. Morton Mower
Musée d'Orsay, Paris
Museum of Fine Arts, Boston
Museum of Fine Arts, Springfield, Massachusetts
The National Gallery of Scotland, Edinburgh
The National Gallery, London
The National Museum of Fine Arts, Stockholm
National Gallery of Art, Washington, D.C.
Noortman Master Paintings, Maastricht, the Netherlands
Private collections
Portland Art Museum, Oregon
Staatsgalerie Stuttgart, Germany
Szépmüvészeti Múzeum, Budapest, Hungary
Tel Aviv Museum of Art, Israel
Wadsworth Atheneum Museum of Art, Hartford, Connecticut
The Walters Art Museum, Baltimore

Acknowledgments

Exhibitions such as this are the result of the generosity and assistance of many individuals. BMA Director Doreen Bolger immediately embraced the idea for an in-depth study of the early landscapes of Camille Pissarro and has been a tremendous support. Jay Fisher, BMA Deputy Director for Curatorial Affairs and Senior Curator of Prints, Drawings, and Photographs, and Sona Johnston, BMA Senior Curator of Painting and Sculpture, were unflaggingly enthusiastic about this exhibition from its inception and provided critical guidance and help with loans and the overall concept.

Christopher Lloyd, one of the world's leading authorities on Pissarro and organizer of the artist's seminal retrospective in 1980–81, contributed an enlightening essay on the places where Pissarro painted in his early years and their effect on his compositions. He cheerfully shared his vast wealth of knowledge of the artist and his work, and I am grateful for his many suggestions and insights. Mary Sebera, The Stockman Family Foundation Senior Conservator of Paintings at the BMA, eagerly investigated Pissarro's painting technique during this formative period, revealing new information about his creative process. Gülru Çakmak, graduate student in the Department of Art History and the Humanities Center at The Johns Hopkins University, drafted loan letters, ably researched and wrote thoughtful catalogue entries, and compiled a chronology for the catalogue.

During the last six years, countless individuals have offered invaluable assistance, generously sharing their knowledge of various aspects of Pissarro's life and art. Claire Durand-Ruel Snollaerts and Joachim Pissarro were very helpful in locating works in private collections as well as allowing me a preview of the lesser-known early paintings they discovered in their research for their fascinating new catalogue raisonné of Pissarro's paintings. In addition, we would like to thank our colleagues for all of their assistance, including Richard Armstrong, Lázló Baán, Violette Boulet, Philippe Brame, Sylvie Brame, Michael Brand, David Brenneman, Richard Brettell, John Buchanan, Caroline Campbell, Michael Clarke, Michael Conforti, Philip Conisbee, Christofer Conrad, Desmond Corcoran, James Cuno, Linda Drasheff, Terry Drayman-Weisser, Douglas Druick, Sally Dummer, Christophe Duvivier, Jeremiah Evarts, Peter Fairbanks, Walter Feilchenfeldt, Kaywin Feldman, Jeanette Gerritsma, Helyn Goldenberg, David Gordon, Eric Gordon, William Griswold, Gloria Groom, Torsten Gunnarsson, Dorothee Hansen, Heather Haskell, Deborah Hatch, Wulf Herzogenrath, Willard Holmes, Christian von Holst, Ahuva Israel, David Jaffé, Eik Kahng, Adina Kamien-Kazhdan, Ellen Lee, Serge Lemoine, Katja Lewerentz, Louise Lippincott, Nicholas Maclean, Daniel Malingue, Terence Maloon, Caroline Mathieu, Charles S. Moffett, Philippe de Montebello, Larry O'Connor, Mordechai Omer, Marini Pacini, Timothy Potts, Earl A. Powell, Rebecca Rabinow, Richard Rand, Chris Riopelle, Malcolm Rogers, Carolina V. Saint-George, Iris Schaefer, Scott Schaefer, Jon Seydl, George T. M.

Shackelford, Michael Shapiro, Lewis Sharp, Julie Simek, Charles Robert Saumarez Smith, James Snyder, Solfrid Söderlind, Timothy Standring, Matthew Stephenson, David Stern, Vivian Tandy, Stanton Thomas, Gary Tinterow, Jia-sun Tsang, Gary Vikan, Alice Whelihan, Laurie Winters, Aaron Young, Eric Zafran, and Frank Zuccari.

I am particularly grateful to Philip Wilson, Managing Director; Cangy Venables, Managing Editor; and Norman Turpin, Production Manager of Philip Wilson Publishers Ltd, London; and Misha Anikst of Anikst Design Ltd, London, for their efforts in producing such a handsome publication. I would also like to thank Fronia W. Simpson for her thoughtful and thorough editing of the manuscript.

As always, the staff of The Baltimore Museum of Art provided invaluable assistance in all aspects of this endeavor, including fund-raising, applying for federal indemnification, negotiating loans and shipping, overseeing conservation reports, handling the works, paying the invoices, planning the installation, organizing special educational programs, and preparing for and serving visitors. Melanie Harwood, Senior Registrar, dealt with the often-complicated negotiations concerning loans and transport of works of art with skill and good humor. Judy Gibbs, Deputy Director for Development, and her staff adeptly applied for grants and funding for this project. Becca Seitz, Deputy Director for Marketing and Communication, and her staff have promoted the exhibition in a thoughtful and enthusiastic way. Allison Perkins, former Deputy Director for Education and Interpretation, and her staff have produced a fascinating schedule of programs and have produced intelligent text and interpretative materials that will be much appreciated by our visitors. Michelle Boardman, Director of Creative Services, ably assisted by Chelsey Moore, skillfully oversaw the production of the exhibition catalogue. Karen Nielsen, Director, Exhibition Design and Installation, provided an inspired and elegant setting in which to display the works of art. Laura Albans, Administrative Assistant for the Department of European Painting and Sculpture, enthusiastically assisted in every phase of this exhibition and publication.

Without generous and supportive lenders, public and private, no exhibition is possible. I am grateful to all who have generously agreed to lend paintings to this project. Of course, major support is essential to such a complex and costly enterprise. The Baltimore Museum of Art is immensely grateful to the Florence Gould Foundation; The Alvin and Fanny Blaustein Thalheimer Exhibition Endowment Fund; the corporate sponsor, Citigroup; the Andrew W. Mellon Foundation Publication Endowment Fund; and the Federal Council on the Arts and the Humanities. I am deeply appreciative of their great generosity.

Katherine Rothkopf, Curator of European Painting and Sculpture
The Baltimore Museum of Art

Introduction

If Camille Pissarro had gone on painting as he was doing in 1870, he would have outclassed us all.
—Paul Cézanne[1]

A little-known and unusual work in the collection of The Baltimore Museum of Art, Camille Pissarro's *Strollers on a Country Road, La Varenne-Saint-Hilaire* (cat. 3), was the impetus for this examination of the artist's early landscapes. This small, powerful painting was made in 1864 when the artist was still creating large-scale works for the annual Salons, a period in his career that has not been fully examined. *Strollers on a Country Road* was not included in Ludovic Pissarro and Lionello Venturi's 1939 catalogue raisonné of the artist's work, nor has it been seen in any of the recent monographic exhibitions devoted to the artist. Understanding the context for this intriguing work, which combines Barbizon-type subject matter with a rigorous painting style, has fascinated me for more than six years.

Pissarro: Creating the Impressionist Landscape attempts to redress the imbalance of recent attention to the careers of the Impressionists. Whereas aspects of the oeuvres of Claude Monet and Edgar Degas have been the focus of exhibitions over the last fifteen years, several essential periods in Pissarro's oeuvre have not been fully explored, particularly his early work. What began as a focused exploration of Pissarro's paintings from the mid-1860s expanded to a broader survey of the artist's landscapes to 1874, an intense decade in which Pissarro's technique and style changed dramatically and he produced some of his most compelling works. This project is the first to assess his early landscapes as a group, revealing that he was painting innovative works earlier than previously thought. This exhibition and its accompanying catalogue carefully examine a select group of paintings in which one can trace Pissarro's gradual evolution from Barbizon-influenced style toward modernism, the period in his career when he was most experimental. Many of the paintings considered here have rarely been seen together, and several have seldom been on public view.

Our knowledge of Pissarro's early work has one caveat. An unknown number of his canvases were destroyed during the Franco-Prussian War of 1870–71, when the German army occupied the artist's home in Louveciennes and, according to Pissarro, ruined many of his paintings. Although he claimed to have lost almost fifteen hundred canvases, it is generally thought that the number destroyed was far smaller.[2] The Wildenstein Institute in Paris has recently published a catalogue raisonné that updates the 1939 edition, in which more than two hundred paintings have been added to Pissarro's life's work, including more than fifty compositions from the period of 1864 to 1874.[3]

Traditionally, scholars of Pissarro's career have neglected his production from the mid-1860s to focus on paintings from his Impressionist period and later. This may be due in part to the public's fascination with Impressionism, particularly the works from the mid-to-late 1870s. The seminal retrospective of Pissarro's work organized by the Arts Council of Great Britain in 1980, which traveled to London, Paris, and Boston, reassessed the artist as an important member of the Impressionist group. Subsequent monographic shows, including those in New York and Jerusalem (1994–95), Stuttgart (1999–2000), and Australia (2005–6), have further reconsidered the artist's substantial oeuvre, introducing him to a new public.[4] His work produced in Pontoise was brilliantly discussed in Richard R. Brettell's *Pissarro and Pontoise* (1990),[5] a publication that documents the artist's changing style and subjects in the town with which he is most closely associated in the earlier part of his life. Joachim Pissarro's monograph of 1993 rejected the theory that the artist was a mere follower of his colleagues Monet and Pierre-Auguste Renoir and instead was one of the main innovators in both technique and choice of subject matter.[6] More recently, Pissarro's close relationship with Paul Cézanne was carefully examined in the exhibition *Pioneering Modern Painting: Cézanne and Pissarro, 1865–1885*.[7] Pissarro's early career, along with examinations of more than thirty other artists of the period, was investigated in the large and impressive exhibition *Origins of Impressionism* (1994–95).[8] This was one of the first shows to propose that Pissarro and his colleagues, such as Monet, Alfred Sisley, and Degas, were artists who looked to the French Salon for official recognition and acceptance before deciding to revolt against authority and create their own exhibition system. Our exhibition continues that research more fully, by linking a wider selection of Pissarro's Salon-era paintings with his early forays into Impressionism, and provides a deep and focused look at the artist as he gradually evolved from being a Realist into an Impressionist.

Note: The new catalogue raisonné has retitled many of Pissarro's paintings. In cases where the new title differs markedly from the old one, the historic title has been included in italics on the second line of the catalogue entry for works in this exhibition.

1. John Rewald cites this comment, made to the artist Louis le Bail, in *Cézanne, sa vie, son amitié pour Zola* (Paris: Albin Michel, 1939), 283, translated in Christopher Lloyd, "'Paul Cézanne, Pupil of Pissarro': An Artistic Friendship," *Apollo* 136 (November 1992): 284.

2. In an undated letter to Théodore Duret from London, Pissarro claims that only forty canvases of fifteen hundred that were stored in his home had survived the war. See *Correspondance de Camille Pissarro*, ed. Janine Bailly-Herzberg, 5 vols. (Paris: Presses Universitaires de France, 1980–91), 1:63–65.

3. Joachim Pissarro and Claire Durand-Ruel Snollaerts, *Pissarro: Critical Catalogue of Paintings*, 3 vols. (Paris: Wildenstein Institute Publications, 2005). Cited hereafter as PD-RS.

4. *Camille Pissarro: Impressionist Innovator* (Jerusalem: The Israel Museum, 1994); *Camille Pissarro* (Stuttgart: Staatsgalerie Stuttgart, 1999); and *Camille Pissarro* (Sydney: Art Gallery of New South Wales, 2005).

5. Richard R. Brettell, *Pissarro and Pontoise: The Painter in a Landscape* (New Haven: Yale University Press, 1990).

6. Joachim Pissarro, *Camille Pissarro* (New York: Harry N. Abrams, 1993).

7. Joachim Pissarro, *Pioneering Modern Painting: Cézanne and Pissarro, 1865–1885* (New York: The Museum of Modern Art, 2005).

8. Gary Tinterow and Henri Loyrette, *Origins of Impressionism* (New York: The Metropolitan Museum of Art, 1994).

This map illustrates the region around Paris where Pissarro spent most of his time between 1864 and 1874. Many of the works included in this exhibition have been identified as depicting specific towns, and some of those are illustrated here.

Chennevières

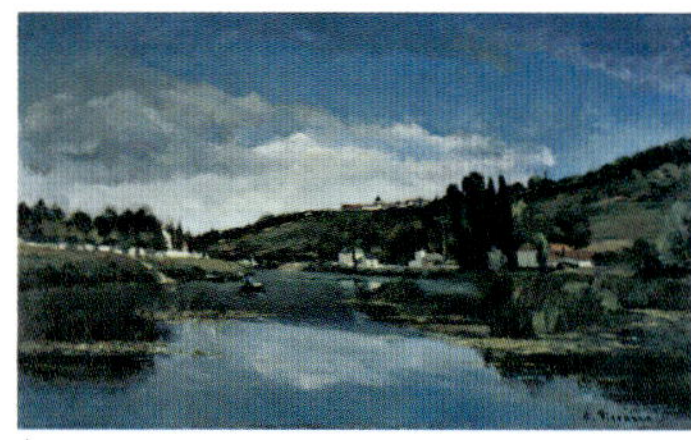
4

La Varenne-Saint-Hilaire

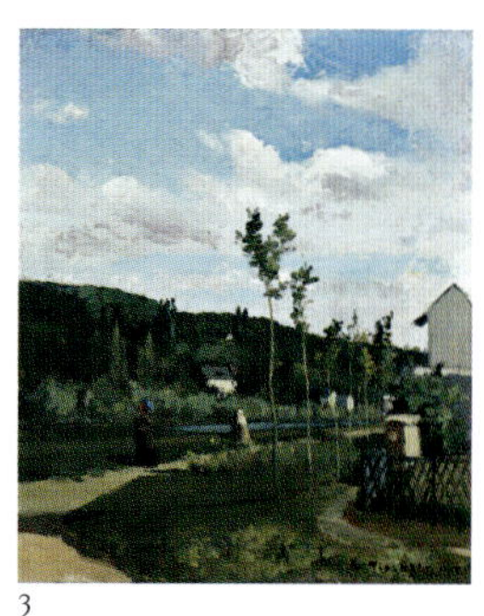
3

Bougival

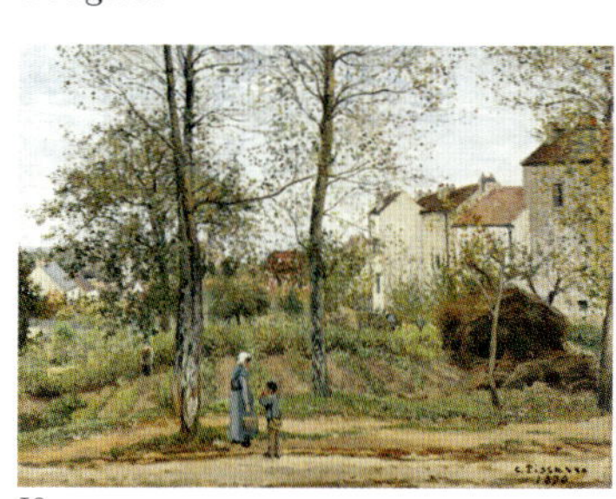
19

Louveciennes

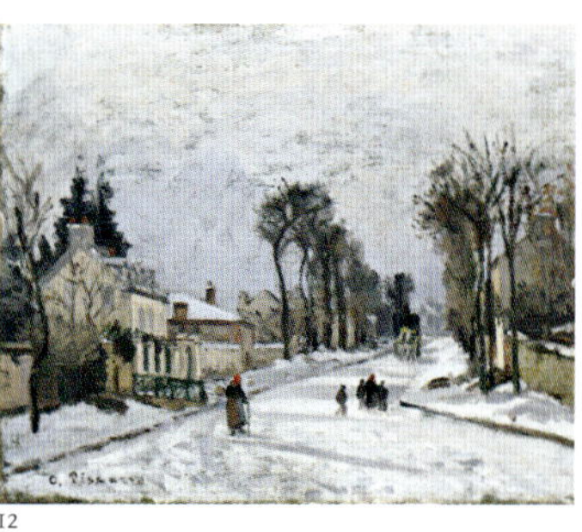
12

Marly-le-Roi

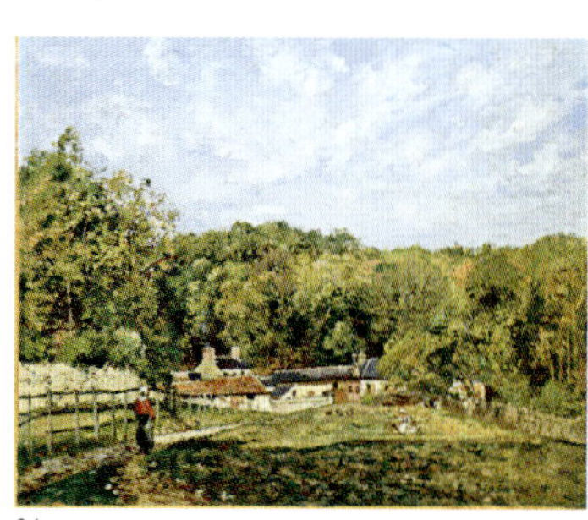
24

Pontoise

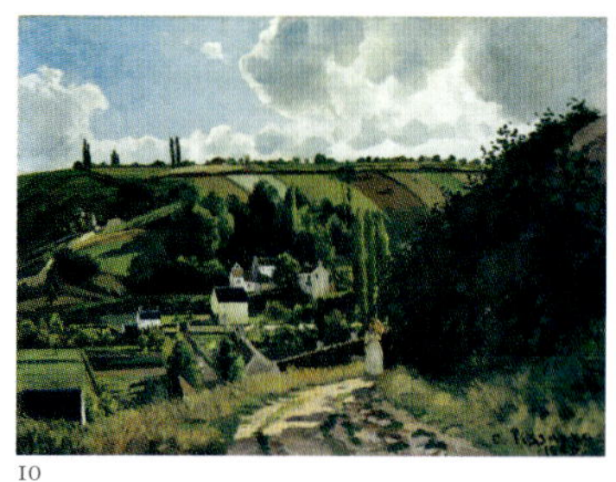
10

Ennery

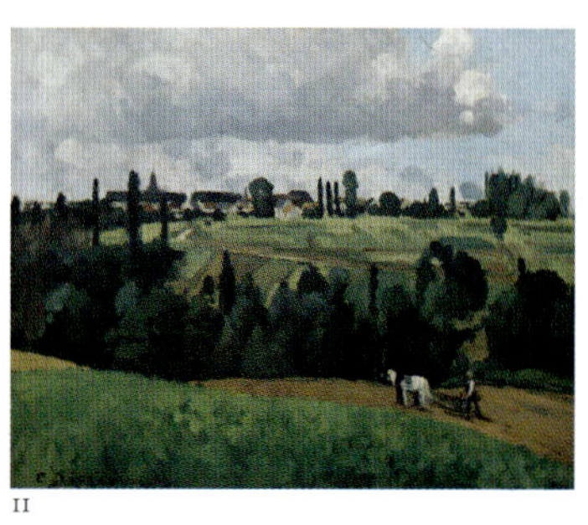
11

Saint-Ouen-l'Aumône

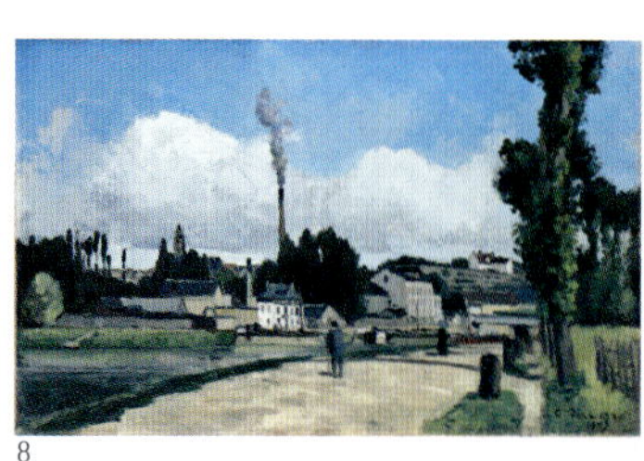
8

Osny

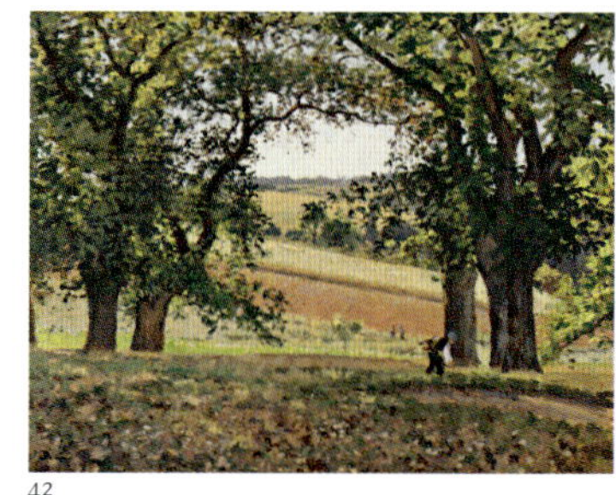
42

French locales where Pissarro painted 1864–1874

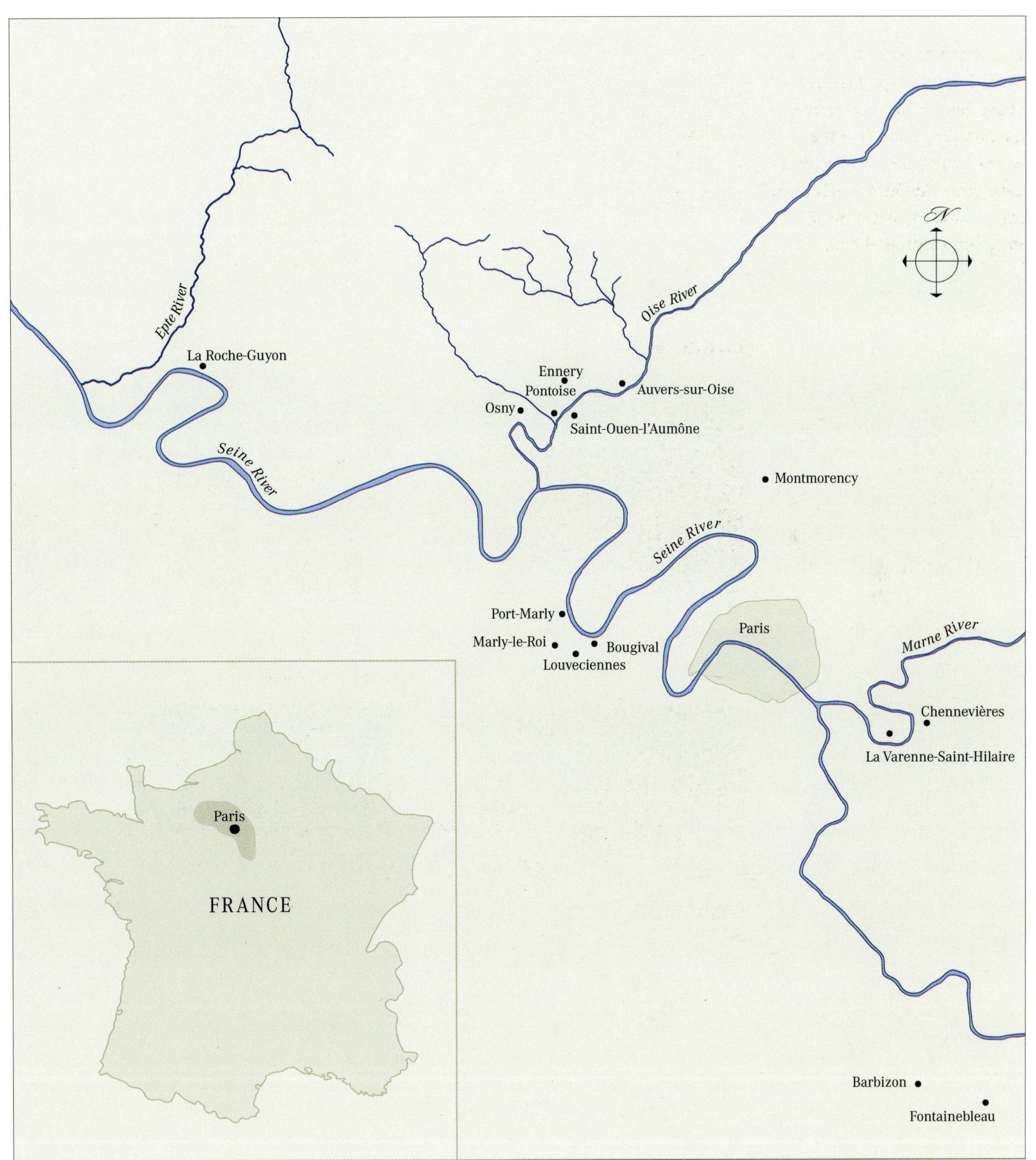

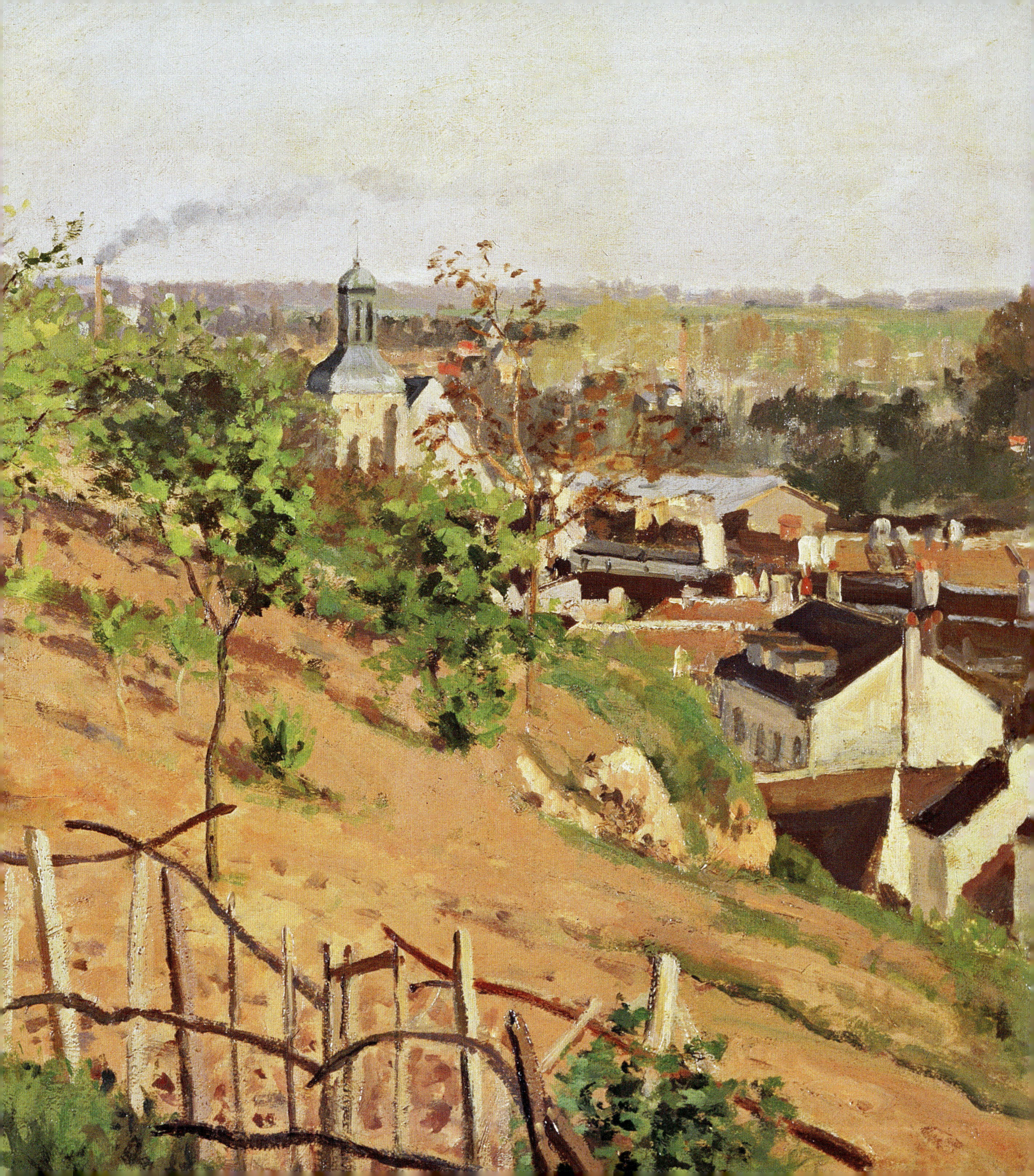

Camille Pissarro and the Essence of Place

Christopher Lloyd

The close association of Camille Pissarro with Impressionist and Post-Impressionist art in France during the second half of the nineteenth century is so well known that it comes as a surprise to realize that he was actually born in the Caribbean on the island of St. Thomas, which now forms part of the Virgin Islands. Pissarro is not an artist who deliberately sought out the exotic at any time during his career, but it would be wrong to ignore the effects that the early years spent so far from France, at such a receptive stage of his life, might have had on his outlook as an artist. Most of all, it brings into question his identity. In the final analysis he came to regard himself as a Frenchman, but at the same time he was somewhat of an outsider with a separate outlook from that of his fellow Impressionist and Post-Impressionist artists.

Although firmly committed to new developments in painting and in many ways pioneering them himself, Pissarro seemed to stand apart, as though preferring to monitor progress from a distance. His reputation for being a moving force—almost literally a father figure—in both Impressionist and Post-Impressionist circles was widely acknowledged, and he was the only artist to exhibit in all eight of the Impressionist exhibitions. Yet, paradoxically, there is a sense of aloofness about the man and his work that can be linked to the degree of objectivity that contemporaries detected in his style and treatment of subject matter, as well as in his politics. Symptomatic of this characteristic is perhaps the placement of Pissarro in the group portrait by Pierre-Auguste Renoir, *The Artist's Studio, rue Saint Georges* (fig. 1). Here he is positioned on the right in the middle distance, half-hidden by another figure. His domed forehead and white beard—an appearance that caused him often to be described in biblical terms—are easily recognizable.

Pissarro's remove from the group of influential artists and writers with whom he was affiliated arguably had its roots in the philosophical anarchism that underpinned his political beliefs. For Pissarro, the basis of a just and fair society was the right to individual thought and independent action. This belief, which he applied to his art as much as to life in general, became increasingly important as he grew older, but it was inherent from the start. It can be seen in his treatment of subject matter with its pronounced emphasis throughout his career on landscape and rural, peasant themes, as well as his calculated decision to live close to Paris although well beyond the city boundaries and its suburbs. Typical of Pissarro is the conscious effort to remain in touch with the capital while also eschewing it, so that from the late 1860s onward his paintings demonstrate a careful balancing of what the more distant areas of the Île-de-France and then of Normandy had to offer in contrast with such large cities as Paris and Rouen.

An explanation for this sense of detachment possibly lies in Pissarro's birth on the other side of the Atlantic Ocean and in the fact that his initial undertakings as an artist took place

Camille Pissarro, *Ruelle des Poulies at Pontoise*, detail (cat. 30)

in the Virgin Islands and in South America. Only after he arrived in France for good in 1855, aged twenty-five, did he become totally absorbed in his adopted country even though he would always regard it at one remove. From the start, then, geography was a determining factor in Pissarro's art, for the physical dislocation he experienced early in life only intensified the sense of place he experienced when he came to paint the French landscape.

The Pissarro family was originally Portuguese-Jewish but had established itself in commerce in France during the mid-eighteenth century. Pissarro's father, Frédéric, was born in Bordeaux and went to St. Thomas to act as executor and to look after the business affairs of an uncle, Isaac Petit, who had died in 1824. While living at Charlotte Amalie, the principal port of St. Thomas, he married his uncle's wife, Rachel Manzana-Pomié, who had been born on St. Thomas. The liaison caused considerable comment on religious grounds and was much debated by the Jewish elders. The marriage was only officially recognized in 1833. Camille Pissarro, the third son of Frédéric and Rachel, was born on July 10, 1830.[1]

The island of St. Thomas (fig. 2) was discovered by Christopher Columbus in 1493 on his second voyage to the New World. Owing to the turbulent history of the West Indies, the island was settled at different times by the British, Dutch, Spanish, and Danish, who ultimately ceded it to the United States of America in 1917. When Pissarro was born, the

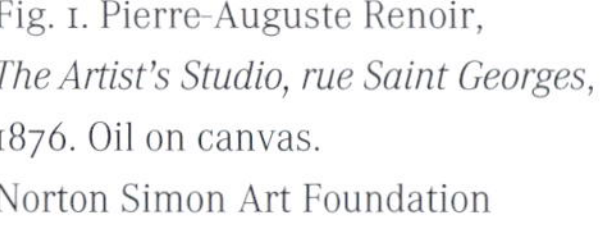
Fig. 1. Pierre-Auguste Renoir, *The Artist's Studio, rue Saint Georges*, 1876. Oil on canvas. Norton Simon Art Foundation

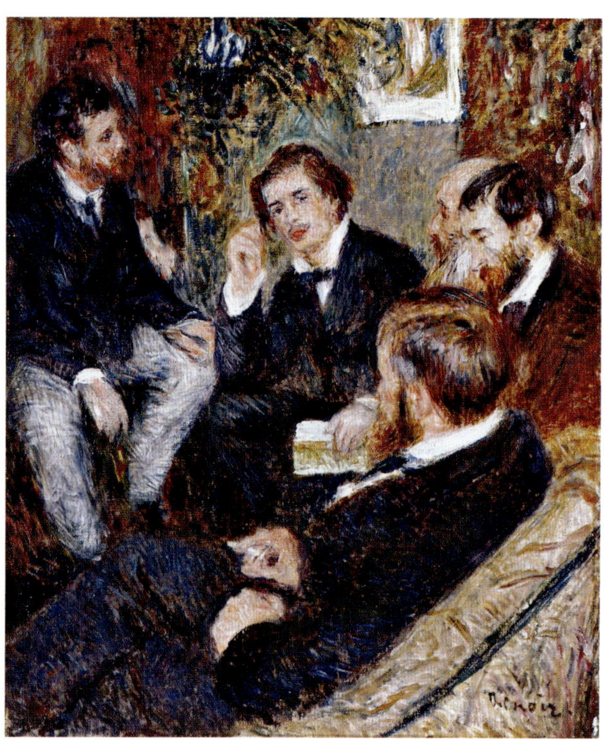

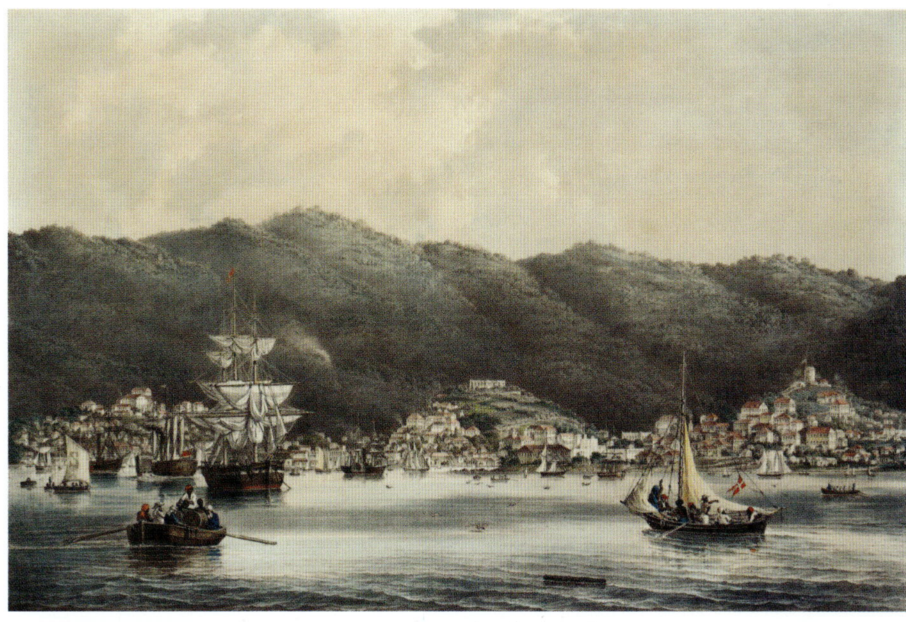

Fig. 2. Tegner and Killendorf, after Fritz Melbye, *St. Thomas*, 1851. Lithograph. The Mariner's Museum, Newport News, Virginia

island was a Danish possession and he was therefore technically a Danish citizen. (He never applied for French citizenship.) St. Thomas owed its significance to its geographical location and its economic prosperity to trade. It offered a sheltered harbor and was essentially an entrepôt for goods of all kinds. Although the island was only thirteen miles long, it supported a population of between thirteen and fourteen thousand, most of whom lived in Charlotte Amalie. An official report written for the Colonial Institute in London and published in 1889 records, "Between 1850 and 1873 the demand for goods of every kind was very great for distribution . . . and fortunes were rapidly realised. Charlotte Amalie became one of the busiest towns in the Western Tropics, and in providing amusement and spending money not at all the most backward."[2] Frédéric Pissarro's time on the island coincided with this last boom in its financial fortunes, before advances in marine technology and modern communications led to its decline. Only in recent years has the tourist industry brought money again to the island.

St. Thomas, however, was by no means an idyllic place. One of the most vivid descriptions of its delights and drawbacks is provided by the British novelist Anthony Trollope. "Let it be understood by all men," he wrote, "that in those latitudes the respectable, comfortable, well-to-do route from every place to every other place is via the little Danish island of St. Thomas." He describes the island as an emporium for "cigars, light dresses, brandy, boots and Eau-de-Cologne."[3] The setting, according to Trollope, is memorable.

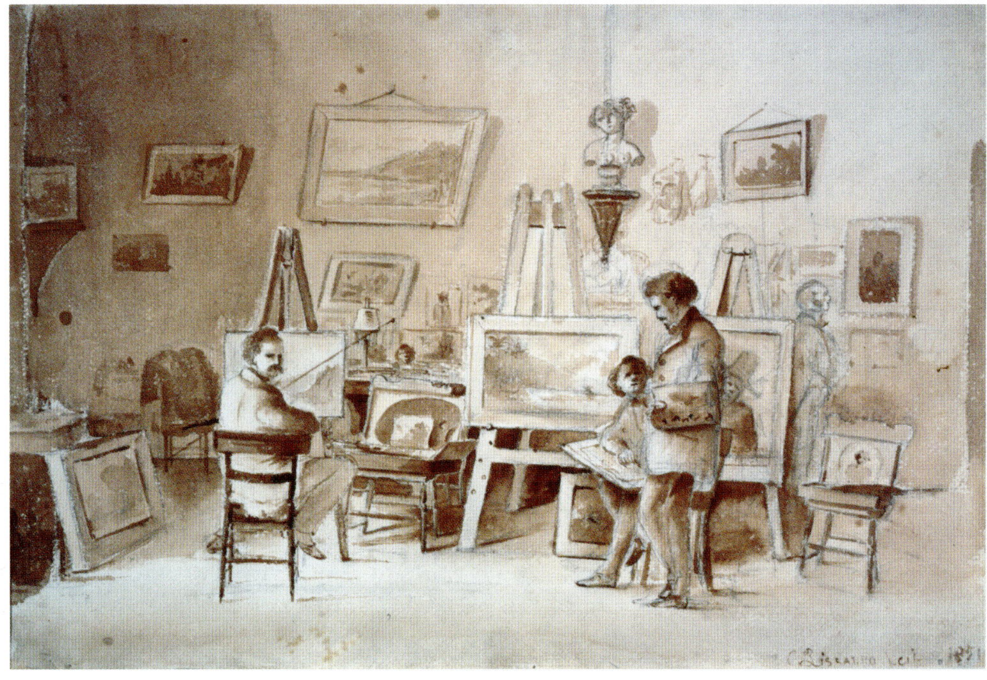

Fig. 3. Camille Pissarro, *The Artist's Studio in Caracas,* 1851. Brown wash over graphite. Collection of Banco Central de Venezuela

> Seen from the water St. Thomas is very pretty! It is not so much the scenery of the island that pleases as the aspects of the town [Charlotte Amalie] itself. It stands on three hills or mounts, with higher hills, green to their summit, rising behind them. Each mount is topped by a pleasant, cleanly edifice, and pretty-looking houses stretch down the sides to the water's edge. The buildings do look pretty and nice, and as though chance had arranged them for a picture. Indeed, as seen from the harbour, the town looks like a panorama exquisitely painted. The air is thin and transparent, and every line shows itself clearly.[4]

This description makes St. Thomas sound like Prospero's Isle in *The Tempest* by William Shakespeare, but Trollope spoils the effect by declaring that on landing all this beauty suddenly vanishes. The harbor of Charlotte Amalie was landlocked, and the stagnant water was distinctly malodorous, quite apart from being a breeding ground for mosquitoes. The terrain itself was barren, there was a shortage of drinking water, and the facilities on land were negligible. Most people only passed through, and many of those were of dubious character. Places of amusement were few and there was no proper school. A library and reading room in the Athenaeum founded in 1839 was reported to be well stocked with journals, periodicals, and newspapers from Europe and the United States. But, generally speaking, cultural opportunities and distractions were severely limited.

Pissarro's first efforts as an artist date from his time on St. Thomas. Although sent away to school in Passy, then on the outskirts of Paris, from 1842 to 1847, Pissarro began to develop his personal artistic credo independently in the environment of St. Thomas.[5] Scenes of local life—peasants at work in the fields, washerwomen, markets—were dispassionately observed in strong sunlight against a backdrop of tropical vegetation throbbing with intense colors. A number of paintings and drawings done on the island either in 1852 or in 1854–55 have survived. These reveal Pissarro's concern at an early stage to combine the direct observation of nature with his instinct to record it all spontaneously. Such works were done while he was employed as a clerk in his father's office, where it was assumed that he would pursue a career in the family business or in something related to it. Later Pissarro expressed his horror at this prospect in a letter to one of his collectors, Eugène Murer, dating from 1878. He wrote, "Living in St. Thomas in 1852, [although] employed in a well-paying business, I could not endure the situation any longer, and without thinking, I abandoned all I had there and fled to Caracas, thus breaking the bonds that tied me to bourgeois life."[6] Even though written retrospectively, this letter indicates how quickly and how soon in his life Pissarro's commitment to art emerged. Furthermore, the political overtones of the letter suggest the particular outlook on life and art that can be equated with his interest in philosophical anarchism.

The trip to Venezuela referred to in the letter of 1878 lasted almost two years (November 1852–August 1854) and was undertaken in the company of the Danish artist Fritz Melbye (1826–1896), the younger brother of the more famous marine painter Anton Melbye, who had been trained at the Academy of Fine Arts in Copenhagen. The time spent in Venezuela enabled Pissarro to test out and improve on those virtually self-taught precepts that he had acquired on St. Thomas. The experience of Melbye undoubtedly provided Pissarro with an example to follow, and the growing city of Caracas, capital of an emerging nation in South America, exposed him to the practicalities of being a professional artist, such as setting up a studio and winning commissions in order to earn an income. This was Pissarro's first experience of the realities of making a living from his chosen profession. One of the requirements in this new situation was to broaden his repertoire by attempting portraiture in addition to landscape compositions and genre scenes (fig. 3).[7]

When Pissarro and Melbye landed at the port of La Guaira in November 1852, they explored the coast for two months. It was not a pleasant place. The heat radiated off the Silla mountains rising above La Guaira, which made being on land unbearable, and the sea offshore was permanently rough. The road over the mountains afforded some relief from the heat and was remarkable for the spectacular tropical vegetation that abounded on either side. Caracas itself lay in a verdant valley, and the view on approaching the city impressed all travelers.[8]

The setting was the subject for several paintings and drawings by Pissarro and Melbye. Pissarro's compositions, some of which were done after he left Venezuela and St. Thomas, reveal a surprising maturity in the arrangement of the constituent elements and the establishment of the spatial intervals (fig. 4). Control, order, and objectivity are the stylistic characteristics that are readily apparent, achieved by what seems to be an innate, instinctive sense of geometry. Similarly, the intermittent use of freely applied watercolor symbolizes Pissarro's heightened and excited response to the tropical vegetation (fig. 5). Such luminaries as the famous explorer, scientist, and man of action Alexander von Humboldt had also memorably responded to the South American flora: "Nowhere perhaps can be found collected together, in so small a space of ground, productions so beautiful, and so remarkable in regard to the geography of plants."[9] Of Venezuela as a whole von Humboldt significantly remarked, "Civilisation has in no other part of South America assumed a more European physiognomy."[10] It was in these fairly sophisticated circles, therefore, that Pissarro and Melbye endeavored to thrive as artists, perhaps working in partnership.

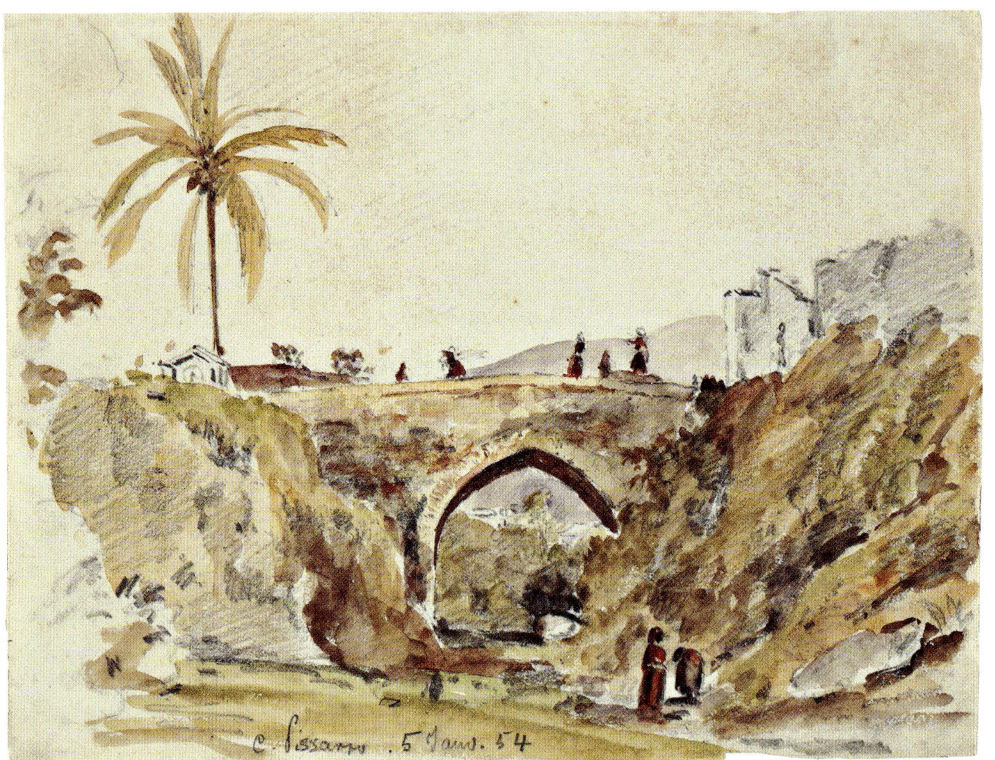

Fig. 4. Camille Pissarro, *The Bridge at Caracas*, 1854. Watercolor over graphite. National Gallery of Art, Washington, D.C., Collection of Mr. and Mrs. Paul Mellon, 1985.64.108

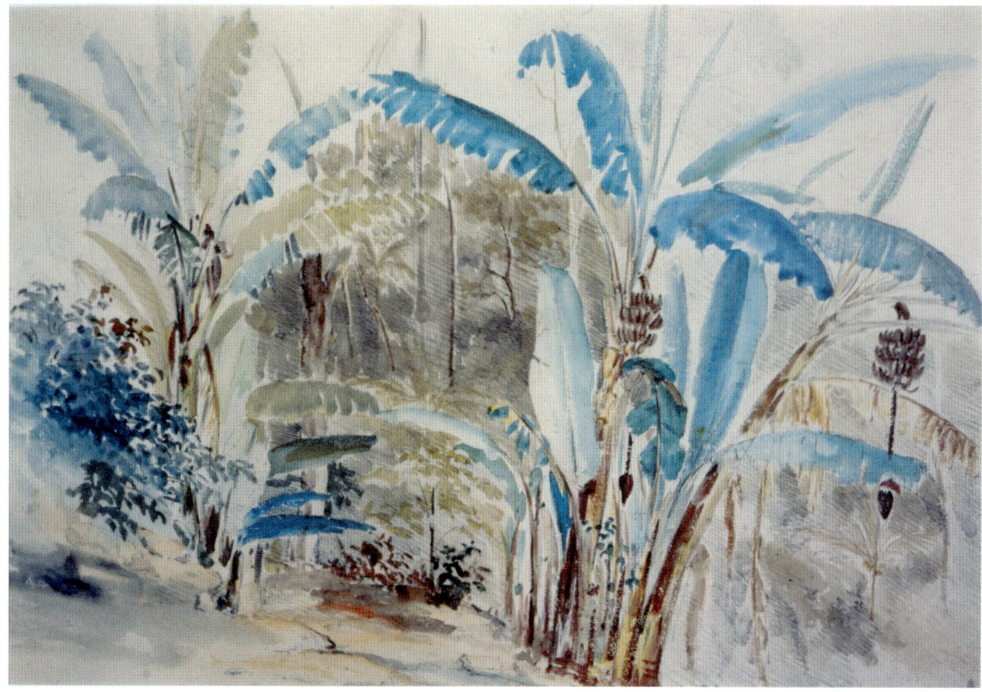

Fig. 5. Camille Pissarro, *Banana Trees*, c. 1852–54. Watercolor over graphite. Collection of Banco Central de Venezuela

South America during the nineteenth century had a considerable impact on several different areas of life. The experience of the sublimity of nature in its pure, untrammeled state on a relatively unknown and unexplored continent was one of the ways in which man could discover more about himself and the world in which he lived. Pissarro's participation in this exploration may have been marginal, but it is noteworthy that many of his early drawings, together with examples by Melbye, are to be found today in the collection of the Luminist painter Frederic Edwin Church, in his house at Olana (Hudson, N.Y.). Church was also traveling in South America during the 1850s and was influenced by the theories of von Humboldt and Charles Darwin.[11] At the same time, too, the renowned geographer and anarchist philosopher Élisée Reclus was also in South America to set up an experimental, ideal commune in Sierra Nevada (now part of Colombia). Later, Pissarro came to know Reclus at a time of political turmoil in France in the 1890s, but he was almost certainly aware of his published work before then.[12]

Understanding the formative years Pissarro spent in the Caribbean is essential for an appreciation of his mature work. Venezuela was a more sophisticated version of St. Thomas, but the subjects he tackled in his art were comparable. Nature held sway and genre scenes dominated by peasant life increasingly fascinated him. By contrast, more traditional or popular forms of painting—portraiture, still life, and domestic themes—were pursued only to satisfy the local clientele. This situation does not really change at later stages in Pissarro's life. The years in St. Thomas and Venezuela therefore anticipate future developments. Even the degree of commitment to his art and the determination with which he set out for Venezuela reveal an independent cast of mind that foreshadows the radicalism of his mature years, when he would explore different styles—the evolution of Impressionism in the late 1860s and early 1870s, the interest in Neo-Impressionism about 1885 to 1890, and the return to a refined form of Impressionism during the 1890s—in the search for the best means of recording those sensations that he experienced before nature.

Paul Cézanne once remarked in conversation with Joachim Gasquet that:

> we learned everything we do from Pissarro. He had the good luck to be born in the Antilles where he taught himself to paint without a teacher. So he told me. As early as '65 he had eliminated black, and bitumen, sienna and the ochers; it's a fact. He told me never to paint with anything other than the three primary colours and their immediate derivatives. It's he who was really the first Impressionist.[13]

In other words, Pissarro was from an early age able to follow his own instincts in terms of style, subject matter, and technique, thereby defining for himself his role as an artist long before he went to France as an adult.

Before his arrival in France in 1855, Pissarro had been only intermittently exposed to developments in European art. At Passy during the 1840s he was undoubtedly encouraged, but actual instruction was probably limited, although he was able to visit the studio of the minor landscape painter Auguste Savary, who was related to owners of the Pension Savary, where Pissarro was at school.[14] On St. Thomas and in Caracas, journals and periodicals, or possibly even drawing manuals, were available on a sporadic basis, but these did not amount to any sustained form of art tuition even on a self-help basis. Fritz Melbye would have been of assistance in explaining the basic aspects of academic practice as a result of his own training, and this is perhaps reflected in Pissarro's early compositional procedures, his techniques of painting and drawing, and his use of a variety of media. He therefore gleaned his knowledge of the academic tradition indirectly, and it was only when he arrived in Paris in 1855 that he was able to measure his progress by visiting the Salon exhibitions or attending private classes at the École des Beaux-Arts. Indeed, he reached France just in time to see the Universal Exposition of 1855 authorized by Emperor Napoleon III, at which there were spectacular displays of the work of Jean-Auguste-Dominique Ingres and Eugène Delacroix, who represented the polarities of French art in the mid-nineteenth century.

During the first few years in France, Pissarro took stock of his situation and adjusted to new possibilities. This period of uncertainty is reflected in his movements and choice of locations. Links with Paris were important for both professional reasons and family ties, but it was not long before Pissarro began to investigate the countryside surrounding the capital. Access to these areas was facilitated by the development of the railway network in France beginning in the mid-1840s. People living and working in central Paris could now escape the turmoil of city life and indulge in recreational pursuits out in the country, particularly on weekends. The pleasures of walking, boating, eating and drinking at restaurants, picnicking, and sightseeing were now open to all segments of society.[15] The pursuit of pleasure became a condition of modernity, and it was one that the Impressionists allied themselves with and chose to depict. Writers as well as artists were attracted to these popular locations out of the city, and a whole sub-branch of travel literature flourished in the form of guidebooks and illustrated topographical descriptions. Although derived from the tradition of Baron Taylor's *Voyages pittoresques et romantiques dans l'ancienne France* (1820–78) and Jules Janin's *La Normandie* (1844), such publications as Louis Barron's *Les Environs de Paris* (1886) and *Les Fleuves de Paris* (1889) were written for a wider audience and illustrated in a less historical vein.

While examining these outlying areas, away from the center of Paris, Pissarro at first rented accommodations for parts of the year; this gave him the freedom to move from one place to another. Because Pissarro's proclivities lay with landscape subjects, he began by looking carefully at artists associated with the village of Barbizon and the Forest of Fontainebleau, particularly Camille Corot, Charles-François Daubigny, Jean-François Millet, and Théodore Rousseau. During the 1830s these artists had painted motifs in the Forest of Fontainebleau, which is located about thirty-eight miles southeast of Paris. The clearings, avenues, rocks, quarries, gorges, and oak trees of the forest provided the basis for a new type of landscape painting, which advocated the direct transcription of nature as personally experienced by the artist. Landscape painting therefore became a vehicle for individual expression, which is why the emerging younger generation of artists—specifically Claude Monet, Pissarro, Renoir, Alfred Sisley—were attracted to the Forest of Fontainebleau. Pissarro himself was strongly influenced by Corot, whose paintings maintain a perfect balance between the architectural elements and the patterns of nature; by Daubigny's riverscapes with their low horizons, towering skies, and gentle undulations; and by Millet, whose depictions of rural life in paintings, pastels, and drawings became open to interpretation as the nineteenth century advanced. Seeking out where these artists had worked was as important as looking at their paintings, and the adoption of their subject matter was a way of gaining public approbation. Chailly, close to the village of Barbizon on the western edge of the Forest of Fontainebleau, was one such place where Pissarro began to set out his credentials as a landscape painter, and it is perhaps not surprising that it is a name closely linked with Millet.

Directly to the north of Paris was the Forest of Montmorency, which, apart from its connection with the eighteenth-century philosopher Jean-Jacques Rousseau, offered motifs similar to those of the Forest of Fontainebleau. Just as popular during the Second Empire, Montmorency presented wonderful walks, good views, restaurants, and donkey rides. It is a place that seems to have absorbed a considerable amount of Pissarro's attention judging by the number of drawings he made there in 1859. His first picture to be accepted by the Salon jury was a landscape made in this forest.[16]

At the same time, to the east of Paris but nearer to the city and on the banks of the River Marne, Pissarro explored Chennevières. For this he rented property at La Varenne during the early 1860s. He made several paintings of the River Marne on different scales, but two in particular demonstrate Pissarro's growing confidence—*Banks of the Marne at Chennevières*, about 1865 (cat. 4), and *The Banks of the Marne in Winter*, 1866 (cat. 5), both intended for and accepted by the Salon. The setting of Chennevières, with its dramatic hillside and terraces, was striking and, according to Louis Barron, was considered by Louis XIV as a possible site for a palace until his eye fell on Versailles. Of La Varenne Barron writes: "Opposite the delightful banks of Varenne-Saint-Maur, the hillsides of Ormesson, Sucy, and Bonneuil rise up forming an amphitheater; simple villages are encircled by châteaux, and there are wonderful panoramic views toward Paris and over the surrounding countryside."[17]

Another place that Pissarro explored during these same years was to assume even greater importance in his life. La Roche-Guyon (fig. 6), a village on the north bank of the River Seine approximately halfway between Paris and Rouen, had a topography that he examined in detail.[18] This part of the River Seine, which flows beyond Rouen to the sea

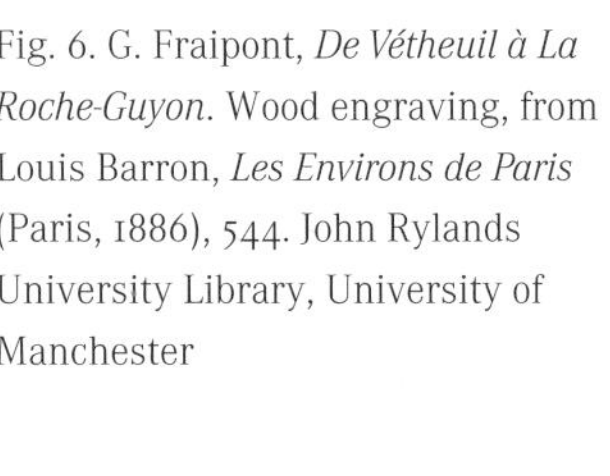

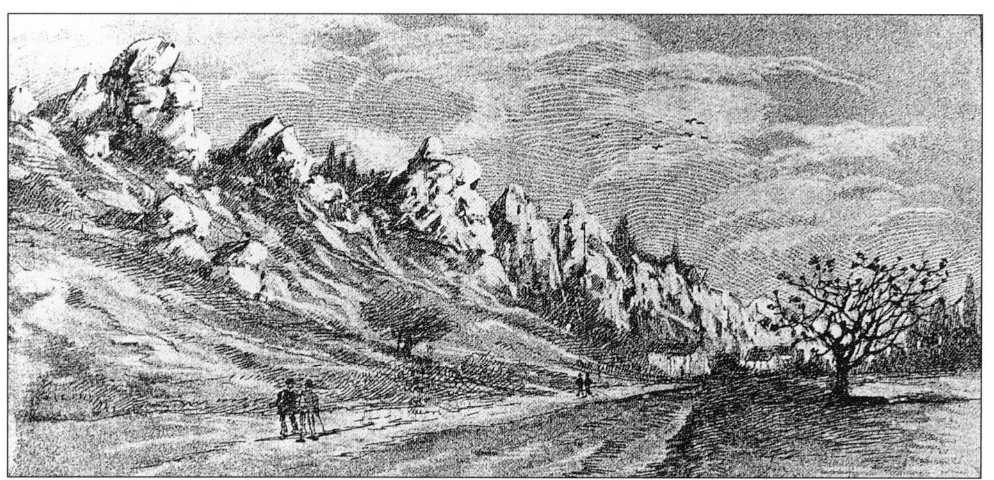

Fig. 6. G. Fraipont, *De Vétheuil à La Roche-Guyon*. Wood engraving, from Louis Barron, *Les Environs de Paris* (Paris, 1886), 544. John Rylands University Library, University of Manchester

Fig. 7. Camille Pissarro, *Donkey Ride at La Roche-Guyon*, c. 1865 (PD-RS 105). Oil on canvas. Tim Rice, London

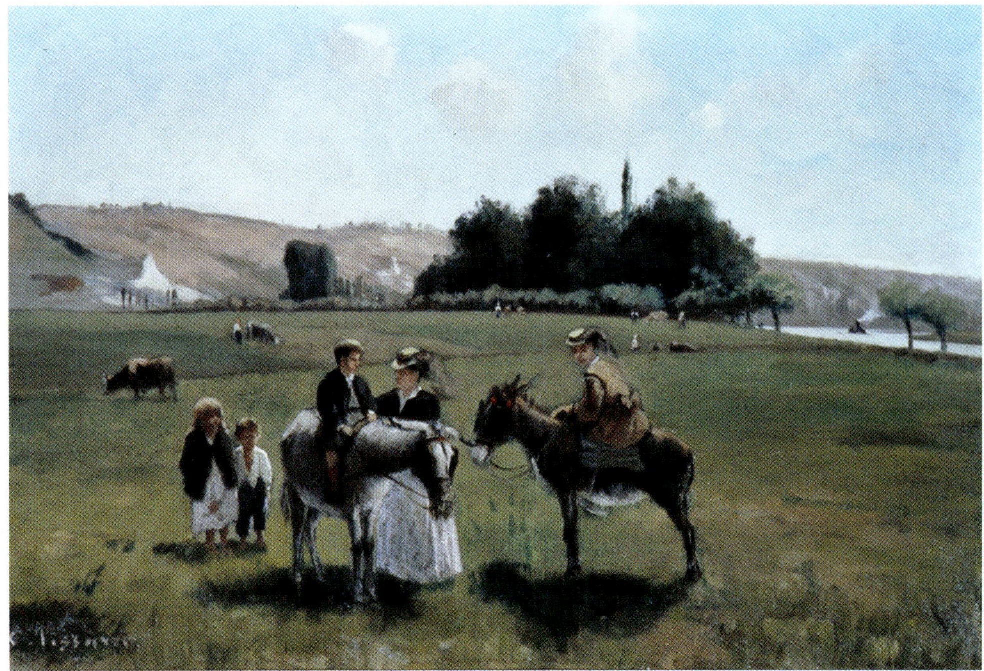

at Le Havre, was developed during the mid-nineteenth century as a picturesque route undertaken by steamer or, alternatively, later by train. The stretch of river at La Roche-Guyon is notable for the steep chalk escarpment that forms a backdrop to the buildings dominated by the medieval keep rising over the château where La Rochefoucauld is said to have written his *Maximes*. The writers Alphonse de Lamartine and Victor Hugo also stayed at the château, which during the closing stages of World War II was used by General Rommel as his headquarters. Pissarro is first documented at La Roche-Guyon in 1857, and its principal topographical features can be seen in several paintings, drawings, and prints. A painting of this site, *Donkey Ride at La Roche-Guyon*, about 1865 (fig. 7), shows a distant view of the hamlet as a backdrop to a subject that was perhaps inspired by Gustave Courbet.[19] By contrast, *Square in La Roche-Guyon*, about 1865 (Rothkopf essay, fig. 5), with its taut composition and use of the palette knife attest the start of the artist's friendship with Cézanne, whom he had met at the private Académie Suisse in Paris in 1861. The dominant motif of an early etching of La Roche-Guyon features one of the outcrops of the escarpment, which is used to emphasize the bend in the road at that point.[20] This use of the road as a compositional device was repeated in paintings of the late 1860s such as *Côte des Jalais, Pontoise*, 1867 (cat. 10). It was explored further by Cézanne again at La Roche-Guyon in the mid-1880s, an example of the continuing artistic interaction between

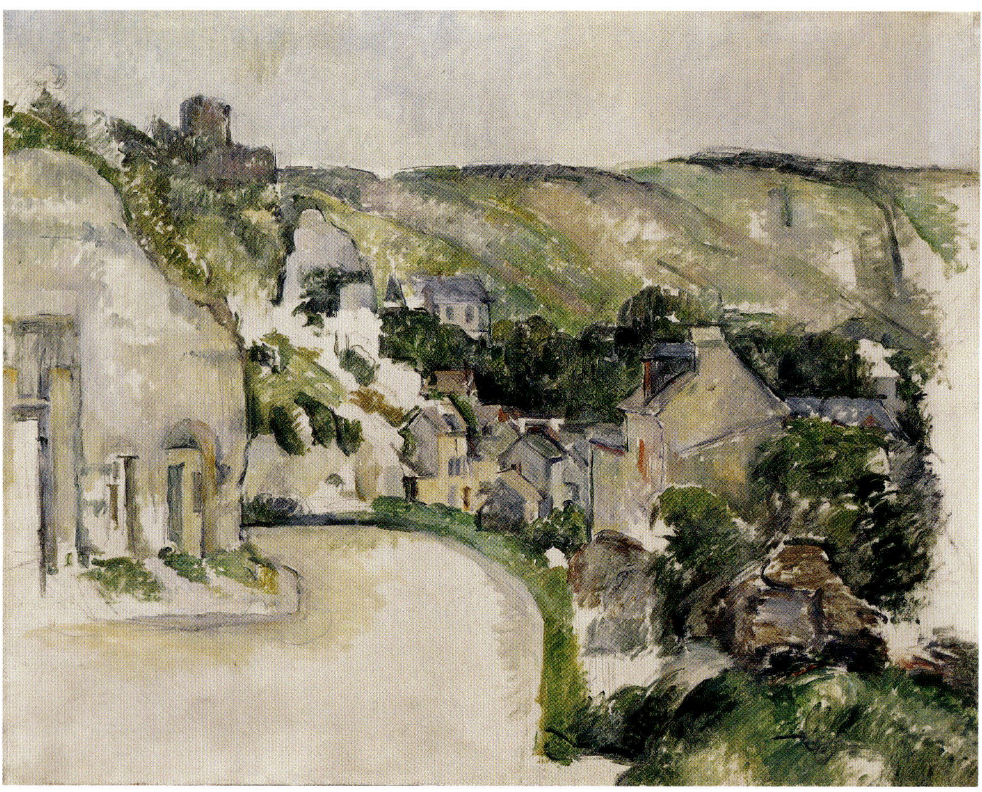

Fig. 8. Paul Cézanne, *A Turn in the Road at La Roche-Guyon*, c. 1885. Oil on canvas. Smith College Museum of Art, Northampton, Massachusetts. Purchased with the Tryon Fund SC1932:2

the two painters (fig. 8).[21] Other artists were interested in depicting the motifs presented by this road along the banks of the River Seine: Monet, after he moved to Vétheuil in 1878; and Renoir, who spent the summers of 1885 and 1886 at La Roche-Guyon (in the company of Cézanne on the former occasion). At the beginning of the twentieth century and inspired in part by Cézanne's late style, Georges Braque visited La Roche-Guyon, where, in the fusion of architectural and natural forms that characterize the hillside, he saw the possibility of creating the Cubist style of painting (fig. 9).[22] As a result of this visual progression extending from Pissarro through Cézanne to Braque, it is no exaggeration to see La Roche-Guyon as a locus classicus of modern painting.

Pissarro's experience at La Roche-Guyon allowed him to appreciate the advantages of closely examining a particular place in great detail. Thereafter, this procedure became a central tenet of his artistic method, which he substantiated and refined during the late 1860s and early 1870s. What began in a small way at La Roche-Guyon was developed at Louveciennes (1869–70 and 1871–72) and in London (1870–71). The stylistic and thematic continuity of Pissarro's output from these years reveals even more about the way in which he recorded his surroundings. There is an added intensity about the rigorous inspection of the artist's immediate locales in Louveciennes and London. Single motifs—usually streets or roads with dramatic perspectives—are frequently repeated, especially in Louveciennes, although seen from different viewpoints and under changing atmospheric conditions dictated by the seasons or the time of day. The artist seems literally to be squeezing the motif from the landscape and subjecting it to a purifying process that enables him to see his environment more clearly, as though experiencing it for the very first time. Significantly, a number of preparatory drawings were made in connection with the paintings done in Louveciennes and London. Recording the landscape in this concentrated way meant in essence creating an incipient series, which Pissarro and Monet—and to a lesser extent Sisley—were engaged in doing at Louveciennes and Argenteuil by the early 1870s. As is well known, the concept of the fully fledged series came to fruition

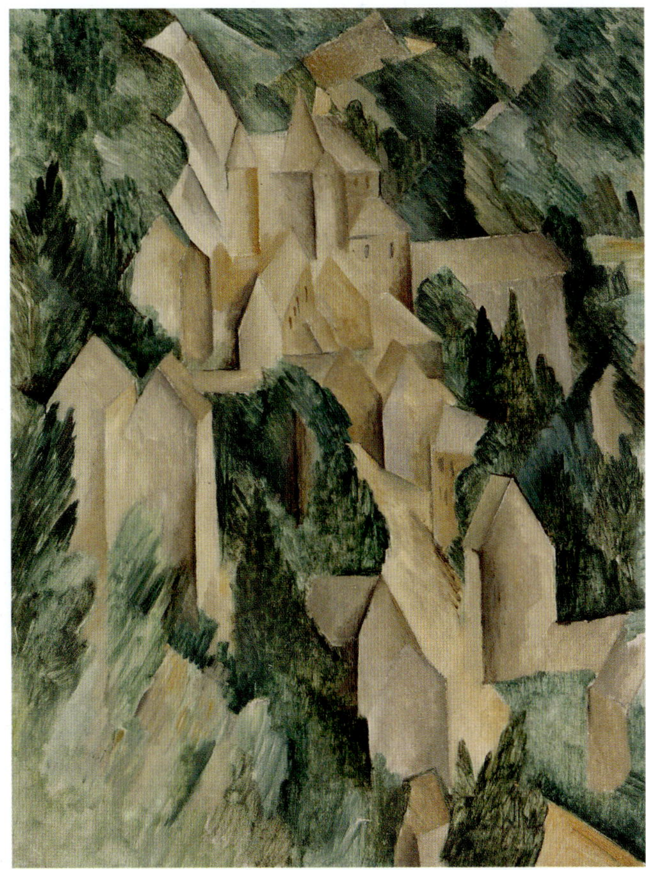

Fig. 9. Georges Braque, *La Roche-Guyon: Le Château*, 1909. Oil on canvas. Moderna Museet, Stockholm

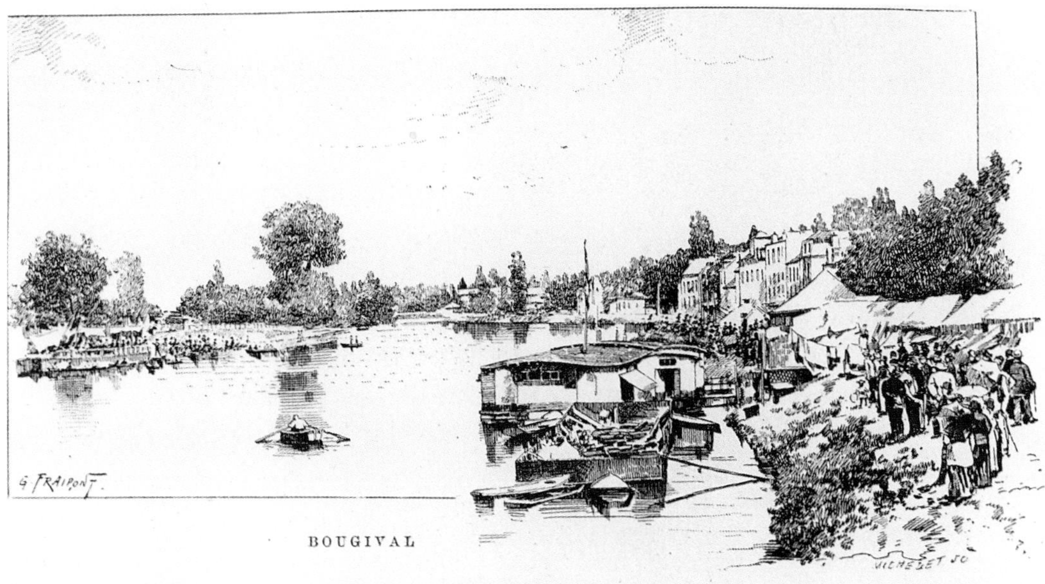

Fig. 10. G. Fraipont, *Bougival.* Wood engraving, from Louis Barron, *Les Environs de Paris* (Paris, 1886), 467. John Rylands University Library, University of Manchester

during the 1890s notably with Monet at Giverny, but also with Pissarro in Rouen, Paris, Dieppe, and Le Havre, and Sisley at Moret-sur-Loing.

The significance of what happened at Louveciennes during the late 1860s and early 1870s goes beyond considerations of style or technique. Pissarro's paintings of these years are of a modern landscape, exploring those places along the River Seine to the west of Paris—Suresnes, Asnières, Argenteuil, Chatou, Bougival, Port-Marly—that were gradually being transformed from hamlets and villages into the suburbs of Paris. Proximity to the capital was a mixed blessing. Local economies thrived in what was essentially a growing service industry. Areas once of natural beauty were now overwhelmed by factories, sewage plants, floating restaurants, boatyards, yachting marinas, market gardens, and villas. It was against such a varied background that the crowds from Paris escaping the city sought their pleasure activities. Such a transformation may not seem shocking or unusual today, but in the mid-nineteenth century it was sufficiently striking to engage the attention of artists and writers. A mutual dependency grew up between Paris and its outlying districts. The latter provided the capital with food and essential supplies, while those who lived in the city could relax and enjoy the leisure facilities being developed away from the metropolis.

The potency of this encroaching suburbanization also stemmed from the association with the eighteenth century of many of the places on this part of the River Seine stretching from Paris westward as far as Mantes-la-Jolie. This is certainly the case with the meander of the river that includes Saint-Cloud, Bougival (fig. 10), Louveciennes, Port-Marly, and Saint-Germain-en-Laye. It is in this geographical nexus that Louis XIV built his palaces at Versailles and Marly-le-Roi. The contemporary diarist, the duc de Saint-Simon, was no admirer of either Versailles or Marly-le-Roi. Of the former he wrote, "Beauty and ugliness, spaciousness and meanness were roughly tacked together." Although he liked the gardens, he nonetheless asked the question, "Who could help being repelled and disgusted at the violences done to Nature?"[23] Similarly at Marly-le-Roi, where now only the park survives, Saint-Simon questioned Louis XIV's choice of an enclosed site with a difficult access. "Such was the development of a haunt of snakes and vermin, toads and frogs, that was selected solely on the grounds that it would entail no expense. Marly was typical of the King's bad taste in everything, and of the proud pleasure which he found in subduing Nature, from which diversion neither the most pressing needs of war nor religious zeal, could ever turn him."[24] Saint-Simon found both Versailles and Marly-le-Roi to be vulgar and a perversion of nature. A discussion of the sites today, however, would stress the audacity of such a grandiose building program and the organization required to undertake it. There was, for instance, the matter of the supply of water from the River Seine for the fountains and ponds in the gardens of the palace at Marly-le-Roi. A vast pumping house, known as the Machine de Marly, was built at Port-Marly near Bougival on the river, and the water was pumped up the hillside before flowing along the aqueduct at Louveciennes. The machine was constructed in 1681 with fourteen waterwheels and 221 pumps. During the time of Emperor Napoleon III, this mechanism was replaced (1855–59) by a steam-driven apparatus comprising six iron wheels and twelve forcing pumps (fig. 11). The Machine de Marly was pulled down in 1968, but the aqueduct at Louveciennes (originally 707 yards long with 36 arches) still stands. The original inventor of the machine, Arnold de Ville, was rewarded by Louis XIV with a château at Louveciennes, which was later the property of Louis XV's mistress, Madame du Barry. The pavilion built in the grounds of the château by the architect Claude-Nicolas Ledoux was, according to the portrait painter Élisabeth Vigée-Lebrun, "famous for the exquisite taste and richness of its decorations,"[25] which included some of the finest furniture, porcelain, and paintings of the day.

Few of these historical aspects of the area are emphasized in the canvases of Pissarro, Monet, Sisley, or Renoir.[26] Pissarro included the aqueduct at Louveciennes in landscapes that can be more readily equated with modern life.[27] However, he concentrates more on the roads that pass through these historical places together with the buildings (including his own house), market gardens, orchards, and modes of transport that constitute his world, rather than on the past itself. Literally putting the past to one side, he marginalizes it. At Louveciennes Pissarro observed afresh, on a daily basis, the network of roads

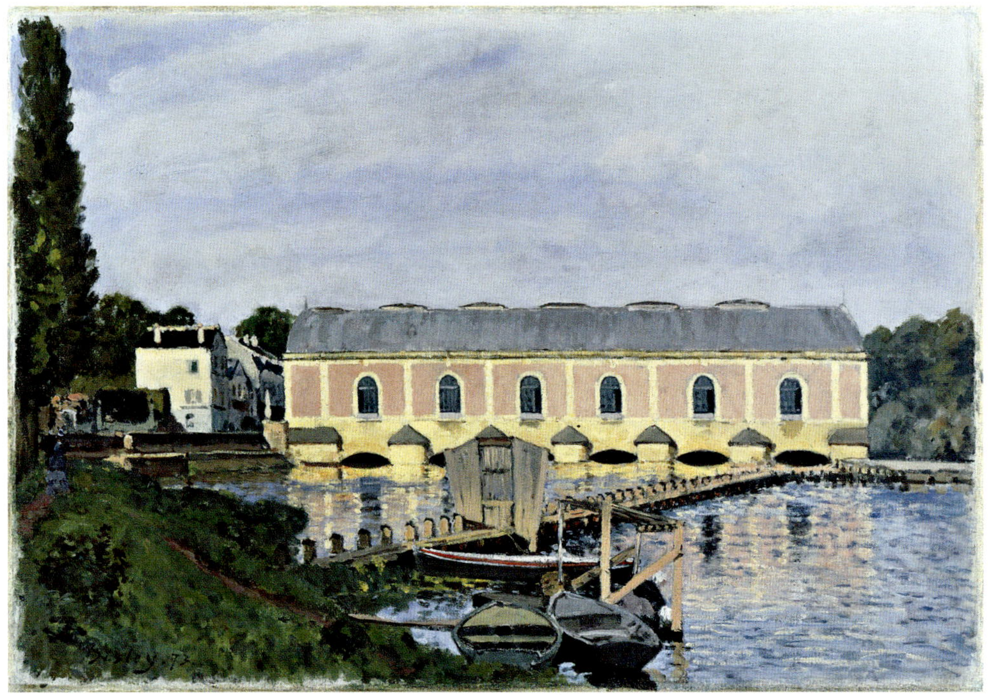

Fig. 11. Alfred Sisley, *The Waterworks at Bougival* (*The Machine de Marly*), 1873. Oil on canvas. Ny Carlsberg Glyptotek, Copenhagen

that by their very names recall the ancien régime and recast the traditional hierarchies of landscape painting. Both Pissarro and Monet—more than Renoir and Sisley—turned their backs on the historical context and concentrated on the quotidian aspects of modern life. This was a reversal of those principles of landscape painting established in France and Italy during the seventeenth century by Claude Lorrain and Nicolas Poussin. It is, if such an expression may be used, the democratization of the historical landscape.

What Pissarro had begun to do in Louveciennes before the outbreak of the Franco-Prussian War of 1870–71 he was able to put to the test in London. Reflecting on his time in London Pissarro stated, "Monet and I were very enthusiastic over the London landscapes. Monet worked in the parks, whilst I, living at Lower Norwood, at that time a charming suburb, studied the effects of fog, snow, and springtime."[28] Norwood lies southwest of central London and was still being developed when Pissarro arrived.[29] His pictures include many new buildings and not just houses but also churches, cemeteries, public institutions, factories, and schools all dating from the nineteenth century. He was aware, too, of the extension to the railway line built in 1865 to improve the service between the Norwood area and central London, and in search of further motifs he ventured to neighborhoods close by, such as Dulwich and Sydenham.[30] This whole part of London was becoming increasingly popular owing to the reopening of the Crystal Palace. Designed by Joseph Paxton to house the Great Exhibition of 1851, this enormous structure was originally erected in Hyde Park, but in 1854 it was moved to Sydenham, where it became an attraction in its own right, before being destroyed by fire in 1936. The Crystal Palace is in many respects the visual counterpart of the aqueduct at Louveciennes but with an essential difference. When it is included in paintings it is only one element within the composition, but its significance is less benign. As a recent revolutionary structure made of cast iron and glass, it had an added relevance in a modern landscape such as Pissarro aspired to paint. This was particularly pertinent since following its removal to Sydenham the building performed a different function. Now it was used more for entertainment. It

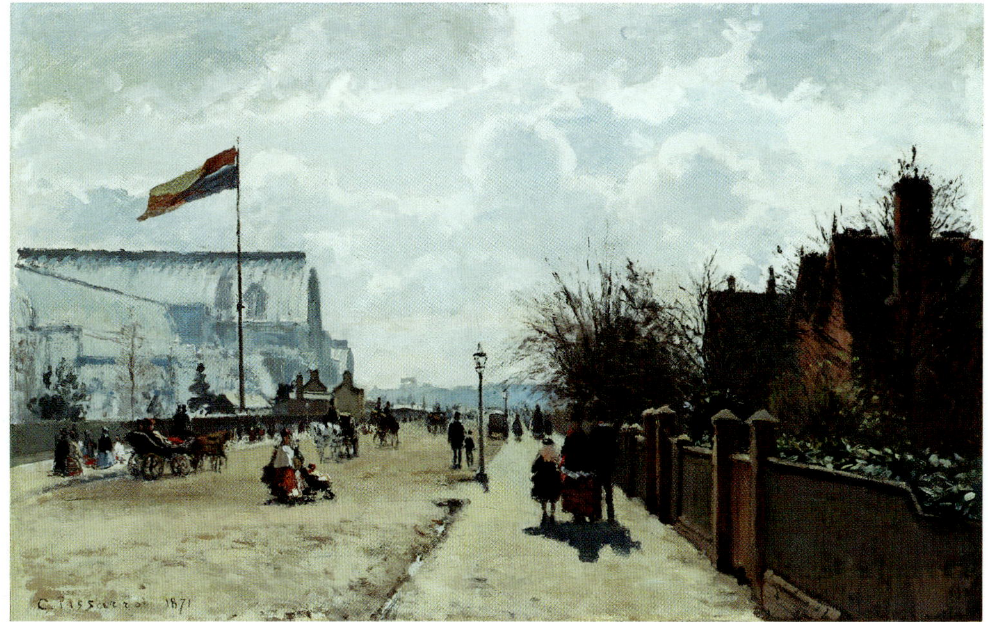

Fig. 12. Camille Pissarro, *Crystal Palace Viewed from Fox Hill, Upper Norwood*, 1871 (PD-RS 183). Oil on canvas. The Art Institute of Chicago, Gift of Mr. and Mrs. B. E. Bensinger, 1972.1164

housed a museum and was frequently a location for musical events. Called "The People's Palace," it enjoyed a prominent position on a hill, which meant that it was visible from a considerable distance, like a medieval cathedral (fig. 12). The Crystal Palace might therefore have been imbued by Pissarro with some political symbolism, but in fact at no time in his career was his treatment of landscape selective in this way. Indeed, the point about his paintings in London is that they are all-inclusive. Their modernity is based on the principle that he painted the spectacle as he saw it in front of his eyes and in all its variety. Some editing or manipulation occurred for pictorial reasons, but not as regards the subject matter, about which there could be no equivocation. As has been written, "Despite the severe circumstances during his seven months in London, Pissarro could hardly have been more inventive, more pictorially daring, or more broad-minded. It was in London that Pissarro's work took a resolutely modern form."[31]

The places in France and England that Pissarro explored during his early maturity were imbued with traditional, historical, and artistic associations. He clearly felt the need to test out their possibilities. In doing this he quickly recognized the potency of a landscape that had literally cradled history but was at the same time able to absorb and to

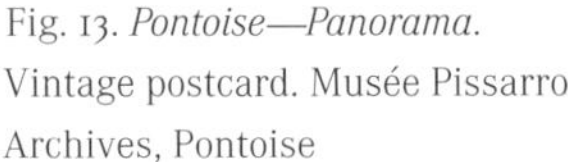

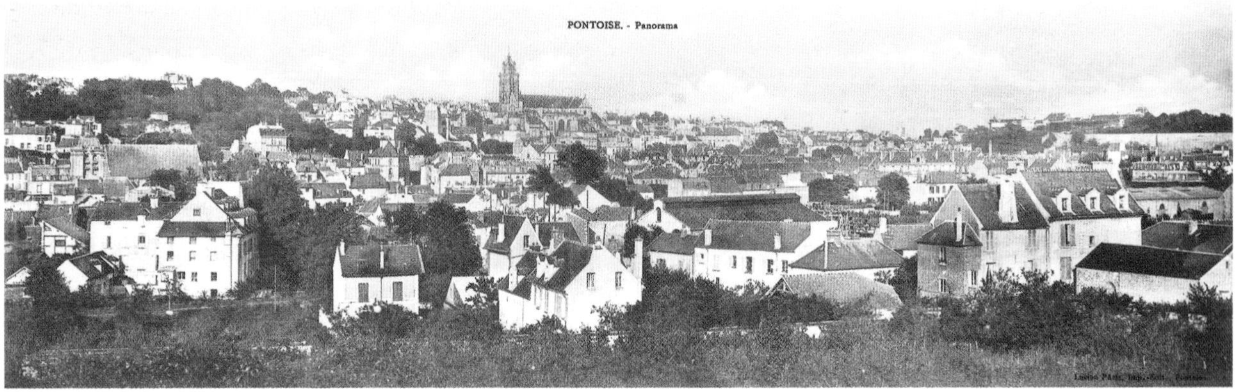

Fig. 13. *Pontoise—Panorama.* Vintage postcard. Musée Pissarro Archives, Pontoise

contain elements of modernity. Pissarro's response was to defuse its historical aspects in favor of the equivalences of contemporary life. This response is even more clearly defined in the context of Pontoise.

Pontoise is the place with which Pissarro is most closely associated and the one that he examined the most intensely during his life. He produced about three hundred paintings of the town and its environs, as well as numerous works in other media. All of this was over a period of some twenty years.[32] His curiosity was first aroused in 1866, when he was exploring the various possibilities presented by the Île-de-France—an area that was as popular with artists in the nineteenth century as the Roman Campagna had been in the seventeenth.[33] Pissarro spent an initial period of two years (1866–68) painting the strong landscapes that were so admired by Émile Zola when they were shown in the Salon.[34] A longer campaign occurred during the ten years that he lived there, from 1872 until 1882. Pissarro's output in Pontoise has been described as "the most sustained portrait of a place painted by any French landscape painter in the nineteenth century."[35]

When he left Pontoise he moved first to the nearby village of Osny and then, in 1884, he established himself farther in the countryside at Éragny-sur-Epte near Gisors, just into Normandy. It was here during the 1890s that he painted the late landscapes that should be seen in conjunction with his urban views of Rouen, Paris, Dieppe, and Le Havre. Pontoise, therefore, presented a specific challenge for the artist. It was one of his own choosing and one that he had not previously faced. The results were not a fully comprehensive or indeed consistent visual record of the town, but in artistic terms it was a thorough examination and it was revealing in its topographical partiality.

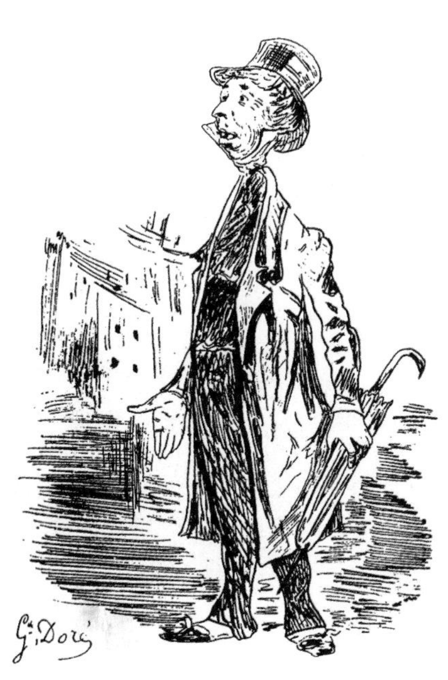

Fig. 14. Gustave Doré, *"I arrive from Pontoise . . ."* Vintage postcard. Bibliothèque nationale de France, Paris

Pontoise is situated nineteen miles northwest of Paris (fig. 13). It lies in a commanding position above the banks of the River Oise, which is a tributary of the River Seine. The main part of the town had great strategic significance in the past, having been built on the edge of the vast plateau extending northward known as the Vexin français. Looking in the other direction, the views are toward Paris. In effect, Pontoise is a nexus between two regenerative forces of French civilization—one medieval and rural and the other modern and urban. Historically, the town played an important role in the dramatic history of France, especially during the Middle Ages. Founded by the Romans, it was favored by the Capetian and Valois kings of France and became for a time the capital of the Vexin français. Louis IX (Saint Louis) fell ill in Pontoise, which was in part an incentive for the seventh crusade in 1244, and during the fourteenth century the town was often contested by the French and the English in the context of the Hundred Years' War. Even though increasingly overshadowed by Paris, Pontoise maintained its historic role during the seventeenth century and for part of the eighteenth, but administrative changes made by Emperor Napoleon I resulted in a downgrading when it was absorbed into the department known as Seine-et-Oise.

Geography and history defined the town of Pontoise. Pissarro did not ignore these aspects when he painted general views, which emphasize its strategic position and incorporated its historic (mainly ecclesiastical) buildings, but it was not his purpose to reinvigorate the Romantic topographical tradition that was the preserve of guidebooks and regional histories. Pontoise had changed its character during the first half of the nineteenth century mainly because of economic developments accelerated by improvements made to the railway line from Paris to Rouen, which had opened in 1843. The line was extended to the more modern part of Pontoise, known as Saint-Ouen-l'Aumône, on the other side of the River Oise, in 1846. Eventually, closer proximity to Paris proved to be a mixed blessing, as Pontoise became more of a suburb than a regional capital. Even so, a drawing by Gustave Doré suggests that people from the town were still regarded as provincials lacking the social wherewithal required for city life (fig. 14).

When Pissarro arrived, the town was flourishing, and this was reflected in the thriving activity of its barge port, its agriculture, and its small industries. The barge port,

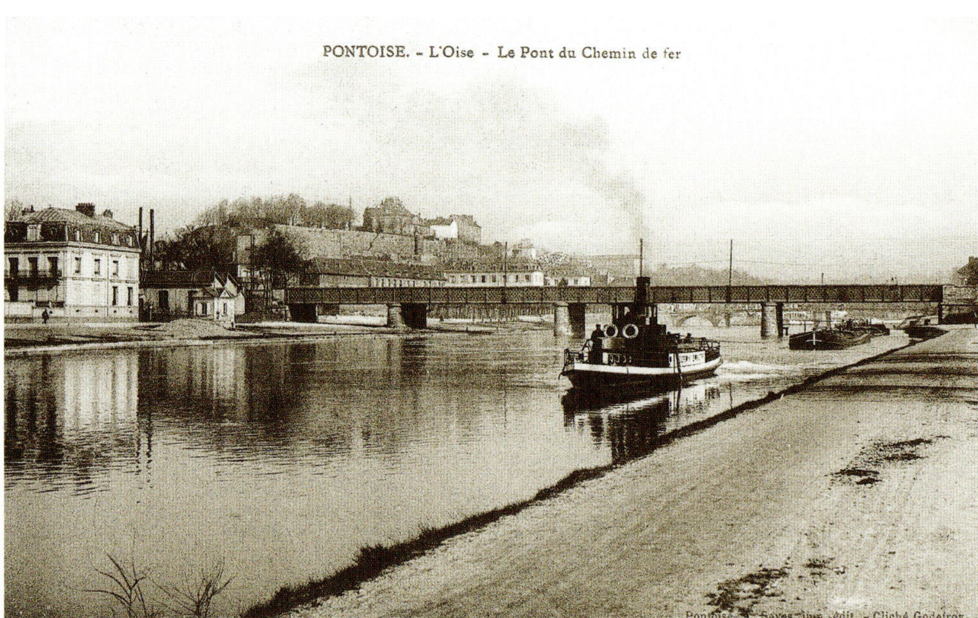

Fig. 15. *Pontoise—The Oise—The Railroad Bridge.* Vintage postcard. Musée Pissarro Archives, Pontoise

which linked the town with the network of canals stretching across the whole of northern France, was enlarged in 1843, the same year that the old stone bridge was renewed. A cast-iron bridge was built in 1863 to accommodate the railway line that was taken across the river from Saint-Ouen-l'Aumône to the main part of the town (fig. 15). Accordingly, a station was constructed for Pontoise from which the rue Thiers (formerly rue Impérial) led steeply up to the statue of the Revolutionary soldier General Leclerc, which stood before the church of Saint-Maclou, whose tower dominated the skyline. This new road therefore joined the upper and the lower parts of the town (fig. 16). Economic prosperity, even though it was to be short-lived, was the result of supplying Paris with essential foodstuffs. The land of the Vexin français produced huge quantities of grain, as well as root crops and fruit. The demand for much of this produce led to advances in agricultural techniques, including more mechanized systems of planting, harvesting, and processing. Traditional aspects of the economy, such as mills, granaries, and tanneries, were also given a new lease on life, and two small factories were opened. Both of these were on the Saint-Ouen-l'Aumône side of the river. One (Châlon et Compagnie) was a distillery for which potatoes and sugar beets were grown, and the other, smaller, one owned by a Monsieur Camille Arneuil, seems to have manufactured commercial paints.[36] This was not so much the rampant industrialization that was happening elsewhere in the region but more of an adjustment in the economic basis of Pontoise.

Alongside these new developments more localized forms of agriculture persisted, and the district of Pontoise to the northeast known as L'Hermitage was famous for its market gardens (*jardins potagers*). These were cultivated close to private homes and tended by families who grew the produce (cabbages, potatoes, peas, fruit) either for their own use or for sale at the local markets and fairs. Not surprisingly, Pissarro depicted several market scenes while living in Pontoise as well as afterward, and these neatly summarize the artist's interest in the social and economic interaction of everyday life in a historic town subject to the forces of modernization.[37] As at Louveciennes, Pissarro juxtaposes the old and the new, giving equal value to each and not declaring a preference for either. The writer Louis Barron also reveled in this visual dichotomy, contrasting the upper town with the lower one, the old buildings with the new, and the industrial with the picturesque. On arriving in Pontoise he tells his readers, perhaps surprisingly, to expect "a striking vision of a Gothic city, almost Oriental-looking" and goes on to compare the quays in the lower part of the town with sights in the Netherlands.[38]

Pontoise was not a place that had attracted a great deal of attention from artists. Although the changes that were being introduced were not exceptional or restricted to that town, it was sufficiently undiscovered to make it noteworthy that an artist such as Pissarro should be giving it his undivided attention as a result of identifying with it so closely, in making it his own. He was attracted by the fact that as a town it was in transition. Without setting out to be comprehensive or, indeed, without being photographic in his approach,

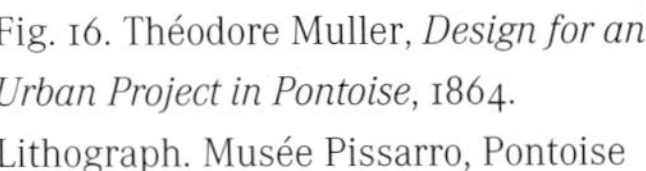
Fig. 16. Théodore Muller, *Design for an Urban Project in Pontoise*, 1864. Lithograph. Musée Pissarro, Pontoise

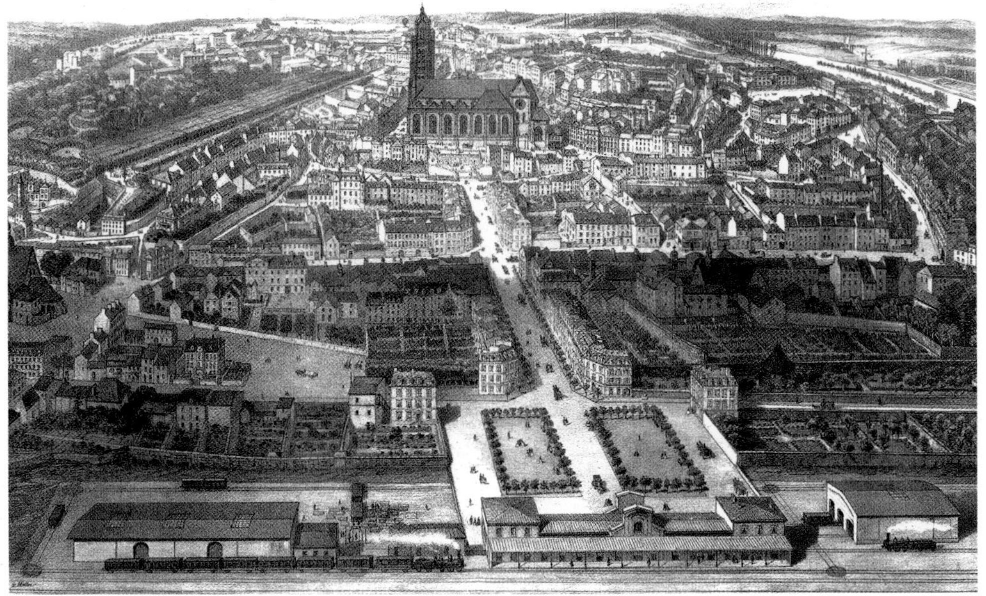

Pissarro does succeed in depicting the essential Pontoise—its location, various buildings, its public spaces, its streets, its environs, its character. So strong is the visual impact of this personal identification that to a great extent Pissarro's Pontoise is the Pontoise of today (cat. 35).

Pissarro chose to live in the older, more rural quarter of L'Hermitage, which in a small way was undergoing a change of its own in becoming a suburb of Pontoise itself. Of the two streets on which he lived, the rue du Fond de l'Hermitage had no modern amenities, but the rue de l'Hermitage had some new facilities such as cafés, a shop, and gas lamps. L'Hermitage, in short, represents the history of Pontoise in microcosm, just as Pissarro's fascination with the whole town reveals so much about him as an artist.

Having settled in France permanently in early adulthood, it took Pissarro some time to identify closely with one particular place that could serve as a base in a rapidly fluctuating world. The sense of belonging and the need to examine somewhere in such detail and with such intensity are most probably the direct consequence of his *Wanderjahre*. The search enabled Pissarro to find himself and to anchor himself, unlike Paul Gauguin, for example, who restlessly traveled the world throughout his life. In Pissarro's case even the choice of place is telling insofar as it defined his artistic credo. Because Pontoise was relatively unknown, the artist could assess it objectively. He belonged there, but he also kept his distance; he immersed himself in it, but he also stood back from it. The same distancing is apparent later in Pissarro's attitude to Rouen, Paris, Dieppe, and Le Havre. The duality he experienced in Pontoise mirrors his relationship with those other places. Paradoxically, one of the reasons that Pissarro is so difficult to categorize as an artist is not the partiality of his vision but its breadth, incorporating at different times rural and urban themes, figurative painting, and pure landscape.

Pontoise was where Pissarro began to fulfill himself. It was part of a landscape that had many associations with painters he admired: Corot at Ville d'Avray, Antoine Chintreuil at Igny, Daubigny at Auvers-sur-Oise, and Honoré Daumier at Valmondois. In addition, there were those artists of the Barbizon school who had been inspired by the Forest of Fontainebleau and were Pissarro's initial artistic exemplars after he arrived in France. Pontoise therefore amounted to a new departure within a familiar context.

It is a characteristic of Pissarro's art that he could discover the new in the old and that he could observe the habitual as though for the first time. This is why his paintings are in the real sense of the word a revelation—the result of an exploration by a painter determined to be true to his own individuality. Only a handful of artists has ever succeeded in this aim of lifting the mundane onto the level of the universal. Pissarro is one of a select number, who in the words of the first verse of William Blake's *Auguries of Innocence* was able

To see a World in a Grain of Sand
And Heaven in a Wild Flower,
Hold Infinity in the palm of your hand
And eternity in an hour.

The successful outcome of Pissarro's representation of Pontoise proved to be influential in its own way. It was here that he showed Cézanne how to treat landscape motifs with a satisfactory degree of objectivity.[39] In fact, not only did Cézanne benefit from Pissarro's advice, but Gauguin also learned from him at the outset of his career by examining the landscape between Pontoise and Auvers-sur-Oise, which was a walkable distance along the river to the east. Vincent van Gogh, too, became intrigued by Auvers-sur-Oise in the last year of his life, when he was being treated by the homeopathic doctor Paul Gachet, who was befriended by so many artists. This key moment in the development of European painting toward the end of the 1870s and the very early 1880s was as short-lived as it was geographically circumscribed. Gauguin was to leave France for more exotic climes and Cézanne returned to Provence, which he hardly left after the mid-1880s. Pissarro, however, stayed in the north, preferring the ever-changing light of the Île-de-France to the unrelenting brightness of the Mediterranean sun. He did so, though, in the knowledge that in those small hamlets between Pontoise and Auvers-sur-Oise with such names as Le Chou, Chaponval, and Valhermeil he had laid the foundations for the birth of modern art.

1. On the origins of the Pissarro family and the artist's early life, see Ralph E. Shikes and Paula Harper, *Pissarro: His Life and Work* (London: Quartet Books, 1980), 17–20, and Joachim Pissarro, *Camille Pissarro* (New York: Harry N. Abrams, 1993), 18–37.
2. C. W. Eves, *The West Indies* (London: Sampson Low & Co., 1889), 283–85.
3. Anthony Trollope, *The West Indies and the Spanish Main* (London: Chapman and Hall, 1859), 2.
4. Ibid., 235.
5. It was the custom for the children of successful merchants to leave the island to be educated. Camille Pissarro's grandparents, as well as other members of the family, were living in Paris.
6. *Correspondance de Camille Pissarro*, ed. Janine Bailly-Herzberg, 5 vols. (Paris: Presses Universitaires de France, 1980–91), 1:122–23, as translated in Pissarro, *Camille Pissarro*, 7.
7. On the period in Venezuela, see especially Alfredo Boulton, *Camille Pissarro en Venezuela* (Caracas: Editorial Arte, 1966), and *Pissarro in Venezuela: Works in Venezuelan Collections of Camille Pissarro's Venezuelan "Oeuvre" (1852–1854)* (Caracas: Editorial Arte, 1997), which includes a fully illustrated catalogue raisonné of those works in Venezuelan collections, 133–49. Also see *Art in Latin America: The Modern Era, 1820–1980*, ed. Dawn Ades (New Haven: Yale University Press, 1989).
8. "Looked down upon from the mountain, Caracas with its flat-tiled roofs, has the appearance of a brick-yard surrounded by a garden; the only noticeable break in its uniformity being one white cathedral and its little Plaza. The valley is fertile and cultivated. . . . Clusters of houses, lines of straight, tapering willows. . . bright streams milling through the valley and. . . tall palm-trees scattered over the plain, paths dotted with strings of donkeys stretching over the neighboring heights, the contrast between the rough, scarred mountains and the rich vegetation in the valley they wall in—all serve to produce a pleasing and picturesque effect." Thus an anonymous writer described the scene, *Harper's New Monthly Magazine* 17 (1858): 188.
9. Alexander von Humboldt, *Personal Narrative of Travels to the Equinoctial Regions of the New Continent during the Years 1799–1804. . . .* , trans. M. Williams (London: Longman, Hurst, Rees, Orme and Brown, John Murray, H. Colburn, 1818), 3:489. This seminal work was first published in French.
10. Ibid., 472.
11. For a discussion of the material at Olana State Historic Site, see Richard R. Brettell and Karen Zubowski, *Camille Pissarro in the Caribbean, 1850–1855: Drawings from the Collection at Olana* (St. Thomas: Lilienfeld House; New York: The Jewish Museum, 1996).
12. Christopher Lloyd, "Camille Pissarro and the Caribbean," *Horizontes: Revista de la Universidad Catolica de Puerto Rico, Ponce* 28, no. 56 (April 1985): 23.
13. *Conversations avec Cézanne*, ed. P. Michael Doran (Angers: Collection Macula, 1968), 121. An English edition with the same title was published by the University of California Press in 2001, 122.
14. For the Pension Savary, see Kathleen Adler, *Camille Pissarro: A Biography* (London: B. T. Batsford, 1978), 12–13, and Shikes and Harper, *Pissarro: His Life and Work*, 11–23.
15. The most stimulating survey of these themes remains Robert L. Herbert, *Impressionism: Art, Leisure, and Parisian Society* (New Haven: Yale University Press, 1988), but also see the exhibition catalogue Richard R. Brettell et al., *A Day in the Country: Impressionism and the French Landscape* (Los Angeles: Los Angeles County Museum of Art, 1984).
16. *Paysage à Montmorency* (Salon no. 2472) has been identified as *Donkey in Front of a Farm, Montmorency*, c. 1858 (PD-RS 37), oil on canvas, Musée d'Orsay, Paris.
17. Louis Barron, *Les Environs de Paris* (Paris, 1886), 172: "Vis-à-vis les rives délicieuses de la Varenne-Saint-Maur s'élèvent en amphithéâtre les coteaux de Chennevières, d'Ormesson, de Sucy et de Bonneuil, rustiques villages environnés de chateaux, merveilleux points de vue sur Paris et la campagne parisienne."
18. See Christopher Lloyd, "Reflections on La Roche-Guyon and the Impressionists," *Gazette des Beaux-Arts* 105 (1985): 37–44.
19. Gustave Courbet, *The Young Ladies of the Village*, 1851, oil on canvas, The Metropolitan Museum of Art, New York.
20. Loys Delteil, *Le Peintre-graveur illustré*, vol. 17, *Pissarro, Sisley, Renoir* (Paris: chez l'auteur, 1923), D 5, c. 1866.
21. Compare *The Winding Road at La Roche-Guyon*, c. 1885, in John Rewald, *The Paintings of Paul Cézanne: A Catalogue Raisonné*, 2 vols. (New York: Harry N. Abrams, 1996), no. 539. Also see Rewald no. 490, which belonged to Monet. A print by Pissarro (D 27, c. 1880) of

La Roche-Guyon demonstrates his continuing interest in the motifs first explored in the 1860s.

22. Braque's three paintings of La Roche-Guyon date from 1909: these are now in the Moderna Museet, Stockholm (fig. 9); the Stedelijk van Amsterdam, Eindhoven; and a private collection.

23. *Saint-Simon at Versailles: Selected and Translated from the Memoirs of M. le Duc de Saint-Simon* by Lucy Norton (London: Hamish Hamilton, 1958), 262.

24. Ibid., 266.

25. *Memoirs of Madame Vigée-Lebrun*, trans. Lionel Strachey (London: Grant Richards, 1904), 50.

26. For the history of Louveciennes, see *Bulletin d'Accueil de Louveciennes* (1989).

27. Prime examples are PD-RS 158, 201, 207, and 233.

28. Quoted in Wynford Dewhurst, *Impressionist Painting: Its Genesis and Development* (London: George Newnes, 1904), 31–32.

29. On Pissarro in London, see Martin Reid, "Camille Pissarro: Three Paintings of London; What Do They Represent?" *Burlington Magazine* 119, no. 889 (1977): 251–61; John House, "New Material on Monet and Pissarro in London in 1870–1," *Burlington Magazine* 120 (1978): 636–42; Martin Reid, "The Pissarro Family in the Norwood Area of London, 1870–1: Where Did They Live?" in *Studies on Camille Pissarro*, ed. Christopher Lloyd (London: Routledge and Kegan Paul, 1986), 55–64; Kathleen Adler, *Pissarro in London* (London: National Gallery, 2003); and Charles C. Frankiss, "Camille Pissarro, Théodore Duret and Jules Berthel in London in 1871," *Burlington Magazine* 146 (2004): 470–72.

30. Nicholas Reed, *Camille Pissarro at Crystal Palace*, 2nd rev. ed. (London: privately printed, 1993).

31. Pissarro, *Camille Pissarro*, 86.

32. Richard R. Brettell, *Pissarro and Pontoise: The Painter in a Landscape* (New Haven: Yale University Press, 1990), is the definitive publication on this subject and an outstanding contribution to Impressionist studies. What follows is dependent on this book.

33. Ibid., 3.

34. Principally PD-RS 119–121 and 125. For Zola's criticism, see Émile Zola, *Le Bon Combat de Courbet aux impressionnistes*, ed. J.-P. Bouillon (Paris: Hermann, 1974), 74, 106–10.

35. Brettell, *Pissarro and Pontoise*, 1.

36. Ibid., 22–25, and chap. 3, 73–97.

37. Ibid., 25–28. Pissarro's treatment of market scenes extends beyond his time in Pontoise, but for general observations, see Christopher Lloyd, "The Market Scenes of Camille Pissarro," *Art Bulletin of Victoria, Melbourne*, no. 25 (1985): 17–32.

38. Barron, *Les Environs*, 565, supplemented by the same author's *Les Fleuves de Paris: La Seine* (Paris, 1889), 328.

39. For the relationship between Pissarro and Cézanne, see the exhibition catalogue Joachim Pissarro, *Pioneering Modern Painting: Cézanne and Pissarro, 1865–1885* (New York: The Museum of Modern Art, 2005).

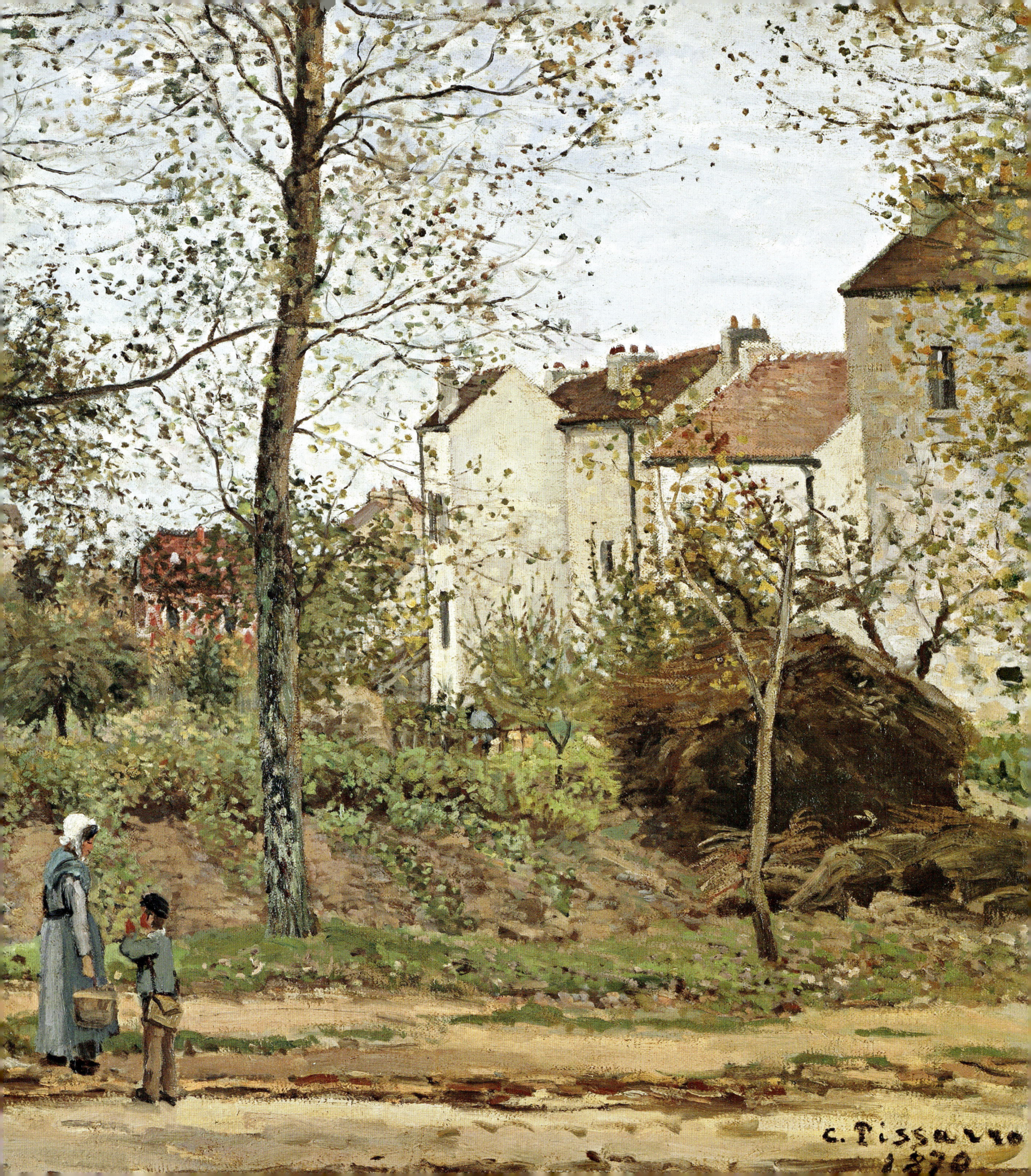
C. Pissarro
1870

Camille Pissarro: From Barbizon Student to Impressionist Innovator

An Overview of His Painting Style from 1864 to 1874

Katherine Rothkopf

One can make such beautiful things with so little. The motifs that are too beautiful sometimes appear even theatrical . . . . Happy are those who see beauty in the modest spots where others see nothing. Everything is beautiful, the whole secret lies in knowing how to interpret. *Camille Pissarro*, 1893[1]

When looking at Camille Pissarro's career as a whole, it is apparent that some of his most innovative landscape paintings were produced in the early 1870s, just as the Impressionist movement was beginning to take shape as a serious challenge to the art establishment in France. The work of his early Impressionist period can be characterized by experimental and varied brushwork, an interest in depicting shadow and changing light and weather effects, a colorful palette, and carefully structured compositions that turn modest views of the French countryside into compelling images of modern life. However, just a few years earlier, in the mid-1860s, he was fully engaged with the Barbizon artists, a group of the previous generation who were interested in depicting nature as a rural paradise and treated their subjects with poetic feeling for color, light, and atmosphere. Pissarro's Barbizon-inspired works are conservative in style, featuring a somber palette and a broad, painterly technique. To fully appreciate his revolutionary Impressionist paintings of the 1870s, a closer look at the decade that preceded this breakthrough is needed. During the 1860s Pissarro was creating inventive, small-scale compositions at the same time that he was trying to please the official Salon jury with more conventional pictures. As one carefully examines the smaller paintings of this early period, a distinct thread of experimentation emerges, one that follows the painter from the banks of the Marne in 1864, to Pontoise from 1866 to 1868, to Louveciennes in 1869, to London from 1870 to 1871, and finally back to Pontoise in 1872, where the artist found a landscape that he made his own.

During the years explored in this exhibition, from 1864 until the first Impressionist exhibition in 1874, he collaborated closely with Claude Monet (1840–1926) and Paul Cézanne (1839–1906), each artist learning from the other as they formed their individual styles. The story of Pissarro's early groundbreaking period serves as a template for his stylistic evolution throughout a long and productive career. He continued to look to artists of the past for inspiration, even as he was pioneering the course of landscape painting with his new techniques and vision. Retaining an interest in the direct observation of nature, Pissarro portrayed elements of everyday life in his compositions. His motivation was to record as accurately as possible on canvas those feelings (*sensations*) he experienced in front of nature, and his varied stylistic changes attest to his willingness to experiment.

Camille Pissarro, *Houses at Bougival*, detail (cat. 19)

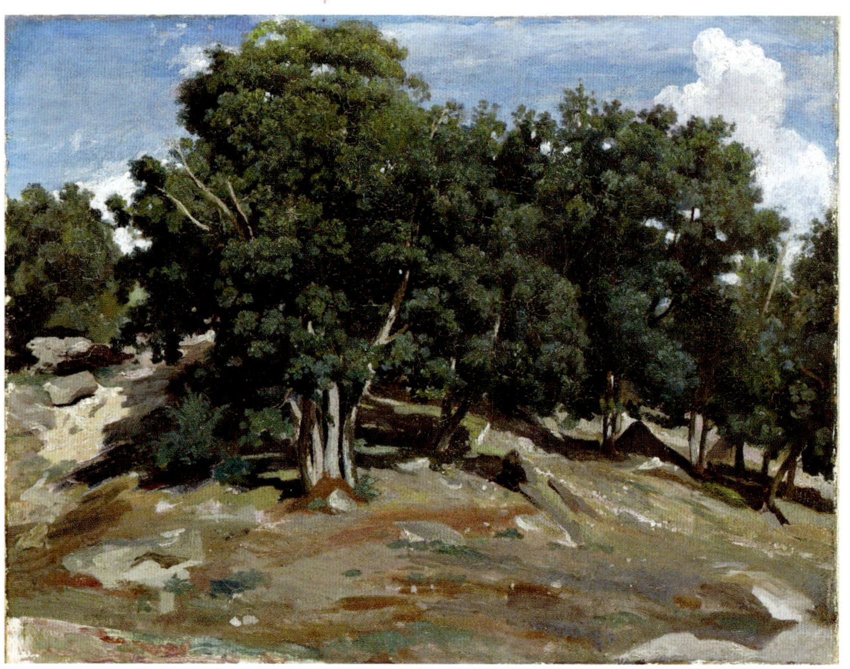

Fig. 1. Jean-Baptiste-Camille Corot, *Fontainebleau: Oak Trees at Bas-Bréau*, c. 1832–33. Oil on paper, mounted on wood. The Metropolitan Museum of Art, Catharine Lorillard Wolfe Collection, Wolfe Fund, 1979 (1979.404)

Artistic Beginnings

Arriving in Paris from St. Thomas in 1855, Pissarro spent his first year exploring his new artistic surroundings. He was profoundly impressed by the paintings of Jean-Baptiste-Camille Corot (1796–1875) whose work he saw at the Universal Exposition of 1855. At the start of the nineteenth century, landscape painting had been considered one of the lesser genres, with figural representations given the highest level of esteem. In 1800 Pierre-Henri Valenciennes (1750–1819) published *Élémens de perspective pratique à l'usage des artistes* (Elements of Practical Perspective for Artists), a treatise that provided important lessons for artists interested in landscape. Corot closely followed the lessons of Valenciennes, and his success at mining the countryside for motifs made him one of the most significant landscapists of the nineteenth century. As both a painter and a teacher, Corot influenced two generations of artists over the course of his long career.

Soon after settling in Paris, Pissarro became an informal pupil of Corot through the assistance of Anton Melbye (1818–1875), the brother of his friend Fritz Melbye who had been his travel companion to Venezuela.[2] Anton, a successful marine painter, soon became a close friend and advisor. Pissarro attended private classes at the École des Beaux-Arts in 1856 and in 1861 registered as a copyist at the Musée du Louvre. At the same time, he began taking classes at the informal Académie Suisse, where he met, among others, Cézanne and Monet. Pissarro's works from the late 1850s and early 1860s can be characterized as modest landscapes, farm scenes, and portraits. Thickly and sometimes awkwardly painted, they display a marked influence of Corot in the choice of subject. In addition, Pissarro derived from the older master his treatment of light and tonal nuance. Although Corot also inspired Pissarro's colleagues, only Pissarro openly claimed him as his mentor, listing Corot as his teacher in the Salon *livrets* of 1864 and 1865, thus becoming the crucial link between the two generations.[3] His respect for Corot continued throughout his career, and he often included him among those the younger generation should follow: "my dear Lucien, for the art of 1830 is that of Corot, Courbet, Delacroix, Ingres. And it is eternally beautiful!"[4] The following year, he acknowledged the influence of Corot on his early development: "I knew Corot very intimately. I passionately admired him, and it's not surprising that his influence can be felt in my early work."[5]

Corot was best known for his large studio compositions in the classical tradition, paintings that were generally considered old-fashioned by Pissarro and his colleagues. However, his unpretentious landscapes on a smaller scale, usually painted directly from nature, had a sense of freedom and looseness that appealed to the younger artists as they searched for their own reality in the world around them. A composition such as Corot's *Fontainebleau: Oak Trees at Bas-Bréau*, about 1832–33 (fig. 1), was typical of those that might have influenced the young Pissarro. This oil study of the forest, like many others, was produced *en plein air* and features a brilliant blue sky juxtaposed with the deep, rich green of the leaves, not unlike some of Pissarro's efforts from the 1860s. Corot would incorporate this tree into a historical painting, *Hagar in the Wilderness* (1835, The Metropolitan Museum of Art), a subject with little interest for Pissarro, who preferred to depict the contemporary landscape.[6]

Exhibiting at the Salon

During his first years in France, Pissarro moved frequently from town to town, always remaining relatively close to Paris. From 1863 to 1866 he lived periodically in La Varenne-Saint-Hilaire,[7] a small town southeast of the capital on the banks of the Marne River that provided an ample source of motifs. The rustic environs inspired him to produce a group of significant riverscapes, including those he submitted to the Salons of 1864, 1865, and 1866 (see fig. 2 and cats. 4, 5). During this period, his paintings became more inventive, losing some of his dependence on Corot's example in subject matter that had been apparent in the preceding years.[8] He continued to study works by artists of the previous generation and freely incorporated their lessons into his personal vision of nature, often interweaving their multiple influences into the same painting. As the critic Émile Zola

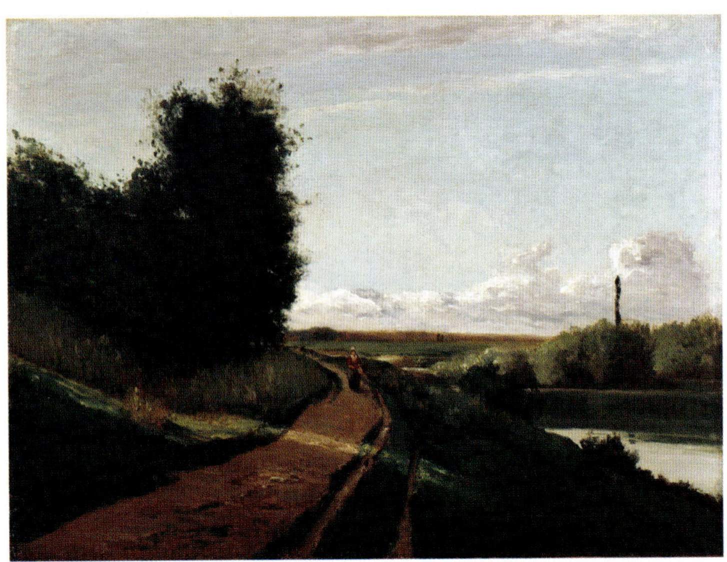

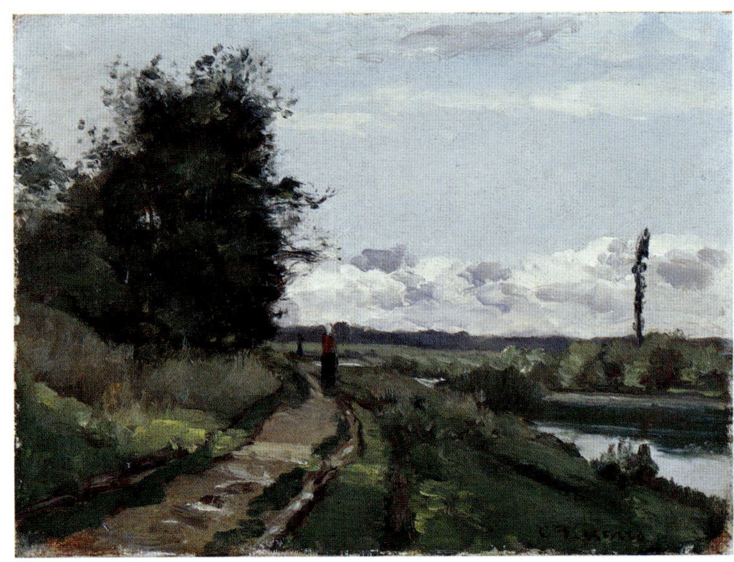

wrote in 1868: "Camille Pissarro is one of the three or four great painters of the time. He possesses solidity and breadth of touch, he paints handsomely, following tradition, like the masters. I have rarely encountered a science more profound."[9]

Pissarro's landscape subjects of 1863–64, in both large and smaller compositions, can be characterized as rural, with views of paths, banks of rivers, and meadows prevailing. These themes remained of great interest to him throughout the decade, providing countless motifs to explore. Although he exhibited for the first time in the Salon of 1859,[10] it was his entry in the exhibition of 1864 that can be considered his first Salon success. *Banks of the Marne* (fig. 2) is a rare Salon painting for which there is a surviving oil sketch (fig. 3). In the exhibition catalogue, the artist described himself as a student of both Anton Melbye and Corot. However, on the basis of motif and technique, it seems that the riverscapes of Charles-François Daubigny (1817–1878) provided a more profound inspiration for young Pissarro.[11] Daubigny, a painter of pure landscape and an important member of the Barbizon group, was more devoted to plein-air painting than any other artist of his generation. Well known for his riverscapes and unconventional, rural views—subjects that appealed to Pissarro as well—Daubigny achieved notable success for his realistic depictions of nature. In his Salon review of 1859, Charles Baudelaire complimented Daubigny's ability to convey "immediately to the viewer's soul the original feeling that pervaded" his views of the countryside,[12] and Théophile Gautier called his paintings "pieces of nature cut out and set into a golden frame."[13] By the late 1860s Daubigny's importance as a painter was overshadowed by his appointment to the Salon jury, where he was often criticized for his

Fig. 2. Camille Pissarro, *Banks of the Marne*, 1864 (PD-RS 90). Oil on canvas. Glasgow City Council (Museums)

Fig. 3. Camille Pissarro, *Banks of the Marne, Study*, c. 1864 (PD-RS 89). Oil on canvas. Fitzwilliam Museum, Cambridge

overwhelming support of the new style of the younger group of painters, including Pissarro.

The oil sketch for *Banks of the Marne* was painted on a fresh canvas. On several occasions in the 1860s, Pissarro reused canvases,[14] so it seems unusual that he would sacrifice a new one for a simple sketch. One explanation may be that Pissarro was simply following standard academic procedure when making a full compositional oil sketch for a large Salon work. It is also possible that the artist conceived it as one of many small independent paintings and only later returned to the motif for the larger composition. The sketch was painted out of doors, which accounts for its freshness and sense of immediacy. His interest in atmosphere and shadow is apparent, notably in the way he paints light falling on the path with pale greens, tans, and whites. The Salon version and the smaller study are so similar in composition and feel that it seems as though Pissarro was attempting to break down the distinction between "painted sketch" and "finished painting,"[15] rather than relying on the sketch to produce a satisfactory larger composition, a notion that was permanently shattered by Pissarro and his colleagues in their early Impressionist years.

A lesser-known canvas from 1864 that is relatively small in size but has more of the assurance of a "finished" work is *Strollers on a Country Road, La Varenne-Saint-Hilaire* (cat. 3). Here Pissarro has combined some of the compositional lessons of Corot, including his choice of subject of the curving path, with the painterly insistence and confidence of Gustave Courbet (1819–1877), who had a deep impact on the artist's early career. From his example, Pissarro learned to paint with assurance, energy, and unconventional methods and motifs, particularly the free use of the palette knife, seen here in the sky. In 1855, when Pissarro first arrived in France, Courbet staged his own one-man exhibition in Paris, a revolutionary display that was completely independent of the state-sponsored Universal Exposition. Among the forty-one paintings was *The Studio—A Real Allegory Representing Seven Years of My Artistic Life* (1854–55, Musée d'Orsay, Paris), a vast composition that includes a self-portrait of Courbet as well as a large landscape, the centerpiece of the work. For the young Pissarro who would devote most of his efforts to landscape painting, this example must surely have made a strong impression.

For his Salon entry in 1865, Pissarro submitted *Banks of the Marne at Chennevières* (cat. 4), an expansive and powerful work that also reflects the influence of Daubigny in the choice of motif. With its wide view and riverside site, Daubigny's *Village of Gloton*, 1857 (fig. 4), represents the artist's signature style that Pissarro was trying to emulate. But differences between the two paintings become clear on careful inspection. The younger artist uses the basic elements of Daubigny's model—sky, water, land—but minimizes the narrative. As he often did, Daubigny provides a clear storyline for the viewer—a farmer

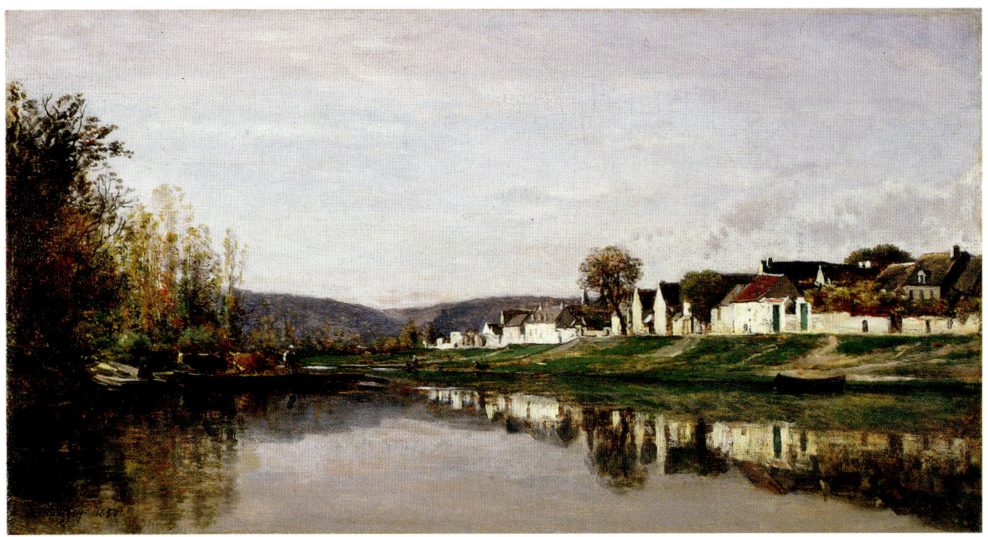

Fig. 4. Charles-François Daubigny, *The Village of Gloton,* 1857. Oil on panel. Fine Arts Museums of San Francisco, Museum Purchase, Mildred Anna Williams Collection, 1940.4

leads his animals across the river—but Pissarro focuses on the solid construction of the composition, abstracting the components, including a small group of figures, to their basic forms.[16] The subtle influence of Courbet's technique is also apparent in the scumbled paint surface visible in the marshy areas of the water, as well as in the use of a palette knife for the architectural elements.

Pissarro discovered the creative possibilities of working more extensively with a palette knife in *Square in La Roche-Guyon* of about 1865 (fig. 5). A technique for which Courbet was well known, it provided Pissarro with a tool to build up his compositions literally, and it also allowed him to experiment with the paint itself, which he applied in thick patches. He was determined to set down his own vision of the landscape around him, whether beautiful or ordinary, a lesson also learned from Courbet's works of the 1850s. In this urban scene, a rare subject in this early phase of Pissarro's career, the sky, a component that normally plays a major role in his work, is hardly present. Here he has applied the paint like mortar, and the viewer is aware of the texture of the paint as well as the scene it depicts. His brushwork is quick and spontaneous, particularly in the reflections in the windows formed with just a few rapid strokes.

In the Salon of 1866, Pissarro exhibited the ambitious *Banks of the Marne in Winter* (cat. 5), a daring and realistic view of a gloomy winter day that produced the first important reviews of his career. After having identified himself as a student of Corot and Anton Melbye in the previous two Salon *livrets,* in 1866 he listed himself only as a pupil of Melbye, probably because Corot was not in favor of the bolder color and stronger tonal contrasts that were appearing in Pissarro's work. In his Salon review, Zola recognized Pissarro's lack of appeal for the more conventional critics, given his bleak choice of subject and rough technique, but praised his solemnity, his force of will, and his profundity:

> You must know that no one appreciates your work and that your painting is deemed too bare and too black. Then why in the devil's name are you so very clumsy as to study nature and paint it in a plain and forthright manner! See here: you selected a winter scene; you put in it a mere portion of an avenue, then a small hill at the back, and empty fields extending to the horizon. This is no feast for the eyes. It is an austere and serious painting, showing an extreme concern for the truth and correctness, a bleak and strong will. What a clumsy fellow you are, sir—you are one artist I like.[17]

For the first time in his career, Pissarro had produced a large-scale work that was completely original, without relying on conventional subject matter or color scheme for inspiration. As in his Salon entry from the previous year (cat. 4), the artist had featured a wide vista, but the radiant sky and delightful calm of a summer day have been replaced by the dreariness of winter. The palette is quite dark, with the green grass at right, the red kerchief of the female figure on the path at left, and the strong highlights on the buildings in the distance the only bright elements in the canvas. The small bit of river at the far left is barely discernible, and

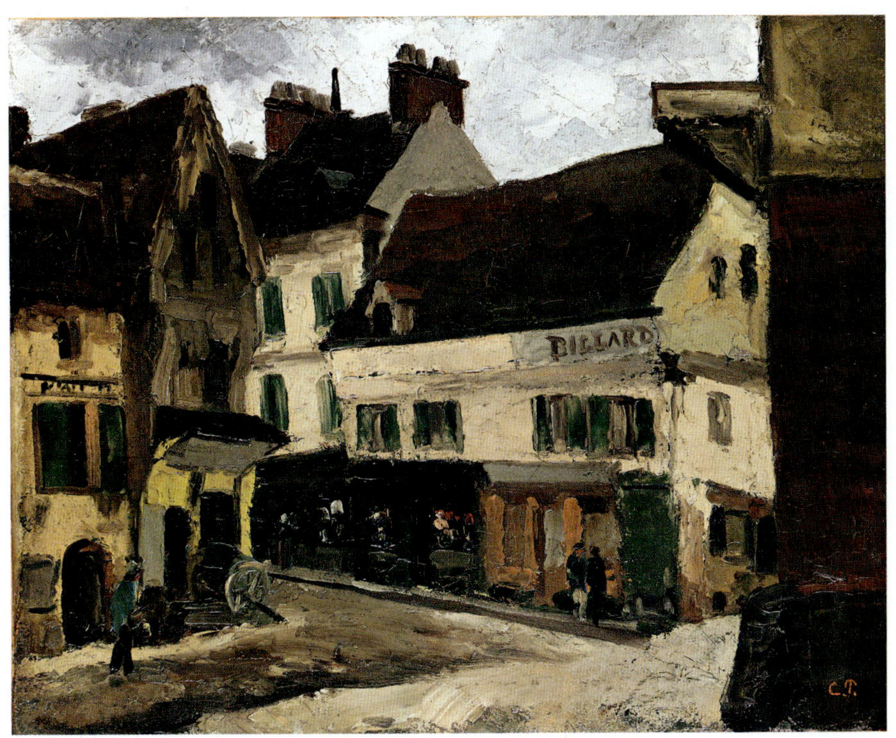

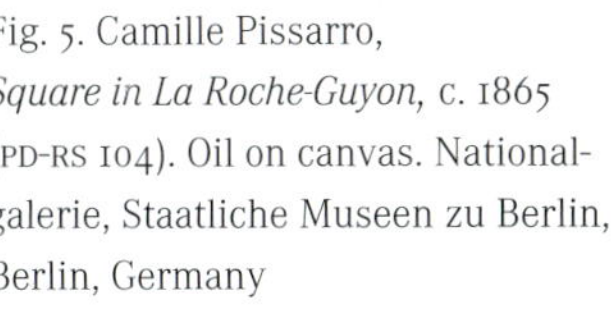
Fig. 5. Camille Pissarro, *Square in La Roche-Guyon,* c. 1865 (PD-RS 104). Oil on canvas. Nationalgalerie, Staatliche Museen zu Berlin, Berlin, Germany

the foreboding sky does not permit reflections in the steel gray water. The artist has used both palette knife and brush, and the scumbled, rough area on the right edge is reminiscent of Courbet's technique. This work must have been immensely important to Pissarro, as it remained in his personal collection until his death, surviving the invasion of his home in Louveciennes by the German army in 1870–71.

At the same time that he was painting large compositions for the Salons of 1865 and 1866, Pissarro also experimented with subject matter and technique in a range of small works. Perspectival street scenes with an emphasis on the blocky nature of the architecture (cat. 7) feature stone walls and cramped roadways, in a rejection of the broad expanses of his Salon entries for a more confined spatial construction. Such early investigations of the rural townscape reflect Corot's influence and prefigure Pissarro's views of the route de Versailles in Louveciennes that he began in 1869 and continued both before and after the Franco-Prussian War of 1870–71 (see cats. 12, 14, and 15). These images of thoroughfares are portraits of the neighborhood where Pissarro was living and allow a glimpse of what he saw every day. *The House of Père Gallien, Pontoise*, of 1866 (cat. 6), also displays a style, structure, mood, and scale that differ markedly from his Salon entries. The palette is fresh and bright, and the innovative use of broken brushwork, particularly in the budding tree in the center, seems to anticipate the Impressionist style that surfaced in his production in the early 1870s.

In 1867 Pissarro continued to explore new subjects and modes of expression in his smaller paintings. In *Banks of the Oise at Saint-Ouen-l'Aumône* (cat. 8), he depicts a dynamic townscape that includes a factory smokestack towering above a grove of trees, spewing its smoke into a beautiful blue sky as two figures walk along the bank on the opposite side of the river. The artist has employed a combination of techniques, with heavily weighted strokes defining the sandy path, more delicate touches for the foliage, and areas of pigment applied with a palette knife in the representation of the buildings. He addresses the encroachment of industrialization again in *The Chemin de l'Écluse and the Pontoise Bridge* (cat. 9), but here the factory is quiet, surrounded by a group of earth-toned buildings. He focuses his attention on a bourgeois couple who stare out at the viewer, stopped in their tracks, surrounded by a somber scene of contemporary life.

Pissarro was the first of his colleagues to include elements of the changing nature of the suburban landscape in his paintings. The choice of a factory as the central theme in his views of Pontoise from the late 1860s was extremely modern. In the 1850s and 1860s major improvements to roads and rivers, as well as the expansion of the railroads throughout the country, changed the way that people lived. For the first time, one could quickly travel from Paris to the suburbs by train, allowing people to commute to jobs in the city from relatively long distances. In addition, members of the working class were able to travel to riverside locations for relaxation on the weekends. Factories appeared in formerly rural locations, where land was cheaper and goods could be easily transported to their destinations. Monet, often credited with being a more progressive artist than Pissarro in subject and technique, did not begin to consider the industrialization of the French countryside in his canvases until the early 1870s with a series of railroad paintings and views of the banks of the Seine in Argenteuil that include factories.[18] Pissarro incorporated representations of this new France in many compositions of the 1860s and 1870s, although later in his career he embraced the more rustic nature of the country in his figure paintings. This change in subject may be considered a product of his growing interest in politics, particularly in philosophical anarchism, which may have stimulated him to feature peasant figures as a symbol of the pure, humble nature of the farming community. However, in his earlier townscapes, he accepts the influence of commerce on the suburban scene and includes it as an element of modern life.

Pissarro's experimentation in style and subject matter in his smaller paintings of this period may have prompted the Salon jury to reject his submission in 1867, after accepting his work for the previous two years. This negative response prompted him to look for an approach that would satisfy both the judges and his own creative needs. He soon began a series of grand compositions that has often been considered the culmination of his efforts in the late 1860s, known informally as the Jalais Hill series. His depictions of this area in L'Hermitage, a group of five large-scale and two smaller works, are admired

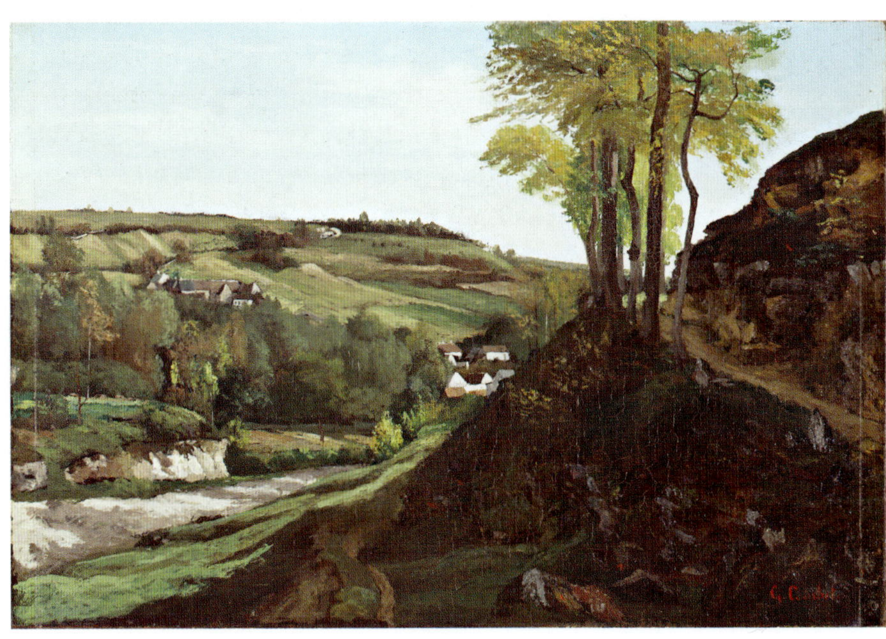

Fig. 6. Gustave Courbet, *The Valley of Ornans*, 1858. Oil on canvas. Saint Louis Art Museum, Museum Purchase

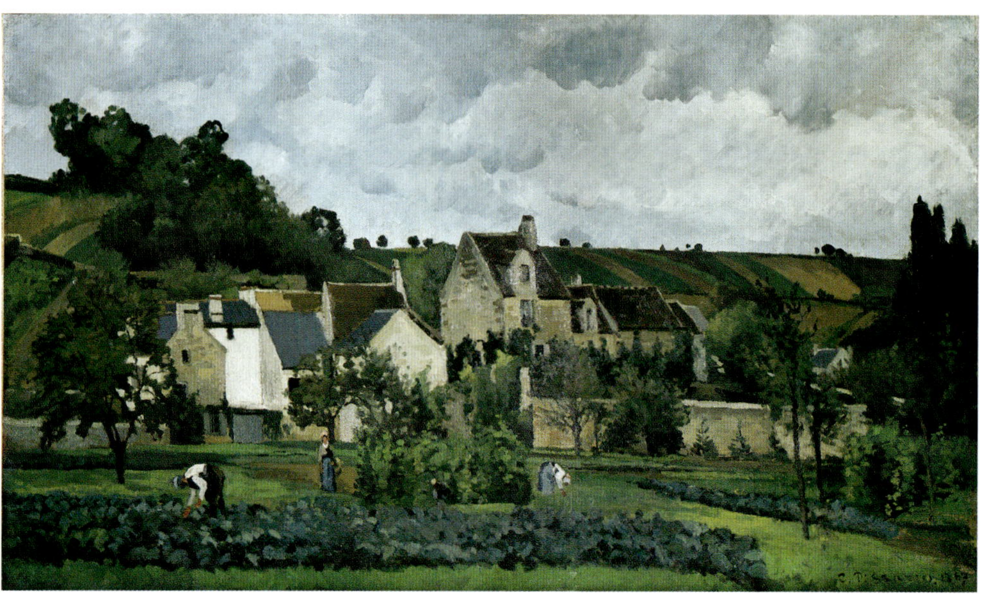

Fig. 7. Camille Pissarro, *L'Hermitage at Pontoise,* 1867 (PD-RS 119). Oil on canvas. Wallraf-Richartz-Museum/Fond. Corboud, Cologne, Germany, WRM 3119

for their exploration of geometric structure, unique quality of light, and bold use of the palette knife.[19] These compositions allowed him to incorporate his previous experimentation with this technique into a more acceptable Salon format. Their broad view and bold painting style are reminiscent of Courbet's landscapes of the previous decade, such as *The Valley of Ornans*, 1858 (fig. 6), but Pissarro has rejected the somewhat artificial image of nature that Courbet had portrayed, where the sky and land seem unconnected. In Pissarro's works from this series, he produced a more authentic, truthful view of nature, harmoniously integrating the elements of sky, land, and air.

When two of the L'Hermitage paintings were exhibited in the Salon of 1868, Zola was extremely enthusiastic about the realistic and honest interpretation of nature that Pissarro was presenting. In comments that could refer to *Côte des Jalais, Pontoise*, 1867 (cat. 10), Zola wrote: "The artist concerns himself with the truth only, with consciousness; he places himself before a wall of nature, he devotes himself to the work of interpreting the horizons in their severe breadth, without seeking to put there the least delight of his invention. He is neither poet nor philosopher, but simply a naturalist, maker of skies and land."[20] For the first time, Pissarro did not identify himself as a pupil of Corot or Melbye in the Salon *livret* but simply listed his name and place of birth.

L'Hermitage at Pontoise, 1867 (fig. 7), is one of the most spectacular paintings from the series. Here the artist has focused on integrating the architecture into the surrounding landscape, juxtaposing the strict geometry of the buildings and the cultivated fields with the nonrectilinear forms of the clouds and foliage. Pissarro employs a wide range of brushwork throughout, making the foliage in the foreground and the clouds in the sky with thick, full strokes. The palette knife that was used to form the buildings produced a coarse effect along their edges, seemingly rough-hewn like the houses that the artist is depicting.[21]

When Pissarro's early career is considered as a whole, there is a seemingly abrupt change in style and scale between the grandeur of the paintings in the Jalais Hill series and his more modestly scaled proto-Impressionist views of Louveciennes of the subsequent years. However, in the smaller paintings produced in Pontoise in 1867–68, such as *Landscape at Ennery near Pontoise* (cat. 11), one can see hints of the future. The careful construction and commitment to geometry apparent in the series has disappeared, and the unique quality of a painting produced in the open air has begun to emerge. Pigment is applied to the canvas in thick, animated brushstrokes. The trees are rounded and organic, serving almost as reflections of the clouds above. It is this sort of intimate, fresh, and immediate composition, along with *Strollers on a Country Road, La Varenne-Saint-Hilaire* (cat. 3) and *Banks of the Oise at Saint-Ouen-l'Aumône* (cat. 8), among many others, that foretell his future as an Impressionist.

Louveciennes: The Birthplace of Impressionism

In 1869 Pissarro moved from Pontoise to Louveciennes, a close suburb of Paris that was easily accessible by train. Monet was living in nearby Saint-Michel, Pierre-Auguste Renoir (1841–1919) in Voisins, a hamlet of Louveciennes, and Alfred Sisley (1839–1899) was also frequently in the area. Pissarro probably settled there to be close to his colleagues.[22] The family lived at 22, route de Versailles, and after a series of snowstorms in the winter of 1869–70, Monet and Pissarro produced a remarkable group of views of this street, including *The Corner of the Route de Versailles and the Chemin de l'Aqueduc, Louveciennes* (cat. 12). With a new focus on light and atmosphere, this series of road scenes can be considered the start of the movement that was to become Impressionism. In these works, both artists incorporated the traditional seventeenth-century Dutch compositional device of a road leading the viewer's eye into the painting. When compared with Monet's view of the thoroughfare (fig. 8), it is apparent that Pissarro chose not to utilize the strict geometry that his friend preferred, in which the perspectival axes meet in the center of the canvas. Instead, he recorded the road curving gently to the right or left, placing his easel to the side of the path. For Pissarro, this collaboration with Monet was the start of a lifelong interest in depicting nature during all types of weather, including snow and rain.[23] Their partnership also influenced Pissarro's brushwork, which became loose and experimental, with more fluid strokes used for the stone buildings and the snow, and thinner, coarser strokes used for the bare trees.

Pissarro's predilection for portraying the roads that ran through Louveciennes formed

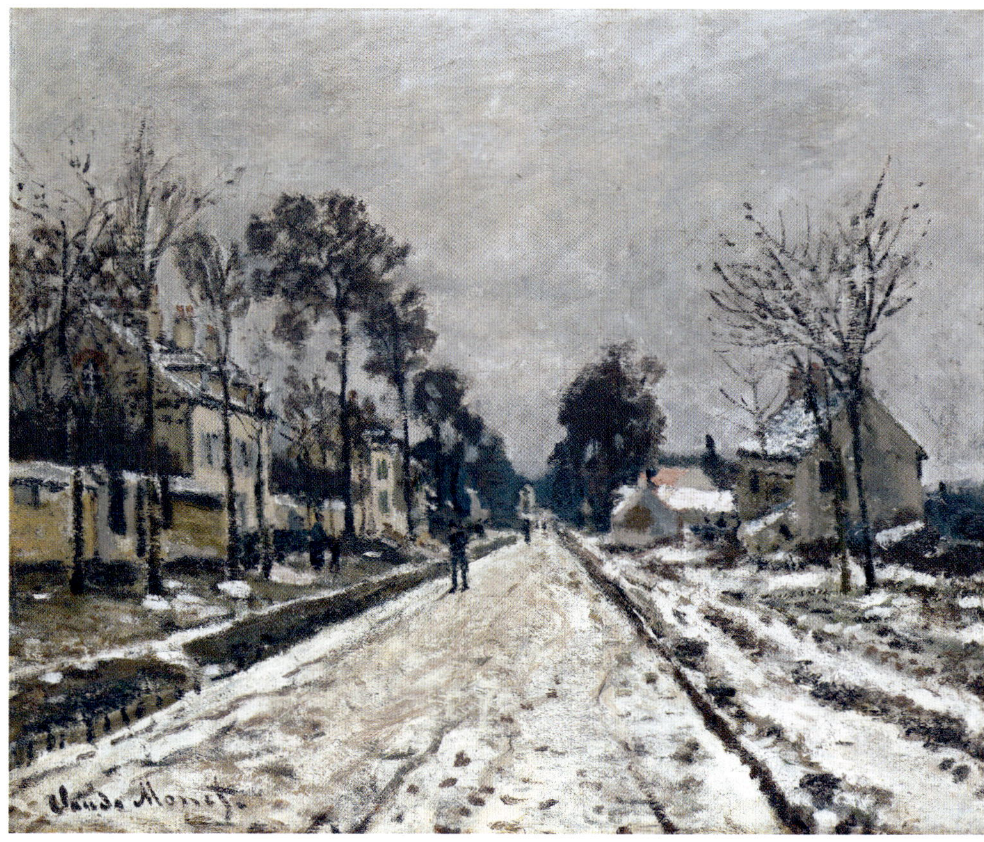

Fig. 8. Claude Monet, *Road to Versailles, Snow Effect,* 1869–70. Oil on canvas. Private collection

an important series of small canvases well after Monet left. This interest in thoroughfares was certainly not a new motif in French landscape painting; Corot had featured the theme in numerous paintings throughout his career.[24] In Pissarro's paintings of roads, the light is luminous, and shadows play an important role. Rather than relegated to a random figure or tree, their dark forms provide overall structure and pattern to the compositions. In 1870 Pissarro painted *Houses at Bougival* (cat. 19), his largest and most ambitious view of the Seine valley to date. It is thought to have been his entry for the Salon of 1870, the last of the state-run exhibitions in which he participated. Here the artist alters the familiar motif of a street scene receding into the distance by rotating the path so it is parallel to the picture plane, a view that allows a glimpse of the gardens behind the houses in the town. The rigid, geometric structure of the road, the tall trees, and the architecture is offset by the graceful shapes of the leaves on the trees and in the gardens that dominate the composition. The cool, crisp atmosphere of an autumn day is accurately and sensitively portrayed in this monumental landscape.

London

The outbreak of the Franco-Prussian War in July 1870 brought an end to Pissarro's first creative period in Louveciennes. The war caused a profound disruption to his life, as well as to the lives of his colleagues. Édouard Manet (1832–1883), Edgar Degas (1834–1917), Renoir, and Frédéric Bazille (1841–1870) all served in the French army (Bazille was killed in action), whereas Pissarro and Monet went abroad. Pissarro and his family escaped first to Montfoucault, in the Mayenne region on the border between Brittany and Normandy. After several months, the family traveled to London, where they remained for the duration of the war. They lived in Upper Norwood, in the southern suburbs of the British capital, from December 1870 until July 1871. Despite its short duration, this period marked a change in Pissarro's oeuvre, in which new subjects, a lighter palette, and varied techniques were fully explored. In addition, this suburban locale, where Pissarro produced all of his works during his stay, provided him with motifs very different from those of rural Louveciennes.

Although Monet had also fled to London, the two artists did not rekindle their creative collaboration of the previous winter. Instead, they often met at museums and were notably

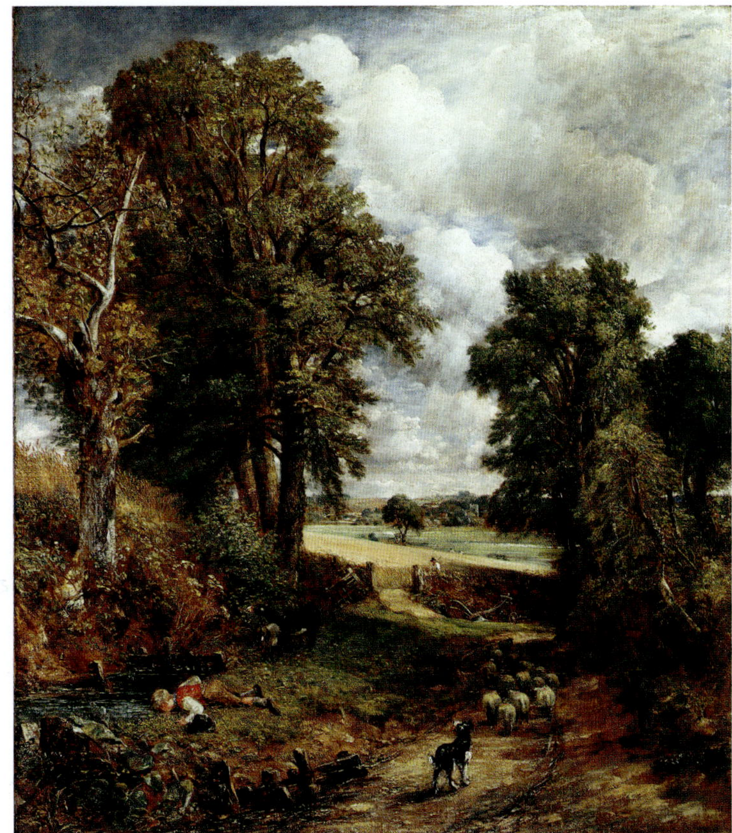

Fig. 9. John Constable, *The Cornfield*, 1826. Oil on canvas. The National Gallery, London, NG8090

impressed by the poetic depictions of nature by the British artists Joseph Mallord William Turner (1775–1851) and John Constable (1776–1837) (fig. 9).[25] Pissarro later described their time in London: "Monet worked in the parks, whilst I, living at Lower Norwood, at that time a charming suburb, studied the effects of fog, snow, and springtime. . . . The water-colours and paintings of Turner and Constable, the canvases of Old Crome, have certainly had influence upon us."[26] Pissarro's London paintings feature views of roads, local landmarks seen from a distance, and the new suburban train line in the area.

Lordship Lane Station, East Dulwich, 1871 (cat. 21), is one of the most modern works that Pissarro painted during his sojourn abroad. This train station, on the Crystal Palace Line, opened in 1865 to serve the popular recreation and exhibition center. In keeping with the Impressionists' interest in portraying modern life, his handling of the subject focuses on the transformation of the suburbs by urbanization. Steam from the railway engine drifts to the sky, and the track, lined with new houses, cuts a deep trench through the hills. This remarkable use of plunging perspective was a breakthrough for Pissarro, possibly influenced by Turner's famous *Rain, Steam, and Speed—The Great Western Railway*, before 1844, that was on view at the National Gallery during his stay in the city (cat. 21, fig. 1). *View of Alleyn Park, West Dulwich* (cat. 23) also features a train in motion. It, however, is barely visible beneath a canopy of interlocking trees that grace the foreground of the composition, producing a more gentle interpretation of the intersection of modernization and suburban life.

In London, Pissarro also returned to the familiar motif of street scenes, although his use of perspective became more assertive and direct. *The Avenue, Sydenham* (cat. 20) feels quite different from the simple rural roads in Louveciennes or Pontoise. Here he focused on a busy thoroughfare, complete with proper sidewalks and several groups of figures in city attire walking or driving on the road on a sunny day. The palette has shifted to embrace brighter hues, including a vivid blue sky, perhaps influenced by works by Turner that Pissarro saw in London (fig. 10).[27] This composition was carefully crafted and considered, with small brushstrokes of paint fully covering the canvas, reminiscent of the formality of a seventeenth-century Dutch landscape.[28]

Return to France

After the war ended in June 1871, the artist and his family returned to Louveciennes for a brief stay of about ten months. Their home had been occupied by the German army during their absence, and a substantial part of Pissarro's oeuvre had been destroyed. He returned to the familiar route de Versailles and other roads leading in and out of the town for his motifs, perhaps to re-create some of the pictures that had been ruined, often experimenting with different types of perspective and varying the angle of the road to the

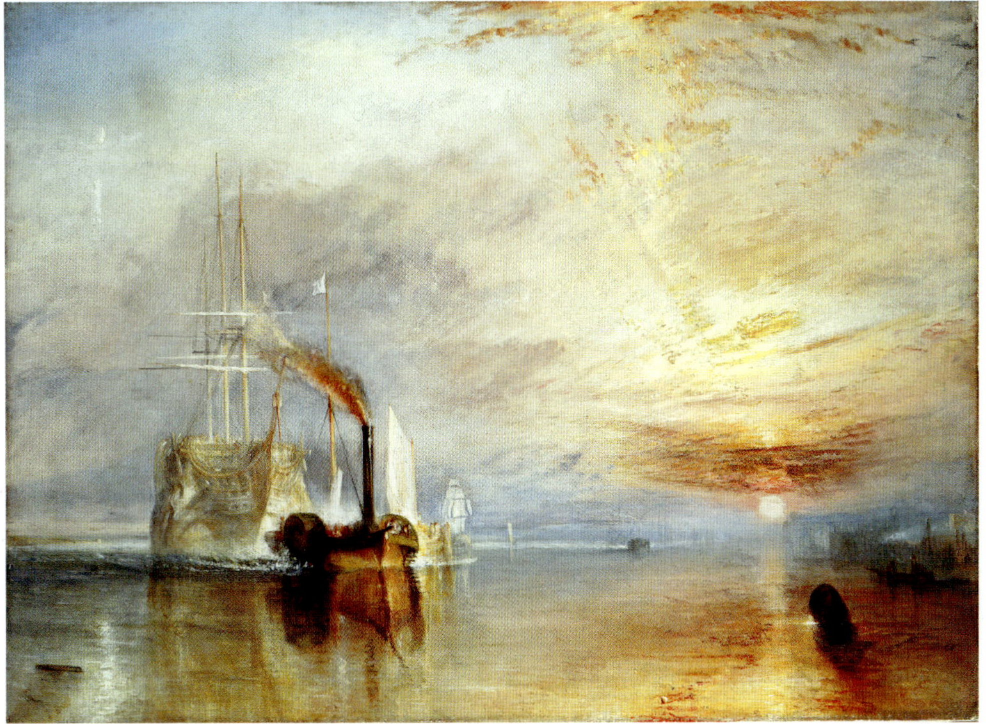

Fig. 10. Joseph Mallord William Turner, *The Fighting Temeraire,* 1838. Oil on canvas. Turner bequest, 1856, The National Gallery, London, NG6236

picture plane in several examples.[29] Some are tightly constructed views (cat. 25), while others show the grand expanse of the street seen from the distance, feature more dramatic vistas, and demonstrate a more balanced relationship between land and sky than those dating from before the war.[30] He worked closely with Sisley, who also was living in Louveciennes. Both artists produced views of the rue de Voisins (cat. 25 and cat. 25, fig. 1) in 1871, each featuring a similar fascination with light and atmospheric effects. Their individual styles during this period were quite alike, as both incorporated soft colors and broken, varied brushwork, although Pissarro's greater focus on structure is evident.

The London experience proved to have a lasting effect on Pissarro's painting style. Varied types of brushstrokes—vigorous, soft, thick, thin—often appear within the same work. His compositions became more complex, more carefully composed and elaborate in feel. Further, his brushwork became increasingly open, often allowing the toned ground to show through lightly painted sections, which gives the composition a sense of illumination. In addition, his paintings during this period demonstrate increasing interest in the rendering of shadows.

Pissarro explored a variety of subjects during this second stay in Louveciennes. A depiction

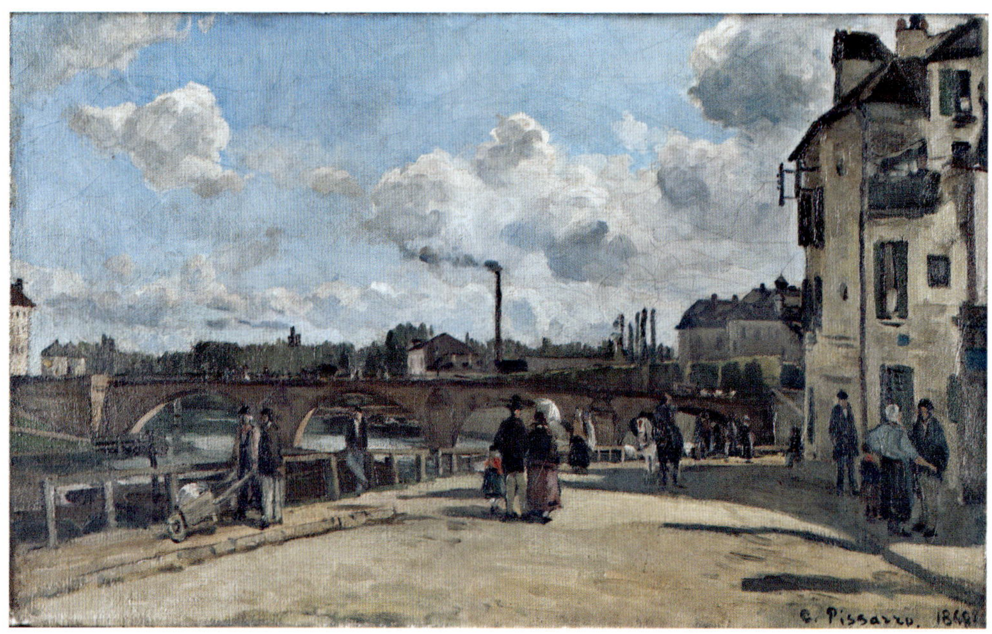

Fig. 11. Camille Pissarro, *Quai du Pothuis, Pontoise*, 1868 (PD-RS 123). Oil on canvas. Kunsthalle Mannheim

of nearby Bougival, produced soon after his return to France, includes the riverside motifs of the previous decade in his new Impressionist style. In *Banks of the Seine at Bougival* (cat. 26), the artist juxtaposes the bourgeoisie who stroll along its banks in their leisure hours with the working barges that are an integral part of the local economy, much as in several of his compositions of 1867 (fig. 11). The Seine was an important subject for many of the Impressionist painters, although Pissarro was more interested in the working aspects of the river than his colleagues were.[31] *The Farm on the Grounds of the Château of Marly* (cat. 24) takes the viewer away from the busy river to a quiet parklike setting on a beautiful early autumn day. The seemingly simple theme of a working farm belies a complex compositional structure, in which the artist uses the two fences on either side of the meadow to funnel the viewer's eye toward the buildings in the distance. Pissarro's interest in exploring different types of light effects are clearly seen here, as he leaves the foreground in shadow, contrasting with bright sunlight in the background.

In 1872 Pissarro received a commission from Achille Arosa, a wealthy Parisian collector, for a series of four large horizontal landscapes of the four seasons to be placed over the doors in his house.[32] *Winter at Louveciennes* (fig. 12) was the first canvas painted, perhaps early in 1872, and the others were completed in Pontoise (figs. 13–15). If they were painted in order of the seasons (winter, spring, summer, and autumn), Pissarro's sense of color became increasingly bolder as he worked. The winter scene, thinly painted with a muted palette, features the most radical and abstract composition. Paint application becomes thicker and more exuberant as the series progresses, as Pissarro's budding interest in light, shadows, atmosphere, and rural life seen in all of its great glory is made manifest in this powerful quartet.

Pontoise

In April 1872 the artist and his family left Louveciennes for Pontoise, where they remained for the next ten years. A much larger town than Louveciennes, Pontoise was formerly an agricultural center, but industrial businesses began to appear in great number during this period. The rich variety of architecture in the town provided endless inspiration for Pissarro's creativity.[33] Soon after Pissarro arrived in Pontoise, Cézanne moved to nearby Auvers in order to paint with him. The period 1872–74 is notable for the intimate working relationship that developed between the two artists. Both openly acknowledged the importance of this friendship and, despite close contact and collaboration, kept his individuality intact. Their relationship encouraged Cézanne to focus on landscape painting for the first time and to lighten his palette. At the same time, Pissarro's works began to evince a renewed focus on geometric forms and structure, influenced by Cézanne's interest in Pissarro's earlier paintings of the region. Many years later, after seeing Cézanne's one-man show at Ambroise Vollard's Paris gallery, Pissarro recalled in a letter to his son Lucien the happy period when the two artists worked together in harmony in Pontoise and nearby Auvers: "Curiously enough, in Cézanne's show at Vollard's there are certain landscapes of Auvers and Pontoise [painted in 1871–74] that are similar to mine. Naturally, we were always together! But what cannot be denied is that each of us kept the only thing that counts, the unique 'sensation'!—This could easily be shown."[34]

Pissarro's compositions from Pontoise are extremely diverse in subject matter and technique. As Christopher Lloyd discusses in his essay in this catalogue, it was in Pontoise that Pissarro made his mark as the painter of a specific landscape, the place with which his work is most associated. His style can be documented as changing, not from year to year, but often from painting to painting. *Ruelle des Poulies, at Pontoise* (cat. 30) features an unusual view of Pontoise seen from a neighboring hill, allowing the viewer to look down on the buildings in the center of town. *Place du Vieux-Cimetière, Pontoise* (cat. 31) highlights a broad, but almost completely empty, plaza on a dazzling sunny day, making the focus of the composition hard to find. Even when he paints a site as open and popular as *The Municipal Garden, Pontoise* (cat. 49), he depicts a large group of figures scattered throughout the garden, seemingly unconnected from one another and somewhat isolated in feeling.

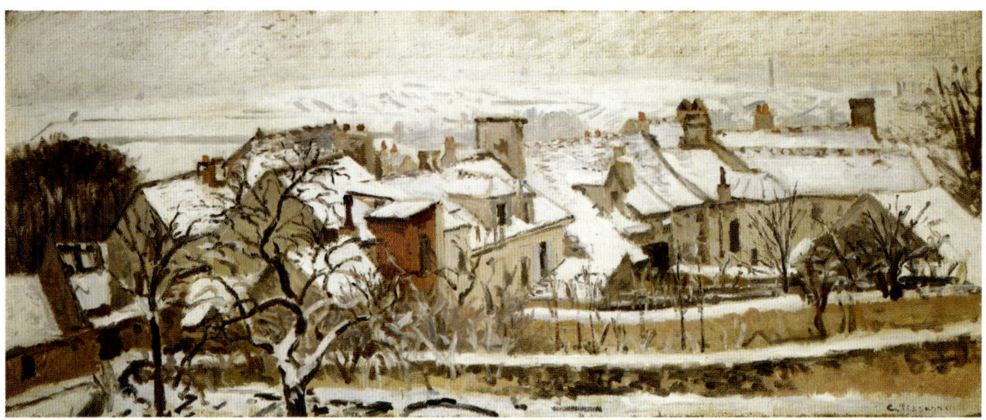

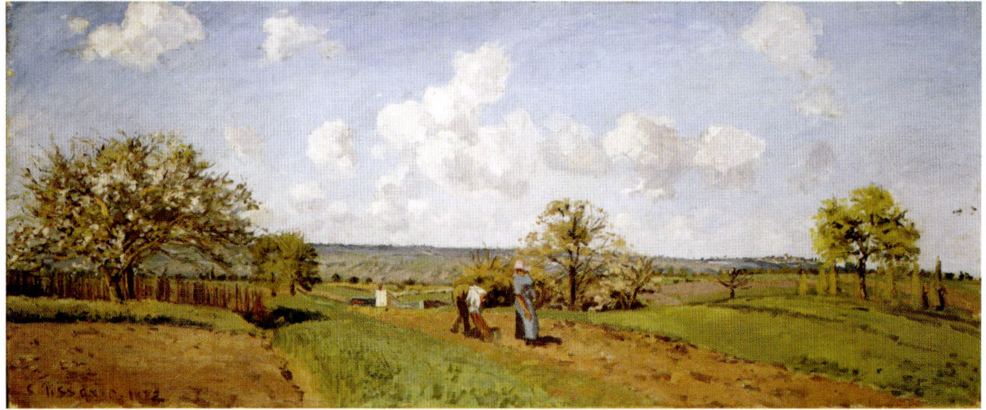

Two of his more "urban" views of the town were painted in winter, a season that inspired him throughout his career. *Rue de la Citadelle, Pontoise* (cat. 34) dates from the winter of 1873, when Cézanne produced his own version of the same street.[35] Given the white sky, there are no shadows to be seen, but Pissarro included footprints in the snow to provide pattern and texture. Probably painted at the same time,[36] *Rue de Gisors, Effect of Snow, Pontoise* (cat. 35) features a curving road filled with figures cleaning up after a snowstorm. Thick, chunky, horizontal brushstrokes are offset by the geometry of the buildings that moves the viewer's eye down the street.

In 1873 Pissarro produced a small group of paintings of the Châlon distillery located on the banks of the Oise (cats. 36–38). This new set of factory buildings allowed him to explore the motif of modernity nestled in a bucolic setting, a subject that had been of interest to him periodically since the 1860s. His devotion to the more rural nature of the French countryside was consistent throughout his career, but in 1867 and 1873, local factories

Fig. 12. Camille Pissarro, *Winter at Louveciennes*, c. 1872 (PD-RS 238). Oil on canvas. Private collection

Fig. 13. Camille Pissarro, *Spring*, 1872 (PD-RS 239). Oil on canvas. Private collection

Fig. 14. Camille Pissarro, *Summer*, c. 1872 (PD-RS 240). Oil on canvas. Private collection

Fig. 15. Camille Pissarro, *Autumn*, c. 1872 (PD-RS 241). Oil on canvas. Private collection

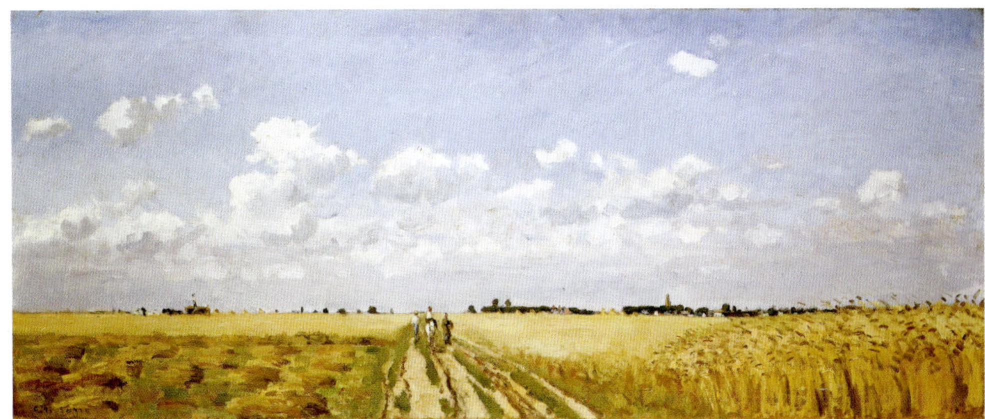

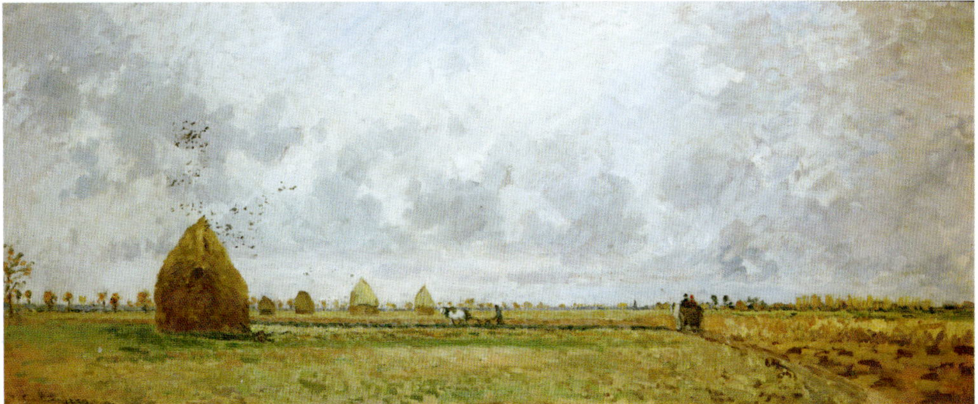

made several substantial appearances in his paintings. In *Route d'Auvers on the Banks of the Oise, Pontoise* (cat. 39), Pissarro focused on a path on the banks of the river, with a chimney and a train speeding by on the opposite side. The energetic brushwork and the brilliant blue of the sky overshadow the relative calm of this suburban landscape, which quietly integrates the rural with the modern. During this period, Pissarro's technique becomes more experimental, with numerous vigorous brushstrokes used to represent motion or energy, or simply to mark the artist's presence, not intended to depict an actual object.

As his painting style evolved into a mature Impressionist mode, Pissarro was continually inspired by artists of the past. Well into the 1870s one can still see the feathery trees of Corot or the compositional toughness of Courbet as an underlying structure for some of his most modern compositions. Jean-François Millet's (1814–1875) images of peasants became more important as Pissarro's interest in figures started to intensify. And the use of bright color that first appeared in his London paintings continued in his later works.

The First Impressionist Exhibition

Because Pissarro had not exhibited at the Salon for several years, he was very eager to show his recent work to the public. As early as 1867, a group of young artists had been talking about organizing their own exhibition. It has been suggested convincingly that the initial idea for an independent group show may have been prompted by the rejection in 1867 of the Salon submissions by Pissarro, Monet, Renoir, Sisley, and Cézanne.[37] Although the group put off the project in 1867, the idea of snubbing the Salon with their own exhibition remained a major objective for Pissarro and his colleagues. Their idea was not to be realized for seven years, however, as the Franco-Prussian War and its devastating aftermath would intervene.

While arrangements were well under way for the first Impressionist exhibition, in January 1874 an auction took place at the Hôtel Drouot that included works by Pissarro, Monet, Sisley, and Degas. The sale was a success. Given the high prices paid for Pissarro's work at the auction, the critic Théodore Duret (1838–1927), a close friend, encouraged the painter not to participate in the first Impressionist show but to return to the Salon. Perhaps due to his progressive leanings and his fondness for his artist colleagues, Pissarro ignored Duret's advice and went on to exhibit in all eight of the Impressionist exhibitions, the only artist to do so.[38]

Although some of the initial organizers were no longer able to participate, on April 15, 1874, the first exhibition of the Société anonyme des artistes peintres, sculpteurs, graveurs, etc. opened in Paris at 35, boulevard des Capucines, the former studio of the photographer Félix Nadar.[39] The show had been actively planned for more than a year, and there was an official charter outlining the members' dues, rights, and responsibilities. Thirty artists took part, including regular exhibitors at the Salon as well as avant-garde independents.[40] The undertaking made history, as the participants chose which of their works to display, without the filter of a jury. The exhibition attracted the attention of the press, both positive and negative, and more than fifty articles were written about the event. The overall reaction to Pissarro's submissions was unenthusiastic, and several reviewers commented on the mundane choice of cabbage fields as the main motif in several of his canvases.

For the exhibition, Pissarro selected five paintings that summarize the range of his interests in 1874; they highlighted different seasons, weather conditions, and public and private locales in and around Pontoise. *Orchard in Bloom* of 1872 (cat. 27) features the familiar subject of a large flowering tree that appeared in his work as early as 1866 (cat. 6). Here the artist displayed his love of shadow, juxtaposed with the strong sun on a brilliant spring day. The two peasants working in the field also recall the compositions of Millet, an artist

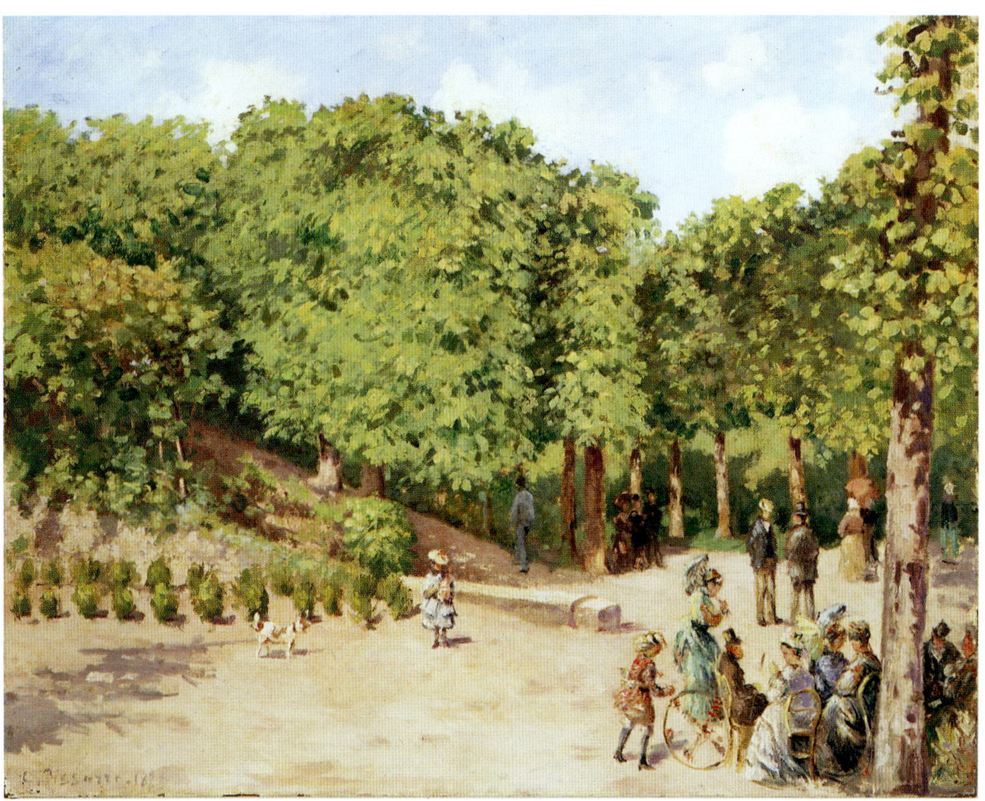

Fig. 16. Camille Pissarro, *The Municipal Garden, Pontoise,* 1873 (PD-RS 309). Oil on canvas. The State Hermitage Museum, St. Petersburg

whose work inspired Pissarro, particularly in his figure paintings, throughout his career.

Chestnut Trees at Osny (cat. 42), probably from 1873, utilizes a traditional motif of a group of chestnut trees with interlocking branches that is reminiscent of one of his London compositions (cat. 23). The subject of intertwined trees recalls the works of the eighteenth-century painter Hubert Robert, among others. *The Municipal Garden, Pontoise* (fig. 16) is one of two works that record the most public place in Pontoise, the city gardens. Here Pissarro showcases his talent for depicting a large group of people within a more cultivated landscape. *Morning in June, Saint-Ouen-l'Aumône* (fig. 17) presents the wide vista of a working field, similar in size and feel to his 1872 *Summer* (fig. 14) from the four seasons cycle. It was the largest of the five works that he entered in the exhibition.

Hoarfrost at Ennery (cat. 43) is the most experimental of the five compositions. In it, a peasant carries a bundle of sticks on his back as he walks through the landscape, a recurring theme in Pissarro's rural scenes of this period, which is reminiscent of some of Millet's paintings. A light frost covers the ground, and the sun is just starting to warm the earth. An

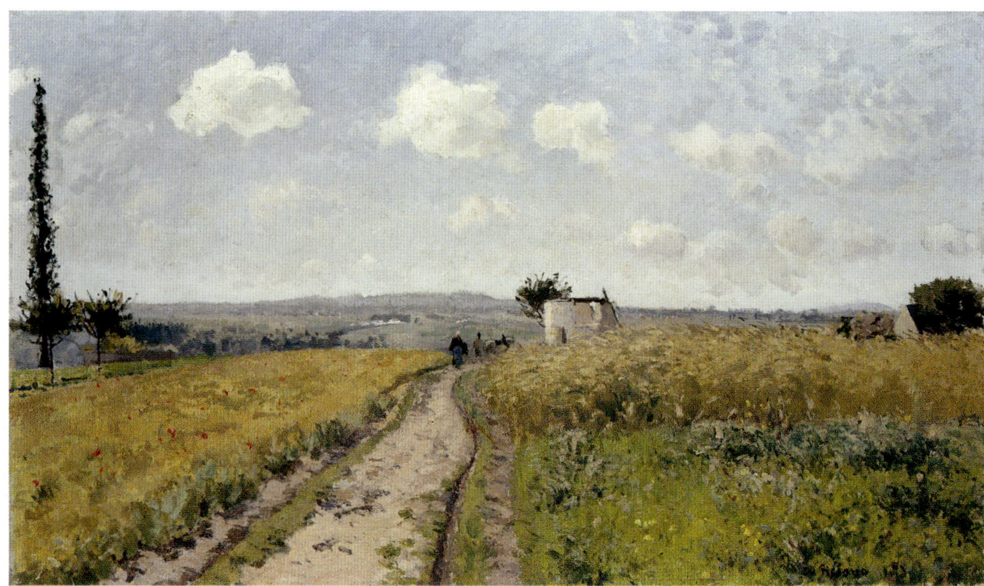

Fig. 17. Camille Pissarro, *Morning in June, Saint-Ouen-l'Aumône,* 1873 (PD-RS 312). Oil on canvas. Staatliche Kunsthalle Karlsruhe

intricate pattern of light and shadow appears in the right foreground, apparently made up of furrows in the field and shadows from trees that are outside the range of the composition. Of the five works that Pissarro exhibited in the show, *Hoarfrost at Ennery* was the most controversial, and it produced significant reaction. In his review, Louis Leroy commented that the painting had "neither head nor tail, top nor bottom, front nor back," a statement that addressed the unconventional construction of the landscape.[41] Pissarro's use of shadows, in particular, caused the greatest stir, forcing even the critic and supporter of the Impressionist movement Jules-Antoine Castagnary to write, "Pissarro is sober and strong. His synthesizing eye embraces at a glance the whole scene. He commits the grave error of painting fields (*Gelée blanche*) with shadows cast by trees placed outside the frame. As a result the viewer is left to suppose they exist, as he cannot see them."[42]

These five works fully explore all of the sites, influences, and techniques that Pissarro had investigated during his stay in Pontoise up to that point. They can be considered an important counterpoint to his Salon entries of the 1860s, in which he was still heavily relying on Corot, Courbet, and Daubigny to help him find the magic formula to display his own "sensation." In the intervening decade, Pissarro became an independent and determined artist, who constantly searched for the perfect motif that would permit him to depict his unique view of the world. By 1874 the lessons of the past had been fully absorbed, and he looked to those masters, and others, for moments of inspiration but no longer relied on them for all of the answers.

Beyond the First Impressionist Exhibition

After the first Impressionist show in 1874, Pissarro had a long and productive career of almost thirty more years of work. Toward the end of the 1870s, he reached a stylistic crisis, painting with small, thick, commalike brushstrokes that often overwhelmed his subjects. In an effort to make a fresh start, he collaborated with Degas on printmaking, and their close working relationship encouraged Pissarro in the early 1880s to turn to figure painting. These compositions in turn inspired Paul Gauguin (1848–1903). In 1885, at the age of fifty-five, Pissarro met Paul Signac (1863–1935) and Georges Seurat (1859–1891), young artists who were working in the Pointillist style, in which complementary colors in precise dots were placed next to each other. This new method of painting appealed to Pissarro, and he devoted several years to exploring this method, proving yet again that he was an artist with an incredible openness and willingness to try new things and take risks. After intense negative response from critics and dealers, and worried that he was losing his connection to nature because of his exclusive work in the studio, Pissarro returned to a more traditional Impressionist technique in the 1890s. In his last decade, he struck a balance between rural subjects near his home in Éragny and urban views of Rouen and Paris.

In 1888, after a continual struggle for financial and critical success, Camille Pissarro described his creative process and his desire to remain true to his vision of the world. In a letter to his son Lucien he wrote: "I do not believe that anyone could devote—if not more talent—more care and good will to the service of his art; it takes me hours of reflection to decide on the slightest detail; is this impatience? . . . I think not! For I do not wish to make a brush stroke when I do not feel complete mastery of my subject, there's the rub—that is the great difficulty; without sensation, nothing, absolutely nothing valid."[43]

1. Camille Pissarro to his son Lucien, July 26, 1893, in *Letters to His Son Lucien*, ed. John Rewald (New York: Pantheon Books, 1943), 212.
2. For more on Fritz Melbye, see Christopher Lloyd's essay in this catalogue.
3. Gary Tinterow, in Tinterow, Michael Pantazzi, and Vincent Pomarède, *Corot* (New York: The Metropolitan Museum of Art, 1996), 296–97, discusses the connection between Corot and Pissarro. He compares Pissarro's *Farmyard*, c. 1863 (PD-RS 69), oil on canvas, private collection, Chicago, and *Village Scene, Women Chatting*, 1863 (PD-RS 70), oil on canvas, private collection, with Corot's *Courtyard of a Bakery near Paris*, c. 1865–70, oil on canvas, Musée d'Orsay, on deposit from Musée du Louvre, R.F. 2441.
4. Pissarro to Lucien, June 28, 1891, in *Letters to His Son Lucien*, 177.
5. Quoted in Paul Gsell, "La Tradition artistique française, I," *Revue Politique et Littéraire*, March 26, 1892, 403–6, quoted and translated in PD-RS, 1:109.
6. For more information on Corot's oil sketch, see Tinterow, Pantazzi, Pomarède, *Corot*, 90–91, 154–57.
7. See Joachim Pissarro, *Camille Pissarro* (New York: Harry N. Abrams, 1993), 39 for a list of Pissarro's various addresses in the 1860s.
8. See PD-RS 55, 57, 61–74 for examples of works that are heavily dependent on Corot's influence.
9. Émile Zola, *Salons*, ed. F. W. J. Hemmings and R. J. Neiss (Paris: Minard, 1959), 48, quoted and translated in Rachael Ziady DeLue, "Pissarro, Landscape, Vision, and Tradition," *Art Bulletin* 80 (December 1998): 726.
10. *Paysage à Montmorency*, no. 2472 in the Salon *livret*, has been identified as *Donkey in Front of a Farm, Montmorency*, c. 1858 (PD-RS 37), oil on canvas, Musée d'Orsay, R.F. 1943-8, a small, modest farm scene featuring a donkey.
11. For more discussion on the influence of Daubigny, see Gary Tinterow and Henri Loyrette, *Origins of Impressionism* (New York: The Metropolitan Museum of Art, 1994), 443–44.
12. Charles Baudelaire, *Oeuvres complètes*, 2 vols. (Paris: Gallimard, La Pléiade, 1975–76), 2:661, quoted and translated in Tinterow and Loyrette, *Origins of Impressionism*, 79.
13. Théophile Gautier, *Exposition de 1859*, quoted and translated in Tinterow and Loyrette, *Origins of Impressionism*, 86.
14. See Mary Sebera's *Technical Notes* in this catalogue for discussion of paintings in the present exhibition that also have another composition under the top paint layer.
15. For a complete discussion of the evolution of the painted sketch in nineteenth-century French painting, see Albert Boime, *The Academy and French Painting in the Nineteenth Century* (London: Phaidon, 1971).
16. See Pissarro, *Camille Pissarro*, 47–48, for a further discussion on this lack of narrative.
17. Émile Zola, "Mon Salon: Adieux d'un critique d'art," 1866, in *Ecrits sur l'art*, ed. Jean-Pierre Leduc-Adine (Paris: Gallimard, 1991), 133; see also Jean Rousseau, "Le Salon de 1866. IV," *L'Univers Illustré* 9 (July 14, 1866): 447, both quoted and translated in Tinterow and Loyrette, *Origins of Impressionism*, 444–45.
18. See *Claude Monet. Biographie et catalogue raisonné*, 4 vols. (Paris: Taschen/Wildenstein Institute, 1996), nos. 153, 219, 221–224, 242, 279, 318, and 319, among others.
19. PD-RS 112, 115, 116, 119, 120, and 121 are depictions of the hills that surround L'Hermitage. PD-RS 125 is a large-scale work of similar style that features Les Pâtis, a hamlet to the west of Pontoise.
20. Zola, *Salons*, quoted and translated in DeLue, "Pissarro, Landscape, Vision, and Tradition," 721.
21. For more information on the creation of this painting, see Mary Sebera's *Technical Notes* in this catalogue.
22. *Camille Pissarro, 1830–1903* (London: Arts Council of Great Britain, 1980), 19.
23. See PD-RS 152, 153, and 155 for examples of road scenes produced during and after a rainstorm. For a survey of his interest in painting snow scenes, see Katherine Rothkopf, "Camille Pissarro: A Dedicated Painter of Winter," in Charles S. Moffett et al., *Impressionists in Winter: Effets de Neige* (Washington, D.C.: The Phillips Collection, 1998), 39–55.
24. See, for example, *The Sèvres Road*, discussed in Tinterow, Pantazzi, and Pomarède, *Corot*, 224–25.
25. Richard R. Brettell, *Pissarro and Pontoise: The Painter in a Landscape* (New Haven: Yale University Press, 1990), 150.
26. Quoted and translated in Wynford Dewhurst, *Impressionist Painting: Its Genesis and Development* (London: George Newnes, 1904), 31.

27. Brettell, *Pissarro and Pontoise*, 215 n. 26.
28. *The Avenue, Sydenham* has been linked to Meindert Hobbema's *The Avenue at Middelharnis*, 1689, a painting that entered the collection of the National Gallery in 1871, at the same time that Pissarro was living in the area. See Christopher Lloyd, "Camille Pissarro and Hans Holbein the Younger," *Burlington Magazine* 117, no. 872 (November 1975), 722–26.
29. See PD-RS 213–15, 221, and 224.
30. PD-RS 195, 196, and 198.
31. See Charles S. Moffett et al., *Impressionists on the Seine: A Celebration of Renoir's "Luncheon of the Boating Party"* (Washington, D.C.: The Phillips Collection, 1996).
32. For more information on this commission, see Christie's, New York, November 3, 2004, lot 33 and PD-RS 238.
33. For more on Pissarro and Pontoise, see Brettell, *Pissarro and Pontoise*.
34. Pissarro to Lucien, November 22, 1895, in *Letters to His Son Lucien*, 276. For more on the relationship between the two artists, see Joachim Pissarro, *Pioneering Modern Painting: Cézanne and Pissarro, 1865–1885* (New York: The Museum of Modern Art, 2005).
35. See John Rewald, *The Paintings of Paul Cézanne: A Catalogue Raisonné*, 2 vols. (New York: Harry N. Abrams, 1996), no. 195.
36. The only snowfall noted for 1873 occurred in February of that year. See "Winter Weather Chronology," in Moffett et al., *Impressionists in Winter*, 224.
37. Paul Tucker, "The First Impressionist Exhibition in Context," in Charles S. Moffett et al., *The New Painting: Impressionism, 1874–1886* (San Francisco: The Fine Arts Museums of San Francisco, 1986), 94.
38. Ibid., 106.
39. For a full account of the context for the first Impressionist exhibition, see ibid., 93–117.
40. Ibid., 105.
41. Louis Leroy, *Le Charivari*, April 25, 1874, quoted and translated in *The New Painting*, 138.
42. Jules-Antoine Castagnary, *Le Siècle*, April 29, 1874, quoted and translated in *The New Painting*, 138.
43. Pissarro to Lucien, April 16, 1888, in *Letters to His Son Lucien*, 124.

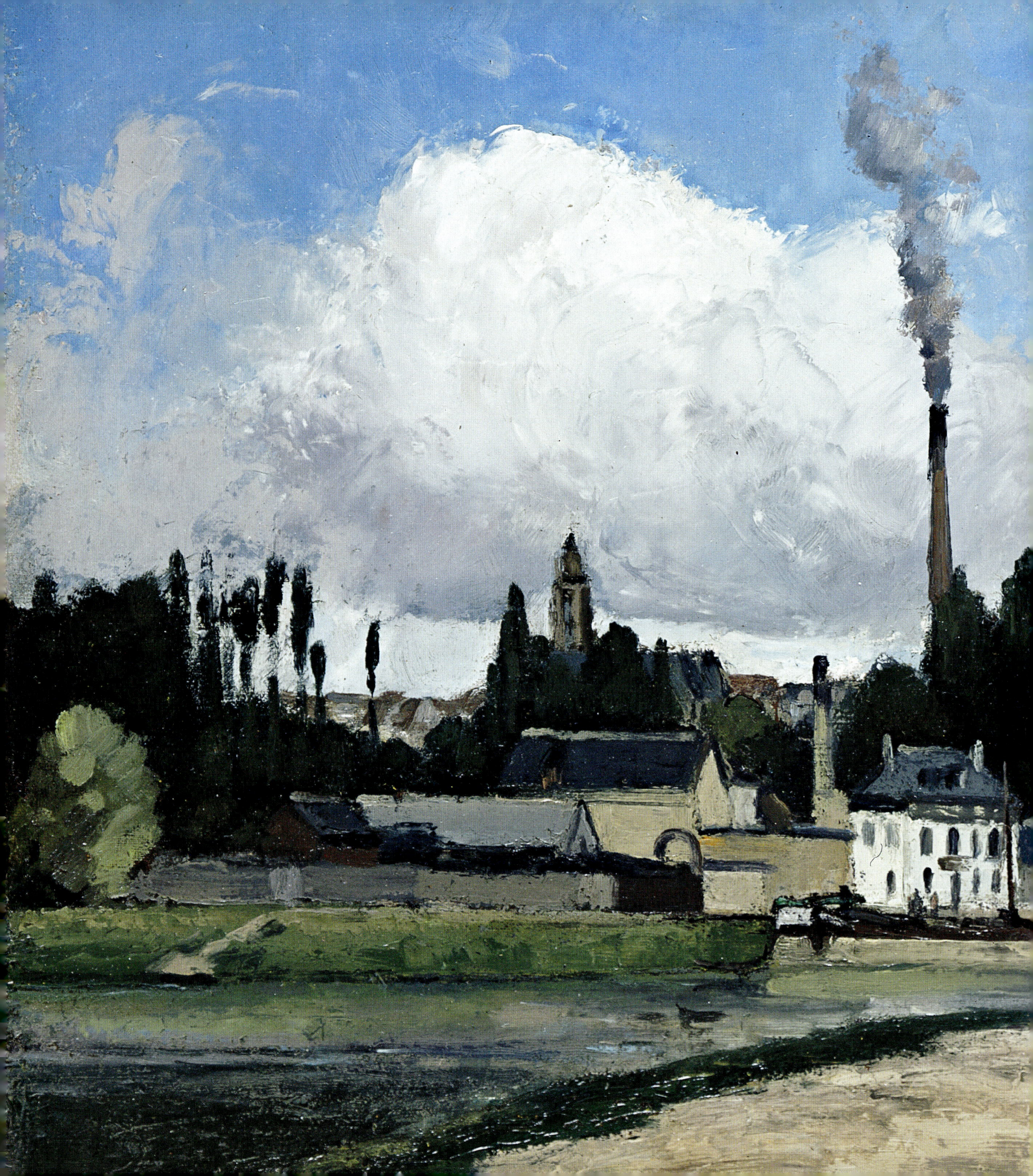

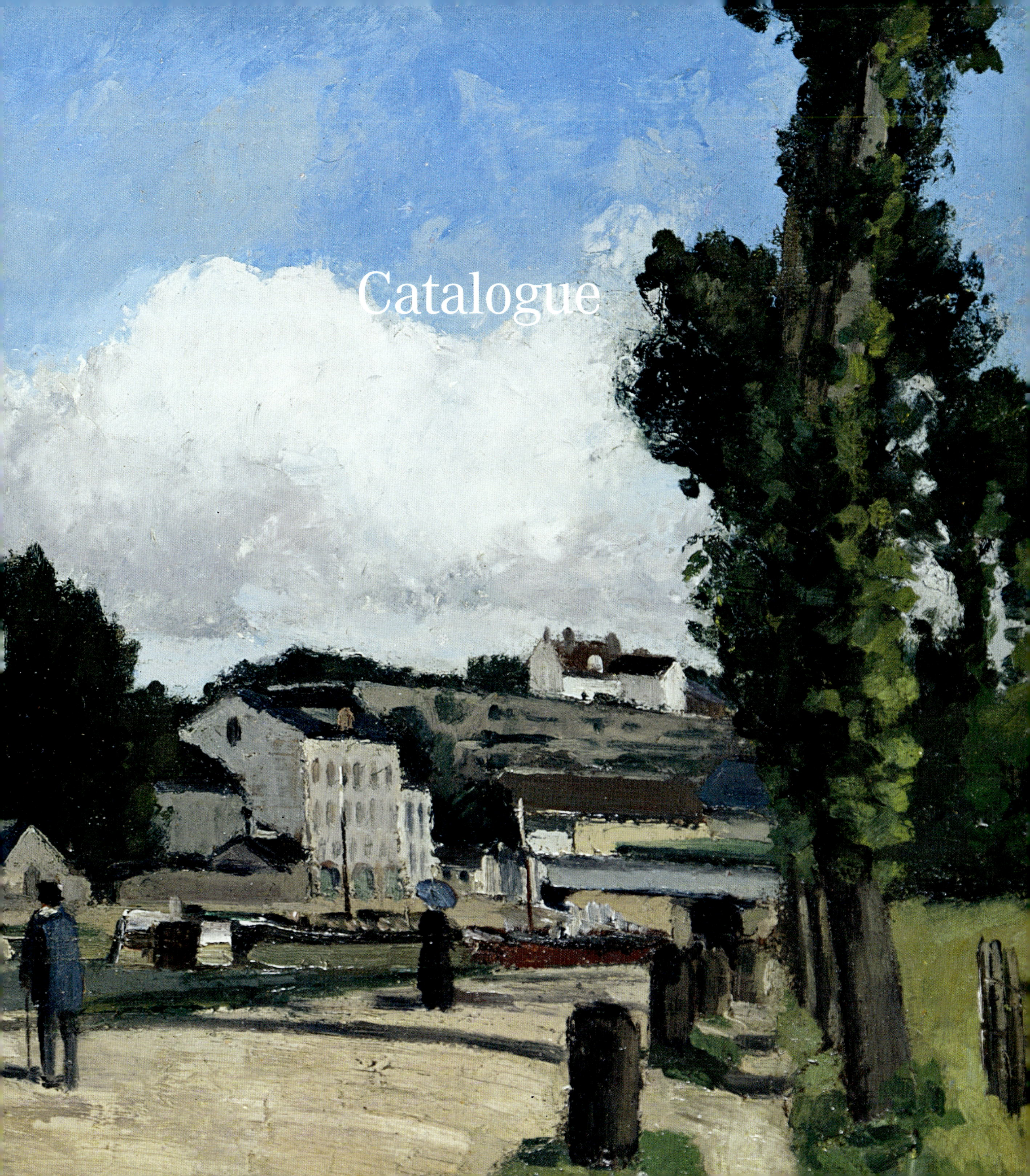

Catalogue

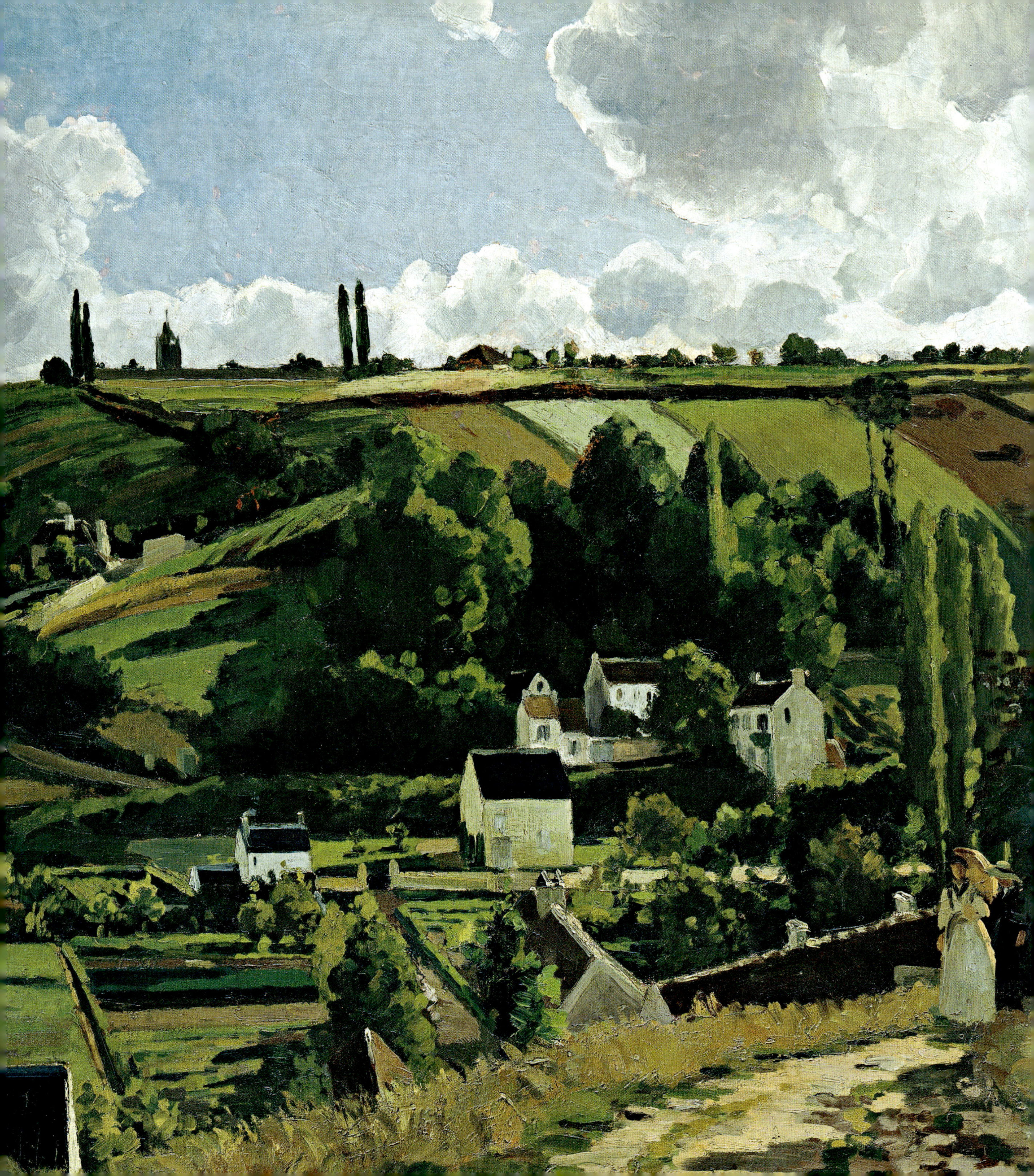

The Salon Years 1864–1868

I

La Varenne-Saint-Hilaire Viewed from Champigny

c. 1863 (PD-RS 74)

Oil on canvas
19 ½ × 29 in. (49.6 × 74 cm)
Szépmüvészeti Múzeum, Hatvany Collection, Budapest, 377. B

Fig. 1. Charles-François Daubigny, *Harvest*, 1851. Oil on canvas. Musée d'Orsay, Paris, R.F. 1972-27

Pissarro painted this view of a meadow in about 1863, just after he began living off and on in the small town of La Varenne-Saint-Hilaire, east of Paris on the Marne River. Here a group of four figures, somewhat dwarfed by the great expanse of land around them, collect wildflowers on a summer day. Although the artist does not supply the faces of the two women and two children with descriptive features, a practice that was typical in his work of this period, their activity and bright clothing provide an important focal point for the composition. Although the foreground is in shadow cast by a tree located outside the picture plane, all four figures are placed in full sunlight. A group of buildings in the distance is almost completely obscured by a row of trees that stretches across the width of the composition.

Most of the paintings Pissarro produced while he was living in La Varenne-Saint-Hilaire are riverside scenes, making this land-based composition unusual. Like many of his works from the early to mid-1860s, this one can be seen as an amalgam of several styles and influences. The broad, mainly horizontal structure of the composition, without any strong diagonal or vertical elements except for the tall tree at the extreme right edge, is very rare in the artist's oeuvre. Pissarro preferred to use a wide variety of elements in his later compositions to form a solid structure of both organic shapes and geometric forms. This painting is reminiscent of Charles-François Daubigny's panoramic landscapes, where the land and sky are carefully separated and the sky takes up more than half of the composition (fig. 1). In addition, the subtle tonalities and delicate brushwork indicate a strong influence from Camille Corot, whom Pissarro credited as his teacher in the catalogues for the Salons of 1864 and 1865. It is clear here that the younger artist is looking to the older master for inspiration, particularly in the delicate depiction of the wildflowers, the bushes on the right side of the foreground, and the trees along the right edge.

KR

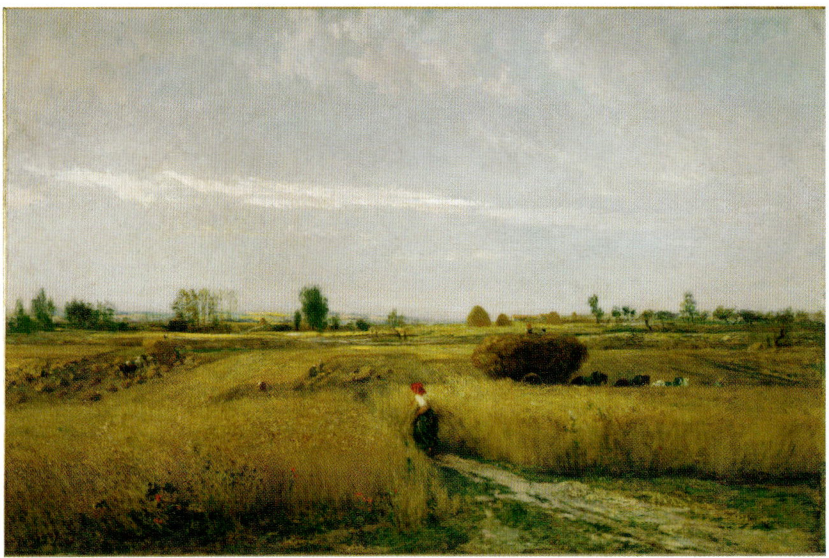

Fig. 1

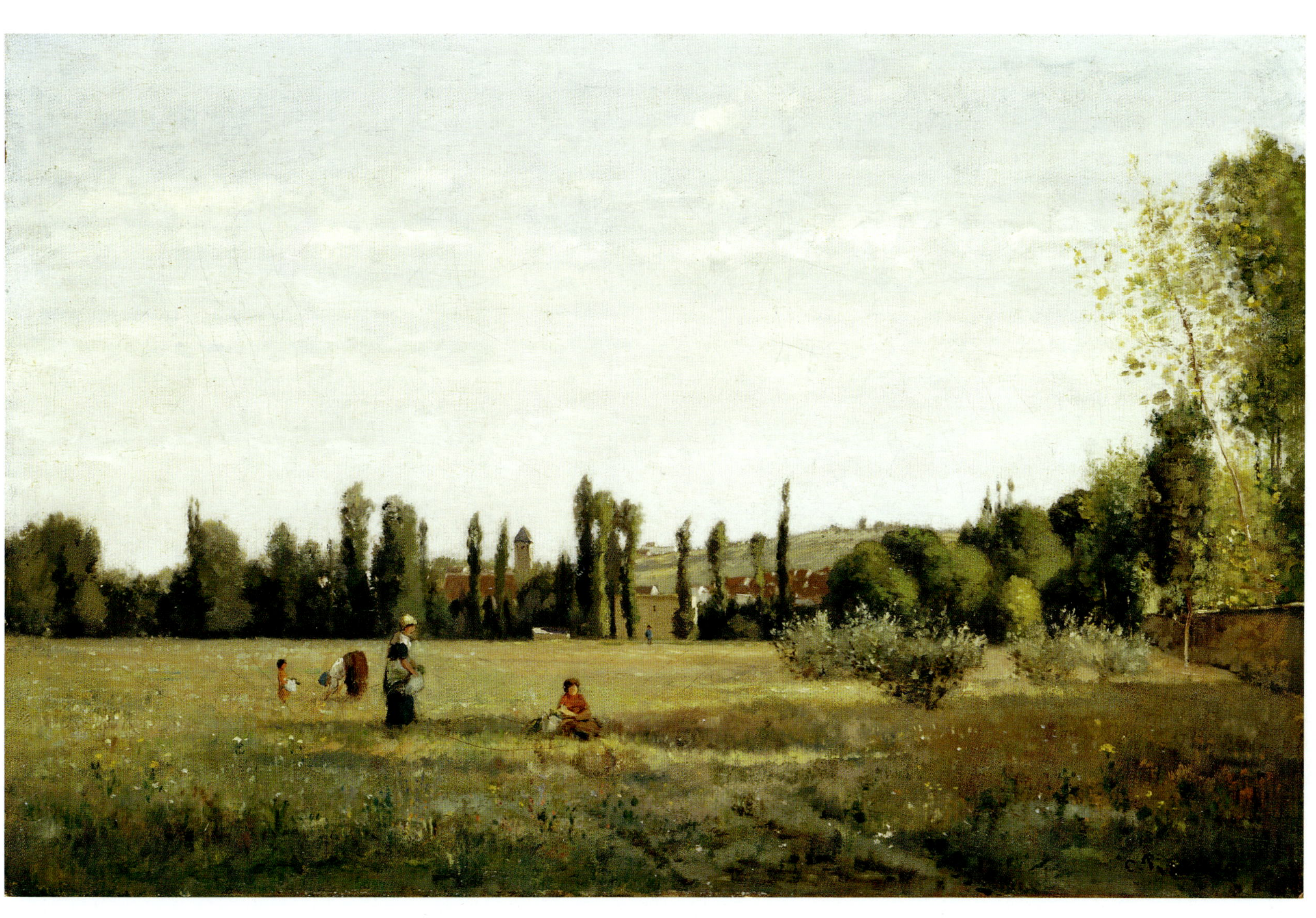

2

A Tree-lined Lane

Road in Perspective

c. 1864 (PD-RS 82)

Oil on canvas
14 × 10 7/8 in. (35.5 × 27.5 cm)
Private collection, Tampa, Florida

In 1864 Pissarro produced five small-scale landscapes in a vertical format, an orientation that he rarely used during his long and productive career.[1] Of that group, four works feature a relatively straight path leading out of a group of trees or buildings in the center of the composition, including *A Tree-lined Lane*. This series of views may have been inspired by the road scenes of Camille Corot, who in turn was motivated by seventeenth-century Dutch examples. Corot's *Ville d'Avray, Entrance to a Wood*, 1823–25 (fig. 1), for example, would have been the type of work that might have encouraged the younger artist to address similar compositional structures in his own paintings. Both are vertical compositions that feature dirt paths that recede into the distance through a group of trees, sunlight filtering through their branches onto the thoroughfare. In the painting by Corot, although the path appears to be somewhat loosely painted, the artist has meticulously depicted the lush branches and leaves of the trees, giving the picture a sense of finish and formality despite its relatively small scale.[2]

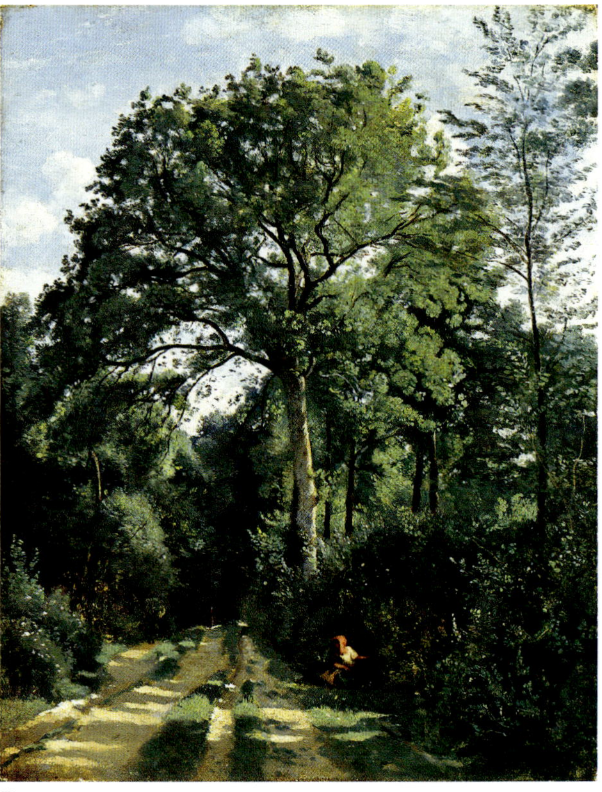

Fig. 1

In comparison, the work by Pissarro has the feel of a rapid sketch, immediate and spontaneous, with a thick, painterly style typical of his early career. The pathway quickly recedes toward the distance, with a quick dab of off-white paint to indicate a sunny area in the far distance. Pissarro used free and enthusiastic brushwork throughout: thick, large strokes of light blue, white, and pink paint in the sky; bold dabs of dark green pigment to approximate the leaves on the trees; and broad strokes of tan and green on the path itself. The vertical orientation allows the artist to elongate the trees to almost the entire height of the canvas, where they seem to dwarf the two figures walking below. These figures are depicted with just a few strokes of paint, without any substantial detail for their clothing or facial features that would distract from the narrow bit of landscape he has chosen to illustrate. In *A Tree-lined Lane*, Pissarro has focused on the lush landscape itself, producing an oil sketch that highlights his experimentation with a variety of painting techniques.

KR

1. See PD-RS 82 (the present painting), 83, 84, 92 (cat. 3), and 98.
2. See Vincent Pomarède, in Gary Tinterow, Michael Pantazzi, and Pomarède, *Corot* (New York: The Metropolitan Museum of Art, 1996), cat. 4, 34–35, where he explains that Corot's original composition included a standing woman with a cow on the right side of the path. The Barbizon artist Narcisse Diaz de la Peña, with Corot's permission, repainted the work after 1850 and replaced the original figures with a seated woman. The landscape elements, however, were not substantially changed.

Fig. 1. Camille Corot, *Ville d'Avray, Entrance to a Wood*, 1823–25. Oil on canvas. The National Gallery of Scotland, Edinburgh

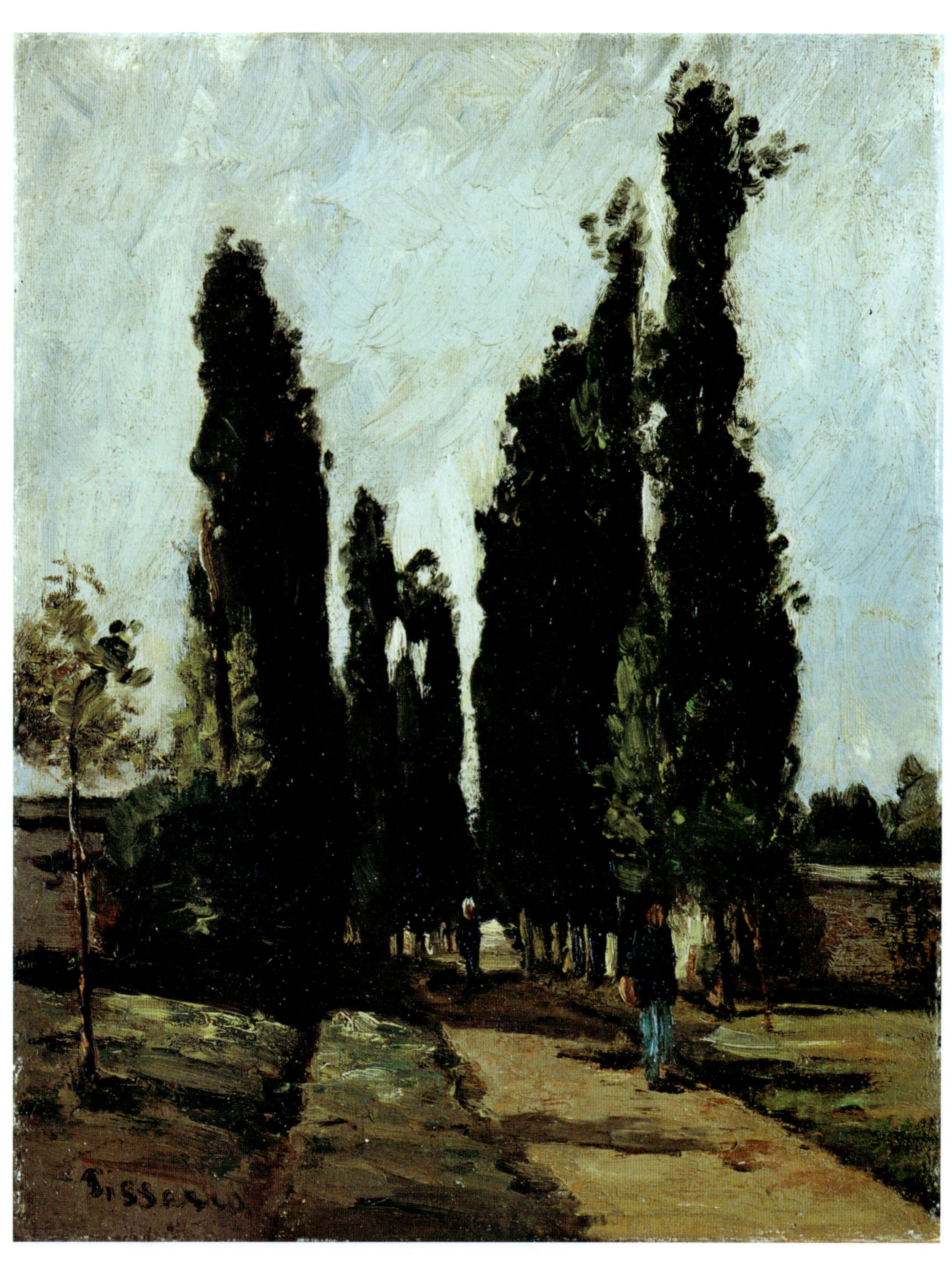
Pissarro

3
Strollers on a Country Road, La Varenne-Saint-Hilaire
Path by the River (near La Varenne-Saint-Hilaire)
1864 (PD-RS 92)

Oil on canvas
22 3/16 × 18 3/16 in. (56.4 × 46.2 cm)
The Baltimore Museum of Art: George A. Lucas Collection, BMA 1996.45.221. Purchased with funds from the State of Maryland, Laurence and Stella Bendann Fund, and contributions from individuals, foundations, and corporations throughout the Baltimore community

In 1864 Pissarro painted *Strollers on a Country Road, La Varenne-Saint-Hilaire,* an intimate and focused view of the countryside near his temporary home on the Marne River to the east of Paris. Despite its small scale in relation to his larger Salon submissions of that period (cats. 4, 5), it is a remarkably assured composition, with little of the hesitation or awkwardness evident in some of his works from the previous year.[1] Here the artist revealed a new confidence and sophistication, and this work is a significant milestone in his evolution from student to innovator. Although painted during another season and from a different vantage point, the picture shows a site closely related to that shown in *Banks of the Marne in Winter* (cat. 5), which can be considered Pissarro's first wholly original Salon painting of the 1860s. Courbet's influence is clearly seen here in Pissarro's carefully structured and solid composition, his use of a palette knife technique in several areas, and in the sharp horizon line that is a frequent feature in the earlier master's landscapes. Pissarro has also adopted Courbet's device of employing a steeply receding path that pulls the spectator forcibly into the scene.[2]

The composition is almost perfectly bisected, with a vigorous rendering of a light blue sky filled with clouds above a lush green landscape. The light source appears to come from the upper right, since shadows are cast to the left. In spite of the bright, clear light, the lower portion of the composition is unusually dark and solid. The right side is extremely crowded, where a building, a fence, and foliage are squeezed into a very small area of canvas. The view opens up toward the left, however, and the artist seems to revel in the various textures and patterns of the verdant foliage across the river.

It is closest in composition to another work from 1864, *Landscape at La Varenne-Saint-Hilaire,* formerly in the collection of Dr. Paul Gachet (fig. 1).[3] It seems likely that the Gachet painting was made first, followed by a reworking of the motif in a slightly larger vertical

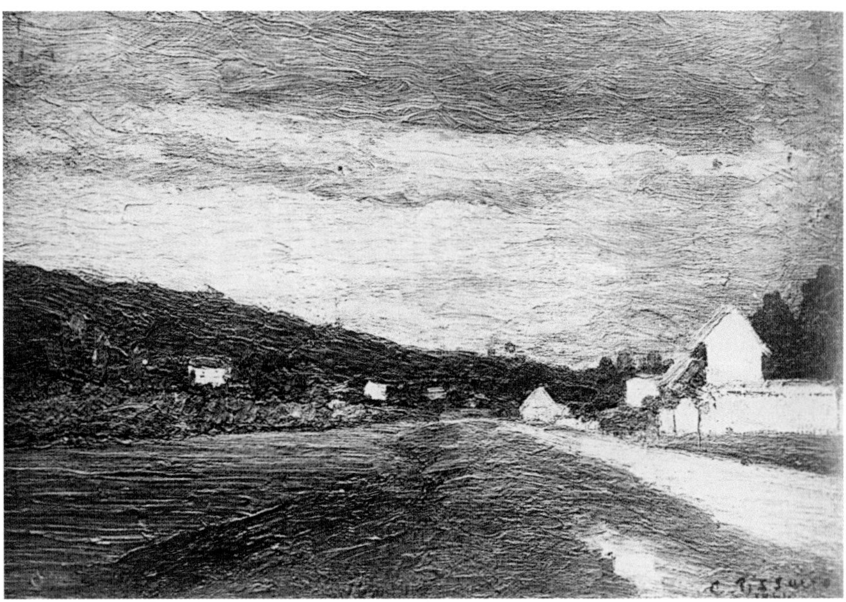
Fig. 1

Fig. 1. Camille Pissarro, *Landscape at La Varenne-Saint-Hilaire,* 1864 (PD-RS 95). Oil on canvas. Formerly in the collection of Dr. Paul Gachet, stolen before 1991

1. See, for instance, *The Telegraph Tower in Montmartre,* 1863 (PD-RS 67), oil on canvas, private collection, and *Farmyard,* c. 1863 (PD-RS 69), oil on canvas, private collection, Chicago (see *Technical Notes,* fig. 3).
2. See, for example, Courbet's *Landscape near Ornans,* 1864, oil on canvas, The Toledo Museum of Art, 74:1937.
3. It contains the motif of the path and the same houses and hillside beyond, but the view is taken further away from the buildings. With its horizontal format and smaller scale, the painting appears less finished a composition when compared with *Strollers on a Country Road, La Varenne-Saint-Hilaire.*

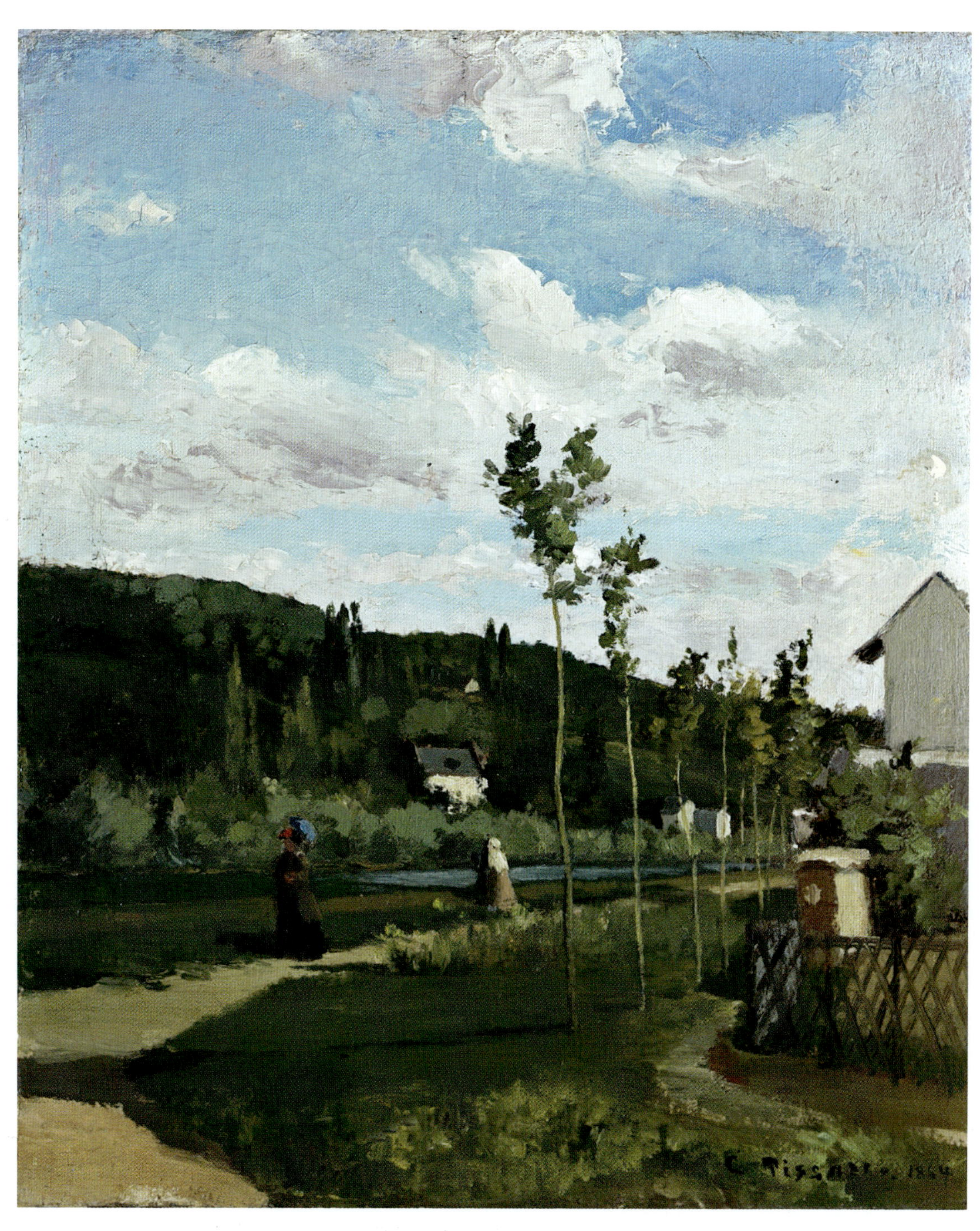
C. Pissarro. 1864

composition in *Strollers on a Country Road, La Varenne-Saint-Hilaire*. Relatively unusual in Pissarro's oeuvre, the vertical orientation of this painting enabled the artist to create a more tightly constructed composition.

X-ray examination of *Strollers on a Country Road, La Varenne-Saint-Hilaire* shows that Pissarro initially employed this canvas for a horizontal painting in which a female figure appears outside a large rustic building, with several farm animals grazing on her right (see *Technical Notes*). The artist may have been unsatisfied with his first attempt and, rather than trying to improve the initial plan, decided to begin anew and rework a familiar landscape in a vertical format. This new orientation enabled him to crop the motif more closely to its bare essentials and focus on the integration of the sky above and the earth below.

Strollers on a Country Road, La Varenne-Saint-Hilaire was not included in the 1939 catalogue raisonné of Pissarro's work, as its location in Baltimore was unknown.[4] With its inscribed date of 1864, it is one of the few paintings from the 1860s that survived the ransacking of the artist's studio by German soldiers during the Franco-Prussian War (1870–71). A little-known painting, it was purchased by George A. Lucas,[5] an American dealer and collector, sometime before 1909 and has remained relatively unstudied by scholars of the Impressionist era.

KR

4. Ludovic Rodolphe Pissarro and Lionello Venturi, *Camille Pissarro: Son art, son oeuvre*, 2 vols. (Paris: P. Rosenberg, 1939).

5. In 1857 George A. Lucas (1824–1909) moved to Paris, where he made his name as agent to a number of American art collectors and dealers. Despite his interest in contemporary French art, Lucas did not acquire many works by the Impressionist painters, preferring the style of the Barbizon artists. However, his purchase of two early works by Pissarro—*Strollers on a Country Road, La Varenne-Saint-Hilaire* and *The Corner of the Route de Versailles and the Chemin de l'Aqueduc, Louveciennes* (cat. 12)—signals his open-minded approach.

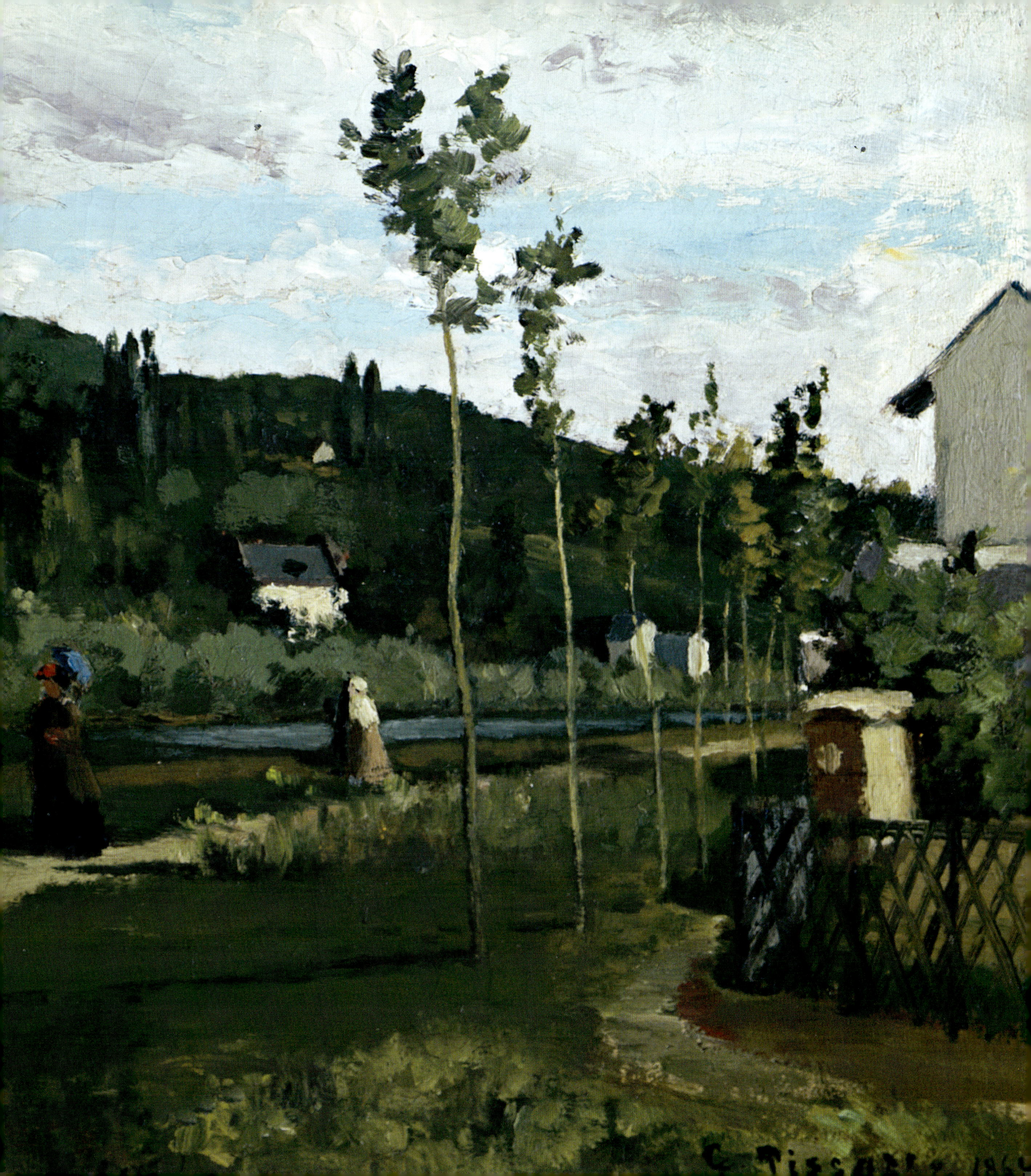

4
Banks of the Marne at Chennevières
The Marne at Chennevières
c. 1865 (PD-RS 103)

Oil on canvas
36 × 57 5/16 in. (91.5 × 145.5 cm)
The National Gallery of Scotland, Edinburgh, NG 2098
Baltimore only

This large panorama of the small riverside town of Chennevières, located opposite La Varenne-Saint-Hilaire on the Marne River, where Pissarro lived intermittently from 1863 to 1866, was the artist's entry for the Salon of 1865. With its broad river view and large scale, it reveals the significant influence that Charles-François Daubigny had on Pissarro's approach at this time. At the previous Salon, Pissarro submitted *Banks of the Marne*, a landscape reminiscent of Daubigny's water views (see Rothkopf essay, fig. 4), but the connection between the two artists becomes even more clear in this example that can be seen as an homage to the older artist's signature style. However, the ever-growing influence of the painting technique of Gustave Courbet, which was to emerge fully in the following years, can also be seen in the scumbled paint surface of the marshy areas in the water, as well as in the use of the palette knife for the architectural elements.

Regardless of the influence of both masters, Pissarro asserts his independence in this major work. Near the center of the composition, Pissarro included what appears to be a large black chimney, which leads the viewer's eye upward toward the buildings on the hill. This may be the first example of his inclusion of the encroachment of modernity on the picturesque French landscape, a subject that interested him throughout this early period of his career.

Despite the somewhat conventional composition, Pissarro's technique, when examined closely, is quite experimental. His knife work is very free and loose, particularly in the white wall along the left side; it has thick impasto, like frosting on a cake. The buildings along the water's edge and in the town above are roughly rendered, without the precision that one might expect from a Salon painting of this period. Unlike *Banks of the Marne*, Pissarro seems not to have produced an oil sketch during the formative stages of this work. He worked directly on the large canvas, as can be seen in the numerous changes apparent along the line of trees. When he first began the composition, the horizon line was higher, but it was subsequently adjusted slightly downward. These alterations, which produced rough dimples, can be clearly seen where the sky meets the land and are obvious across the entire width of the painting. The light seems muted, without an obvious source. The reflections in the water of the sky above are not very convincing, and the water feels hard and solid, lacking the shimmer and finish that Daubigny typically achieved in his paintings. Pissarro has concentrated more of his effort on the rushy areas in the right and left foreground, which were very freely painted, indicating an interest in texture and pattern that was to remain strong throughout his career.

KR

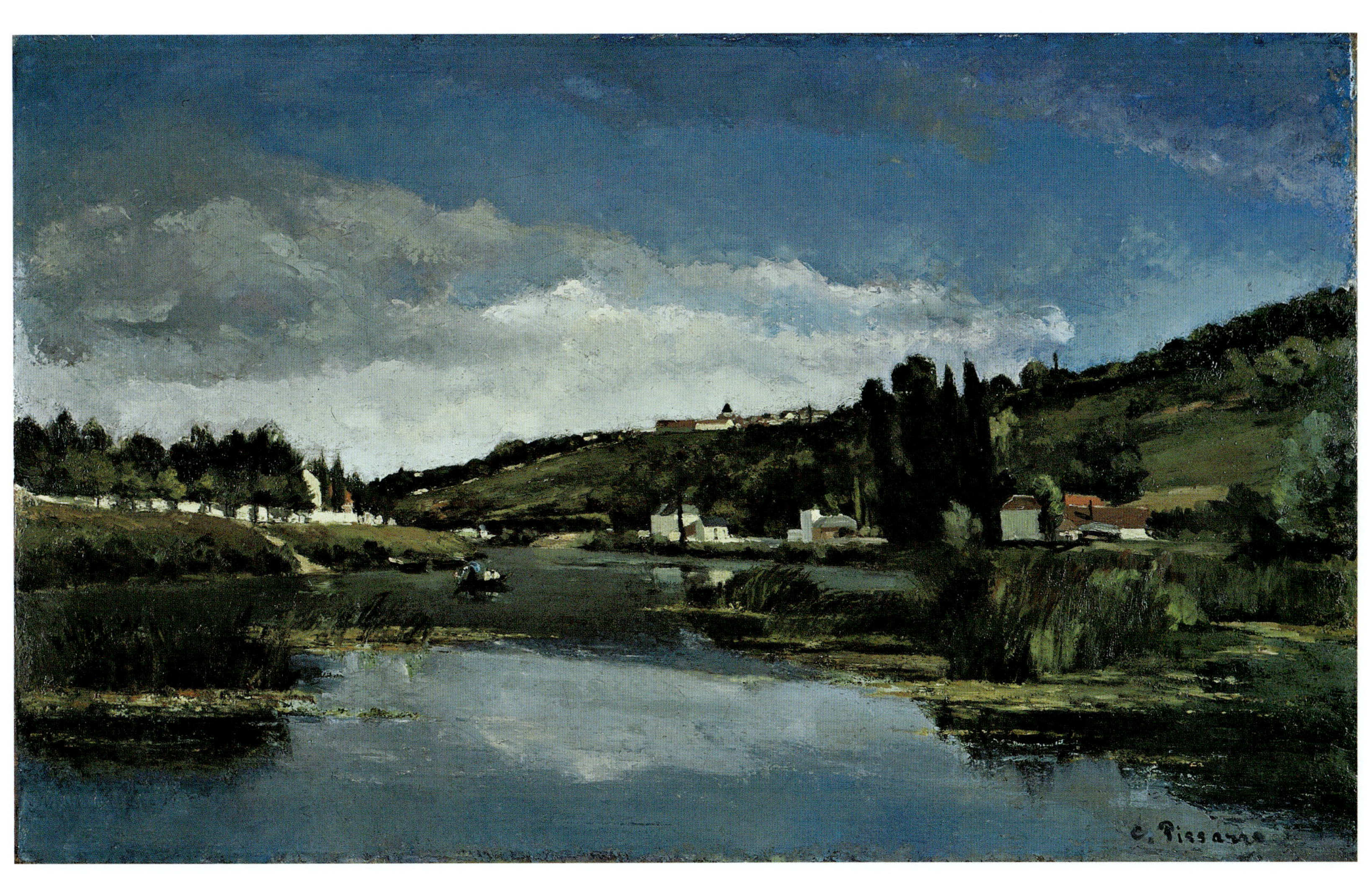
C. Pissarro

5

Banks of the Marne in Winter

1866 (PD-RS 107)

Oil on canvas
36 ⅛ × 59 ⅛ in. (91.8 × 150.2 cm)
The Art Institute of Chicago, Mr. and Mrs. Lewis Larned Coburn Memorial Fund, 1957.306

1. See Ludovic Rodolphe Pissarro and Lionello Venturi, *Camille Pissarro: Son art, son oeuvre*, 2 vols. (Paris: P. Rosenberg, 1939), 1:21.
2. Ibid.
3. Émile Zola, "Mon Salon: Adieux d'un critique d'art," 1866, in *Écrits sur l'art*, ed. Jean-Pierre Leduc-Adine (Paris: Gallimard, 1991), 133, quoted and translated in Gary Tinterow and Henri Loyrette, *Origins of Impressionism* (New York: The Metropolitan Museum of Art, 1994), 444–45.

This ambitious, large-scale painting was shown at the Salon of 1866. Although Pissarro had been exhibiting at the official Salon since 1859, it was with *Banks of the Marne in Winter* that he received his first critical acclaim. In his review, Jules-Antoine Castagnary drew attention to the strength of the handling.[1] Jean Rousseau found the voice of a satirical poet in the artist's depiction of an "ugly" and "banal" scene that lacked a central picturesque motif. According to Rousseau, in this work Pissarro intended to highlight the vulgarity of the contemporary world.[2] It was Émile Zola, however, who singled out Pissarro's work as exemplifying the ideals of a new generation of painters: "Thank you, sir. . . . Then why in the devil's name are you so very clumsy as to study nature and paint it in a plain and forthright manner! . . . It is an austere and serious painting, showing an extreme concern for the truth and correctness, a bleak and strong will. What a clumsy fellow you are, sir—you are one artist I like."[3]

This painting, admired for its honest view of winter when it was first exhibited, is organized according to a strict perspectival system. As the sharp recession of the path on the left briskly pulls the viewer's gaze into the distance, the foreground is left open to the barren field. Once reaching the end of the path, a series of brightly lit details of a banal and everyday nature commands the viewer's attention in the middle distance: a small horse cart, the thin stripe of snow, the intricate structure of the imposing farmhouse, and small white buildings emerging from the darker foliage at the foot of the hill. All of this takes place in a delicately orchestrated arrangement of dark and light, partially lit by the sun, which breaks through the darkened sky from behind the hill.

Pissarro's initial idea for this composition seems to have been more pastoral in nature. X-radiograph studies have revealed that he painted over a partially completed composition underneath, with a cow in the foreground (see *Technical Notes*). When he started working on the canvas, it was positioned vertically on his easel. Turning the canvas horizontally, he began anew, subordinating figures, now diminished in size, to a rigorous geometric structure. Broad white walls and houses by the Marne River had attracted Pissarro's attention as early as 1864. *Strollers on a Country Road, La Varenne-Saint-Hilaire* (cat. 3) is an earlier example where contours and darker tones of nature and foliage are juxtaposed against the white wall of a house, its prominent arrowlike chimney accentuating its flatness. Despite the obvious differences in size and function, one being a small-scale landscape probably produced to be sold to a dealer and the other a large Salon painting, *Strollers on a Country Road, La Varenne-Saint-Hilaire* and *Banks of the Marne in Winter* share a common set of tools Pissarro formulated to explore human presence and experience in the rigorously structured world of his landscapes.

GÇ

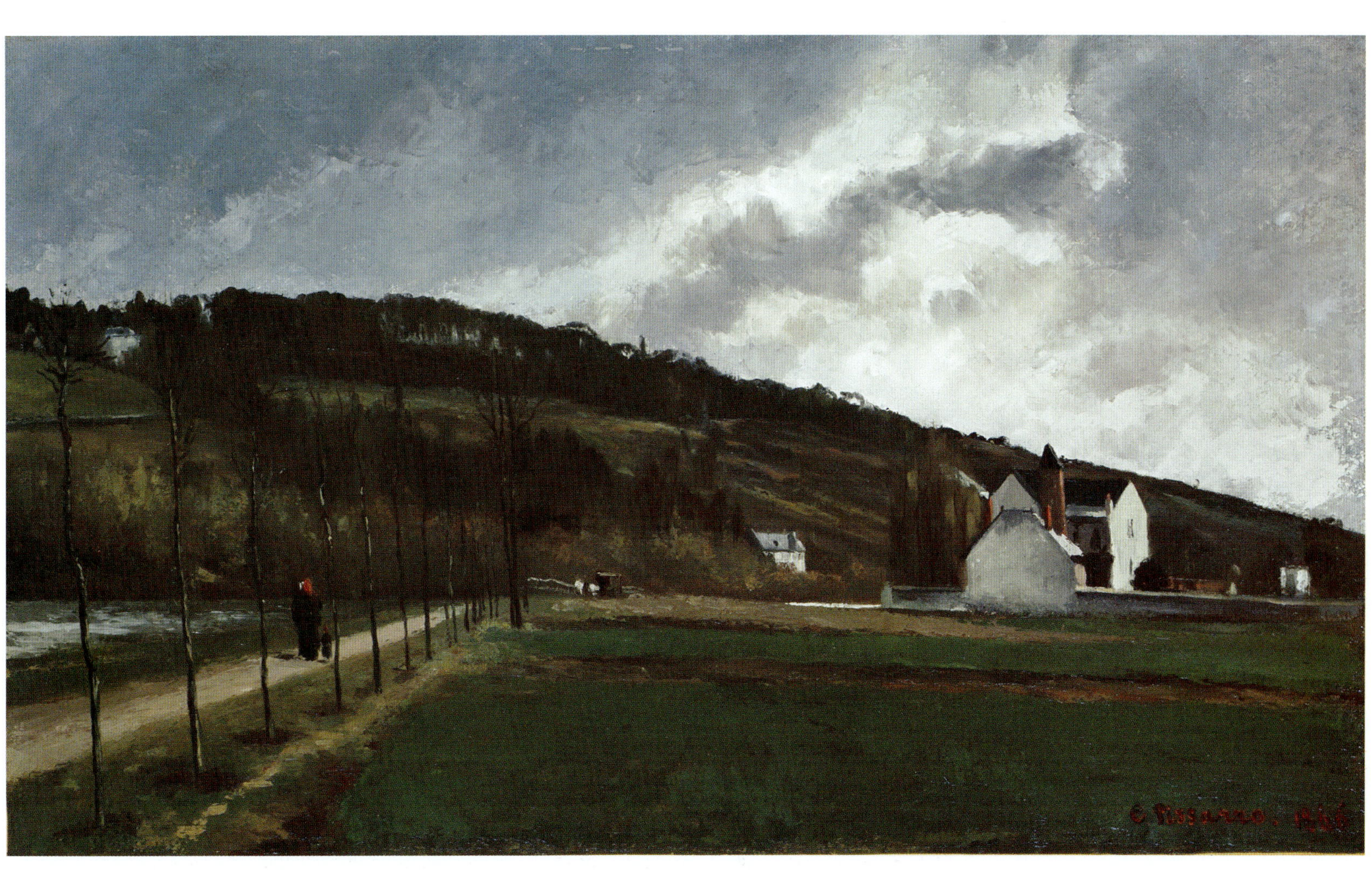
C. Pissarro.

6

The House of Père Gallien, Pontoise

Père Gallien's House, Pontoise

1866 (PD-RS 111)

Oil on canvas
15 7/8 × 21 3/4 in. (40.3 × 55.2 cm)
Ipswich Borough Council Museums and Galleries, Acquired with the assistance of the Museums, Libraries, and Archives Council

Pissarro painted this work just after he and his family moved to Pontoise in the spring of 1866. It features an elegantly dressed couple walking along a dirt path underneath a large, budding tree that dominates the composition. In the distance a group of female figures in more humble attire walk near a group of houses. Pissarro produced a similar composition of the same site two years later that is more freely painted.[1] The large house on the left is named for its owner, Jean-Pierre Gallien, and is located on the rue de Gisors, a main street in Pontoise.[2]

Despite the relatively bright conditions of this spring day, the artist has not included any shadows, a compositional element that becomes increasingly important in his paintings starting in late 1869. The lack of shadows produces a somewhat flat and muted atmosphere. Almost half of the canvas is covered by the tree in the foreground, which is composed of a variety of expressive brushstrokes. The branches are painted with dark calligraphic marks that are almost inklike, a technique that appears more frequently in his work of the early 1870s, when he was fully engaged with Impressionism, therefore making this work a very early precedent of his later style. A second layer of softer, lighter strokes was painted on top, with pink and white highlights added as a final gesture. The delicate and detailed brushwork of the foliage and the grass in the foreground is contrasted with the more cursory depiction of the grass in the field, as well as with the buildings and stone wall beyond. The artist has carefully sculpted the architectural elements that line the back of the composition with broad, flat strokes. Their geometric perfection and solidity are typical of Pissarro's works from Pontoise.
KR

1. See PD-RS 128.
2. See PD-RS 111 for more information on this site and other paintings by Pissarro that include this house.

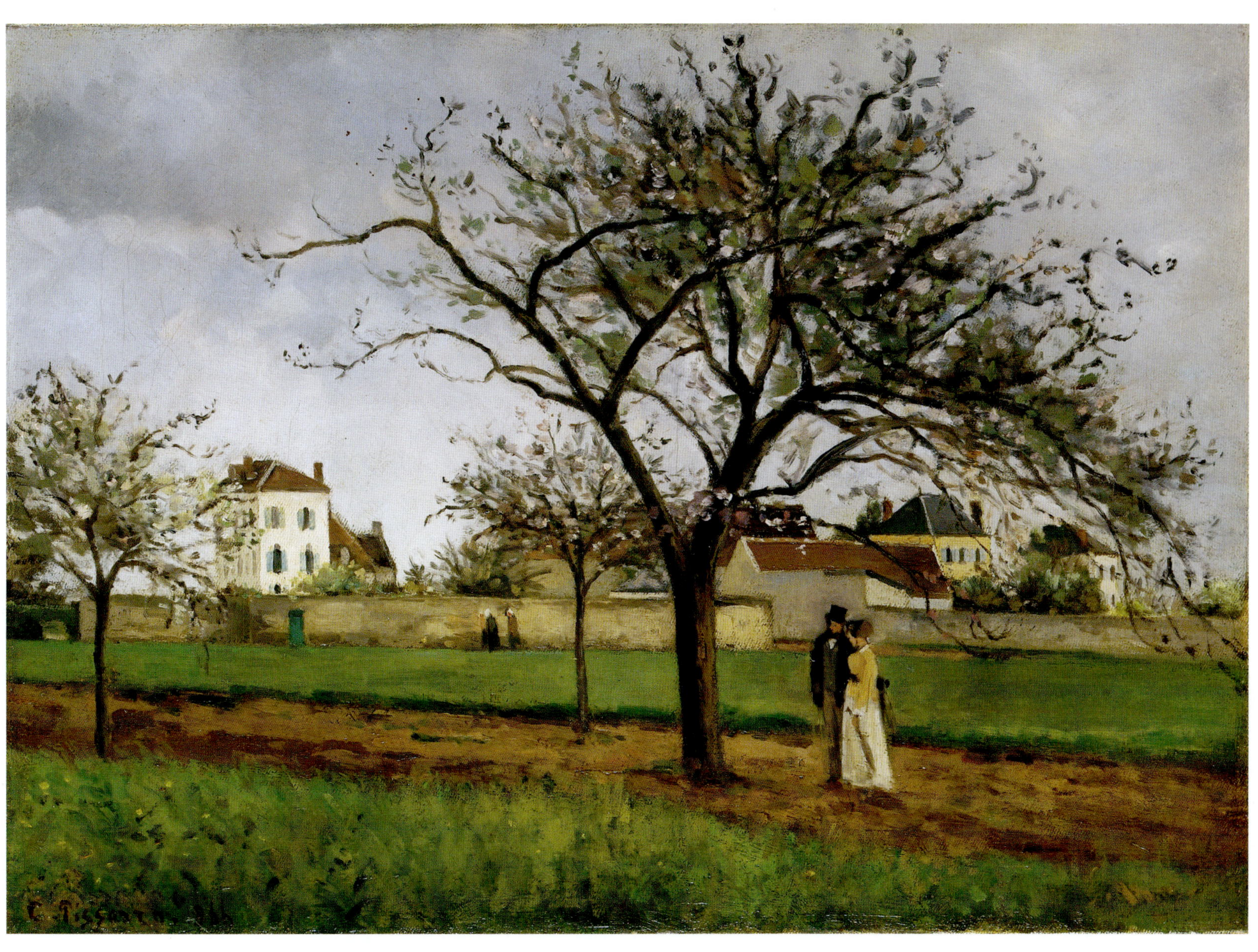

7
Rue de l'Hermitage, Pontoise
c. 1866 (PD-RS 109)

Oil on canvas mounted on panel
15 × 18 5/16 in. (38 × 46.5 cm)
Collection of the Tel Aviv Museum of Art, Bequest of Lilli Schocken, Jerusalem–New York, 1959, TAMA2463

Unlike his colleague Monet, who occasionally traveled to distant and exotic places for inspiration for his landscapes, Pissarro did not enjoy being far from home. He restricted his painting trips to relatively nearby destinations in France (Rouen, Le Havre, Dieppe, Paris) or combined them with family or social visits (Montfoucault, London), preferring to find motifs close to home. Pissarro lived in Pontoise, the place with which his work is most closely associated, from 1866 to 1868 and again from 1872 to 1882. While there, he and his family lived in L'Hermitage, a small hamlet just north of the town, for almost their entire stay in the area.[1] Pissarro was inspired by the intimate nature of life in L'Hermitage, where houses were built very close to each other. He painted more views of L'Hermitage than any other part of Pontoise during his two stays in the area.

This is a view of the rue de l'Hermitage, a street that ran through the small neighborhood. When he painted this work, Pissarro and his family were living on the older rue du Fond de l'Hermitage, which was a curved road that ran parallel to the rue de l'Hermitage. The rue de l'Hermitage took on a special significance in Pissarro's career, as he painted many views of it over the course of more than ten years, with each work including different details of the location as well as new painting techniques.[2]

Here the artist has focused on the cramped street itself. The foreground is in shadow, and a barely defined building or stone wall is at the right, with a group of trees hanging over the edge. To the left, the artist has included a small part of another building, cropping most of it out of view. As in many of his road scenes, the thoroughfare leads the viewer's eye quickly into the distance, with the aid of the long stone wall on the left side of the composition. Two female figures, dressed in the somber attire typical of the rural community, walk toward the viewer. In a similar view of the rue de l'Hermitage, though facing the other direction, Pissarro depicts a sunnier and brighter scene (fig. 1). Both works feature a blond palette and have a sense of freedom and spontaneity that indicate that they were probably painted out of doors.

KR

1. Richard R. Brettell, *Pissarro and Pontoise: The Painter in a Landscape* (New Haven: Yale University Press, 1990), 101.
2. According to the new catalogue raisonné of Pissarro's paintings, the street also appears in PD-RS 110, 349, 352, 412, 509, 528, 539, 592, and 616. See PD-RS 109 for more information.

Fig. 1. Camille Pissarro, *Rue de l'Hermitage*, c. 1865 (PD-RS 110). Oil on canvas. Private collection

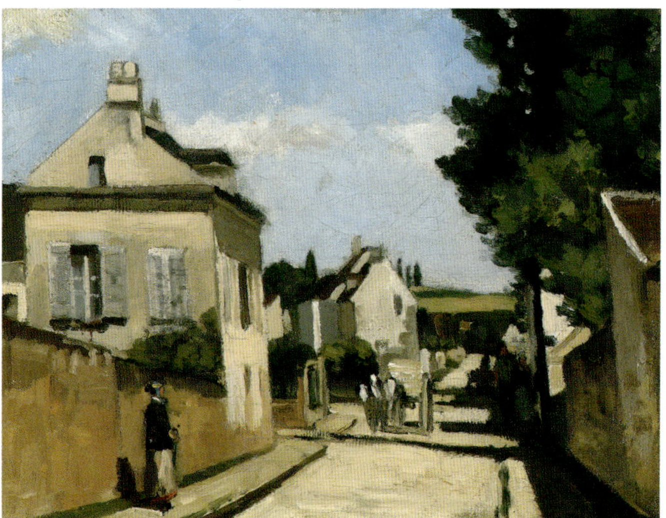

Fig. 1

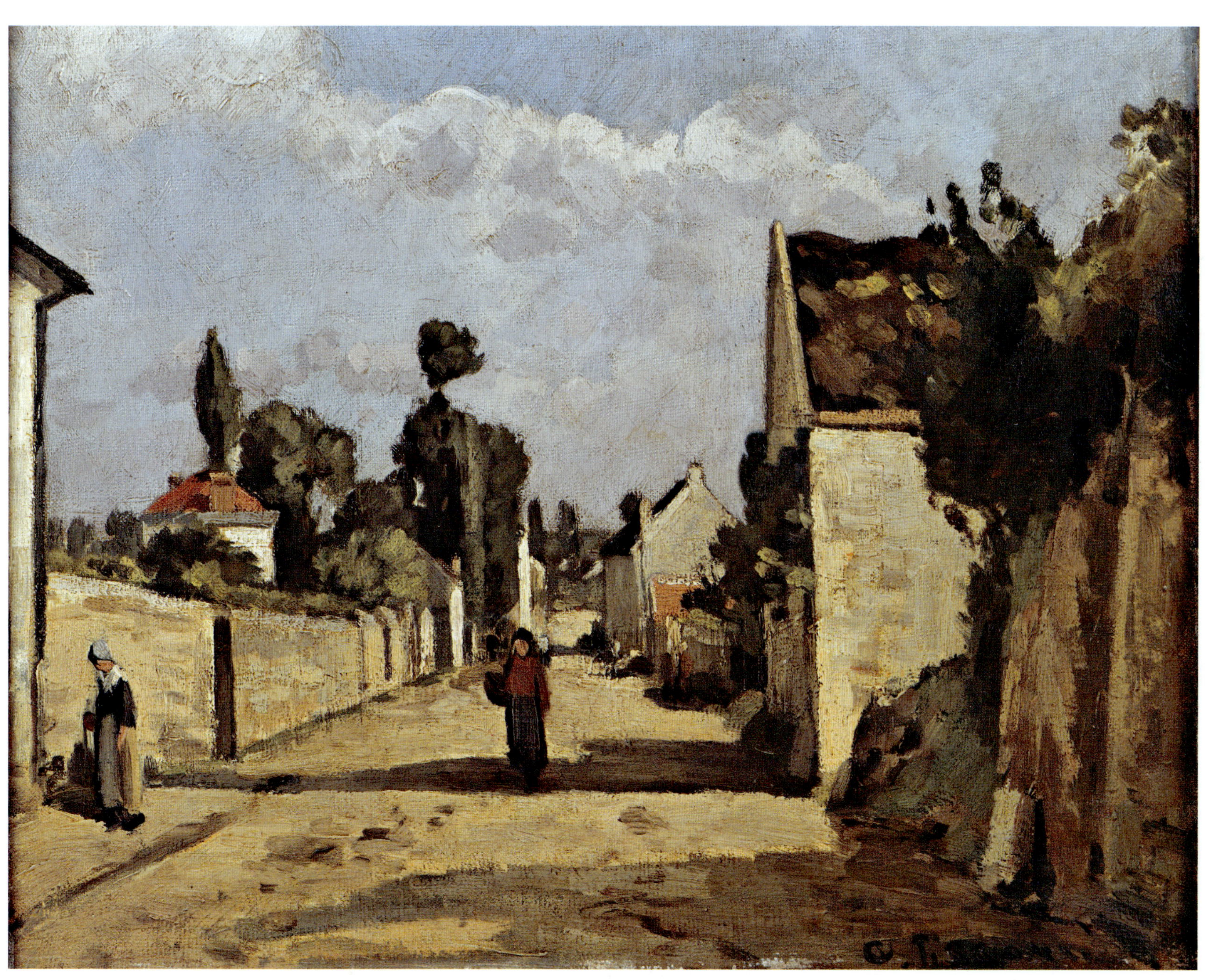

8

Banks of the Oise at Saint-Ouen-l'Aumône

Banks of the Oise at Pontoise

1867 (PD-RS 117)

Oil on canvas
18 × 28 ⅛ in. (45.7 × 71.5 cm)
Denver Art Museum Collection, Gift of the Barnett and Annalee Newman Foundation in honor of Annalee G. Newman, 2001.310

1. See T. J. Clark, "The Environs of Paris," in *The Painting of Modern Life: Paris in the Art of Manet and His Followers* (Princeton, N.J.: Princeton University Press, 1999), 147–205.
2. In *Quai du Pothuis, Pontoise*, 1868 (PD-RS 123), oil on canvas, Kunsthalle Mannheim, he depicts a similar view of the Pontoise townscape with a smoking factory chimney in the background (see Rothkopf essay, fig. 11). In cat. 9, no smoke is coming out of the chimney.

Fig. 1. Camille Pissarro, *Banks of the Oise at Saint-Ouen-l'Aumône*, 1867. Pencil. Private collection

The countryside around Paris underwent a transformation beginning in the 1850s, as the railway made leisure travel more accessible for various social classes.[1] Because of this great change, in the 1860s French artists started to rethink what a contemporary landscape painting could represent. People strolling on the banks of the Seine River in towns near Paris on a Sunday afternoon were often depicted near factory buildings, symbols of the growing presence of industry and the changing society. In the 1870s these industrial motifs began to appear in the works of Monet and Sisley. Many of their paintings of Argenteuil and Louveciennes from the 1870s pictured nature at the junction of leisure and industry.

Pissarro explored industrial motifs in a series of cityscapes of Pontoise several years earlier than his colleagues, in 1867 and 1868.[2] In *Banks of the Oise at Saint-Ouen-l'Aumône*, promenading figures take in the sights of an industrial-looking townscape. Nature and modernity easily coexist in this serene scene. When compared with a drawing made at the same spot that highlights Pissarro's talent as a precise draftsman (fig. 1), the view represented here is one of bold geometry and simplification. In the drawing, the river receding diagonally in space provides a clear, linear, perspectival structure, whereas in the painting the river almost disappears in the crowd of diagonal and horizontal bands of vibrant color. The buildings delineated with clear outlines in the drawing are transformed in the painting into abstract bands loaded with color. Pissarro's love of structure and geometry can be clearly seen in this carefully considered composition.

The artist has included two figures that serve important functions. A man with a walking stick seemingly stares at the smokestack across the river, while a woman sheltered by an umbrella walks farther down the path toward the vanishing point. When human figures populate the artist's semi-abstract landscapes, they attract the viewer's attention, induce her to come closer to the picture surface, and show her details on the densely painted surface. Pissarro would explore this function of figures further in the course of the 1870s (see cats. 30, 31, 48, and 49).
GÇ

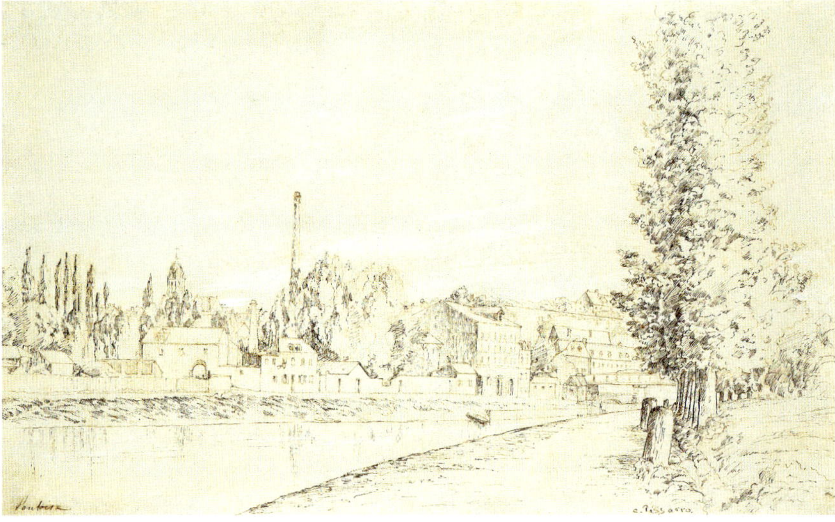

Fig. 1

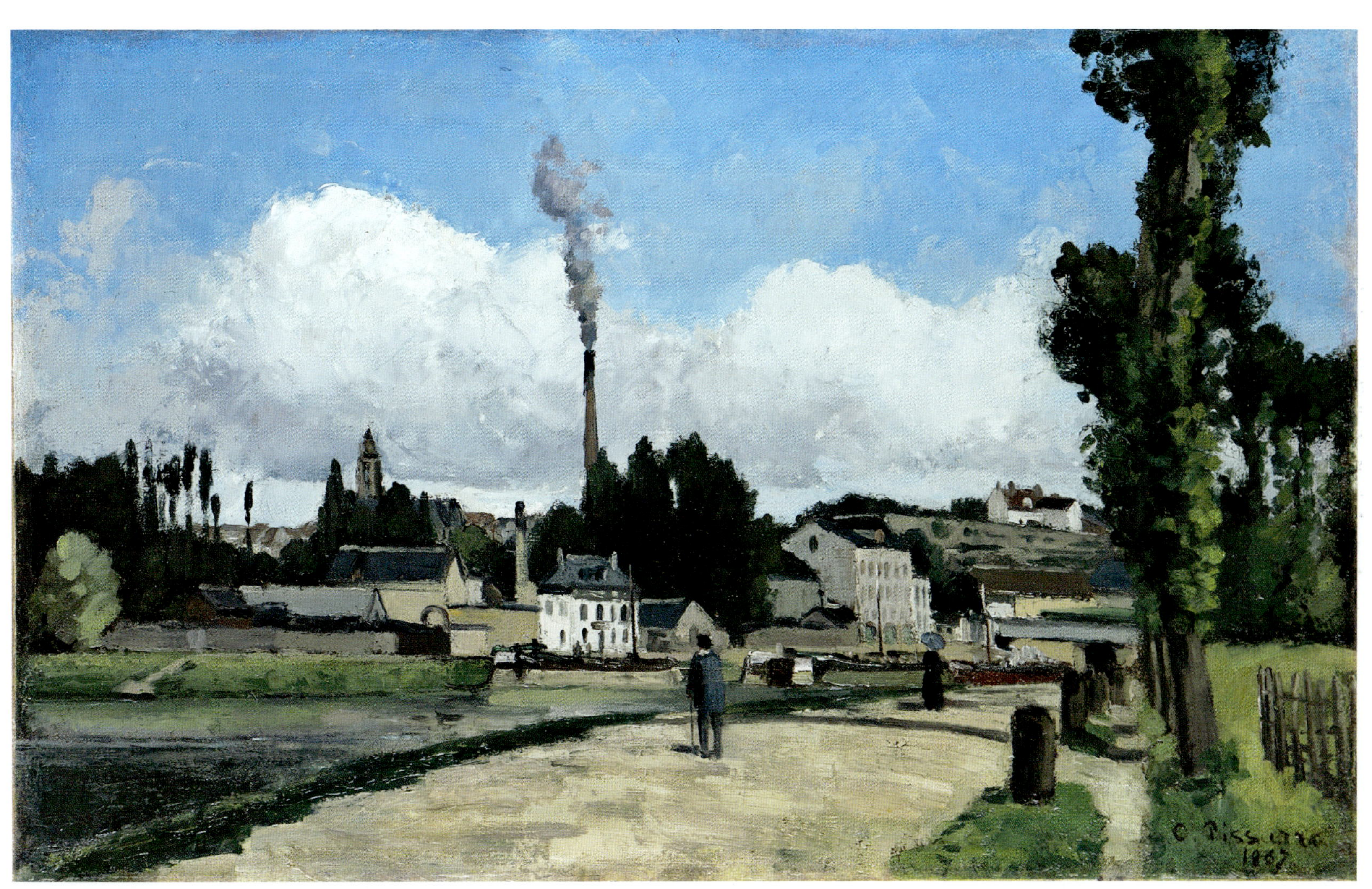
C. Pissarro

9
The Chemin de l'Écluse and the Pontoise Bridge
1867 (PD-RS 122)

Oil on canvas mounted on panel
12 3⁄16 × 17 15⁄16 in. (31 × 45.5 cm)
Collection of the Tel Aviv Museum of Art, Bequest of Lilli Schocken, Jerusalem–New York, 1959, TAMA2462

1. The site has been identified in PD-RS 122.

Although best known for his rural images of the French landscape, Pissarro produced a small but important group of townscapes during the period 1864–74. His interest in depicting the industrialization of the countryside can be seen as his way of coming to terms with his own feelings about the changing nature of France, a topic about which he was ambivalent. This early "metropolitan" view of Pontoise from 1867 features the stone bridge over the Oise that was built in 1843 and one of its quays. In the central distance, the smokestack of the Pontoise pumping plant can be seen.[1] The compositional structure is similar to that of *Banks of the Oise at Saint-Ouen-l'Aumône* of the same year (cat. 8) but depicts the opposite side of the river.

Unlike his well-known series of factory scenes of 1873 (cats. 36–38), which feature the Châlon distillery during working hours, here the chimney is not emitting smoke and is surrounded by earth-toned buildings. These buildings, on the far side of the river, are portrayed with thick, loose brushstrokes, that are, in a way very different from the clearly defined and precise technique used for the building in the right foreground. The bottom half of the composition is very densely painted, an analogue to the solidity of the architecture and surrounding foliage. The sky, consisting of white clouds with a few hints of blue, is more thinly portrayed, with the texture of the canvas visible through the paint. The bridge gracefully crosses the river with a series of arches; however, the artist ignores the potential reflective qualities of the river in favor of an opaque gray paint. Rural nature, a subject that normally preoccupied the artist, has been overwhelmed by man-made domestic and industrial architecture.

One of the most unusual aspects of the composition is the inclusion on the quay of a relatively large-scale bourgeois couple, dressed in fashionable black and white. The stark colors of their attire contrast strongly with the subtle earth tones of the surrounding townscape. Here, as he often did, Pissarro did not fully define their facial features, giving them a somewhat ominous quality as they stare at the viewer. Unlike some of his rural figures in his countryside motifs who often are on their way somewhere, this couple seems stopped in their tracks as they face the artist, not permitting entry for the viewer.
KR

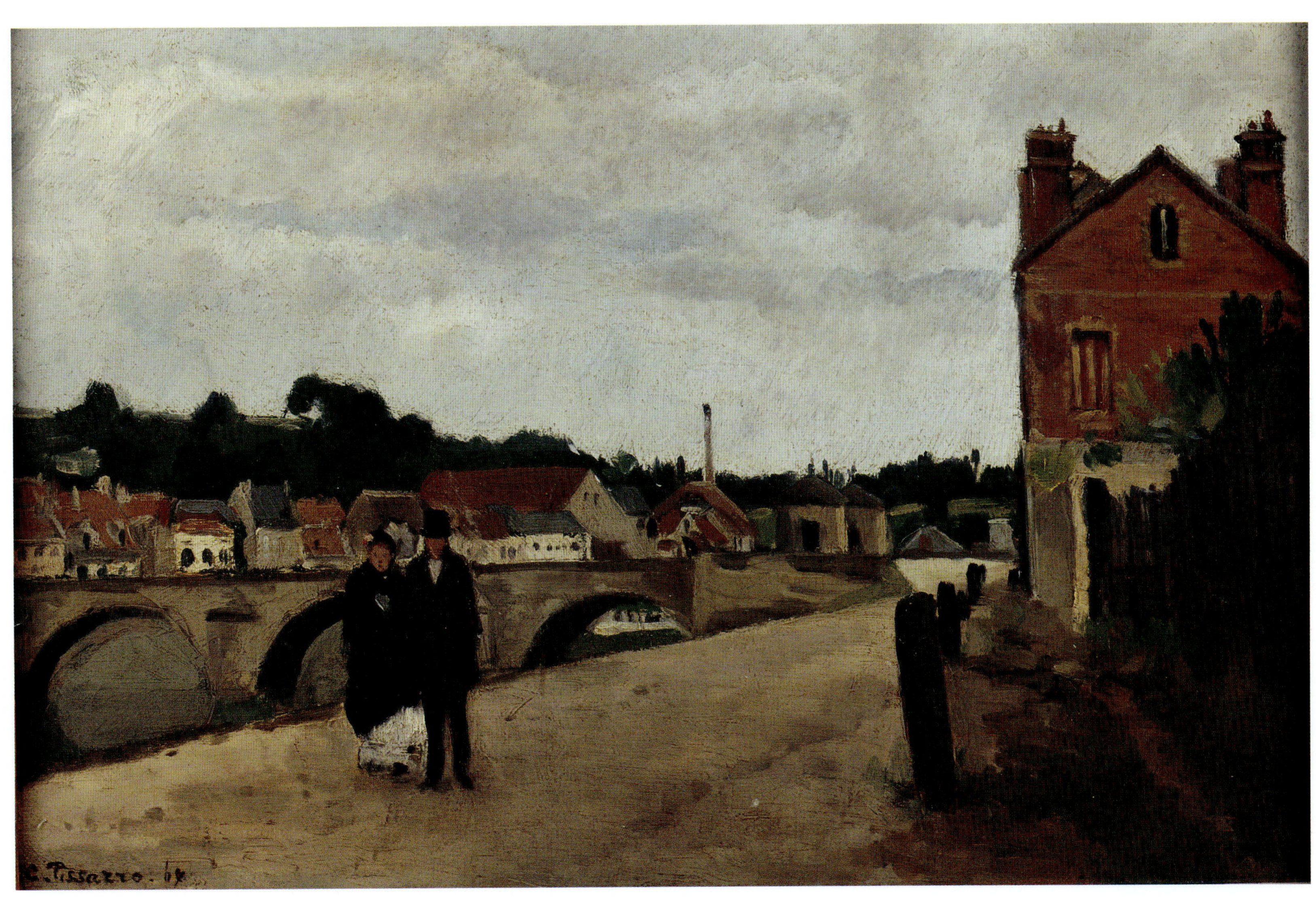
C. Pissarro. 67

10

Côte des Jalais, Pontoise

Jallais Hill, Pontoise

1867 (PD-RS 116)

Oil on canvas
34 ¼ × 45 ¼ in. (87 × 114.9 cm)
Lent by The Metropolitan Museum of Art, Bequest of William Church Osborn, 1951 (51.30.2)

In 1867 Pissarro began a series of works that featured the hills surrounding the hamlet of L'Hermitage in Pontoise, informally known as the Jalais Hill paintings. This group of seven compositions, often described as the culmination of the artist's early period, allowed Pissarro to explore his growing interest in geometric structure and atmosphere.[1] Despite their similarities in site and style, each work emphasizes a different aspect of the integration of man-made buildings into the natural surroundings. Some versions have architecture as the main focus,[2] whereas others let the hillside and surrounding fields play a larger role.[3]

This painting, along with another from this series, was exhibited in the Salon of 1868.[4] The more progressive critics encouraged this new direction in the young artist's work. In his review of the Salon, Odilon Redon, a critic who later became an important Symbolist painter, praised Pissarro's subdued palette and geometric style, as well as his honest interpretation of nature:

> *L'Hermitage* and the *Côte du Jallais* [*sic*] are very strong subjects and do not lack in character. The color is a bit dull, but it is simple and very true. His peculiar talent seems to brutalize nature. He paints it in an apparently rudimentary manner, but this indicates above all sincerity. M. Pissarro's vision is simple; the sacrifices he makes in his coloring only express the general impression more vividly, and this expression is always strong because it is simple.[5]

Émile Zola, in his review for the Salon, was passionate in his reaction to this painting, recognizing the poetry and simplicity of the artist's vision that was both unique and truthful:

> This is the modern country. One feels that man has been here, digging the ground, dividing it, creating a dejected landscape. This small valley, this little hill possess a heroic simplicity and candor. If it were not so great, nothing would be more banal. The temperament of the painter has drawn a precious poem of life out of ordinary truth.[6]

Here Pissarro focuses on two women walking on a path, enjoying a beautiful sunny day, surrounded by a majestic view of hills and fields. Whereas some of the other works in this series were composed with a palette knife, here Pissarro has abandoned that tool for thick, luxuriant brushstrokes, particularly in the verdant foliage to the right of the path and on the roadway itself. Much larger and flatter strokes are used to convey the rectangular fields on the hill in the far distance. Although a broad expanse of countryside is depicted in the distance, the space in the painting as a whole seems constricted. The curving road with a large mass of foliage on the right makes the far hillside seem to come down on top of the two figures, who are pinned in place by the tall poplars, producing a confined sense of space amid a magnificent panorama.

KR

1. See PD-RS 112, 115, 116, 119–121. PD-RS 125 is a large-scale work of similar style that features Les Pâtis, a hamlet to the west of Pontoise.
2. See PD-RS 119 and 120.
3. See PD-RS 115, 116, and 125.
4. According to the 2005 catalogue raisonné of Pissarro's work, the second painting was *The Jardin de Maubuisson, Pontoise*, c. 1867 (PD-RS 115), oil on canvas, National Gallery, Prague.
5. Odilon Redon, *Critiques d'art*, ed. Robert Coustet (Bordeaux: W. Blake & Co., 1987), 57, quoted and translated in Gary Tinterow and Henri Loyrette, *Origins of Impressionism* (New York: The Metropolitan Museum of Art, 1994), 446.
6. Émile Zola, "Mon Salon: Les Naturalistes," in *Écrits sur l'art* (1868), ed. Jean-Pierre Leduc-Adine (Paris: Gallimard, 1991), 205, quoted and translated in *Origins of Impressionism*, 446.

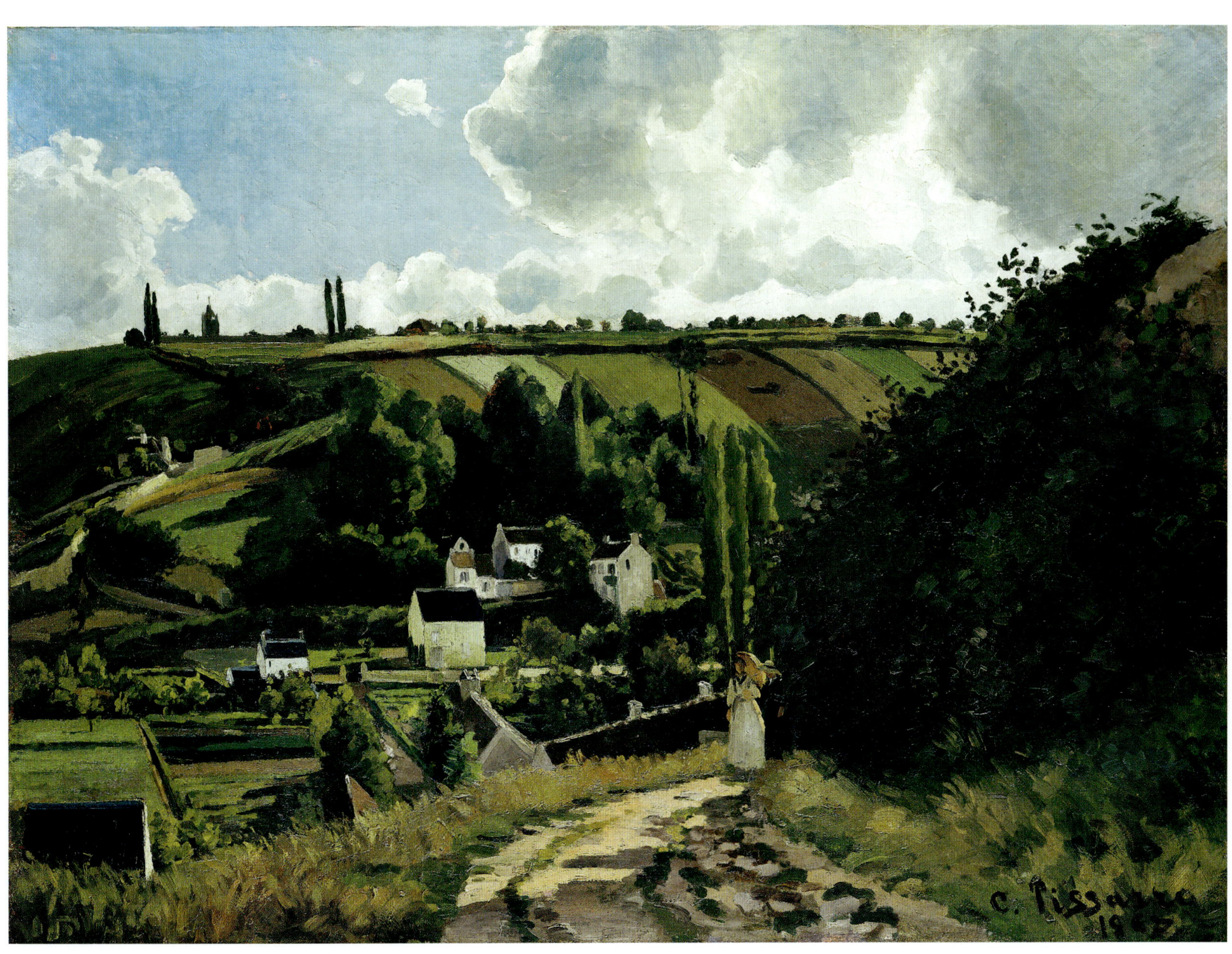

11

Landscape at Ennery near Pontoise

1868 (PD-RS 131)

Oil on canvas
15 × 18 5/16 in. (38 × 46.5 cm)
Kunsthalle Bremen—Der Kunstverein in Bremen

1. See PD-RS 46.

This intimate landscape was produced at the same time that Pissarro was painting his series of large-scale views of the hills that surrounded L'Hermitage. Although it retains some of the overall geometric structural elements of these monumental paintings (such as cat. 10), with its broad panorama and general theme of working fields on a hillside, it reveals a new immediacy and looseness that foreshadow his Impressionist works of the following decade. The palette knife technique that Pissarro used frequently in his Jalais Hill series has been replaced by large, thick brushstrokes, generously applied across the canvas. It cannot be considered simply a sketch, as there is no larger work that is particularly close to the composition, and by this point in his career Pissarro typically preferred to work out his compositions directly on the canvas, forgoing preliminary studies. Instead, this is a fully realized small painting in which the artist has allowed himself the freedom to explore the subject completely.

Here the artist has divided the canvas into a series of three carefully composed sections, structured into horizontal bands. The foreground, a large area of grass and field, is populated by a working farmer. The middle section is made up of a group of dark green, lush, rounded trees that separate the foreground from the hillside beyond that is covered with more fields, demarcated into rectangular forms by thick strokes of green and brown pigment. A curving path leads up the hill to the town, which is peppered with small cube-like houses and tall trees. The third section is the sky, filled with a long mass of clouds that takes up almost the entire width of the canvas. The rounded forms of the clouds are mirrored below in the loose band of trees in the middle ground.

The figure following a horse pulling a plow appeared in Pissarro's work as early as 1860[1] and continued to be of interest throughout his career. Given his anarchist political leanings, his numerous depictions of farmers and working-class figures may be considered a statement of his preference for the common man as subject over the bourgeoisie or aristocracy, classes of society for which he felt little sympathy. With his own financial hardship during this period, as he struggled to sell his work and care for his family, it is no wonder that he felt a closer relationship to members of the working class, who also labored hard for success.

KR

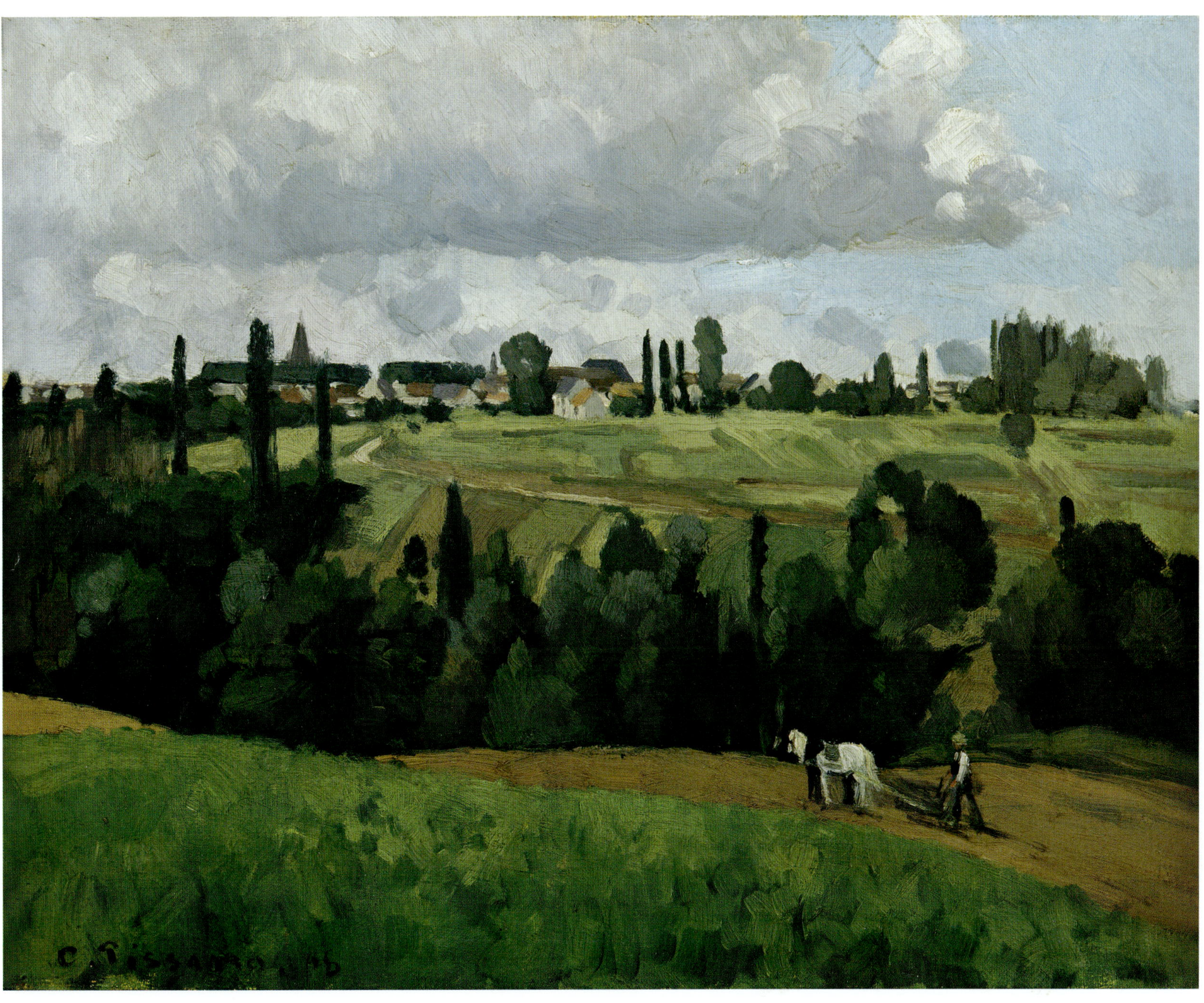

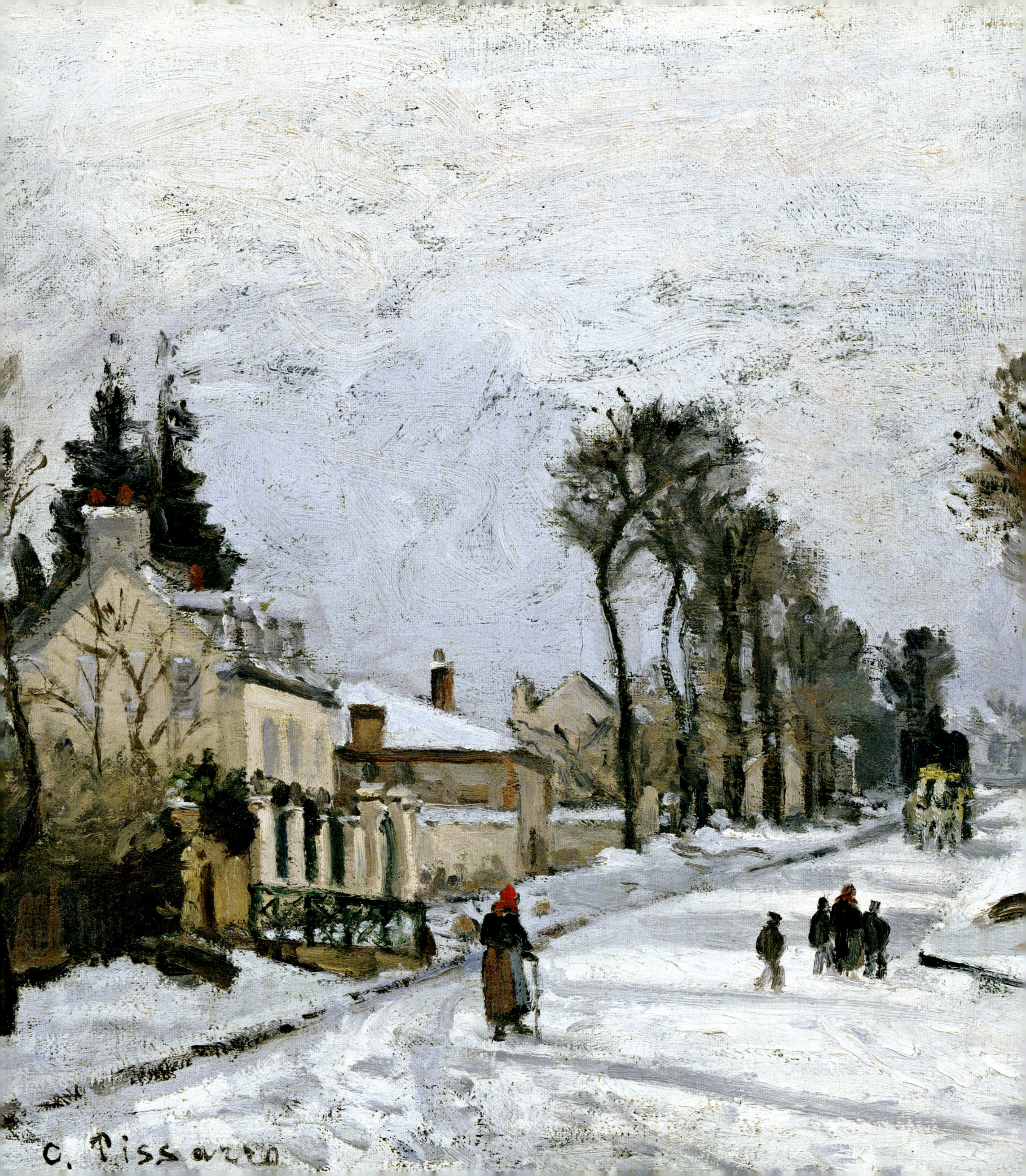
C. Pissarro

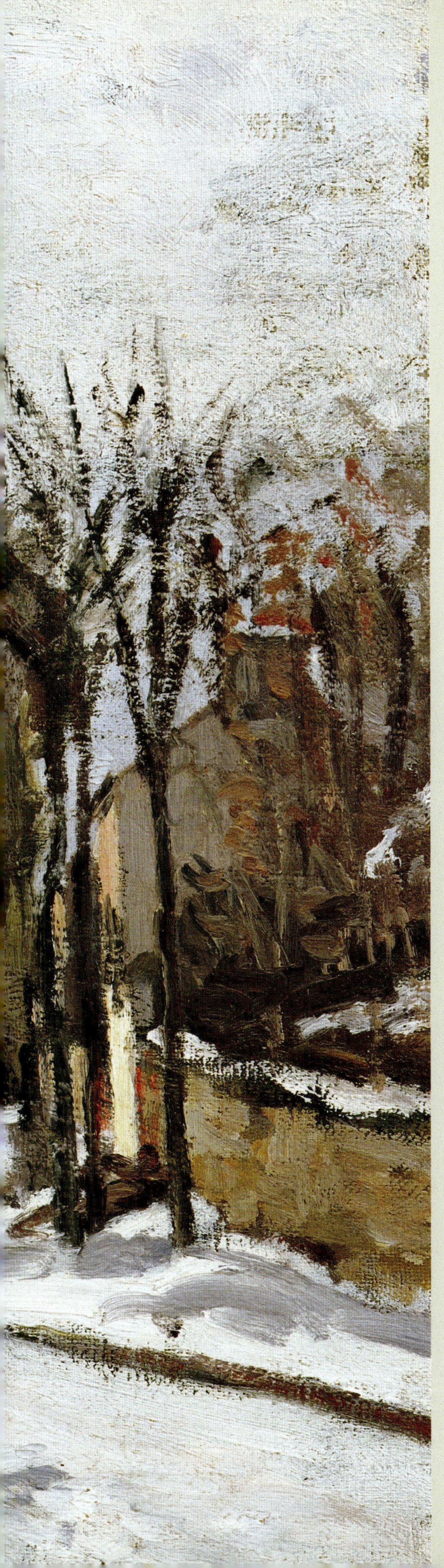

Louveciennes and the First Forays into Impressionism 1869–1870

12

The Corner of the Route de Versailles and the Chemin de l'Aqueduc, Louveciennes

The Versailles Road at Louveciennes (Snow)

c. 1869 (PD-RS 138)

Oil on canvas
15 ⅛ × 18 ⅛ in. (38.4 × 46.4 cm)
The Walters Art Museum, Baltimore, Maryland: The George A. Lucas Collection, 37.1989

In early 1869 Pissarro left Pontoise for Louveciennes, a small town west of Paris on the Seine River. He rented a large house on the route de Versailles, a main thoroughfare, where he remained for about eighteen months. Over the following year, Pissarro's friends and colleagues also began to frequent the region. Claude Monet and Pierre-Auguste Renoir painted together during the summer of 1869 in nearby Bougival, and Alfred Sisley visited the area, eventually moving to Voisins de Louveciennes in the fall of 1870.

In December 1869 Monet went to Louveciennes to paint with Pissarro. A heavy snowfall inspired the two artists to produce a series of works depicting the unique qualities of the winter landscape. Monet, who had painted his first snow scene in 1865,[1] completed three views of the snow-covered route, and Pissarro produced six, including *The Corner of the Route de Versailles and the Chemin de l'Aqueduc, Louveciennes*.[2] These were among Pissarro's earliest snow scenes, and they were the start of a lifelong interest in creating landscapes during all types of weather. *The Corner of the Route de Versailles and the Chemin de l'Aqueduc, Louveciennes* can be considered Pissarro's first foray into the style that eventually became known as Impressionism. With its quick brushwork, responsive to recording changes in weather and atmosphere, and its small scale and sense of immediacy, this painting was the start of a new phase in his career. The motif of a village street became a fascination for him, and he depicted the simple country paths and suburban roads of the towns where he lived for the rest of his career. The transformation of Pissarro's style in 1869–70 has long been credited to Monet's direct influence; however, it seems more likely that each contributed equally to a metamorphosis that occurred for both. Together, the artists learned a great deal from one another during that winter, and their successful experiments in Louveciennes encouraged them to continue searching for the ideal motif.

Here Pissarro placed his easel on the right side of the street, where it intersects with another thoroughfare. A thickly painted white sky, highlighted by streaks of pale yellow, orange, and passages of gray, hovers over the quiet setting. The heavy, wet atmosphere of the snowy day is articulated by the scumbled paint and rough texture visible throughout. A horse-drawn carriage moves along the road toward the viewer. A group of villagers walks toward the carriage, followed by a woman who stands alone, attempting to walk in the road with her walking stick. Whereas Monet placed the street in the very center of the composition in one of his views of this site so that it recedes quickly toward the horizon line (see Rothkopf essay, fig. 8), Pissarro placed his perspectival axes slightly off center, allowing for a slower recession into the distance.

The Corner of the Route de Versailles and the Chemin de l'Aqueduc, Louveciennes was purchased just weeks after its completion by one of Pissarro's first dealers, Père Martin. Martin, in turn, sold it in January 1870 for twenty francs to the American collector and dealer George A. Lucas.[3] Lucas, who lived in France for most of his life, was a great supporter of contemporary French artists, particularly of the Barbizon school. When he died in 1909, Lucas had amassed a collection that numbered more than twenty thousand works, including two remarkable early paintings by Pissarro (see cat. 3) that show his evolution toward Impressionism.
KR

1. Claude Monet, *A Cart on the Snowy Road at Honfleur*, 1865, oil on canvas, Musée d'Orsay, Paris, R.F. 2011.
2. See PD-RS 139–142, 145, and the present work.
3. *The Diary of George A. Lucas: An American Agent in Paris, 1857–1909*, ed. Lillian M. Randall, 2 vols. (Princeton, N.J.: Princeton University Press, 1979), 1: fig. 102, 2:313.

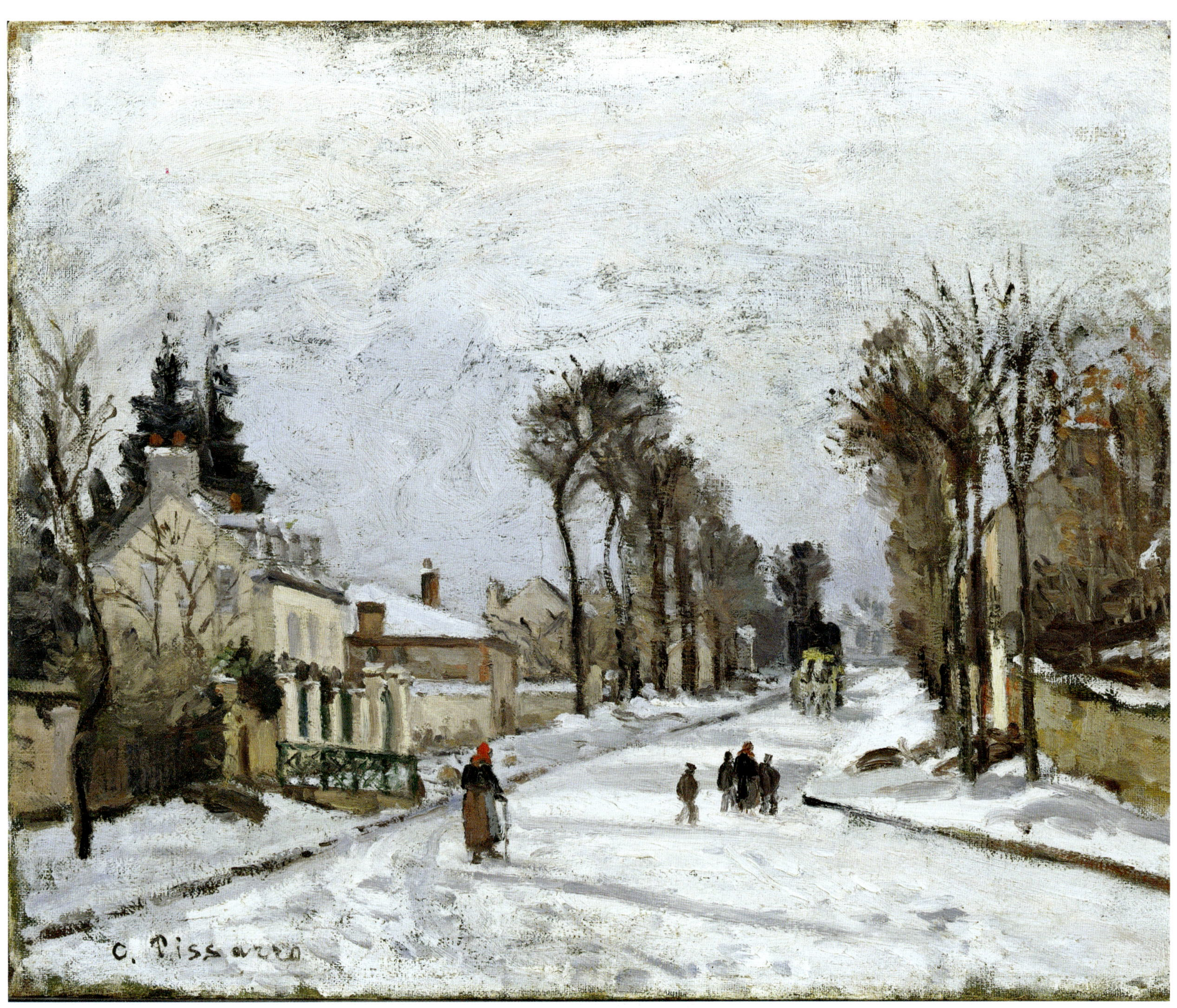
C. Pissarro

13
Route de Marly, Louveciennes
Road to Louveciennes
C. 1870 (PD-RS 178)

Oil on canvas
15 × 18 1/8 in. (38.1 × 46 cm)
High Museum of Art, Atlanta, Georgia, Purchase with the High Museum of Art Enhancement Fund, funds from the Livingston Foundation, Hambrick Bequest, Alfred Anstell Thornton in Memory of Leila Anstell Thornton and Albert Edward Thornton, Sr., and Sarah Miller Venable and William Hoyt Venable, the Phoenix Society, and Mr. and Mrs. Jerome Dobson, 2001.1

This undated painting belongs to a series of Louveciennes road views that Pissarro undertook between 1869 and 1870, before he left for England in December 1870 (see also cats. 12 and 14–16). In these works the artist depicted a variety of fleeting atmospheric and light effects in a well-structured world established on strict rules of perspective. In a letter he wrote to Lucien on May 8, 1903, he remarked on the centrality of observation of natural daylight during this early period: "This Mr. Dewhurst [author of essays that were eventually published in 1904 as *Impressionist Painting: Its Genesis and Development*] understands nothing of the impressionist movement, he sees only a mode of execution . . . ! He says that before going to London [in 1870] we [Monet and Pissarro] had no conception of light. The fact is that we have studies which prove the contrary."[1]

This is a view of the route de Marly, a street that linked Louveciennes to Marly-le-Roi to the north and Versailles to the south. The entrance to the château de Marly can be seen in the foreground at the right, but the artist has depicted the everyday street rather than the elegant château. Here the subject is shown from a low vantage point, where the viewer is dwarfed by the imposing tree on the left whose top branches go beyond the edge of the canvas. The diagonal road, too, extends beyond the framed view in the lower right corner. Its other end disappears at the horizon, providing a vanishing point and suggesting a further expanse. By inserting these cues on this fairly small canvas, the artist creates the impression of a wide vista.[2] Subtle shadow effects are produced by a sophisticated deployment of color and brushwork. The shadows cast by the house, tree, and figures highlight the textures of soil and the cobblestone road. The soft, subtle palette is typical of Pissarro's work of this period, as is the varied and energetic brushwork. This view is similar to a painting by Monet of the same year that was made after a snowstorm,[3] and, given the close relationship between the two artists at this time, the works share many similarities in style and technique.
GÇ

1. Camille Pissarro to Lucien Pissarro, May 8, 1903, in *Letters to His Son Lucien*, ed. John Rewald (New York: Pantheon Books, 1943), 355–56.
2. See cat. 16, for French and Dutch precedents of the road motif in landscape painting.
3. Claude Monet, *Road at Sunset, Winter Effect*, 1869, oil on canvas, Musée des Beaux-Arts et de la Céramique, Rouen, France.

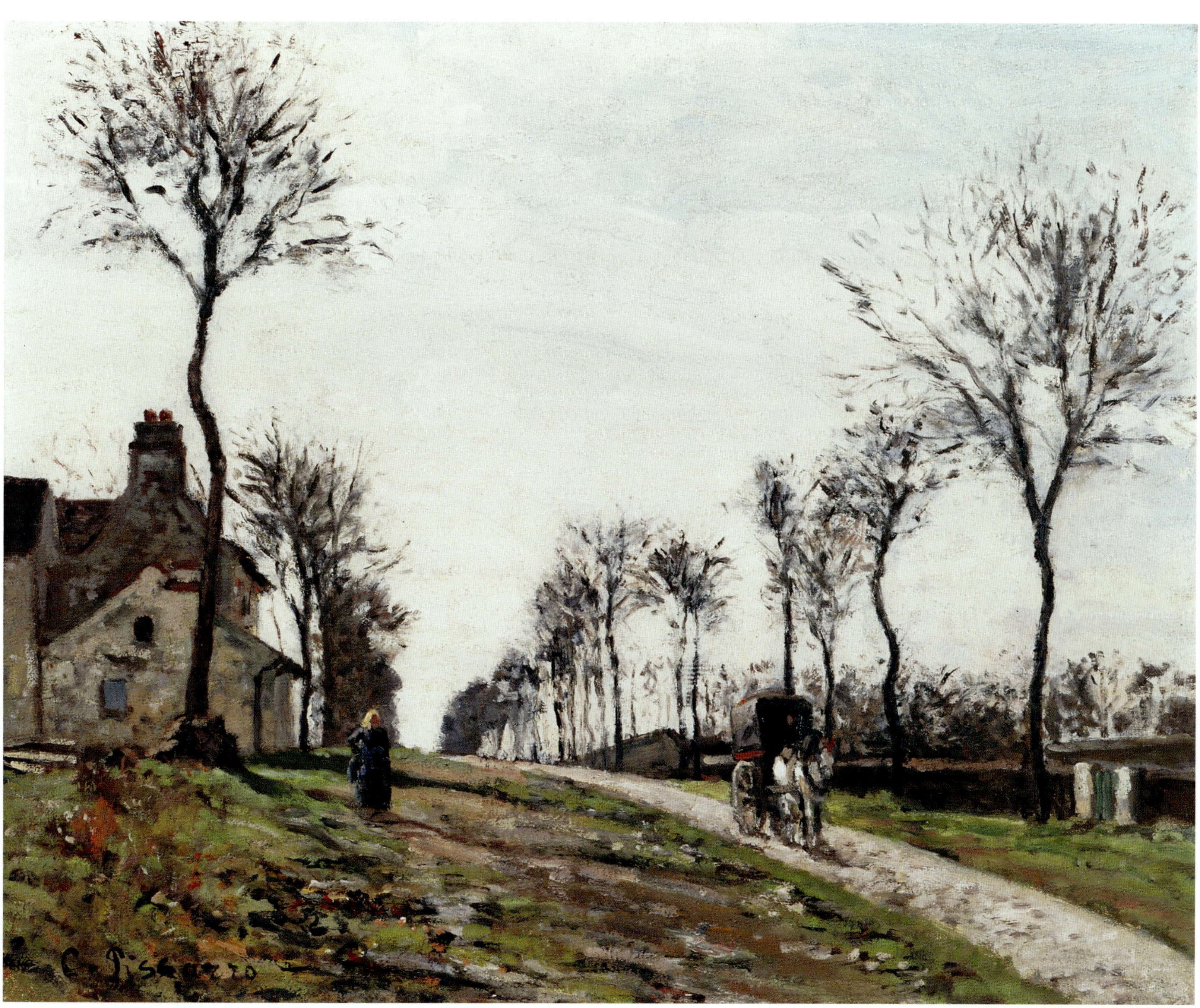

14
Route de Versailles, Louveciennes
The Road to Versailles at Louveciennes
1870 (PD-RS 151)

15
The Road from Versailles to Louveciennes
c. 1872

14
Oil on canvas
12 7/8 x 16 3/16 in. (32.8 x 41.1 cm)
The Sterling and Francine Clark Art Institute, Williamstown, Massachusetts, 1955.828

15
Watercolor over graphite
7 1/2 × 10 in. (19 × 25.2 cm)
National Gallery of Art, Washington, D.C., Collection of Mr. and Mrs. Paul Mellon, 1985.64.107
Milwaukee and Memphis only

Pissarro moved with his family from Pontoise to Louveciennes in 1869, settling in a house on the route de Versailles, a road that he painted several times between 1869 and 1870.[1] In *Corner of the Route de Versailles and the Chemin de l'Aqueduc, Louveciennes* (cat. 12), the artist depicted this street from approximately the same viewpoint as is seen in *Route de Versailles, Louveciennes* (cat. 14) although from slightly farther up the street. This series of paintings focused on the route de Versailles constitute the initial stages of Pissarro's concerted explorations of painting *en plein air*. As part of this project, Pissarro radically changed the range of colors on his palette beginning in 1868. He drastically reduced his use of dark browns, the basic building block of academic studio light, and systematically started to observe the effects of daylight, in which the range of hues is much broader than what could be observed in the artificial light of studio interiors.[2] Developing the technical means and a stylistic language to capture the myriad effects of broad daylight under different atmospheric conditions was an interest he shared with Monet, Sisley, and Renoir.[3]

In *Route de Versailles, Louveciennes*, the composition is enlivened by scattered clusters of color contrasts to depict daylight on a winter day under an open sky. Two complementary colors, creamy yellow and violet-blue, each of them pale on its own, strengthen one another when applied side by side. The house on the left exemplifies this optical effect: the tawny wall color is enhanced by the contrasting light blue shutters. Small, diffused brushstrokes of violet-blue and gray on the road at the lower left evoke the last traces of snow that reflect the color of the blue sky above. Observing atmospheric light effects on an overcast day, for example in *Route de Saint-Germain, Louveciennes* (cat. 16), Pissarro would paint the melting snow by the roadside in a darker tone of gray.

One of the hallmarks of the painting, and of this period in Pissarro's early Impressionist period in general, is the artist's use of shadow. Here, by extending the shadows of the trees that line the roadway onto the surface of the street itself, he provides a subtle pattern of darker pigment that continues in regular intervals into the distance. The depiction of colored shadows, especially those of blue and violet, was one of the most controversial aspects of the Impressionist technique; most critics in the coming years found colored shadows unacceptable. Pissarro, however, did not consider his practice to be a deviation from the tradition. In a letter to his son Lucien, he emphasized the influence of "Claude Lorrain, Corot, the whole eighteenth century [French painting] and Chardin"[4] on his and Monet's studies of light and shadow in the late 1860s and early 1870s.

1. See PD-RS 138–142, 145, 151–153, 155, 159, 163–165, 167, 196, 198, 209, 214, 215, and 224 for other paintings from the same period featuring the same road.
2. For an explanation of the differences between studio light and outdoor light, see Anthea Callen, *The Art of Impressionism: Painting Technique and the Making of Modernity* (New Haven: Yale University Press, 2000), 112, 116.
3. See cat. 12 for more on Pissarro's relationship and common goals with this group of painters, especially Monet, in the late 1860s.
4. Camille Pissarro to Lucien Pissarro, May 8, 1903, in *Letters to His Son Lucien*, ed. John Rewald (New York: Pantheon Books, 1943), 355–56.

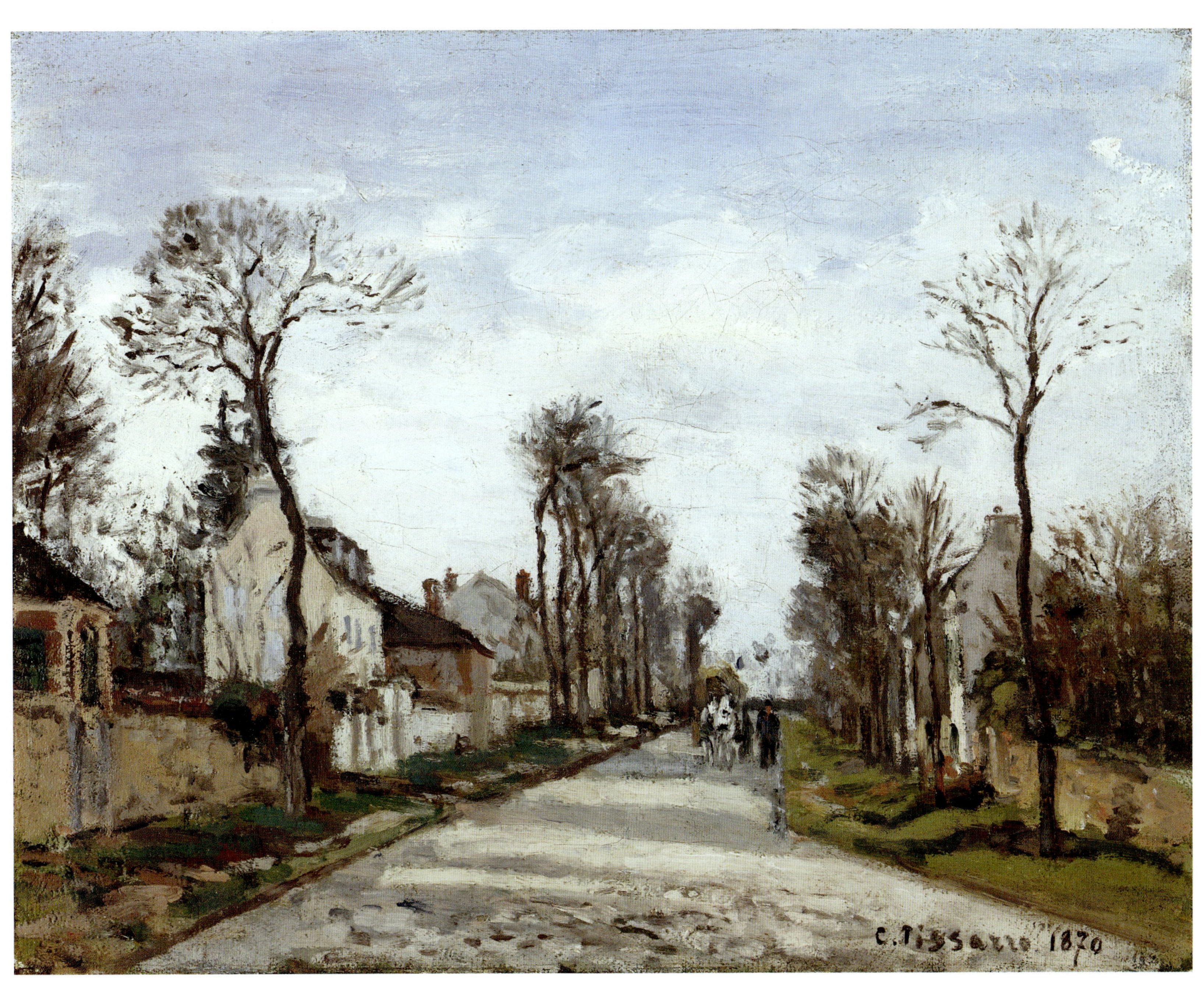
C. Pissarro 1870

The watercolor *The Road from Versailles to Louveciennes* depicts the same road from a different vantage point. Not dated by the artist, it is not clear whether it was made about 1870, before Pissarro left for London, or about 1872, when he moved back to Louveciennes. The latter seems more probable: after the Franco-Prussian War Pissarro became more interested in expanding his graphic means of spontaneous expression. On a cream-colored ground, summary, rapid gestures in purple, red, and green, both sinuous lines and small, multidirectional touches made with the tip of the brush, harmoniously work together with wider areas of washes. Watercolor allowed Pissarro to use freer handling and looser brushstrokes than in his oil paintings, which are more carefully constructed.
GÇ

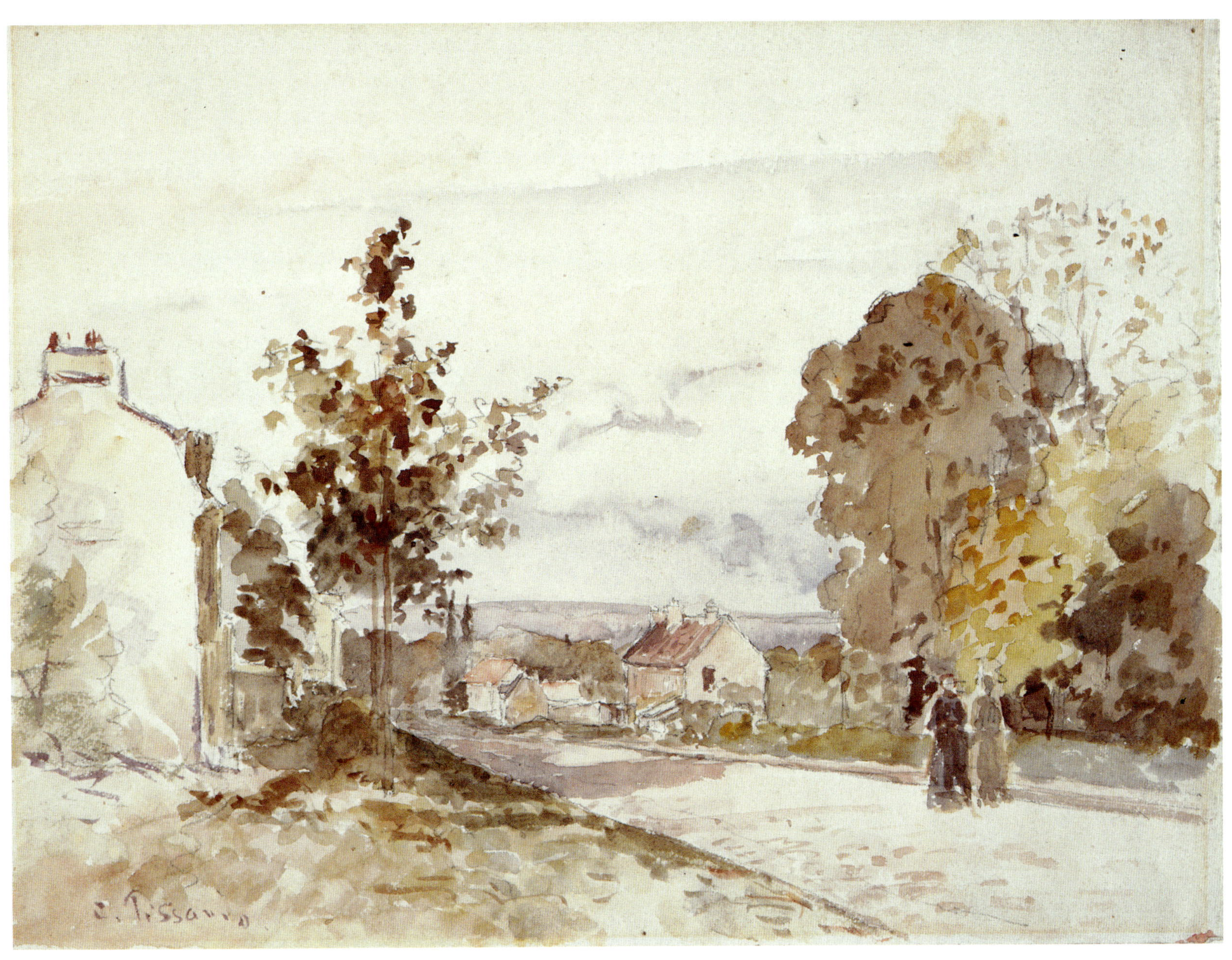

16

Route de Saint-Germain, Louveciennes

The Road to Saint-Cyr at Louveciennes

c. 1870 (PD-RS 146)

Oil on canvas
18 × 21 in. (45.7 × 53.3 cm)
Private collection, courtesy of The J. Paul Getty Museum, Los Angeles
Milwaukee and Memphis only

Route de Saint-Germain, Louveciennes, depicting a country road on a winter afternoon under an overcast sky, was painted before Pissarro and his family left for England in December 1870, fleeing the Franco-Prussian War. On a fairly small canvas, the feeling of a wide space is achieved by a well-sustained tension between horizontal and vertical motifs. Strong vertical forms of trees stretching into the sky and triangular roofs pointing upward are balanced by the broad expanse of the curving road that disappears into the horizon. Although the sky itself is a bright silvery gray, the mood of a dark winter afternoon is conveyed through the silhouettes of trees, roofs, and pedestrians. Snow, depicted by loosely brushed dabs of gray, is melting on the ground by the side of the road. This work was published in the 1939 catalogue raisonné of Pissarro's work as a view of the route de Saint-Cyr, but the authors of the 2005 catalogue raisonné have identified it instead as a view of the route de Saint-Germain in Louveciennes.[1]

Pissarro's interest in road scenes dates from the 1850s, when, as a young artist in Paris, he frequented the studio of Camille Corot. As a compositional formula, the road in perspective dates back to seventeenth-century Dutch landscape painting.[2] The naturalist Dutch tradition was mediated to painters in Pissarro's generation by Corot, who was profoundly influenced by their example (fig. 1). The subject was appealing to Pissarro, as with it he could convey perspective, mass, and volume as well as explore pictorial means to depict changing atmospheric effects within the confines of a firmly structured space. Through this basic composition, the artist produced numerous variations of an orderly world where vegetation and human structures are arranged around a central motif that traverses the landscape toward a vanishing point.

GÇ

1. For more information, see PD-RS 146.
2. See cat. 32 for more on the legacy of the Dutch tradition.

Fig. 1. Camille Corot, *A Road near Arras*, 1853–58. Oil on canvas. Musée des Beaux-Arts d'Arras

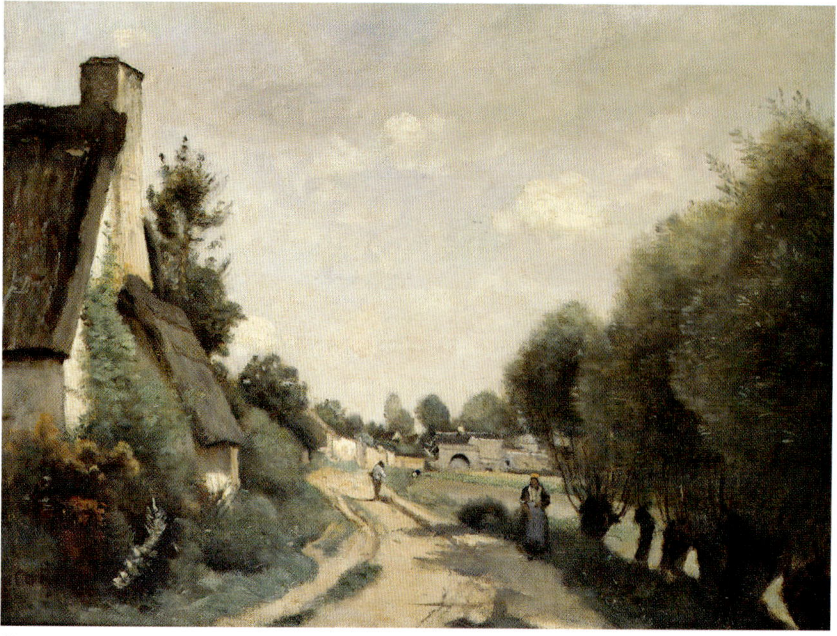

Fig. 1

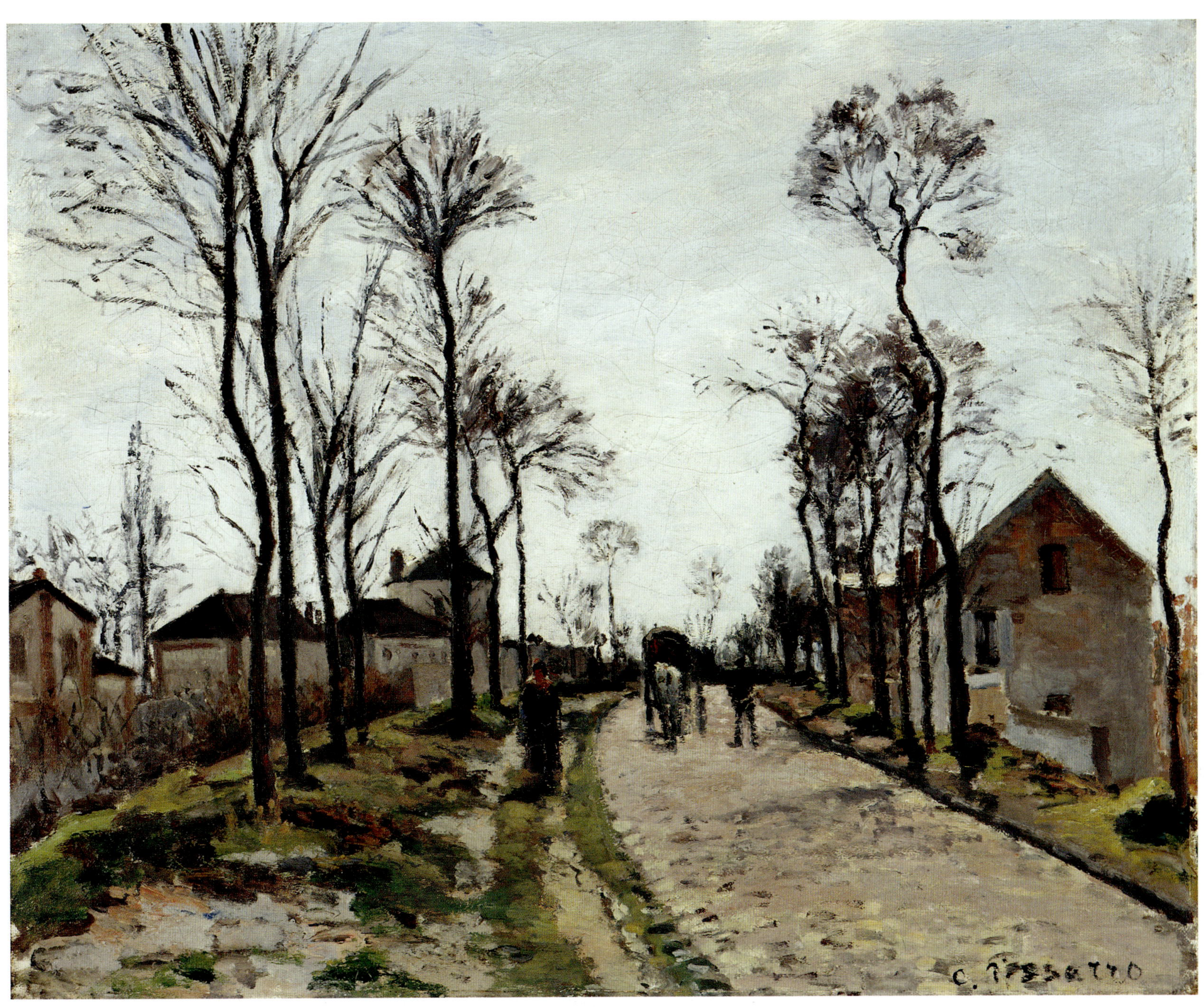
C. Pissarro

17

Grounds of the Château du Pont under Snow, Louveciennes

Snow at Louveciennes

c. 1870 (PD-RS 143)

Oil on panel
12 ¾ × 18 ¹¹⁄₁₆ in. (32.3 × 47.5 cm)
The Art Institute of Chicago, Mr. and Mrs. Lewis Larned Coburn Memorial Endowment, 1973.673

1. See John Rewald, *The History of Impressionism*, 4th rev. ed. (New York: The Museum of Modern Art, 1973), 209–10.

Grounds of the Château du Pont under Snow, Louveciennes might be one of the earliest snow scenes Pissarro painted. Signed but not dated, it is thought to have been produced before he left Louveciennes during the Franco-Prussian War. The broad, sweeping brushstrokes and limited palette suggest an early period in Pissarro's Impressionist technique, perhaps around the time he started attending the artists' meetings at the Café Guerbois in the late 1860s. These discussions on new painting, presided over by Édouard Manet, focused, in part, on the questions of working *en plein air*.[1]

The color scheme, in particular the black and dark earth tones, and the brushwork suggest that this painting was made at a very early stage in the artist's study of snow effects. Black, a noncolor indicating the absence of light, was not discarded from the Impressionist palette right away. Rather, it was gradually replaced, in the course of the 1870s, by colored blacks, obtained by mixing dark blue and red. Pissarro's vocabulary of gestural brushstrokes and his depiction of various states of snow is very limited at this stage. Small areas of snow are suggested by dabs of color deployed on the branches and the wall at left, while larger amounts of snow in the foreground are represented by broad, sweeping gestures of the brush. This brushwork is similar to that found in the sky in another early snow effect made about 1869, *The Corner of the Route de Versailles and the Chemin de l'Aqueduc, Louveciennes* (cat. 12). The color scheme of *Grounds of the Château du Pont under Snow, Louveciennes* is much more limited. A narrow range of blues, grays, and whites is used for the light and shadow effects on snow. Over the next decade, Pissarro introduced a variety of brush techniques, as well as primary and secondary colors, into his snow scenes and shadows, experimenting with complementary color effects. In addition, by introducing different shades of blue and purple as well as pink and orange into the reflections and shadows on snow, he made his depictions of these phenomena more sophisticated (see cats. 34, 35, 43, and 45).

Landscape painters in the Café Guerbois group, including Monet, Sisley, Renoir, and Pissarro, advocated painting in the open air. They believed in the necessity of observing the subtle optical effects produced by natural light and tried to reproduce them without resorting to dark earth tones. They observed that natural daylight revealed colors everywhere, even the areas in shadow. Here, in a scene covered with a blanket of snow, the angle of the light source, the topography of the terrain depicted, and the light reflecting off the snow and surface of other landscape features all produce a myriad of color effects. The painters set themselves the challenge, beginning in the late 1860s, to develop a color scheme that they believed was true to their observations of nature.

GÇ

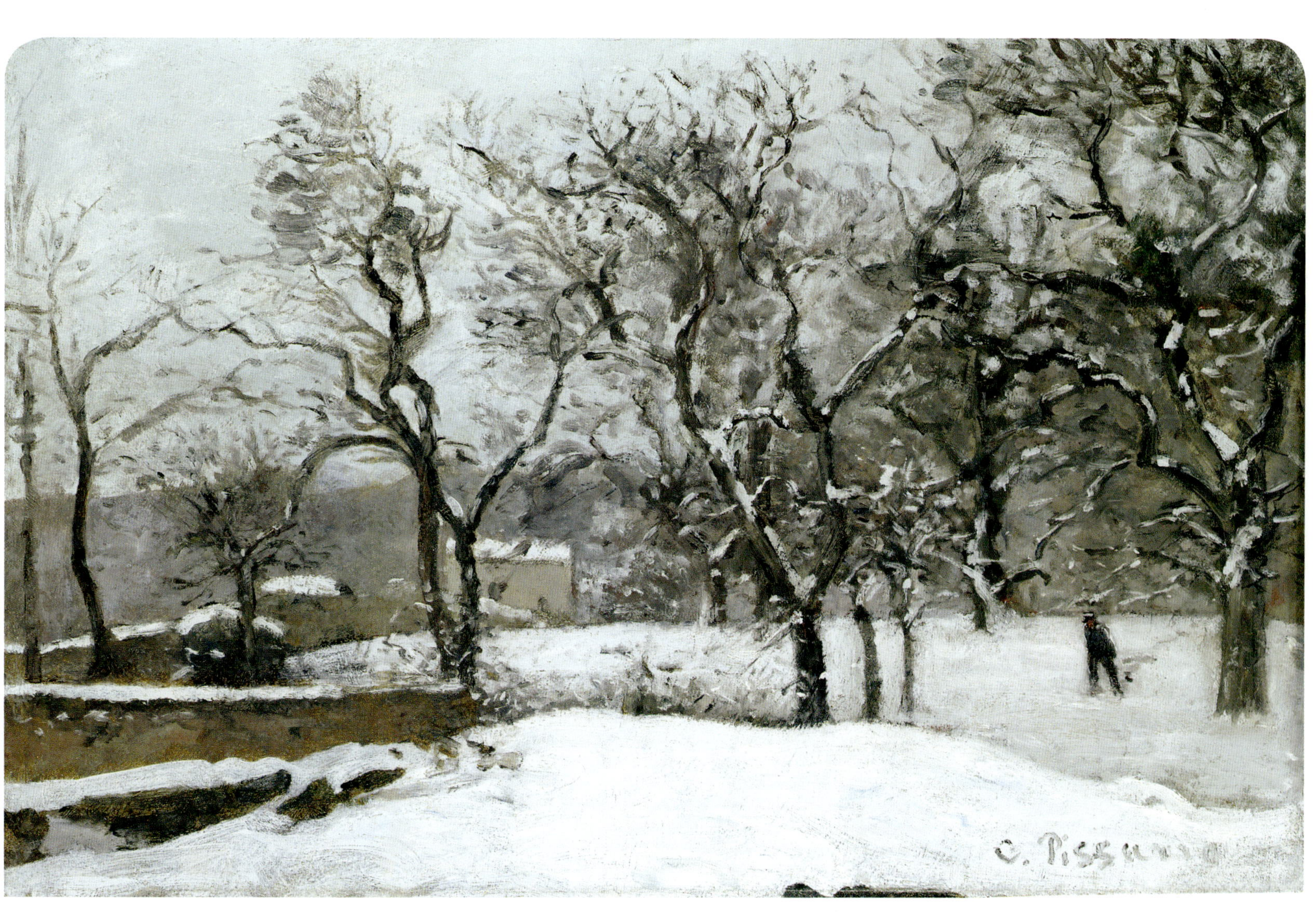

18

View of the Village of Louveciennes

Orchards at Louveciennes

c. 1870 (PD-RS 166)

Oil on canvas
18 × 21 in. (45.7 × 53.3 cm)
Ruth and Bruce Dayton

Trees were among Pissarro's favorite motifs, and he depicted apple blossoms in Pontoise and orchards in Louveciennes in the early 1870s. Although blooming trees are generally associated with rejuvenation in springtime, the critics attacked Pissarro's orchard scenes for their vulgarity and coarseness. His depictions of kitchen gardens and plowed fields, all evocative of agricultural labor, were associated with crude, unpicturesque aspects of everyday life. When *Orchard in Bloom* (cat. 27) was shown at the first Impressionist exhibition in 1874, critics declared Pissarro a simple painter of cabbages. Their criticism derived in part from the contrast between the coarse soil and the delicate foliage, a juxtaposition the artist highlighted as early as 1866 in *The House of Père Gallien, Pontoise* (cat. 6).

Spatial ambiguity is a novel aspect of this work, where Pissarro's general preoccupation with recession verges on transforming landscape features into abstract shapes. This is especially clear in the gold-colored field at the center under the trees: this golden patch oscillates between being a field receding in space and a pyramidal object rising vertically from the foreground. Here the brusque foreshortening of the fields in the foreground produces ambiguity, accentuating the flatness, rather than depth, of these quadrangular zones of color.

In this rich and complex view from his house in Louveciennes, rather than contrasting the worked, barren surface of the earth with blossoming fruit trees, he depicts a world of abundance in a composition unified by a color scheme based on different tones of green and red and an underlying structure made of sharp diagonals and verticals. The palette, as well as the compositional structure, is reminiscent of that of *L'Hermitage at Pontoise* (see Rothkopf essay, fig. 7). In its scale and brushwork, however, *View of the Village of Louveciennes* differs from its grand predecessor. Here the artist uses small, multidirectional brushstrokes to build up the composition, in contrast to the larger strokes of color that constitute the Hermitage paintings.

It is significant that Pissarro revisited a compositional formula he had developed for a Salon painting in this much smaller format in the early 1870s, when he was searching intensively for new compositional structures. Pissarro, as well as his younger colleague Paul Cézanne, would return to Pissarro's Jalais Hill series during the 1870s and 1880s for a number of innovative compositions.[1] *View of the Village of Louveciennes* is significant for being one of the earliest, and most radical examples of the artist's interest in revising his Salon paintings.
GÇ

1. For more on Pissarro and Cézanne's working relationship, see cats. 34 and 48.

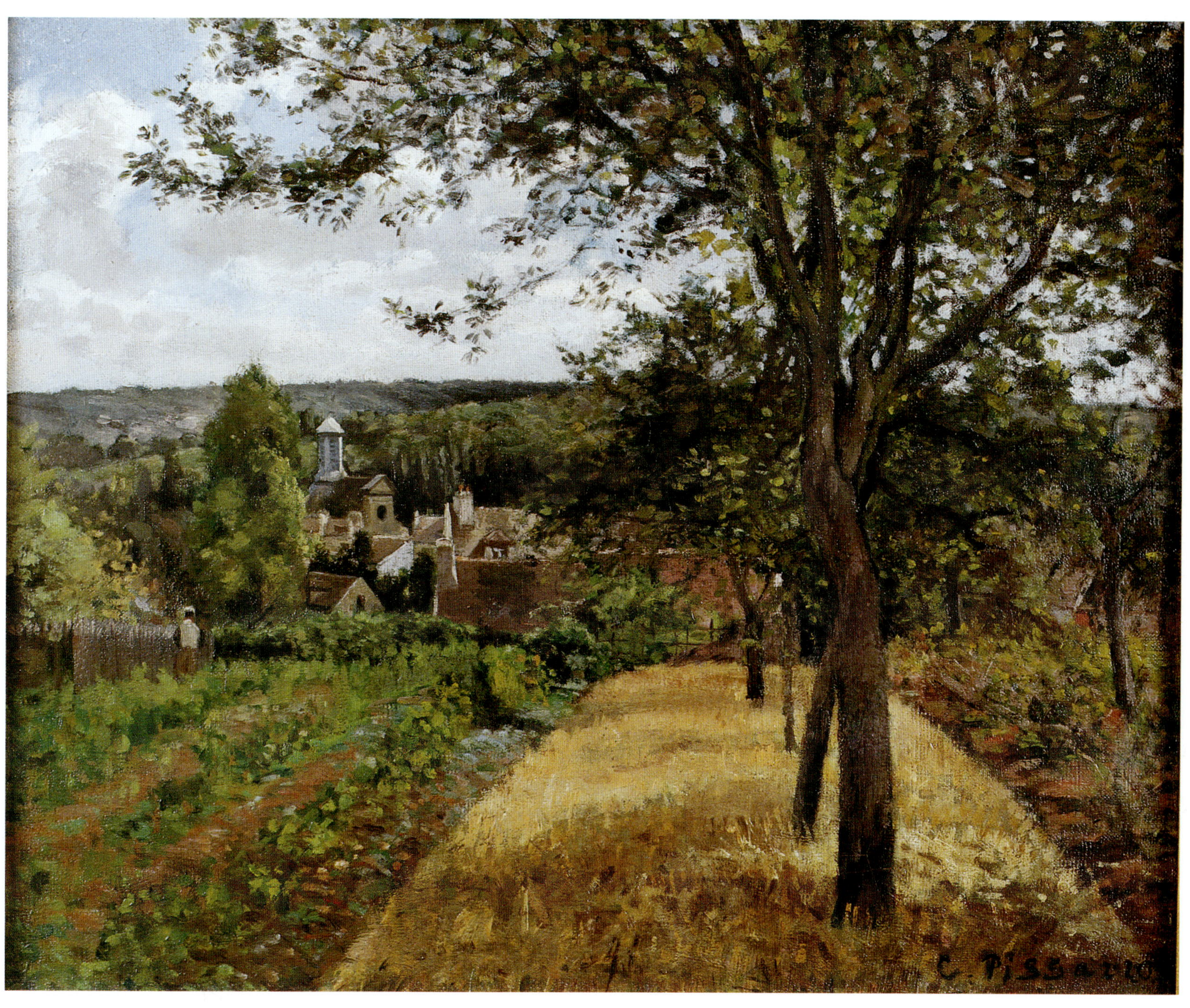
C. Pissarro

19
Houses at Bougival
Landscape in the Vicinity of Louveciennes (Autumn)
1870 (PD-RS 157)

Oil on canvas
35 × 45 ⅝ in. (88.9 × 115.9 cm)
The J. Paul Getty Museum, Los Angeles
Baltimore only

In *Houses at Bougival,* Pissarro depicts an unpretentious scene of peasants, a village garden, and houses. The pathway in the foreground and the row of trees in the middle ground suggest a stagelike setting, offering a vista of a village garden located behind a group of houses and a partial view of the townscape beyond, a compositional structure that differs greatly from his typical perspectival street scenes of this period. The viewer is invited to see the various details in the background through a screen of delicately painted leaves that flicker in broad daylight. Several figures, dwarfed by tall trees and buildings, add an element of intimacy to this fairly large composition.

It has been suggested that *Houses at Bougival* was shown at the Salon of 1870.[1] The relatively large dimensions of the canvas and the highly finished paint handling argue for such a possibility. This exhibition turned out to be the last Salon of the Second Empire, and the last Salon in which Pissarro exhibited. Next to such controversial and highly contrived Salon blockbusters as Henri Regnault's *Salomé* or Pierre Puvis de Chavannes's *Beheading of St. John the Baptist*, Pissarro's modest landscape did not receive much critical attention, except from those art critics in his close circle. Théodore Duret lauded Pissarro's landscape as the exact reproduction of a natural scene and the portrait of a corner of the world that existed in reality.[2]

According to the recent catalogue raisonné of the artist's work, this scene is set in Bougival, a Parisian suburb frequented at the end of the 1860s by the future Impressionists Monet, Renoir, and Sisley, who were in search of motifs for their studies *en plein air.* In the summer of 1869 Renoir and Monet set their easels side by side at La Grenouillère, a popular bathing spot at Bougival, where they produced their seminal Impressionist scenes of the bathing crowd. About a year later, Pissarro would also choose Bougival as the setting for this large canvas, preferring to depict the town's rural character instead. This quiet suburban townscape, featuring a peasant woman and a boy engaged in conversation and another villager working in the field, is radically different from Renoir's and Monet's scenes of leisure featuring fashionably dressed Parisians. Whatever these artists chose as subject matter, during this period Pissarro, Monet, and Renoir developed a growing interest in novel brush technique and color scheme for the spontaneous depiction of their observations *en plein air.* In *Houses at Bougival,* large, separate brushstrokes, employed to render the earth, foliage, and the shimmering light effects produced by the leaves on the trees, exemplify the artist's new technique. This composition is significant for being the earliest Salon-size painting created with the aim to impart the immediacy of the artist's vision.

GÇ

1. See PD-RS 157.
2. See Ludovic Rodolphe Pissarro and Lionelli Venturi, "L'Art de Camille Pissarro: Étude critique," in *Camille Pissarro: Son art, son oeuvre*, 2 vols. (Paris: P. Rosenberg, 1939), 1:25.

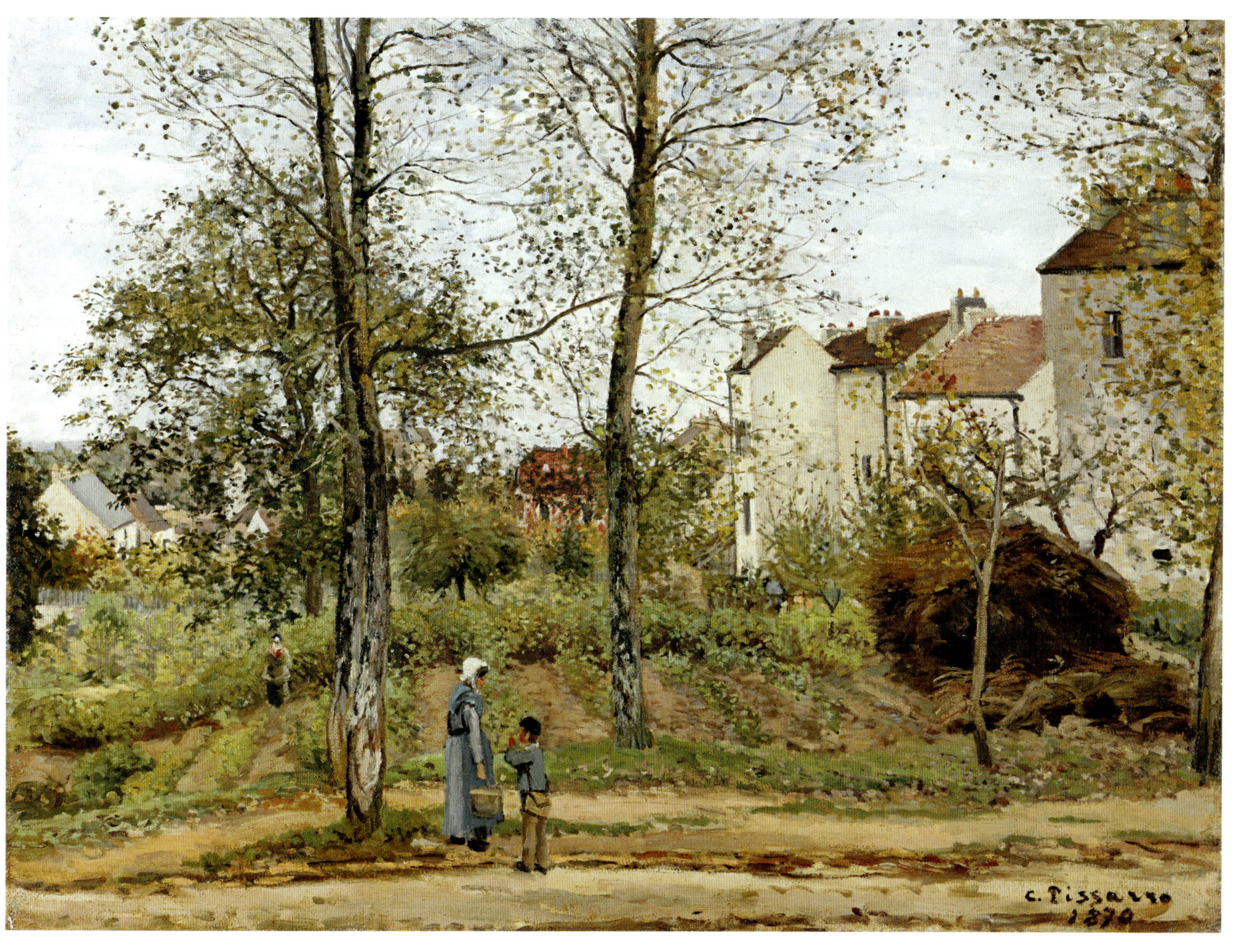
C. Pissarro
1870

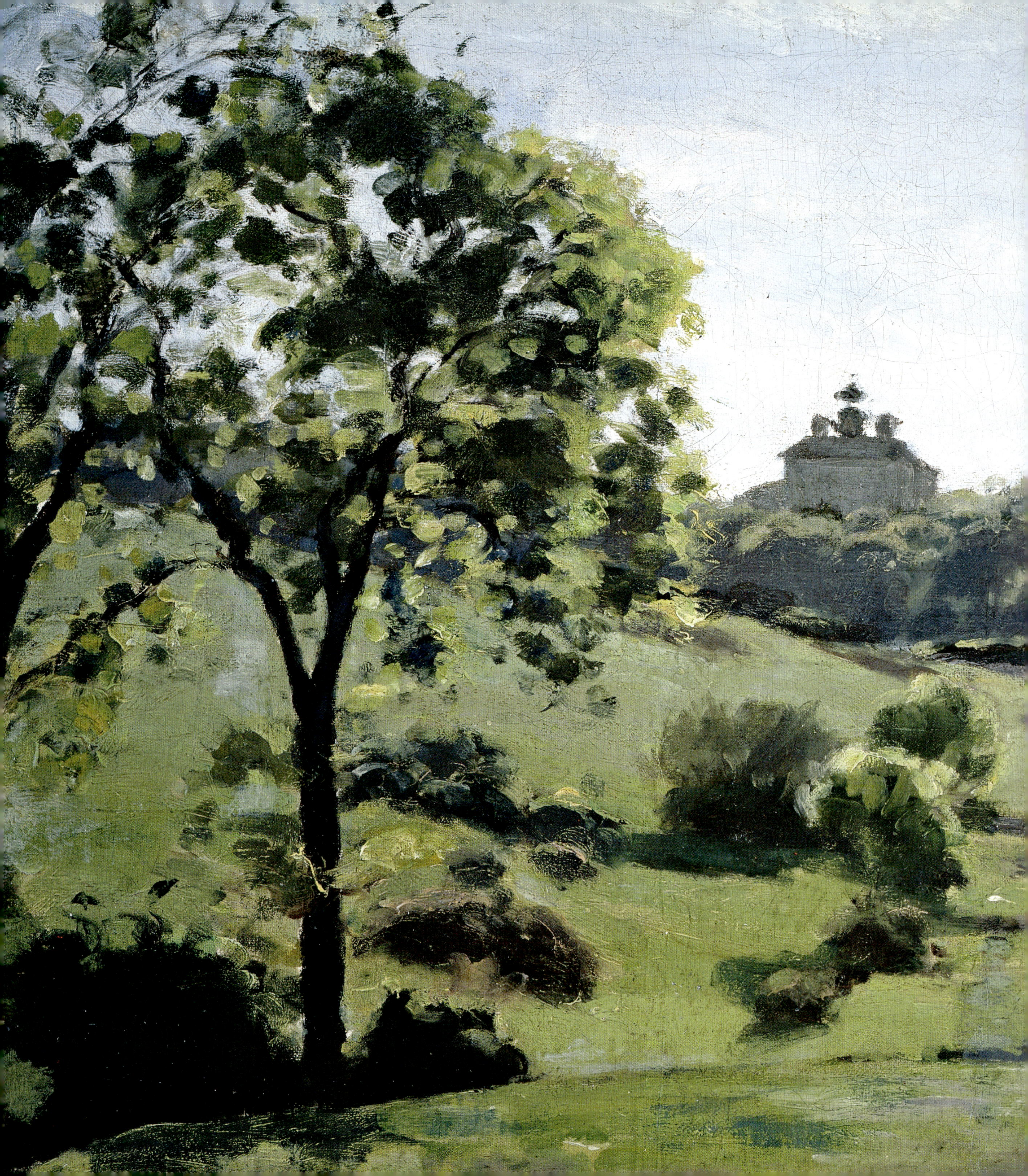

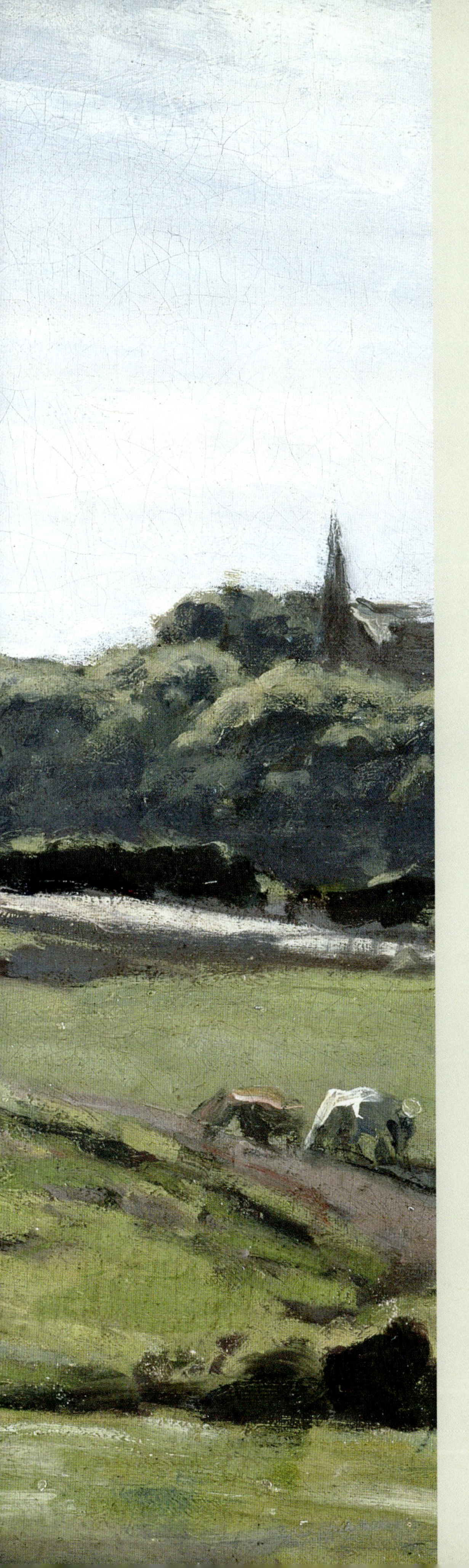

London 1870–1871

20

The Avenue, Sydenham

1871 (PD-RS 188)

Oil on canvas
19 ¼ × 28 ¾ in. (49 × 73 cm)
The National Gallery, London, NG 6493

1. For the identification of this site, see PD-RS 188.
2. Camille Pissarro to Lucien Pissarro, January 1883, in *Letters to His Son Lucien*, ed. John Rewald (New York: Pantheon Books, 1943), 21.
3. Richard R. Brettell, *Pissarro and Pontoise: The Painter in a Landscape* (New Haven: Yale University Press, 1990), 215 n. 26.
4. Christopher Lloyd, "Camille Pissarro and Hans Holbein the Younger," *Burlington Magazine* 117, no. 872 (November 1975): 722–26.
5. For more on the painted-out female figure, see David Bomford et al., *Art in the Making: Impressionism* (London: National Gallery, 1990), 138–39.
6. PD-RS 188 identifies this work as the first painting by Pissarro to be purchased by Paul Durand-Ruel.

Pissarro produced this view of an avenue in the London suburb of Sydenham during his stay in the British capital in 1870–71. Here Pissarro experimented with the traditional landscape format of a receding avenue that long had fascinated him. His highly structured compositions from Louveciennes are markedly different, however, from this wide, graceful street. Rather than featuring simple townspeople in the midst of their daily routines, often on their way to or from work, here Pissarro includes figures in their brightly colored city clothes enjoying a leisurely walk. A horse-drawn carriage complete with two drivers commandeers the center of the road, their fawn-colored uniforms matching the tan color of the street itself. The thoroughfare, known today as Lawrie Park Avenue, is lined with lovely well-built homes, and a church, identified as Saint Bartholomew, stands at the end of the sidewalk to the right.[1] Pissarro later wrote to his son Lucien about his fond memories of working in picturesque London: "I recall perfectly those multicolored houses, and the desire I had at the time to interrupt my journey and make some interesting studies. But it would be a long trip indeed if one stopped at every attractive town or village, at every beautiful motif—although a painter could want nothing better than to be able to stop and then go on his way and always go on and stop."[2]

Not only is the compositional structure more elaborate in this work than in his paintings of roads of Louveciennes but the overall palette has lightened considerably. The grays, tans, and browns of France have been replaced by bright blue and green, a palette that may have been influenced by the works of Joseph Mallord William Turner, which Pissarro saw in London.[3] Christopher Lloyd has suggested that Meindert Hobbema's *The Avenue at Middelharnis*, which was on view at the National Gallery in May 1871, two months before Pissarro returned to France, may have influenced this composition.[4] Hobbema's design of an avenue of trees receding toward the center of the picture is both simple and majestic and may have inspired Pissarro to explore the motif in the London suburbs, although he placed his easel to the right of the roadway.

The Avenue, Sydenham is one of the rare

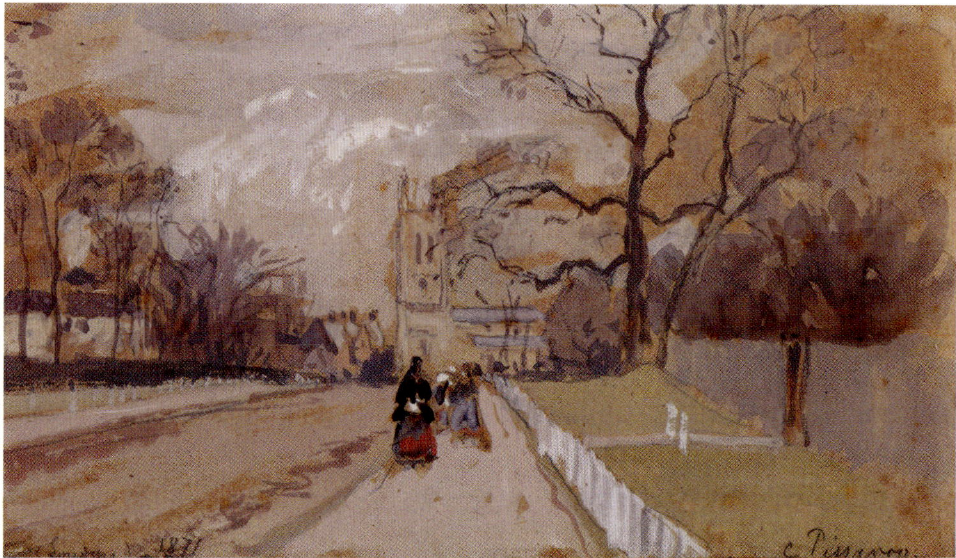

Fig. 1

Fig. 1. Camille Pissarro, *Avenue with a Church at the Far End*, 1871. Gouache. Musée du Louvre, Paris, France, R.F. 28798

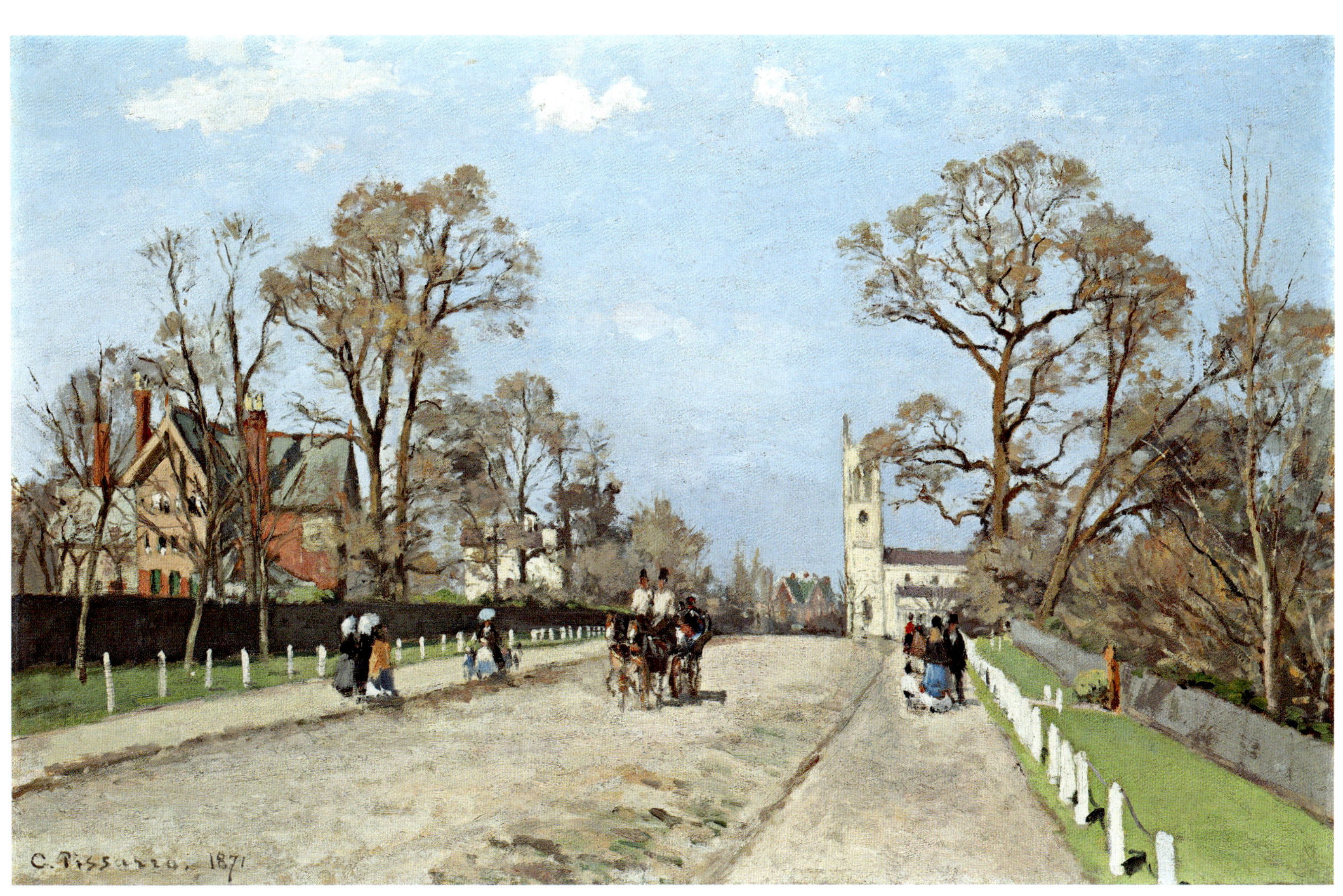
C. Pissarro. 1871

works from Pissarro's early Impressionist period for which there is a surviving watercolor sketch, which allows a glimpse into his working methods (fig. 1). A gouache drawing of the motif produced out of doors helped him to conceive the final work, although the artist continued to modify the view on the canvas. As seen in the sketch, the artist originally intended to have a darkly dressed figure on the sidewalk in the foreground. He initially followed that design on the canvas, but as he refined the composition, he painted out the large female figure in favor of a smaller grouping placed farther up the street.[5] Without a dominant figure near the picture's edge and with more groups of figures placed equally across the width of the composition at a significant distance from the viewer, Pissarro provided a more objective view of the scene.

While living in London during the war, Pissarro was introduced to Paul Durand-Ruel, a Parisian art dealer who was also in exile in the British capital. Durand-Ruel soon became the most important supporter of the Impressionist circle, buying and selling works by Pissarro, Claude Monet, and their colleagues. *The Avenue, Sydenham* was the first work that Durand-Ruel purchased from Pissarro, marking the start of a long and fruitful relationship.[6]

KR

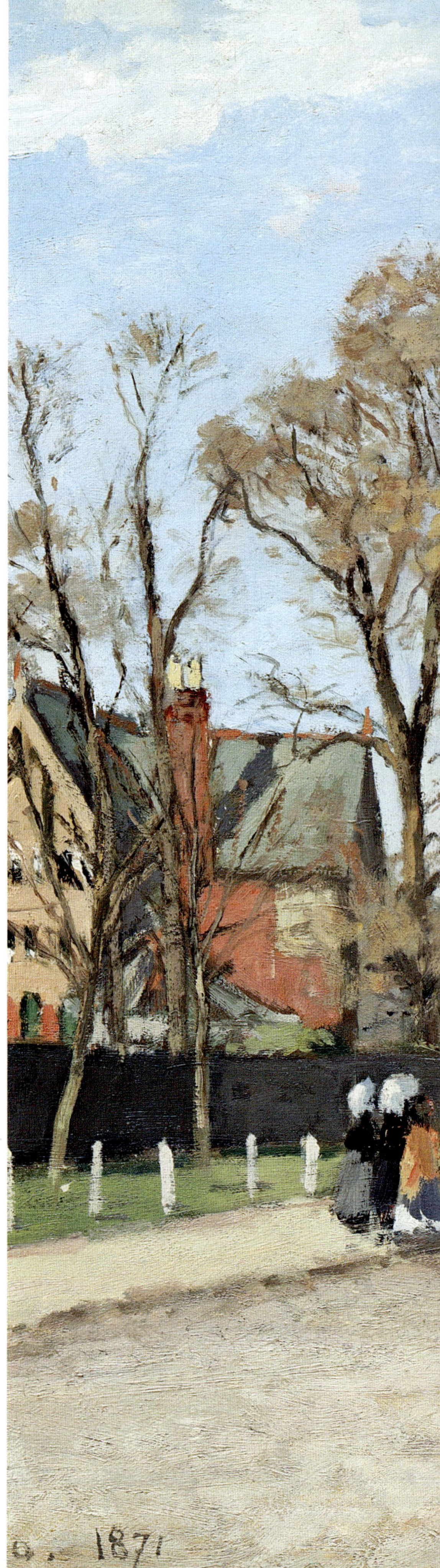

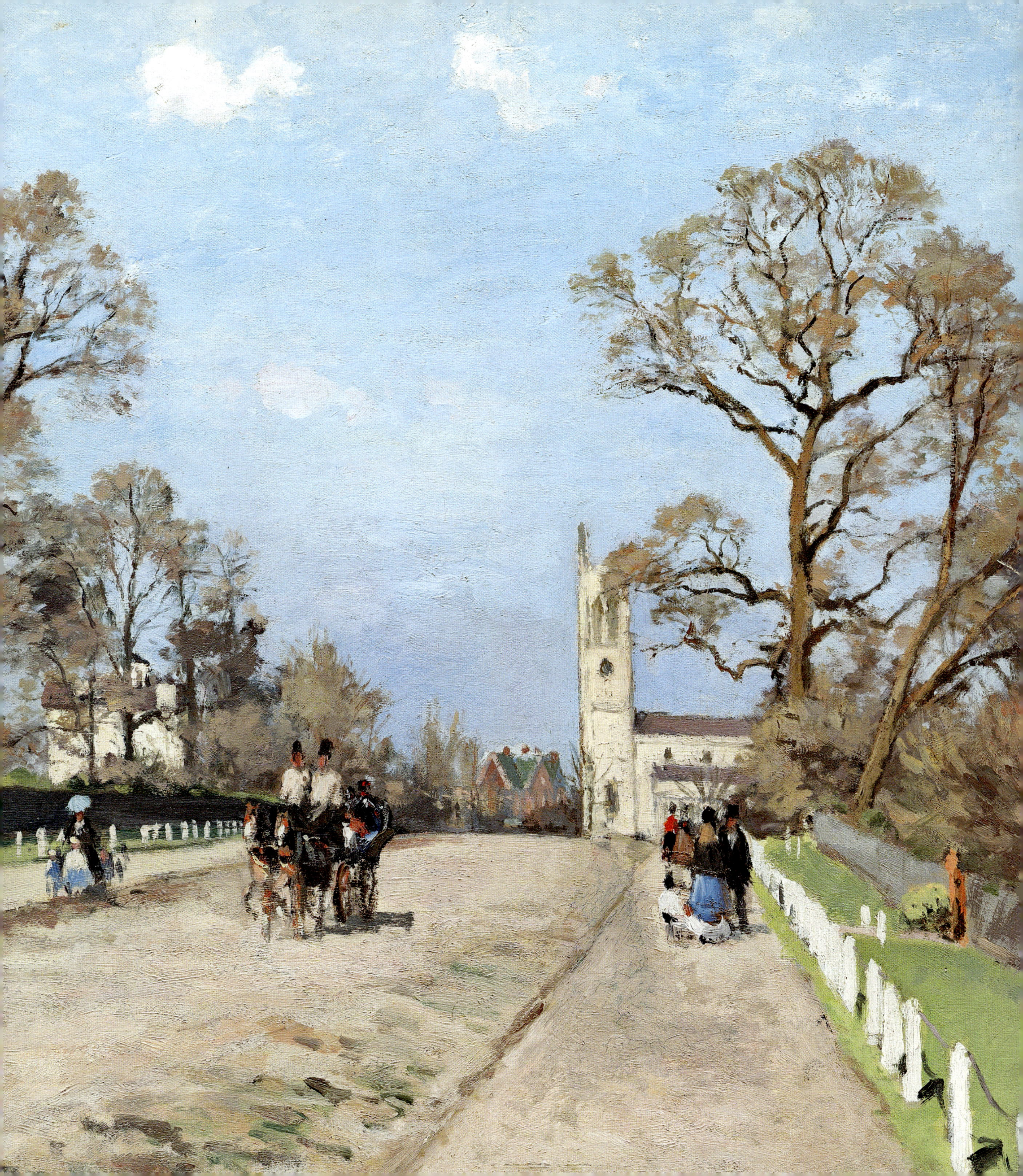

21

Lordship Lane Station, East Dulwich

Lordship Lane Station, Dulwich

1871 (PD-RS 189)

Oil on canvas
17 ½ × 28 ¾ in. (44.5 × 72.5 cm)
The Samuel Courtauld Trust, Courtauld Institute of Art Gallery, London
Baltimore only

This depiction of a train in motion can be considered one of Pissarro's most modern compositions of the early Impressionist period. His seven-month stay in the British capital inspired him to explore new motifs and styles, and his palette brightened considerably when compared with works produced earlier in Louveciennes. Although he had explored the subject of industrialization of the French suburban landscape as early as 1867, in a group of views that included factories amid foliage (cats. 8, 9), he first approached the subject of train travel during his stay in London. While living in Norwood, a suburb south of the city, Pissarro painted subjects near his home instead of venturing into the city to explore its notable landmarks. This work portrays the suburban train line that had opened in 1865 to serve those who wanted to see the Crystal Palace, an enormous exhibition hall made of iron and glass built in 1851 as part of the country's Great Exhibition. Three years later, it was moved from central London to the suburbs, and crowds were enthusiastic to see this incredible feat of engineering. The new train line was located very close to where Pissarro and his family were living and appears in two works from this period (see cat. 23).

Although he spent most of time in London painting outside the city, Pissarro did frequent the National Gallery and the Victoria and Albert Museum, often with his friend Monet. He was particularly taken with the paintings of Joseph Mallord William Turner (1775–1851). More than ten years later, he reprimanded his son Lucien for not being suitably impressed by Turner's work when Lucien was living in London: "You and Esther [Lucien's wife] have been to the National Gallery, you have seen the Turners, yet you don't mention them. Can it be that the famous painting *The Railway, The Burial of Painter Wilkie,* the astonishing *Seascape,* at the Kensington Museum, the *View of Saint Mark in Venice,* the little sketches

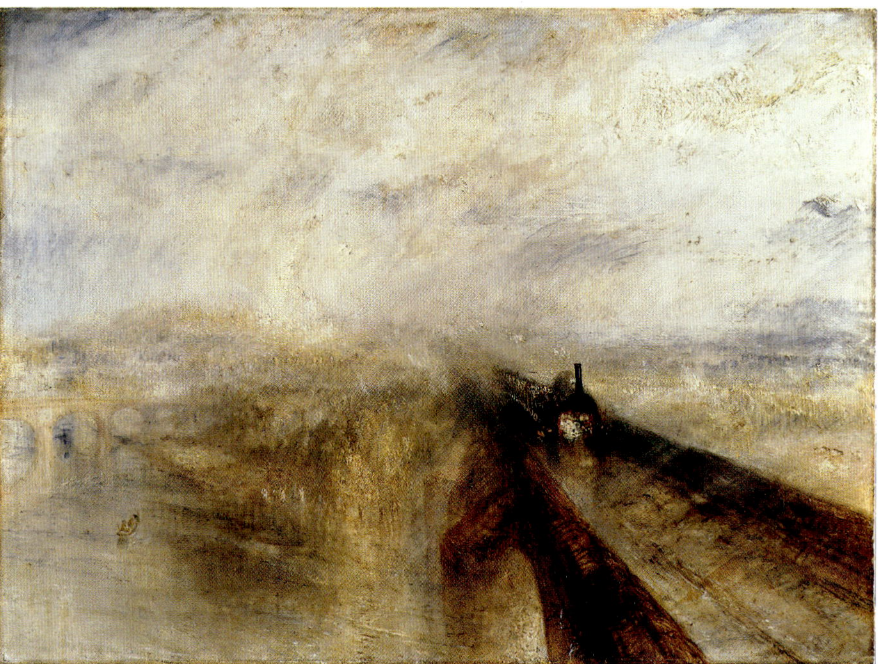

Fig. 1

Fig. 1. Joseph Mallord William Turner, *Rain, Steam, and Speed—The Great Western Railway,* before 1844. Oil on canvas. The National Gallery, London, NG538

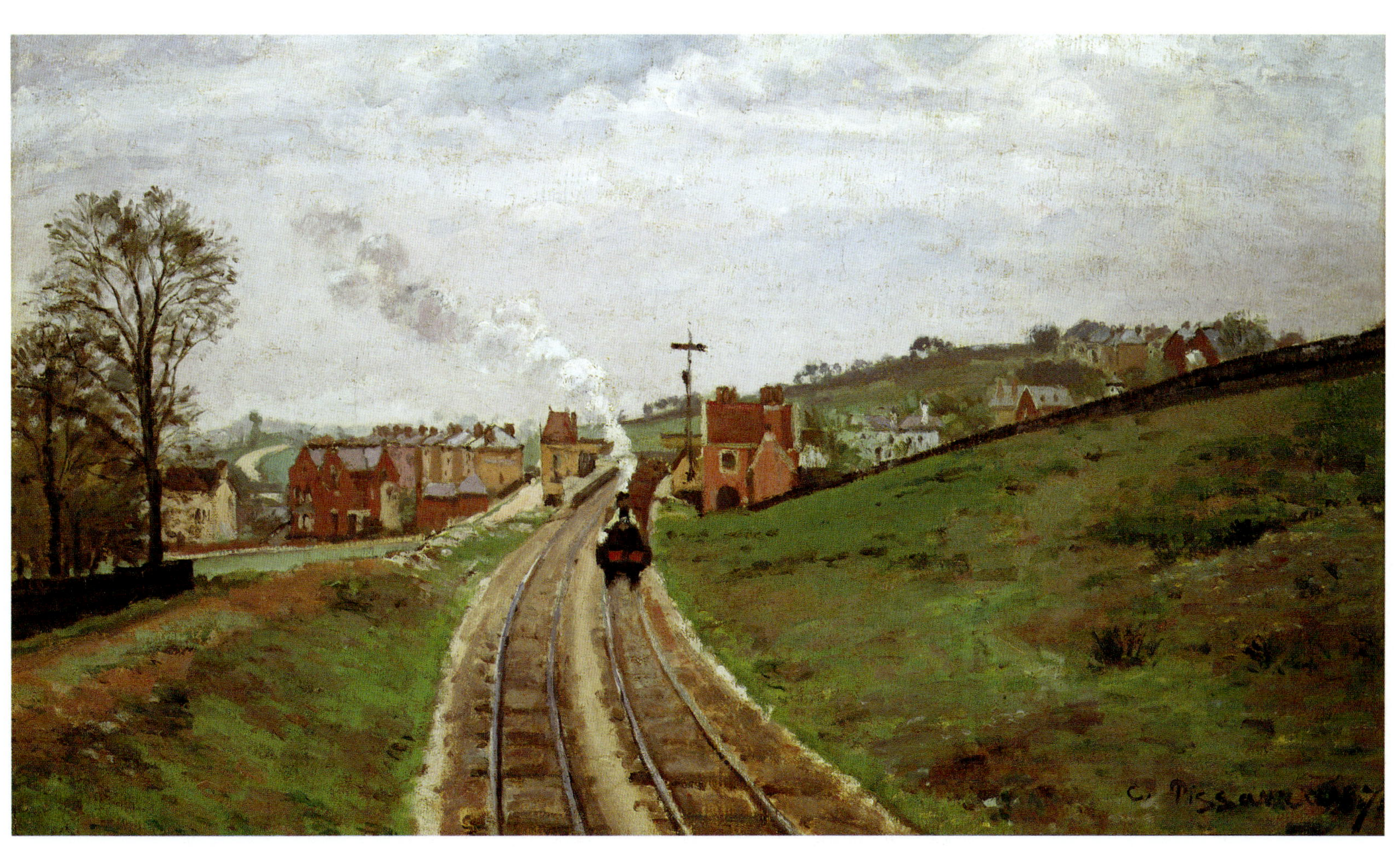

retouched with watercolors of fish and fishing equipment, etc., did not impress you?"[1]

Turner's *The Railway*, properly known as *Rain, Steam, and Speed—The Great Western Railway* (fig. 1), is one of the works that Pissarro remembered from his trip of the previous decade. It may have influenced his decision to update a vision of a train racing through the landscape. Unlike Turner's version, which focuses on the light and atmosphere surrounding a powerful train as it speeds over a bridge, Pissarro's approach addresses issues of modern life. The train, with its red head-lights placed in almost the exact center of the composition, is moving steadily out of the station and toward the viewer, who is seemingly standing on the tracks. The smoke from the train easily merges with the clouds in the sky above. Newly built houses line the railway, and the neatly kept grass in the foreground is another symbol of the encroachment of industrialization on the former countryside. It is one of the rare works by Pissarro without any figures. However, on closer inspection, it is evident that the artist had originally painted a figure with a scythe on the grassy knoll to the right of the tracks, which he later covered up.[2] It is the first Impressionist painting to show a train as the principal subject; Monet was to address the motif later in the 1870s.

KR

1. Camille Pissarro to Lucien Pissarro, February 20, 1883, in *Letters to His Son Lucien*, ed. John Rewald (New York: Pantheon Books, 1943), 22.
2. See object file, Courtauld Institute of Art Gallery.

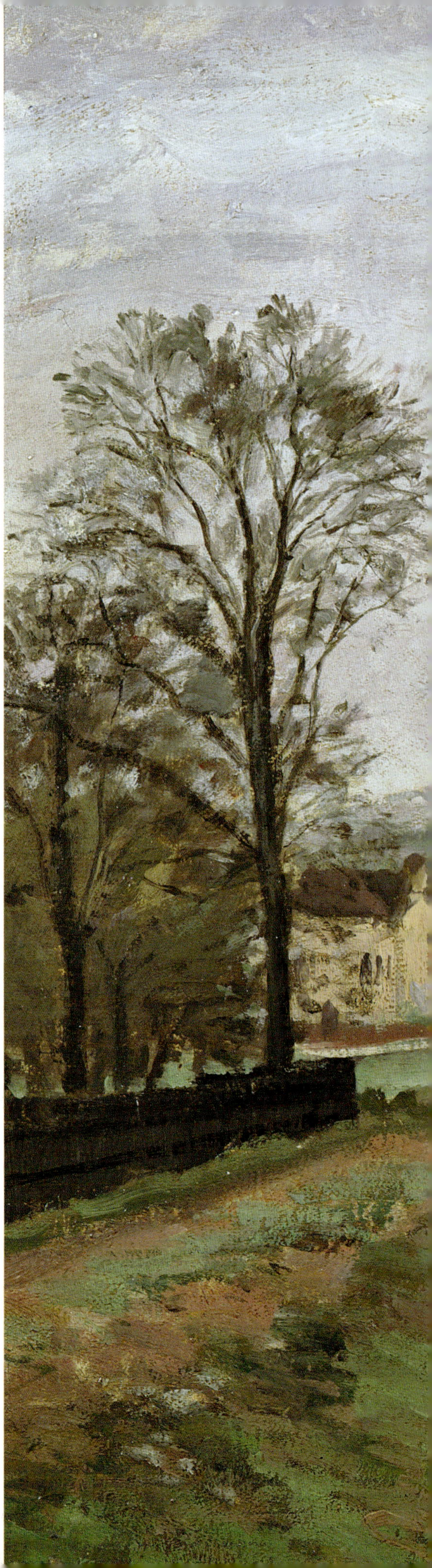

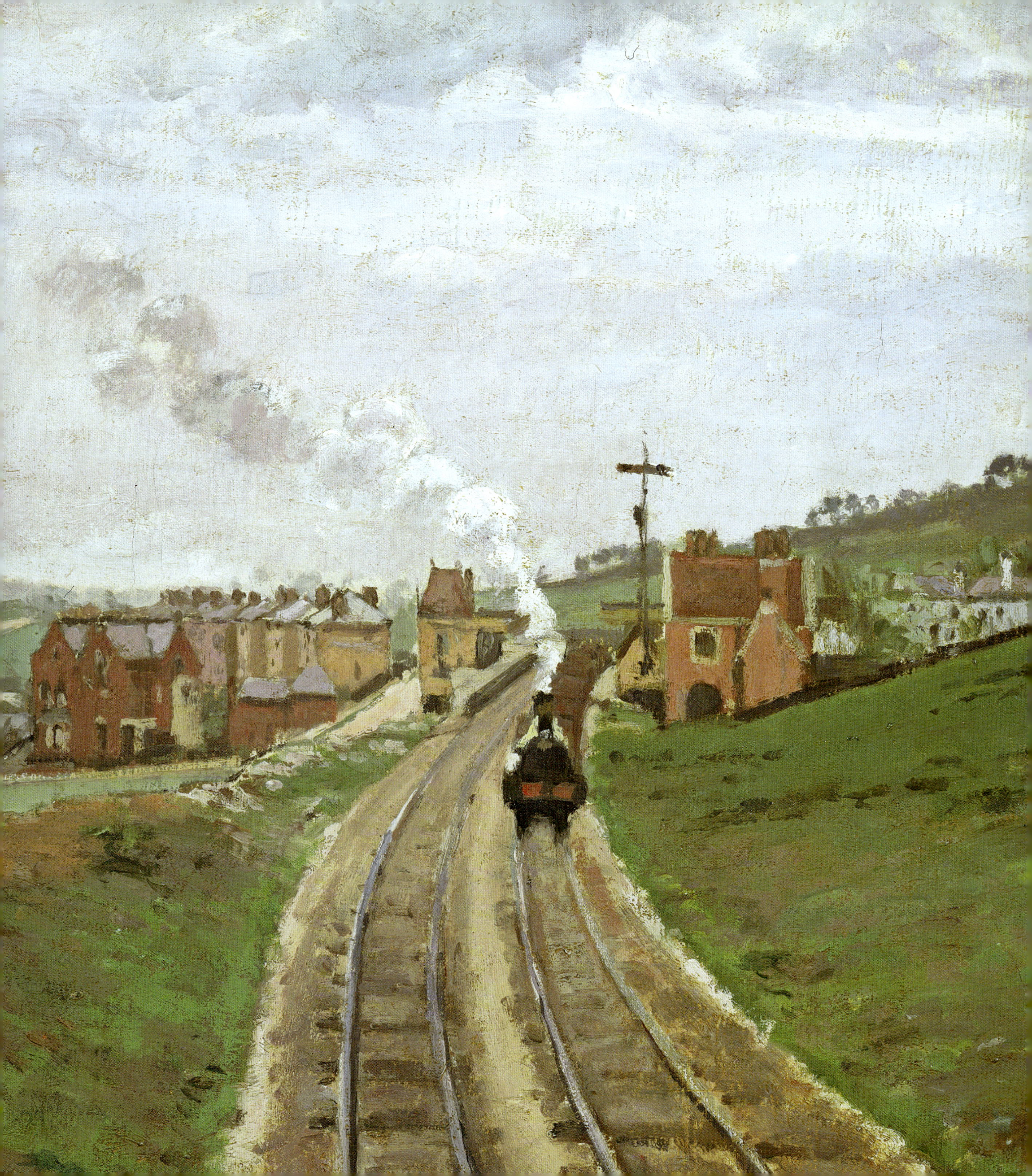

22

South Norwood, Study

Upper Norwood, London

c. 1871 (PD-RS 193)

Oil on canvas
15 ¾ × 19 ¾ in. (40 × 50 cm)
Private collection

1. Nicholas Reed, *Camille Pissarro at the Crystal Palace*, 2nd rev. ed. (London: Lilburne Press, 1995), 18.
2. Ibid.
3. *Correspondance de Camille Pissarro*, ed. Janine Bailly-Herzberg, 5 vols. (Paris: Presses Universitaires de France, 1980–91), 1:64.

Fig. 1. Claude Monet, *Hyde Park*, 1871. Oil on canvas. Museum of Art, Rhode Island School of Design, Gift of Mrs. Murray S. Danforth, 42.218

This is one of fourteen oil paintings Pissarro made during his seven-month stay in London, where he and his family (his wife, Julie Vellay, and their two children) lived during the Franco-Prussian War. They settled in the southern suburbs of the city, where they remained throughout their time in Great Britain. The suburbs were growing rapidly, and many services, including the commuter railway, were expanded to try to accommodate the rapid increase in population.

Because the suburbs were similar to the small villages and towns he preferred to paint in France, Pissarro chose motifs near his home. This view has been identified as Anerley, painted from Upper Norwood.[1] The Pissarro family moved to 2 Chatham Terrace, Palace Road, in Upper Norwood, in April 1871, and the vivid green of the foliage suggests that this work was produced in early summer, soon after their move. The building in the center of the picture has been identified as the North Surrey Industrial School, and the church at right is thought to be Holy Trinity on Croyden Road, the only local church with a spire in 1871, which was destroyed in World War II.[2] These landmarks are just a backdrop to a truly pastoral scene, complete with a group of cows grazing in the grass. It is hard to imagine that this picture was painted in the most populated city in the world, the nexus of the British empire during the middle of the industrial revolution.

Pissarro's friend Claude Monet was also living in exile in London during the war, and the two artists spent a great deal of time visiting the museums and galleries, but they did not work together. Monet painted more traditional city scenes, including views of Hyde Park (fig. 1), Green Park, and the banks of the Thames River. The hiatus abroad provided both artists with the life-changing experience of meeting Paul Durand-Ruel, a Parisian art dealer also in exile who purchased his first works by Pissarro and Monet in London and went on to be one of the most important promoters of the Impressionist movement. Nevertheless, Pissarro did not achieve financial or critical success during his stay in London. In June 1871 he was anxious to return to France, writing to his friend the critic Théodore Duret: "My painting doesn't catch on, not at all; this follows me more or less everywhere."[3]

KR

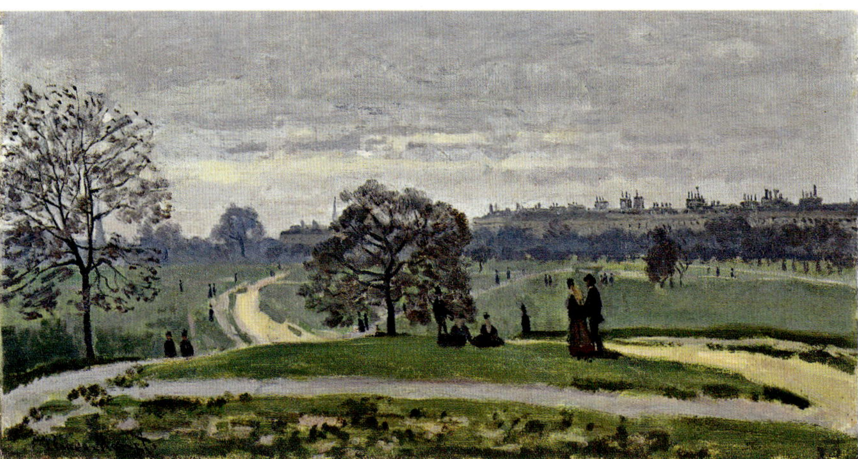

Fig. 1

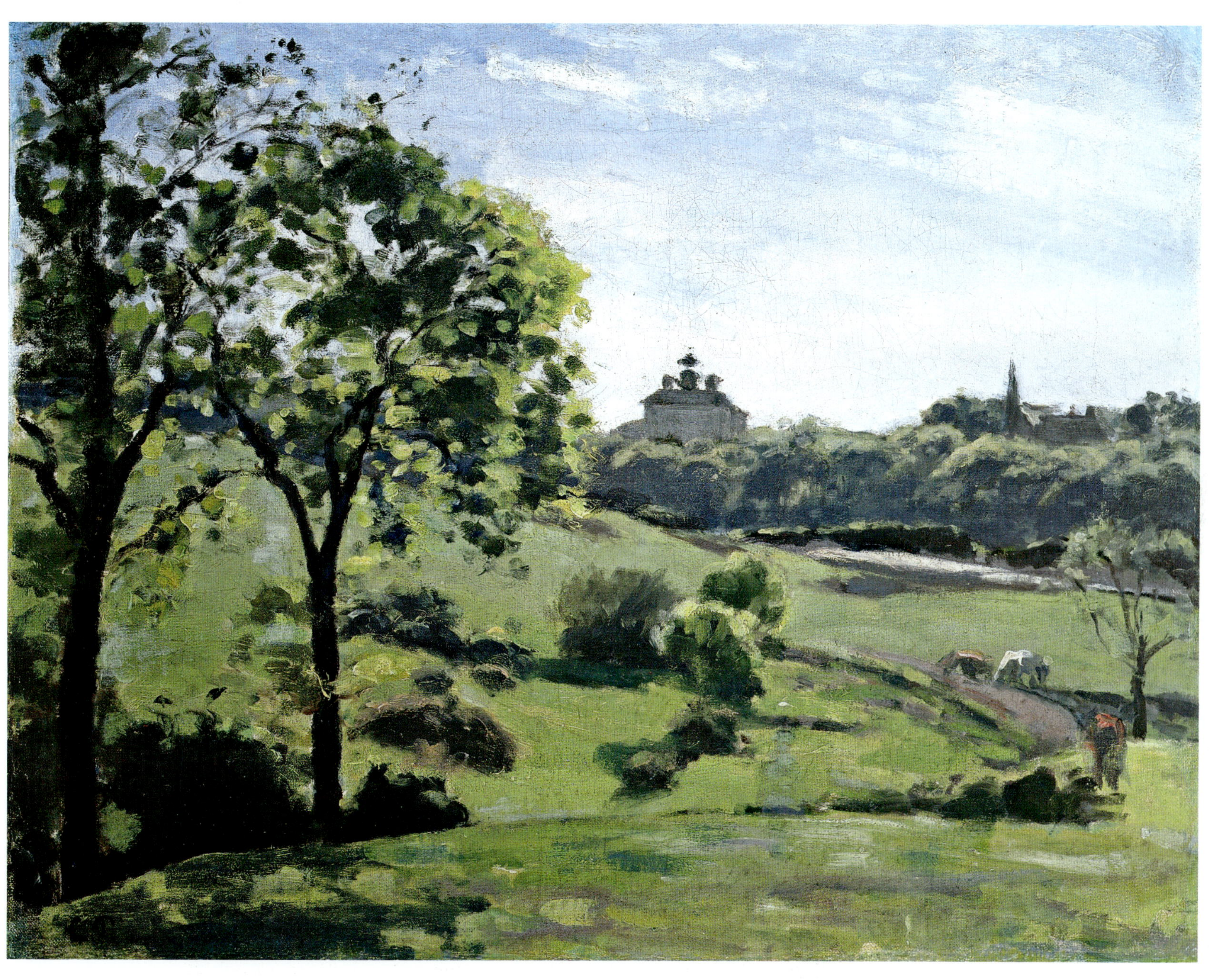

23

View of Alleyn Park, West Dulwich

Near Sydenham Hill

c. 1871 (PD-RS 190)

Oil on canvas
17 × 21 in. (43.5 × 53.5 cm)
Kimbell Art Museum, Fort Worth, Texas

With its strict vertical and horizontal axes, intertwined with baroque foliage effects and plumes of steam emitted by a train, *View of Alleyn Park, West Dulwich* exemplifies the compositional innovations and new themes that emerged in Pissarro's work in the early 1870s.[1] The inscription on the back of the canvas, "To my wife, C. Pissarro," marks this painting as a gift from the artist to his wife, Julie. The couple was married in England, days before the family returned to France, and it is assumed to have been a wedding gift.[2]

This is one of the first known works by Pissarro showing a train in motion. His interest in trains, which emerged during his stay in England, might in part have been generated by his encounter with the Romantic landscapist James Mallord William Turner's painting *Rain, Steam, and Speed—The Great Western Railway* (cat. 21, fig. 1). In the late 1860s and early 1870s, Pissarro, in collaboration with Monet, Sisley, and Renoir, started exploring light and other atmospheric effects in his work. The representation of such evanescent motifs as plumes of steam and smoke belongs to this wider interest. In his otherwise tightly structured compositions with more static motifs, Pissarro took on the challenging task of depicting the fleeting presence of steam, often coming from a moving train, as well as its interaction with wind, clouds, and other atmospheric conditions.

In *View of Alleyn Park, West Dulwich*, trees in the foreground dramatically frame the distant landscape, where a moving train is about to exit the picture space to the right, as is clearly seen in the energetic plumes of smoke it leaves in its wake. The use of *répoussoir* trees seen here, where an artist places a large figure or object in the immediate foreground of a painting to increase the illusion of depth in the rest of the picture, is a compositional device that would have been known to Pissarro from seventeenth- and eighteenth-century precedents, such as Hubert Robert's (1733–1808) *Le Jet d'eau du Bosquet des Muses à Marly*, painted about 1780 (fig. 1). This device is adapted to the values of mid-nineteenth-century French naturalist landscape painting in *View of Alleyn Park, West Dulwich*, which focuses on the everyday in its choice of motifs. Where lush foliage frames Robert's scene of genteel leisure, Pissarro's picture shows barren trees dramatically meeting at the top, raising the curtain and setting the stage for nothing but an undistinguished landscape: a crude wooden fence and beyond it a meadow, the train track on which a train at full speed is disappearing from sight, a single figure watching its passage, and severely schematized houses in the distance, ending with the faint horizon line at the top of the band of hills.[3] The integration of the train, the quintessential sign of modernization, into a traditional compositional formula marks this painting as a bold and original blend of the new and the old.

GÇ

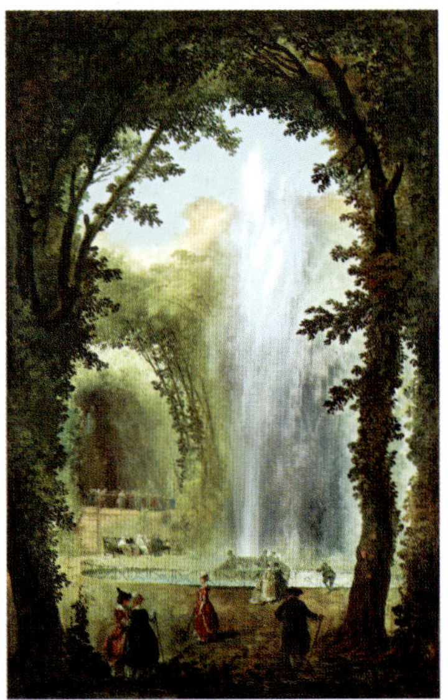

Fig. 1

1. Train motifs were of great interest to Pissarro at this time. For other examples, see cats. 21 and 39. A later example is *The Train at Bedford Park*, 1897 (PD-RS 1181), oil on canvas, private collection.
2. For more information on the inscriptions on the back of the canvas, see PD-RS 190.
3. Apart from these seeming disparities between Robert's and Pissarro's compositions, the latter remains true to the essence of the earlier model: the trees not only envelop the scene in the background, but their shapes echo the landscape. Furthermore, the central motif, which is one in motion, is frozen in time and suspended in air: in Robert's painting, a jet of water spouting from the fountain, in Pissarro's example, clouds of steam released by the locomotive.

Fig. 1. Hubert Robert, *Le Jet d'eau du Bosquet des Muses à Marly*, c. 1780. Oil on canvas. Private collection, France

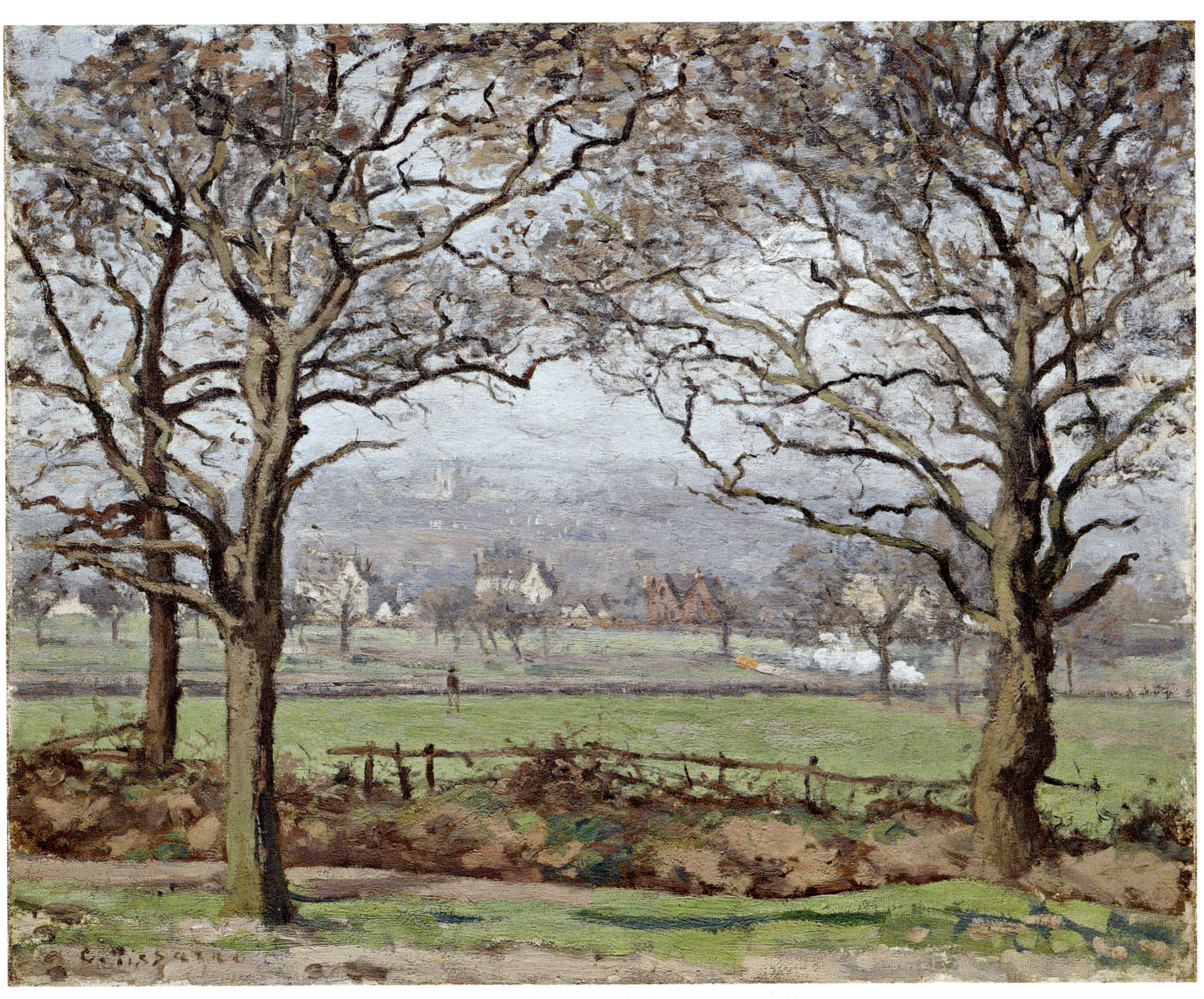

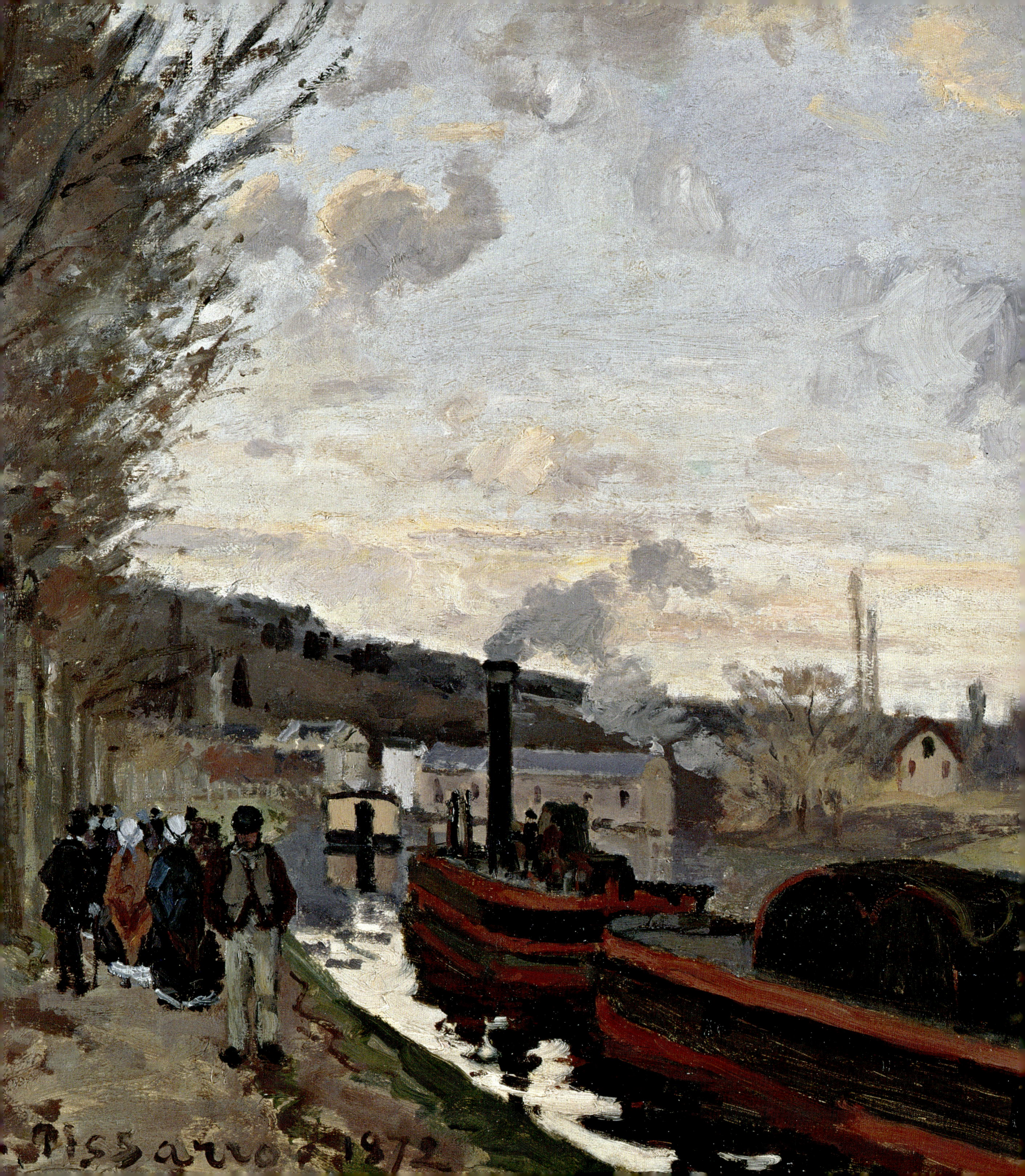
Pissarro. 1872

Return to Louveciennes 1871–1872

24
The Farm in the Grounds of the Château of Marly
Farm on the Edge of the Forest
1871 (PD-RS 205)

Oil on canvas
18 1/8 × 21 7/8 in. (46.5 × 55.8 cm)
Noortman Master Paintings

1. See PD-RS 205 for further information on the site depicted in this painting.
2. *Correspondance de Camille Pissarro*, ed. Janine Bailly-Herzberg, 5 vols. (Paris: Presses Universitaires de France, 1980–91), 1:72.

Produced in Louveciennes soon after Pissarro's return from London, this painting is a view of a farm in early autumn.[1] The leaves have just started to change color, and the smoke from the chimney of the house on the left signifies the apparent need for warmth in a cool interior. A footpath on the left side of the picture, bordered by a split-rail fence, provides a perspectival device that leads the viewer's eye toward the group of farm buildings. A female figure walks on the path toward the buildings, while another figure works in the field at the right, a group of chickens behind her. Another fence runs along the right side of the work; the two fences form a triangular shape that funnels toward the cluster of buildings. Comfortably nestled beneath a canopy of trees, these man-made elements seem to merge into one large structure that is well integrated into the surroundings.

The artist's use of shadow in this painting deserves comment. The entire foreground is in a shadow of dark green, brown, and tan cast by a group of trees that lies outside the picture. Contemporary writers criticized Pissarro's compositions of the 1870s that included this kind of shadow. The large figure on the path, just about to leave the shadow for the bright area of the canvas, contributes an element of anticipation as she is about to break the threshold into the light. This sense of immediacy and interest in the changing effects of light and shadow are notable elements in Pissarro's work of the early 1870s.

The Paris merchant Albert Hecht (1829–1889), the first owner of this painting, was an enthusiastic supporter of the Impressionists and a close friend of Edgar Degas. He purchased it from Louis Latouche (1829–1884), who owned an art supply store on rue Lafayette in Paris and was himself a painter and friend of many artists. Latouche exhibited his own work in the first Impressionist exhibition in 1874. This painting is in all likelihood *La Ferme du parc* that Pissarro had written about to his wife in a letter of January 1872: "Latouche has bought my painting of the farm in the park."[2]
KR

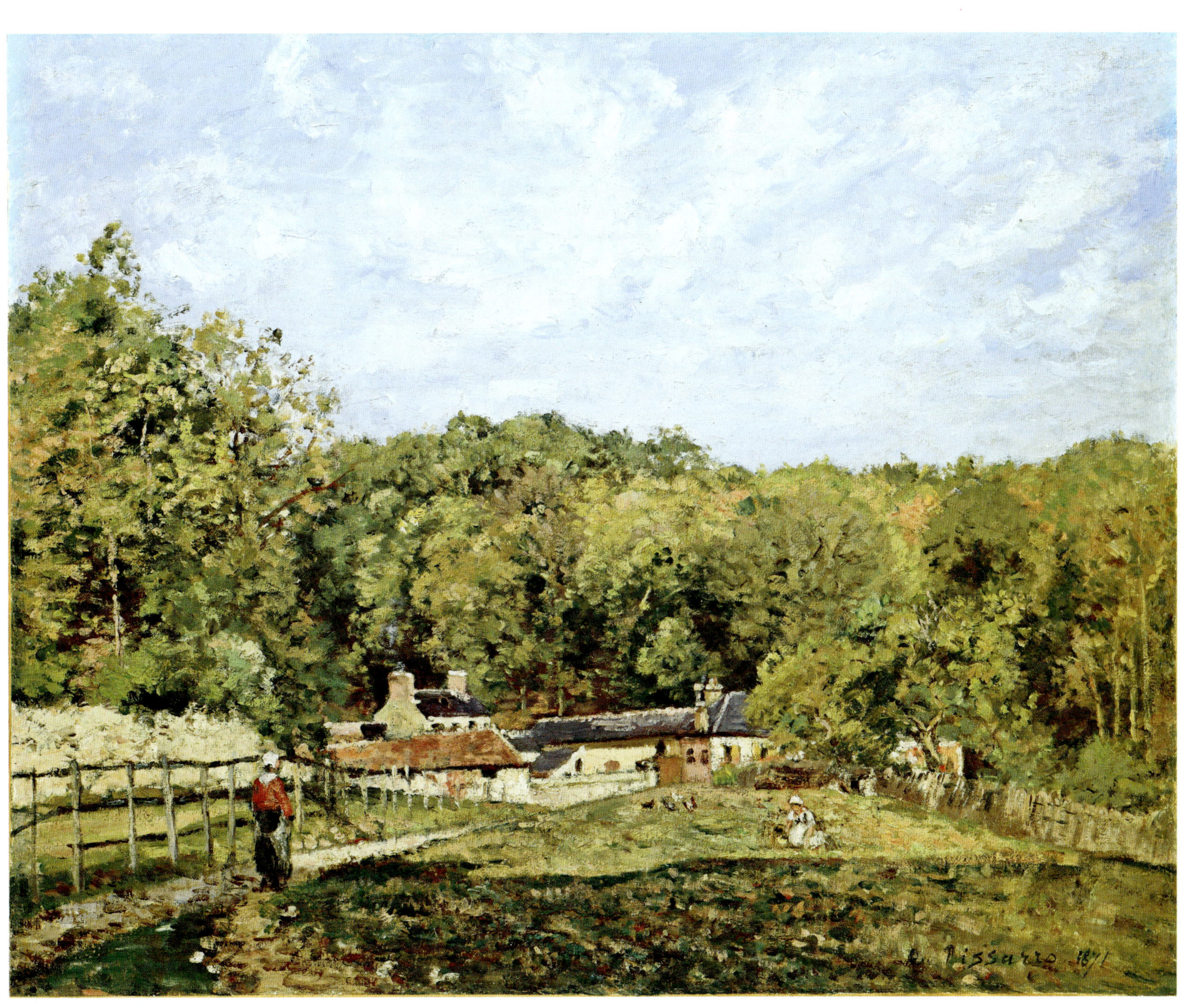
C. Pissarro. 1871

25

Rue de Voisins

Village Street, Louveciennes

1871 (PD-RS 208)

Oil on canvas
18 ⅛ × 21 ⅞ in. (46 × 55.5 cm)
Manchester City Galleries, 1969.67
Milwaukee and Memphis only

1. Christopher Lloyd et al., *Retrospective Camille Pissarro* (Tokyo: Art Life Limited, 1984), 129.

Fig. 1. Alfred Sisley, *Early Snow at Louveciennes*, c. 1870–71. Oil on canvas. Museum of Fine Arts, Boston, Bequest of John T. Spaulding, 48.600

This roadway, the rue de Voisins, was a favorite motif of the Impressionist painters, including Pierre-Auguste Renoir and Alfred Sisley.[1] Sisley's *Early Snow at Louveciennes*, of about 1870–71 (fig. 1), depicts the same subject from a vantage point farther from the houses. This gave Sisley a broader view of the slow curve of the thoroughfare, which relegated the group of buildings to the middle ground. Thus, he could pay concentrated attention to the expanse of the roadway and the snow on the rooftops and the side of the road. Pissarro, moving closer to the houses, focused on the details of their construction, from the materials of which they were made to the color of their shutters and the different styles of chimneys that punctuated their rooftops. Pissarro's composition is more geometric in structure and more tightly compressed than Sisley's example. The street quickly plunges into the distance, pulling the viewer's eye down the hill. His painting style is very typical of the early Impressionist period, with broken strokes and a colorful palette, as is Sisley's. These two pictures clearly demonstrate the similar brushwork that Pissarro and his colleagues used during this period.

Pissarro's portrayal of light and shadow is particularly dramatic in this work. On the left side, a stone wall stands beside a large tree, with its branches and leaves hanging over the architectural structure. The sunny day creates abstract shadows on the wall. On the opposite side of the street, the sun has yet to warm up the blank side of a stone house, which is carefully constructed of strokes of pigment that approximate the texture of the hard material itself. It seems as though the artist has laid down these patches of paint in the same manner that mortar was used to cement the actual stones together. Several figures walk along the street, dressed in the simple attire of local villagers. The sunlight carefully illuminates details of their garments, from their white head coverings to their full skirts.

This painting did not appear in the 1939 catalogue raisonné of the artist's work. It was purchased from the artist by the dealer Paul Durand-Ruel, who subsequently sold it to a British collector, Samuel Barlow, making it one of the first works by Pissarro to enter a British collection.

KR

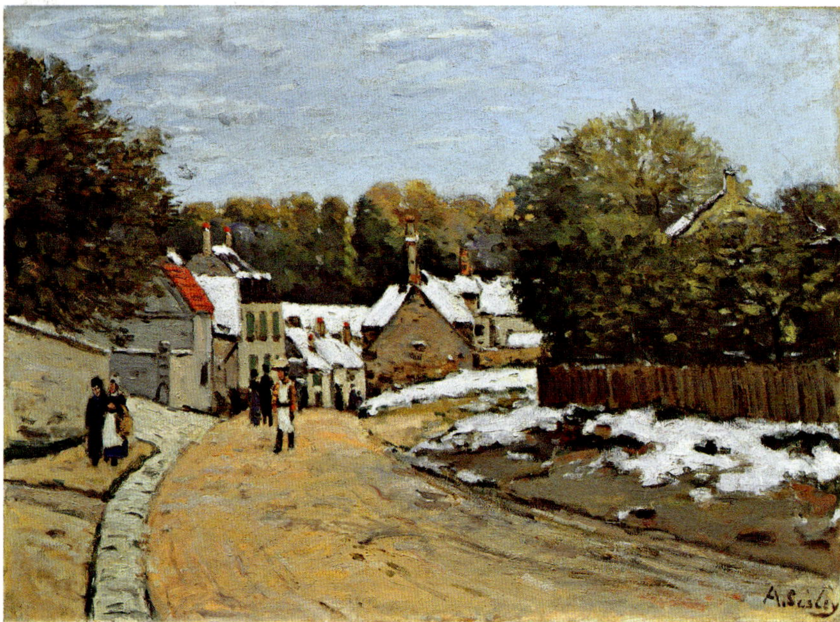

Fig. 1

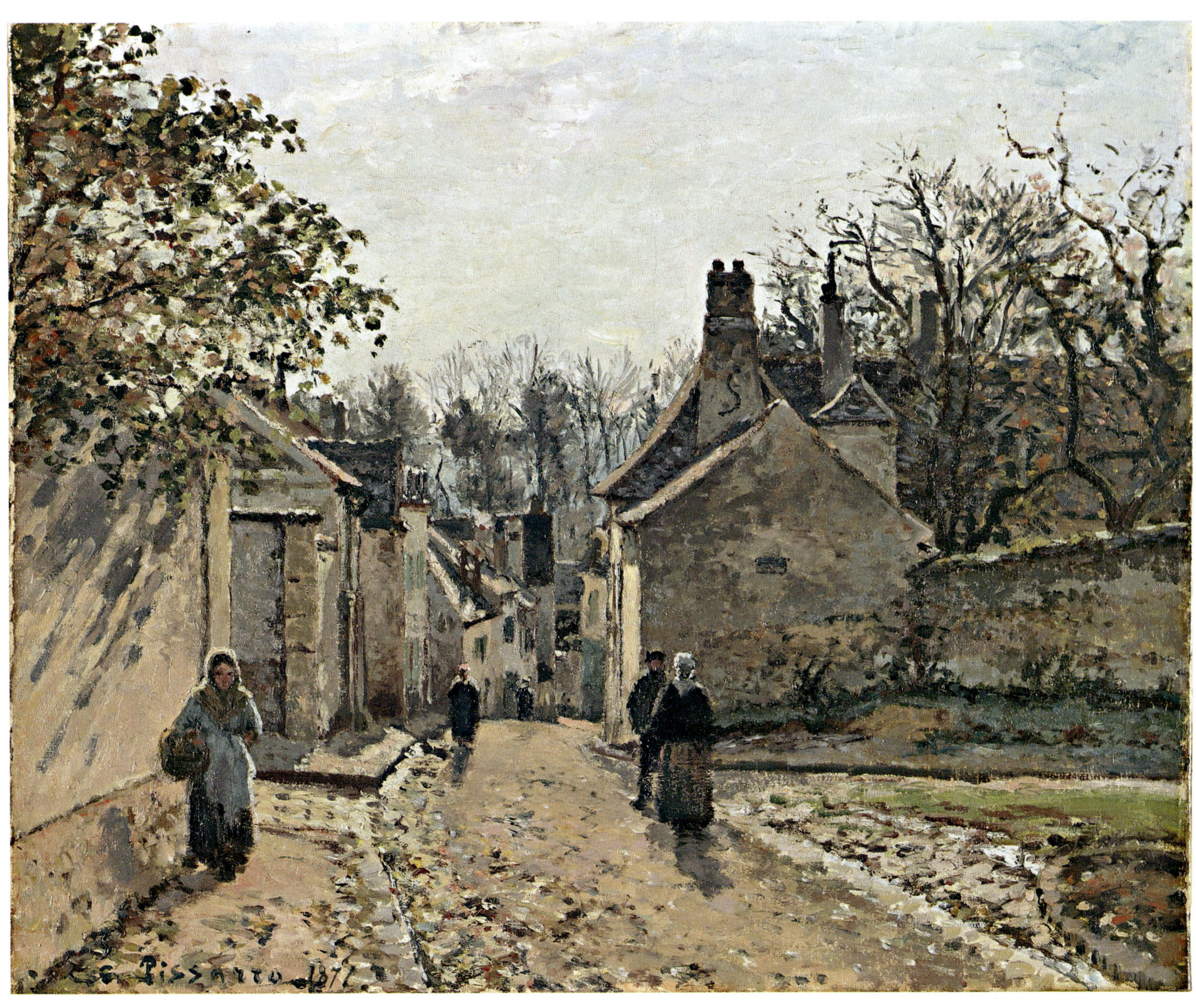

26

Banks of the Seine at Bougival

The Seine at Port-Marly

1872 (PD-RS 234)

Oil on canvas
18 1/8 × 22 in. (46 × 54 cm)
Staatsgalerie Stuttgart, Germany

Riverside subjects appealed to Pissarro throughout his early years, because they provided a wealth of motifs and compositional challenges. When he returned to Louveciennes in 1871 after the war, Pissarro traveled to nearby Bougival to explore the landscape. In this bold and colorful view, Pissarro highlights the commercial side of the river by showing steamboats along the promenade. One boat enters the composition at a bold diagonal from the lower right corner. A worker is on board, surrounded by tools and a large chimney that emits steam. A second boat is stopped in front of it, also spewing smoke freely into the air. The artist has set up his easel on the towpath at the river's edge, which is crowded with figures. Given the rosy glow of the sky, it may be late afternoon, when people are leaving their jobs and returning home. In the background can be seen the Machine de Marly, the pumping station that Sisley also depicted in several paintings.[1] Renovated to use steam power by Napoleon III in the late 1850s,[2] the station, able to pump more than twelve thousand cubic meters of water a day, was considered a technical marvel of its time.[3] In this composition, however, Pissarro highlights the activity on the river's edge rather than the modern pumping station.

The workers on the boats are juxtaposed with the middle-class figures on land, a subject that was of interest to the politically minded artist who claimed a personal preference for the life of an honest laborer. Bougival was a popular weekend destination for Parisians who could take a quick train ride from the city and in a very short time enjoy riverside activities. This was one of the many advances that train travel, and the industrialization of France, offered to the bourgeoisie in the last half of the nineteenth century.

Pissarro used a wide variety of brushwork to make this painting, ranging from the calligraphic, dry strokes in the trees at left to the broad layers of red pigment applied as ornamentation on the steamboats. The most experimental painting occurs in the water itself. Rather than exploring the many reflective possibilities that water can provide, the artist used thick, opaque strokes of light and dark paint in the small space between the water's edge and the boats closest to the shore, which deny any type of reflection. This bold, expressive application of paint can be considered the opposite of the delicate atmospheric explorations for which his colleagues Monet and Sisley were well regarded in their many depictions of water.[4]
KR

1. For more on the Machine de Marly, see Christopher Lloyd's essay in this catalogue.
2. MaryAnne Stevens, ed., *Alfred Sisley* (London: Royal Academy of Arts, 1992), no. 20, 122.
3. Richard Thomson, *Camille Pissarro: Impressionism, Landscape, and Rural Labour* (Birmingham, Eng.: South Bank Centre, 1990), 26.
4. In the new catalogue raisonné of Pissarro's work, this painting is described as unfinished, which may explain the loose brushwork in the treatment of the water. See PD-RS 234 for more information.

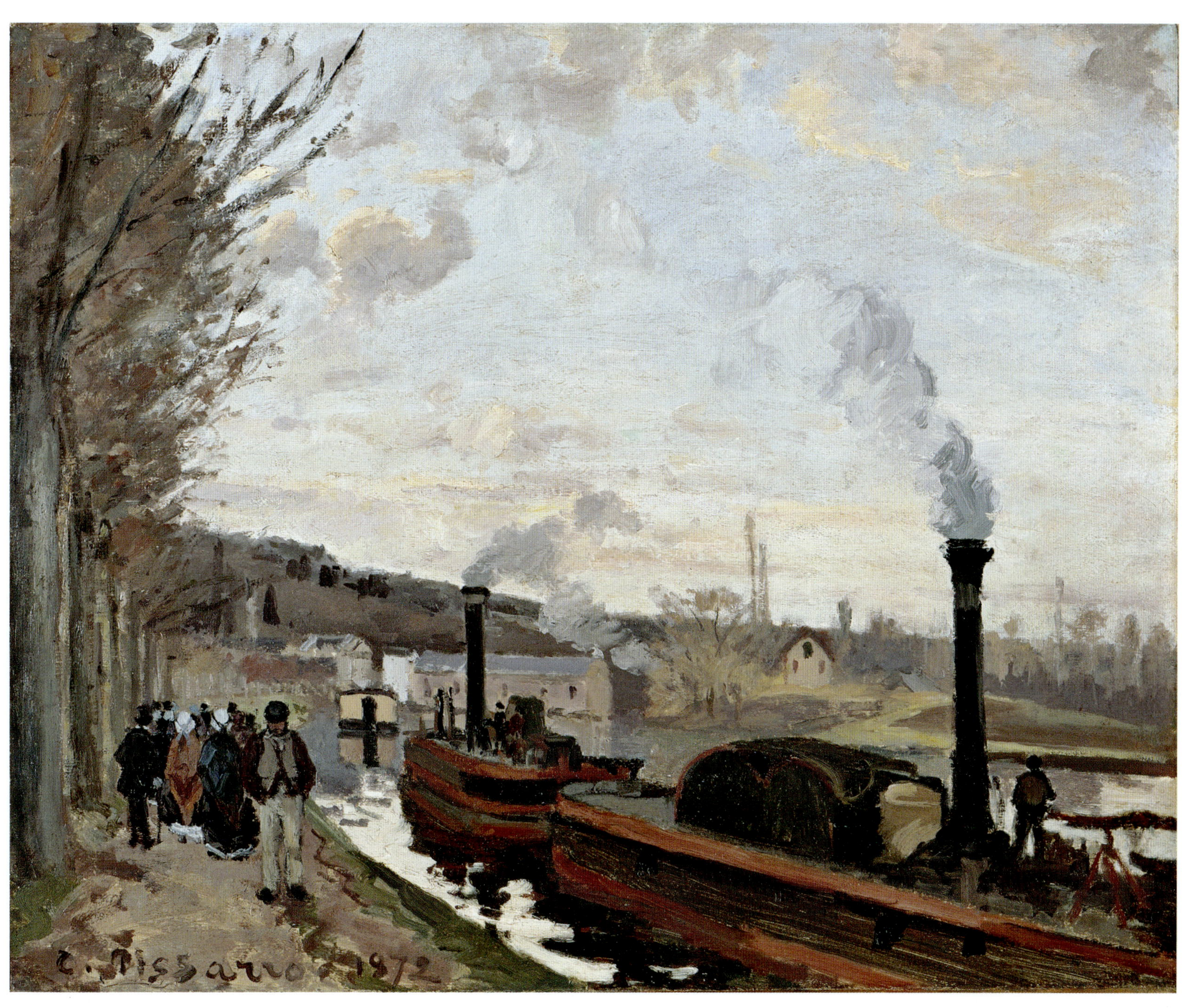
C. Pissarro. 1872

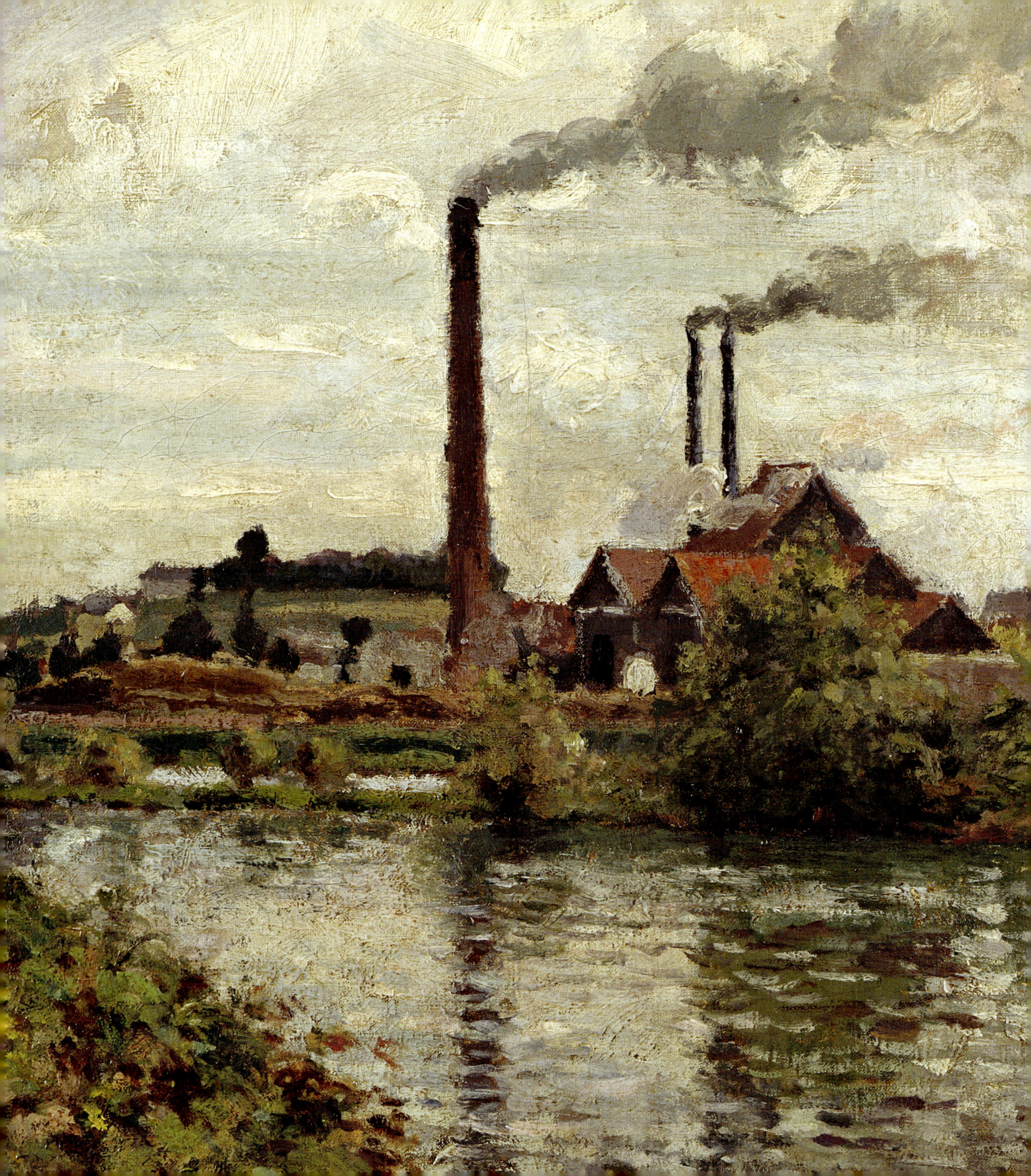

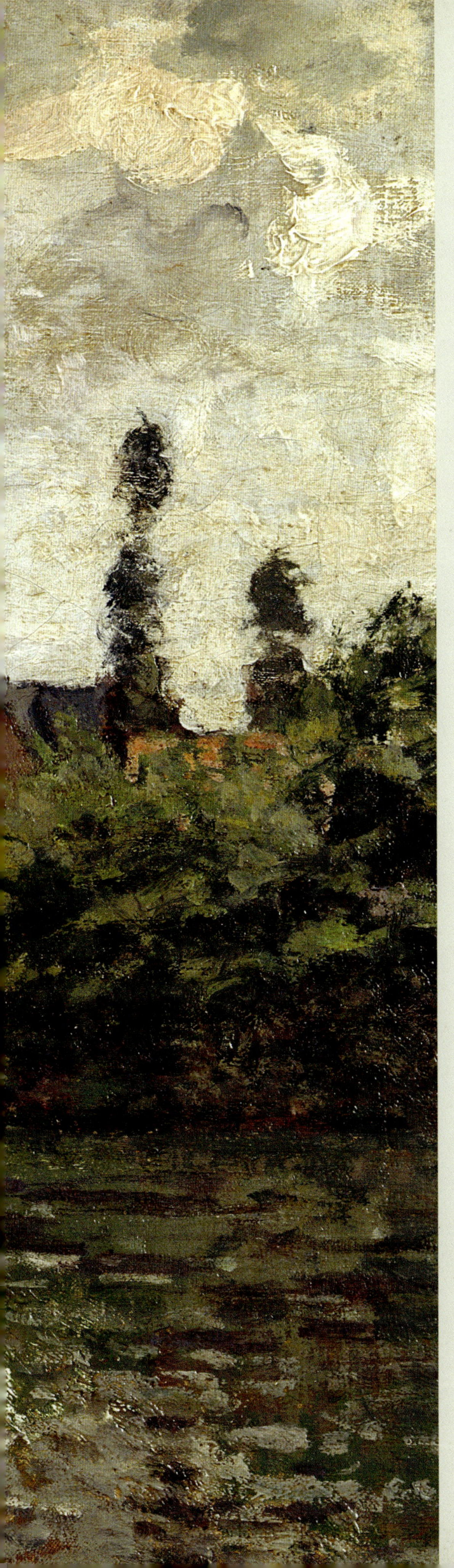

Return to Pontoise and the First Impressionist Exhibition 1872–1874

27

Orchard in Bloom

Orchard in Bloom, Louveciennes

1872 (PD-RS 248)

Oil on canvas
17 ¾ × 21 ⅝ in. (45.1 × 54.9 cm)
National Gallery of Art, Washington, D.C., Ailsa Mellon Bruce Collection, 1970.17.51

Orchard in Bloom was one of five entries Pissarro submitted to the first Impressionist exhibition in 1874. It represents a peaceful spring scene, with two peasants working in the fields. Light flickers delicately across the stack of wood and the bark of the blossoming tree. Feathery leaves and flowers on the tree, created by multiple layers of brushstrokes, convey an impression of substance and verdure, belying the temporality of spring blooms. The healthy tree, the most solid and durable element in this landscape, poses a stark contrast to the still bare branches of other trees as well as to the rough, dry soil. Delicate white dabs of paint scattered in the background echo the white flowers on the blooming tree, imbuing the scene with the promise of spring.

Pissarro shows that the two peasants, wholly engrossed in their work, are in harmony with nature, by rhyming the outlines of their bodies with the surrounding landscape elements. The tree branch immediately above the man on the right duplicates his arching back, a natural surrogate for his body. The left branch of the blooming tree and the tree at right both follow the outlines of the female figure's bent pose.

These central figures clearly recall the peasants depicted by one of the masters of the Barbizon school of landscape painting, Jean-François Millet (1814–1875). The female figure, who seems to be gathering firewood to add to the stack visible behind her, evokes Millet's *Gleaners* (1857), while the man is an amalgam of the older artist's 1866–68 *Willower* and 1850 *Sower*. Pissarro is known to have started his series of large-scale peasant scenes in the 1880s with Millet in mind. In a later letter written to his son Lucien, he noted the necessity to rework the earlier artist's themes in an unsentimental way.[1] In *Orchard in Bloom*, the desire to emulate Millet is apparent. Nevertheless, at this stage this painting is more of an homage to Millet than a challenging reinterpretation, a project that occupied the artist in the 1880s. This may partly explain why the artist chose to include this work in the first Impressionist exhibition.
GÇ

1. Camille Pissarro to Lucien Pissarro, May 16, 1887, in *Letters to His Son Lucien*, ed. John Rewald (New York: Pantheon Books, 1943), 111.

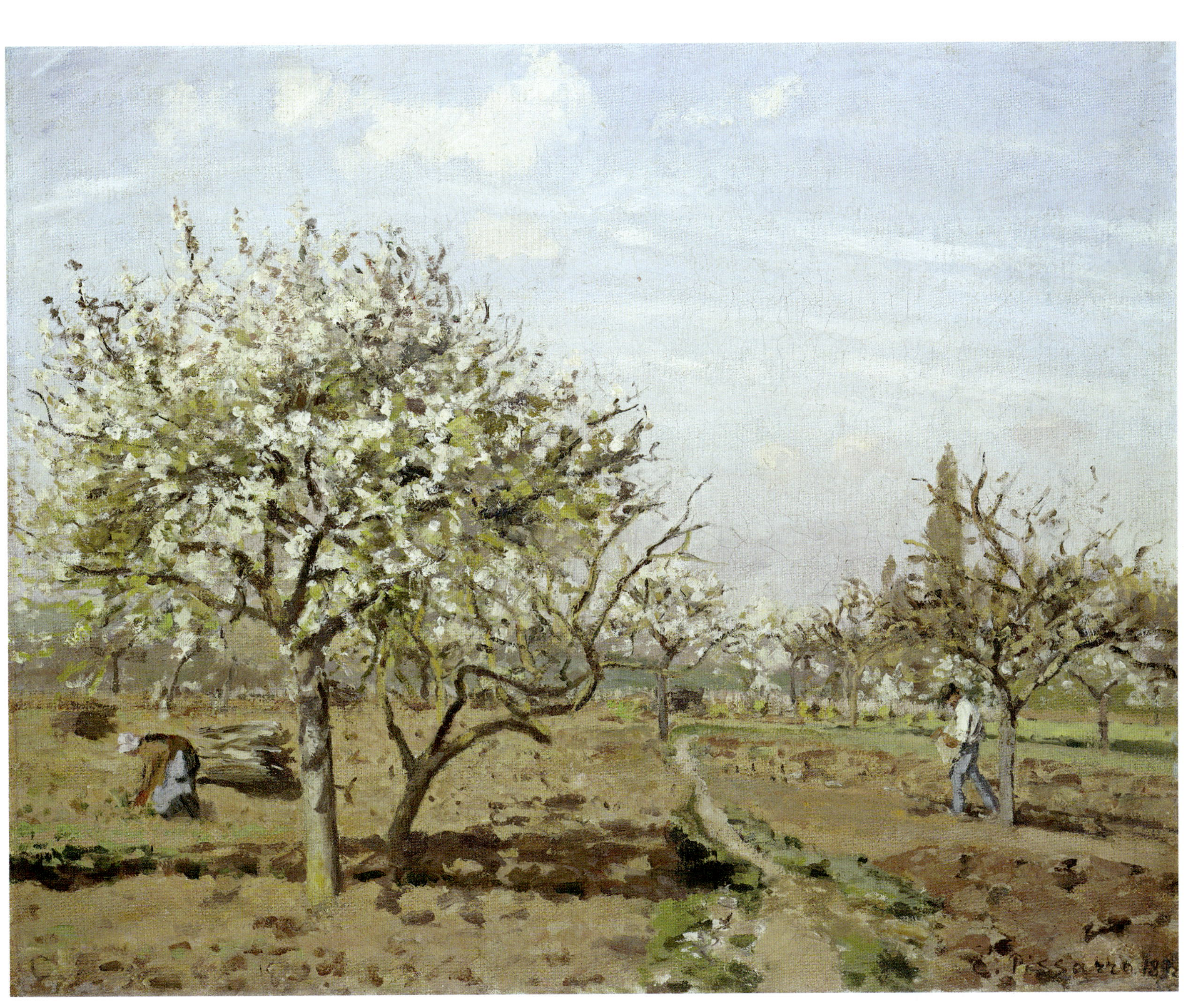
C. Pissarro

28
Rue de Gisors, Pontoise, Winter Effect
The Road: Winter Effect
1872 (PD-RS 279)

Oil on canvas
10 ½ × 16 in. (26.7 × 40.6 cm)
Private collection
Baltimore and Milwaukee only

Throughout his career as a landscape painter, Camille Pissarro produced just over one hundred canvases in which snow or a variant of snow, such as frost or ice, plays a major role. He began this long series of works during the winter of 1869, and he continued to address the many complex issues of representing snow on canvas with oil paint for more than thirty years. These winterscapes have in common Pissarro's enduring love of nature, his fascination with light and shadow, and his interest in humanity; in virtually every painting, he includes a reference to humankind—a house, a fence, or a small figure. These works also allowed him to explore many different, even unusual, effects of color and light. As he wrote to his friend Théodore Duret in 1873: "There is nothing more cold than the sun at its height in the summer, contrary to what the colorists believe. Nature is colored in winter and cold in the summer."[1]

Pissarro produced a record number of eleven snowscapes during the winter of 1871–72 while he was living in Louveciennes.[2] Often featuring the route de Versailles and other roads leading in and out of town, these works allowed Pissarro to experiment with different types of perspective, varying the angle of the road to the picture plane in several examples.[3] Similar in composition, this painting depicts not Louveciennes but Pontoise. The site can be determined by the church of Saint-Maclou, whose recognizable profile can be seen in the distance (fig. 1). It is a clear, crisp winter day, with snow still clinging to the ground. Two figures in the middle ground at the right are conversing, a relatively rare occurrence in Pissarro's rural scenes, as the artist typically isolated his figures as they go about their daily chores. A large group of birds has taken flight on the left, another relatively unusual aspect of this energetic composition, as Pissarro normally omitted birds from his landscapes. In the foreground at the right, thin trees line the sidewalk, their shadows reaching across the width of the roadway. Produced with loose brushstrokes of blues, lavenders, and tans, these shadows are a remarkable example of Pissarro's virtuosity as a painter of light and shadow. In fact, he was chastised two years later during the first Impressionist exhibition by the critic Jules-Antoine Castagnary for his seemingly arbitrary use of shadows in his *Hoarfrost at Ennery* (cat. 43), aspects of his style that are today considered hallmarks of his genius.
KR

1. Camille Pissarro to Théodore Duret, May 2, 1873, *Correspondance de Camille Pissarro*, ed. Janine Bailly-Herzberg, 5 vols. (Paris: Presses Universitaires de France, 1980–91), 1:80.
2. PD-RS 212–221 and 238.
3. See PD-RS 214–216 and 221.

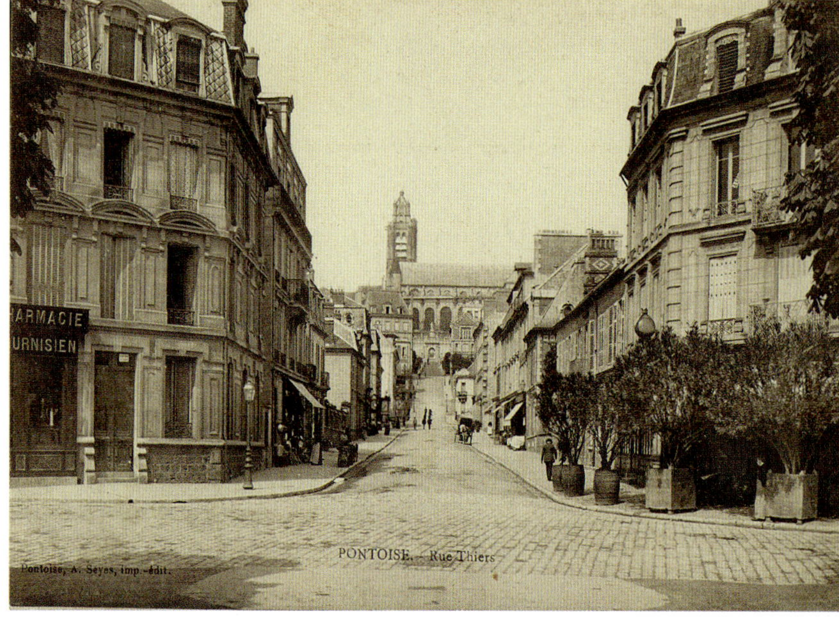

Fig. 1

Fig. 1. *Pontoise—Rue Thiers*. Vintage postcard. Collection of Terence Maloon

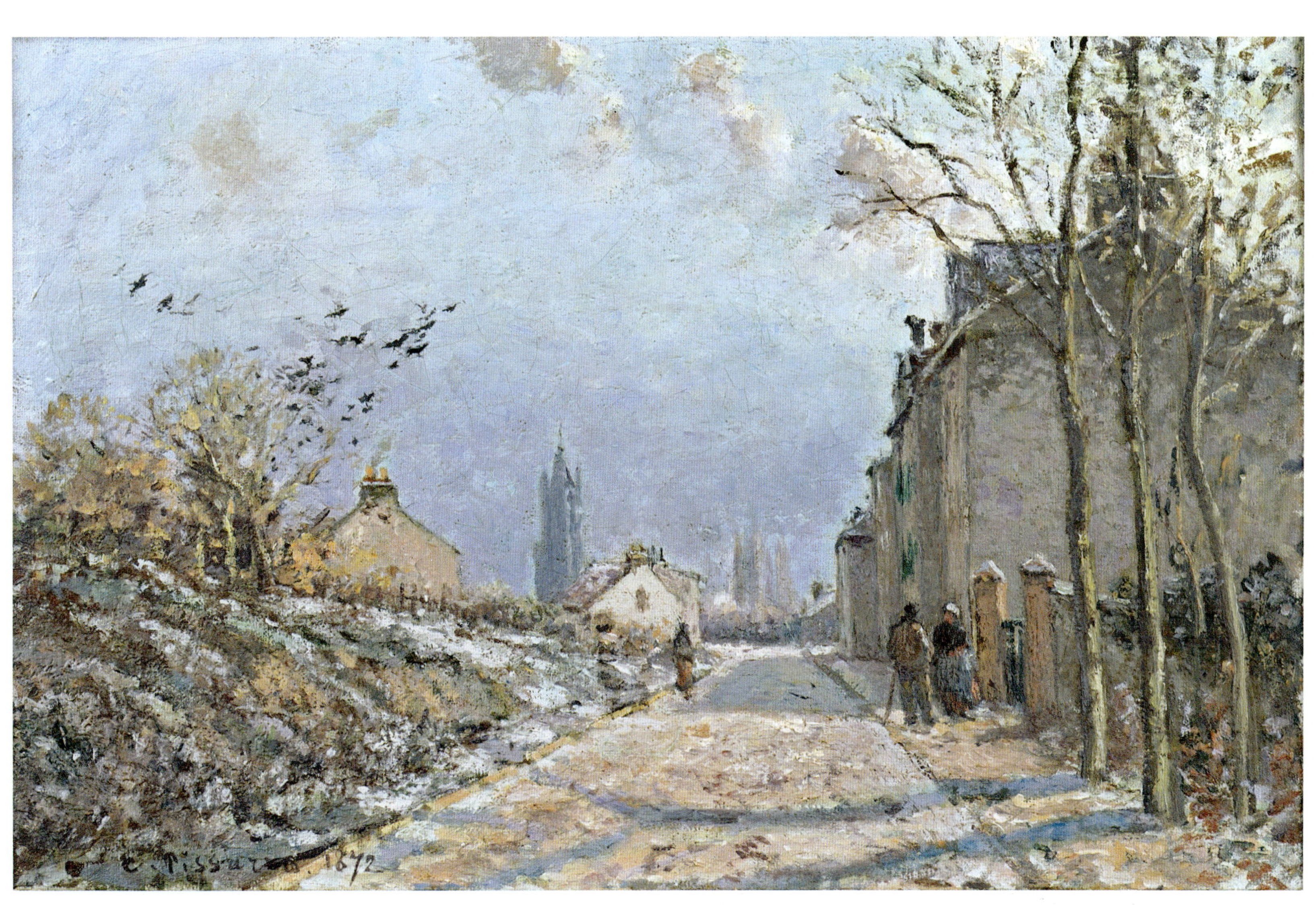
C. Pissarro. 1872

29
Rue de Beaujour, Pontoise
Street at Pontoise
1872 (PD-RS 245)

Oil on canvas
18 × 22 in. (46 × 56 cm)
Carnegie Museum of Art, Pittsburgh; Acquired through the generosity of Mrs. Alan M. Scaife and Family, 65.31

In *Rue de Beaujour, Pontoise*, Pissarro revisits the familiar motif of a road in perspective. His series of Louveciennes street scenes made between 1869 and 1870 systematically explored this subject in different light conditions and atmospheric effects. This painting, however, is a variation of the theme, depicting a turning road rather than one that disappears at the horizon. The curved thoroughfare implies a wider space, one that extends beyond the picture plane. Shadows in the foreground, cast by invisible buildings, contribute to this sense of expanse.

In the two years since he started exploring the possibilities of the road motif, Pissarro broadened his brushwork to evoke a wide range of surface qualities. Color is applied in varied, small clusters that evoke different textures. Cold blue, pink, and beige strokes in different sizes appear on the rough surface of the stone wall to the right, while larger areas of red and green suggest the softness of the grass covering the hill that rises above this wall. The cloudy sky is depicted by even larger and looser patches of gray, blue, and mauve, among other colors. Here Pissarro has not only advanced his painting methods but also developed a way to unify the composition. The result is a densely worked, thick surface, in which even the smallest areas are heavily painted in numerous colors. Elements that occupy different planes are tightly interlocked, as though parts of a three-dimensional picture puzzle.

Dark blues and mauves used in the shadows exemplify an important aspect of Pissarro's and his friends' plein-air aesthetic at this time. Their exploration of colored shadows was a conscious rejection of modeling, the academic chiaroscuro effect that was developed in the relative darkness of the painter's studio, where three-dimensional illusionism was attained by subtle transitions from dark to light. It tended to produce heavy shadows rendered in dark brown tones. Plein-air painters realized that natural daylight illuminated everything in sight. Shadows cast by objects in nature were not black or brown but as colorful as the objects themselves.

The depiction of colored shadows, especially using blue and violet, became one of the most controversial aspects of the Impressionist palette. It remained unacceptable to most critics reviewing their exhibitions, some of whom even assumed the Impressionist painters suffered from pathological eye conditions, since they saw colors and light effects that did not really exist in nature. As late as 1883, in a letter to his son Lucien, Pissarro would complain, "we are accused of having sick eyes, 'the sickness of painters who see blue.'"[1] However, he was convinced that the French painting tradition fully justified the Impressionists' studies of light and shadow. He emphasized the influence of "Claude Lorrain, Corot, the whole eighteenth century [French painting] and Chardin" on their analysis of light effects and colored shadows starting in the late 1860s.[2]
GÇ

1. Camille Pissarro to Lucien Pissarro, May 13, 1883, in *Letters to His Son Lucien*, ed. John Rewald (New York: Pantheon Books, 1943), 31.
2. Camille Pissarro to Lucien Pissarro, May 8, 1903, in ibid., 356.

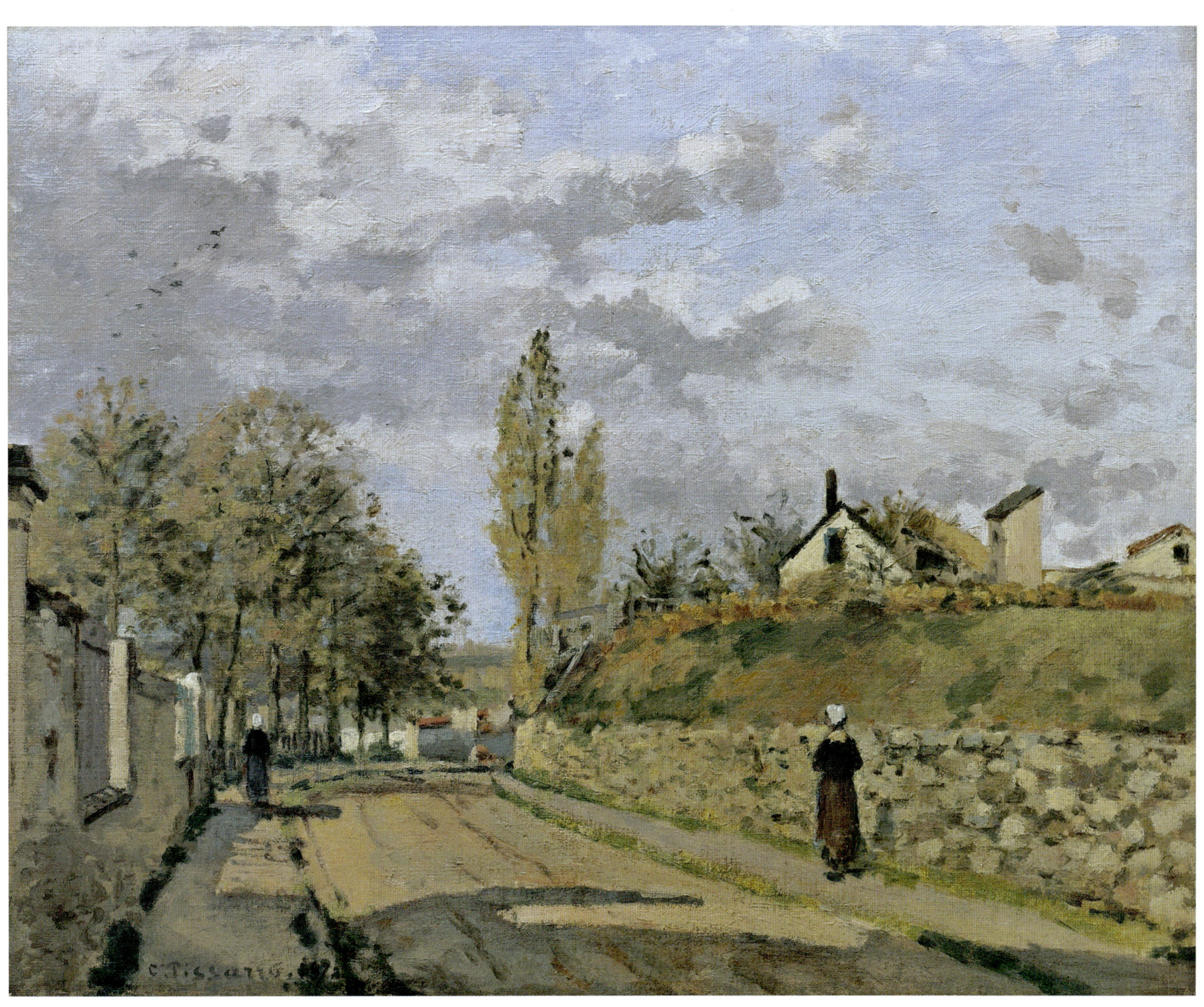

30

Ruelle des Poulies at Pontoise

The "Sente de Justice," Pontoise

c. 1872 (PD-RS 264)

Oil on canvas
20 5/8 × 32 1/8 in. (52.4 × 81.6 cm)
Memphis Brooks Museum of Art, Memphis, Tennessee; Gift of Mr. and Mrs. Hugo N. Dixon, 53.60

This unusual view of Pontoise seen from above highlights the hilly terrain on which the town was built. From this site, Pissarro was able to depict the upper and lower levels of the town in the same composition, producing a more elaborate spatial construction that looks forward to his works of the mid-1870s. It is one of only two known images of Pontoise from this vantage point, both produced in about 1872.[1]

Here the artist has set up his easel on a dirt path lined with grass and small trees, known today as the ruelle des Poulies. It curves in a wide arc along a fence on the left side of the composition, providing a structure that accentuates the steep incline of the hillside that rapidly descends to the buildings below. The careful geometry of the architecture in the center of town is juxtaposed with the more organic forms of the natural world on the hillside. The unusual light, sandy palette, made up of earth tones, the green foliage of the hillside, and the light blue of the sky, is disrupted by the vivid red costume of the woman walking along the path. This splash of color draws the viewer's eye down the path, toward the background.

One of the more recognizable buildings included in this view is the church of Notre-Dame, one of two churches in Pontoise. Its tower rises just above the horizon line in the middle ground. The art historian Richard Brettell has argued convincingly that Pissarro's atheism resulted in his downplaying the religious sites in his depictions of Pontoise.[2] Raised in a Jewish family in St. Thomas, Pissarro was not observant, remaining secular in his lifestyle. Although Pontoise was a predominantly Roman Catholic town, the artist rarely featured the two churches in it. Instead, the familiar images of the churches of Notre-Dame and Saint-Maclou appear as part of the general townscape, without being given any particular prominence. The height of the church tower competes with a factory chimney from the gasworks in the far distance, which spews smoke into the sky.[3]

KR

1. See *Ruelle des Poulies, Pontoise,* 1872 (PD-RS 265), oil on canvas, Musée d'Orsay, Paris. This view of Pontoise seen from above is darker in palette than the present picture and also includes the tower of the church of Notre-Dame in a prominent position.
2. Richard R. Brettell, *Pissarro and Pontoise: The Painter in a Landscape* (New Haven: Yale University Press, 1990), 45–51.
3. For more information on this site, see PD-RS 264.

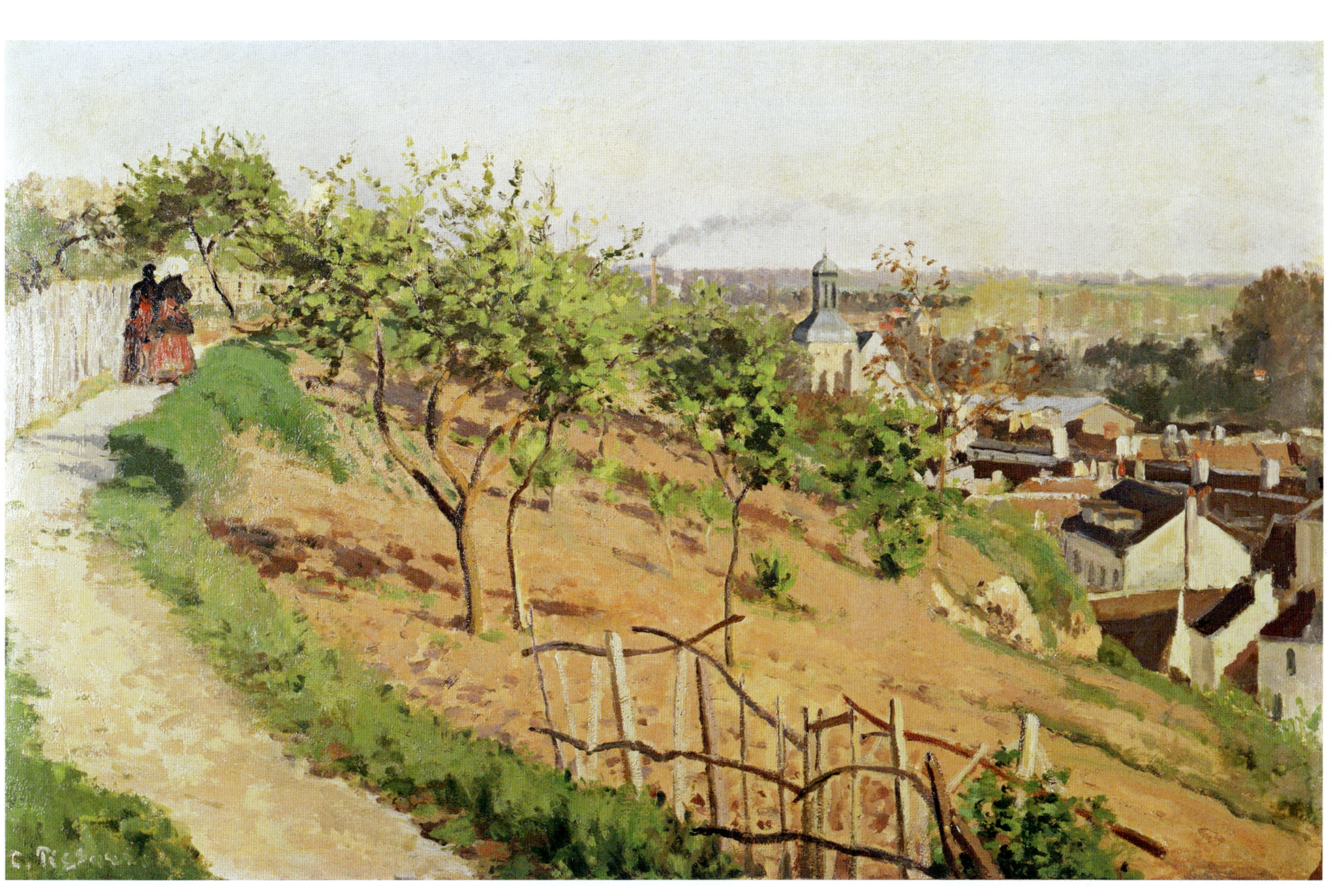

31
Place du Vieux-Cimetière, Pontoise
The Crossroads, Pontoise
1872 (PD-RS 259)

Oil on canvas
21 × 37 in. (54.9 × 94 cm)
Carnegie Museum of Art, Pittsburgh; Acquired through the generosity of the Sarah Mellon Scaife family, 71.7

This was one of many paintings bought from Pissarro by Paul Durand-Ruel, whom the artist met in London in 1871. From 1872 on, Durand-Ruel bought extensively from Pissarro, Monet, Sisley, and Manet, among others, becoming one of the most important dealers of Impressionist paintings. The relative financial security provided by the regularity of this arrangement was suddenly disrupted in 1874, when Durand-Ruel encountered financial difficulties.[1]

For the artist the challenge in this work lay in depicting a deep space on a bright summer day without resorting to the academic technique of chiaroscuro.[2] The imposing sky, which occupies half of the canvas, the wide vista, and the semicircular shape of the foreground contribute to the feeling of a broad expanse, an experience of plein air, where air and daylight circulate freely. Both the composition and color—the bright red and blue accents of clothes, and orange hues of chimneys—draw attention to the presence of the strong, unseen light source.

In addition to bright daylight, Pissarro tries to reproduce light bouncing off the surface of objects. The two figures in the middle ground, a woman and a young child staring at the viewer, strategically attract attention to a minute detail: bright daylight reflecting off the woman's umbrella as well as off the patch of ground in front of her (fig. 1). Here, strong sunlight has a neutralizing effect, for this light does not bring out the color of the earth or of the umbrella.[3] All that is visible is a bright glitter, represented by a few brushstrokes of white paint. The pathos conveyed in the indistinct, yet expressive features of the woman and child as they hold hands and look at the viewer with curiosity induces one to get closer to the picture, and consequently discern Pissarro's delicate light effect.

Pissarro employs in this work the so-called painting in reserve technique.[4] To define the edge of the roof of the house on the right and delineate it from the blue sky, he left bare a thin line of canvas. Between this white line and the blue sky, he ran a stroke of faint violet around the outer ridge of the roof. This technique allows the sky and building to meet without resorting to traditional light and shadow effects.

GÇ

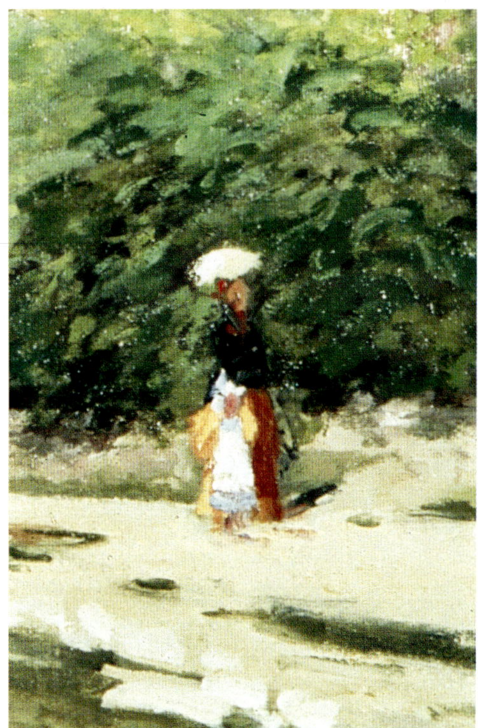

Fig. 1

1. John Rewald, *The History of Impressionism*, 4th rev. ed. (New York: The Museum of Modern Art, 1973), 310–11, discusses Durand-Ruel's near bankruptcy at this time.
2. See cat. 29 for more on the difference between academic chiaroscuro and the plein-air aesthetic.
3. Defining this effect as "neutral surface reflectance," Richard Brown adds, "this reflectance contributes very strongly to our realization of the presence of both the envelope of atmosphere around objects and the dominating light source itself." See Brown, "Impressionist Technique: Pissarro's Optical Mixture," in *Impressionism in Perspective*, ed. Barbara Ehrlich White (Englewood Cliffs, N.J.: Prentice-Hall, 1978), 114–21.
4. For an overview of the application of this technique in Pissarro's and Cézanne's works, see Joachim Pissarro, *Pioneering Modern Painting: Cézanne and Pissarro, 1865–1885* (New York: The Museum of Modern Art, 2005), 52–54.

Fig. 1. Detail of *Place du Vieux-Cimetière, Pontoise*

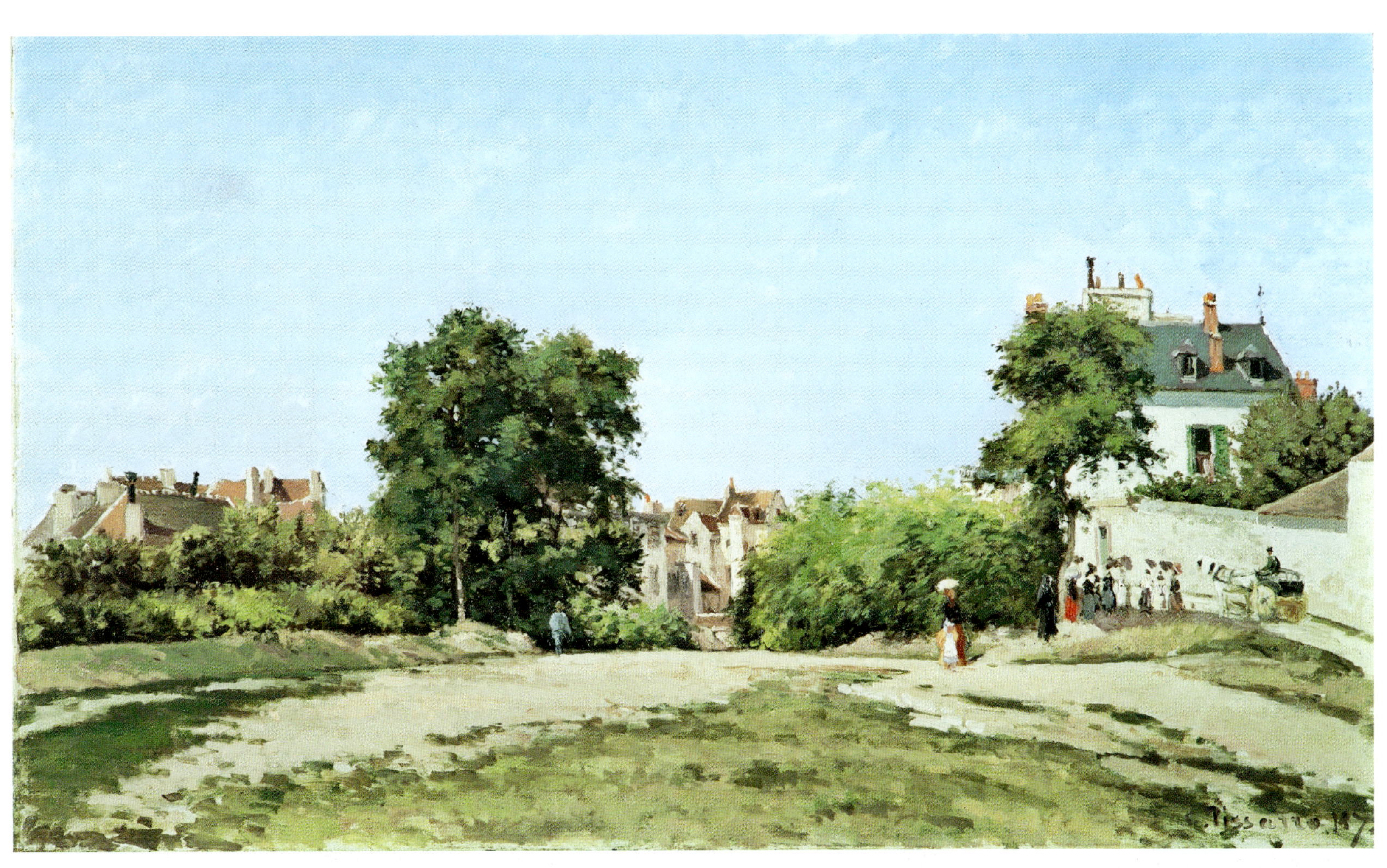

32

The House in the Woods

The House in the Forest

1872 (PD-RS 255)

Oil on canvas
19 $^{11}/_{16}$ × 25 $^{9}/_{16}$ in. (50 × 65 cm)
Dr. and Mrs. Morton Mower

Fig. 1. Meindert Hobbema, *Woodland Road*, c. 1670. Oil on canvas. The Metropolitan Museum of Art, Bequest of Mary Stillman Harkness, 1950 (50.145.22)

Returning from England after the Franco-Prussian War, Pissarro discovered that many of his paintings that he had left in his house in Louveciennes had been destroyed by the Germans. Despite this enormous setback, the artist started painting the landscape around Louveciennes and Pontoise with renewed vigor. He broadened his color scheme and experimented with many technical and stylistic innovations, as can be seen in *The House in the Woods*. The forest motif, with a receding path, stone cottages, and travelers, was a traditional compositional formula with roots in the seventeenth-century Dutch landscape tradition. Meindert Hobbema (1638–1709) was a prolific painter of such scenes, in which footpaths cut across the picture plane, and groups of houses, foliage, and figures are scattered throughout the composition (fig. 1). *The House in the Woods* interprets this theme using an Impressionist technique, presenting a delicate rendering of light effects, as sun filtering through trees flickers on the stone facade of the house, the path, and the meadow in the foreground.

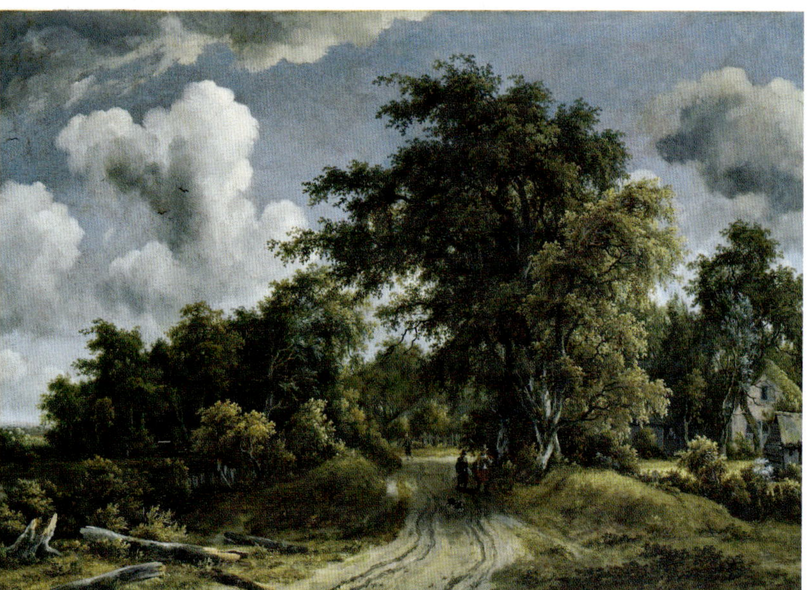

Fig. 1

In the artist's earlier street scenes, such as those from Louveciennes (see cats. 12–16), the motif of a road in perspective provides a bridge between the foreground and the background. The path in *The House in the Woods*, however, does not pull the viewer's gaze into the pictorial space, as it is screened from view by tree trunks and tattered by their shadows. Figures are used as crucial compositional tools to sustain the pictorial illusion, strategically positioned on the road and in the meadow to orient the viewer in the space. The viewer's attention is attracted by small genre scenes: peasant women carrying bundles and baskets, two women stopping in the middle of the road to greet one another, an equestrian figure elegantly framed by two trees, while another person sits on a bench in front of the stone house. Despite their small size and free execution, these figures are noteworthy for the large amount of detail included in their portrayal. They seem to have dropped what they have been doing to turn their heads and look at the viewer.

This painting was once in the collection of Henri Rouart (1833–1912), a successful entrepreneur-engineer as well as an artist who exhibited regularly at the official Salons from 1868 to 1872. Together with Jean-Baptiste Faure (1830–1914), he was one of the early collectors of Impressionist works. Like Faure, Rouart also started by collecting works by the Barbizon artists, especially Camille Corot and Jean-François Millet. He is known to have owned several works by Pissarro. *The House in the Woods* was auctioned by Rouart's heirs in his estate sale in December 1912.

GÇ

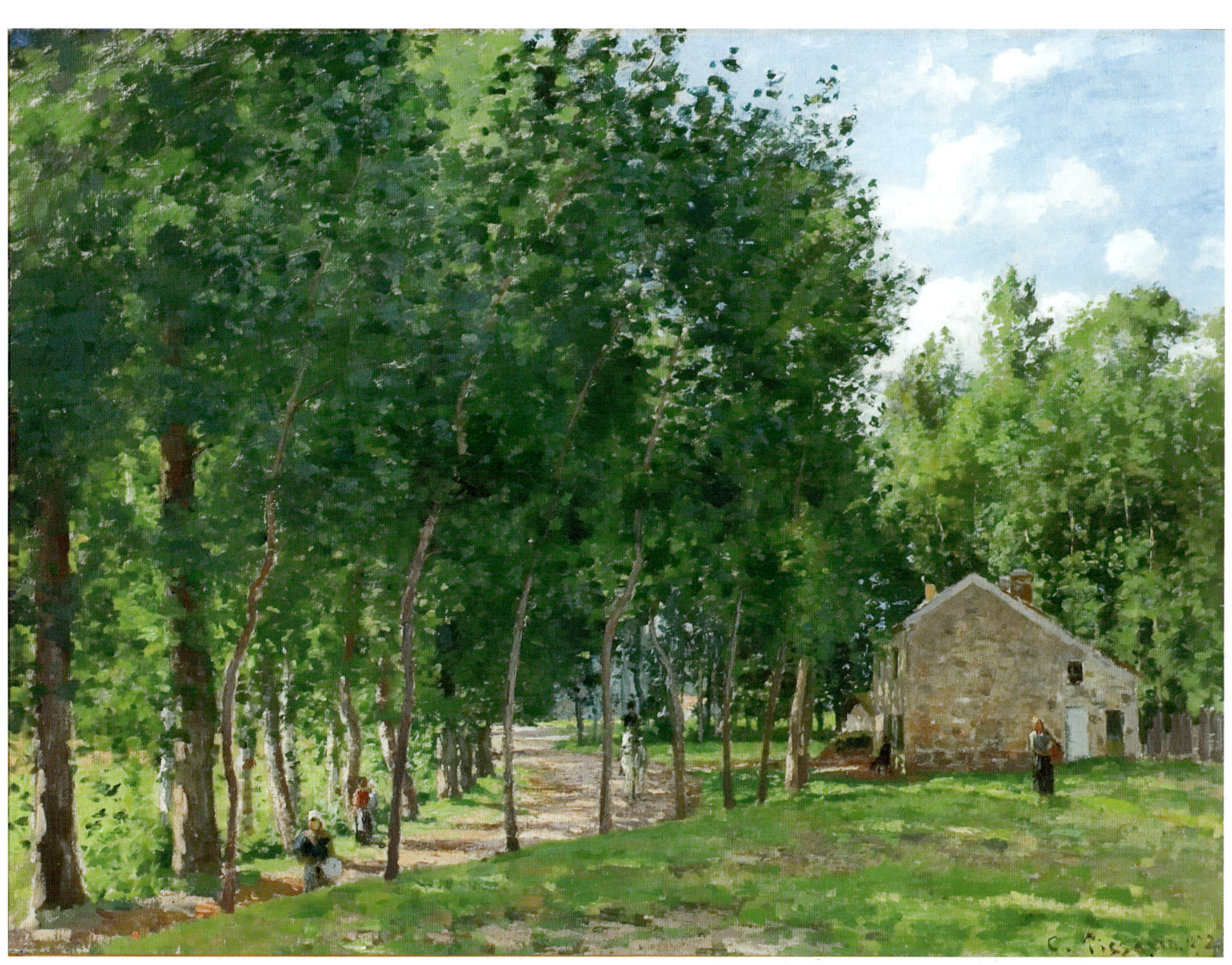

33
Flood at Saint-Ouen-l'Aumône
Landscape with Flooded Fields
1873 (PD-RS 295)

Oil on canvas
25 ½ × 32 in. (64.8 × 81.3 cm)
Wadsworth Atheneum Museum of Art, Hartford, Connecticut, The Ella Gallup Sumner and Mary Catlin Sumner Collection Fund, 1966.315

1. *Correspondance de Camille Pissarro*, ed. Janine Bailly-Herzberg, 5 vols. (Paris: Presses Universitaires de France, 1980–91), 1:79 n. 2.

Fig. 1. Meindert Hobbema, *Windmill at the Riverside*, 1659–60. Oil on canvas. Collection Museum Bredius, The Hague, the Netherlands

Fig. 2. Detail of *Flood at Saint-Ouen-l'Aumône*

In a letter to Pissarro, the art critic Théodore Duret—who was the first owner of *Flood at Saint-Ouen-l'Aumône*—compared this composition to the works of Camille Corot and the Dutch landscape painter Meindert Hobbema (1638–1709).[1] Duret's reference to Hobbema in this context was not arbitrary. During this period in Pissarro's career, when he was searching for technical and compositional innovations and a new definition of what constitutes naturalism in painting, seventeenth-century Dutch precedents provided important models. Hobbema was well known for his compositions of windmills and watermills, in which he depicted the interaction of the world of solid objects and their watery reflections. In *Windmill at the Riverside* (fig. 1), for example, vertical outlines of the reflections of the windmill and the wooden structure on the right link the world of mirrored reflections to the real world. The reflections themselves are demarcated from reality by other solid elements floating on the surface of the water, such as the swan and weeds on the right and the boatman in the center, as well as ripples in the water.

In *Flood at Saint-Ouen-l'Aumône*, Pissarro carries Hobbema's solution of differentiating solid masses from their reflections one step further. The reflection on the water below the tree on the left merges the clouds with the branches of this tree in a dynamic swirl, and the result is a heavily painted area at the lower left of the composition (fig. 2). All of these elements merge in one area on the surface of the water. Here loosely circular brushstrokes are applied irregularly, in a manner radically different from Pissarro's typical brushwork, where regular rectangular patches of color are carefully applied side by side to build up the motif.

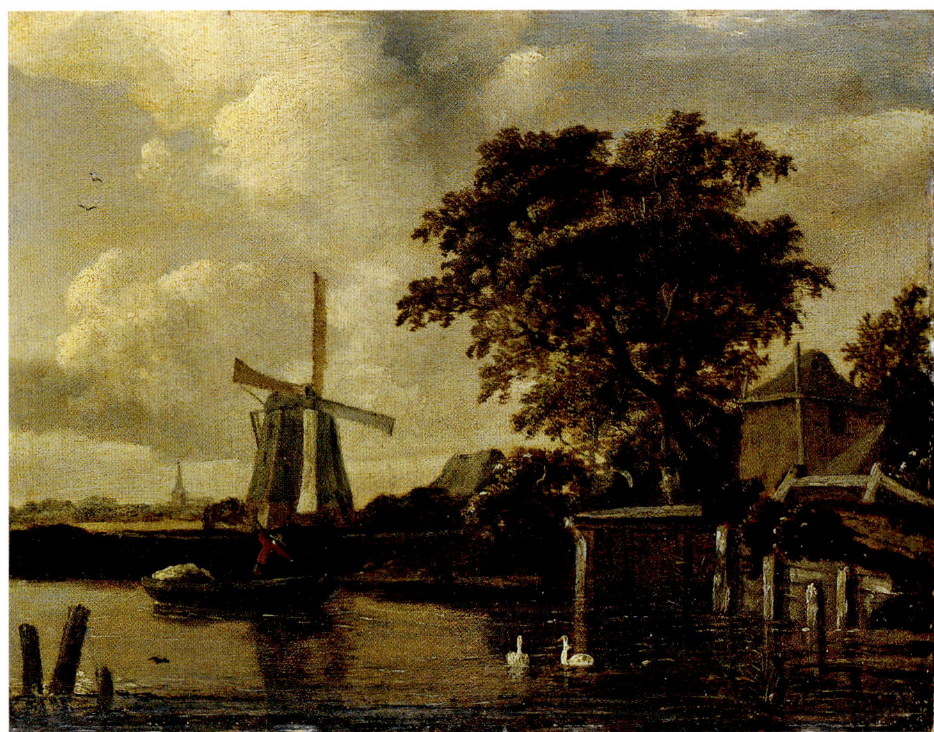

Fig. 1

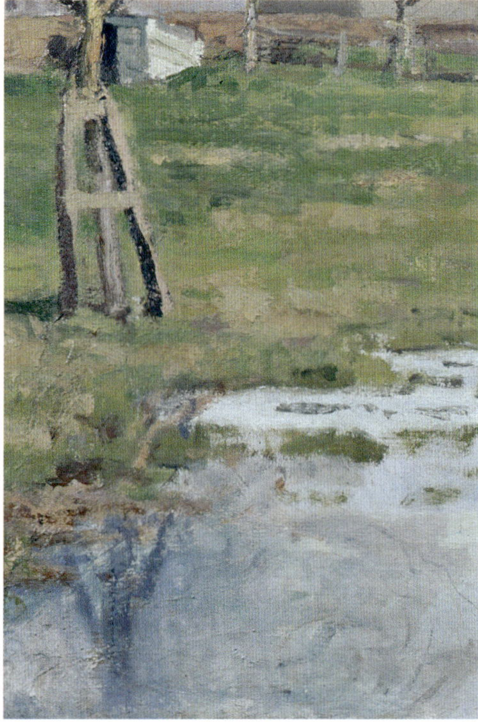
Fig. 2

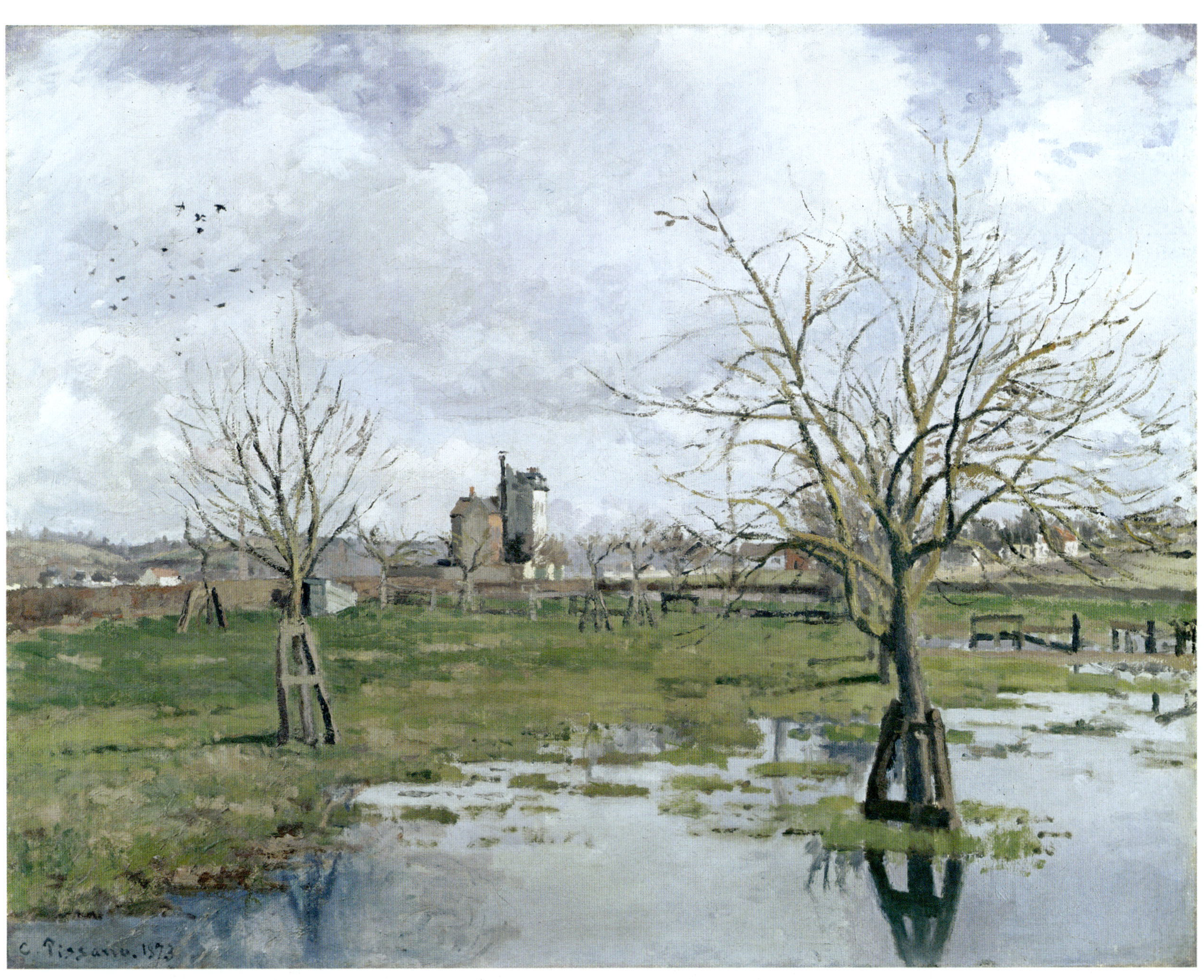
C. Pissarro. 1873

With the inclusion of the tree on the right, Pissarro takes on yet another challenge. How is it possible to demarcate an object from its reflection if the latter is cast on a still surface of water? Without the intervention of waves, birds, or boats to mark the water's surface, how is it possible to tell where the bark of the tree ends and where its reflection begins? Pissarro solves this problem through color. The bark of the tree is rendered with a mixture of greens and browns, whereas its reflection is achieved with a wider range of hues, including purple, light green, and blue. These colors accord with the artist's observation that the water itself is tinted by the color of the earth under its surface as well as by the color of the sky and the clouds above.

GÇ

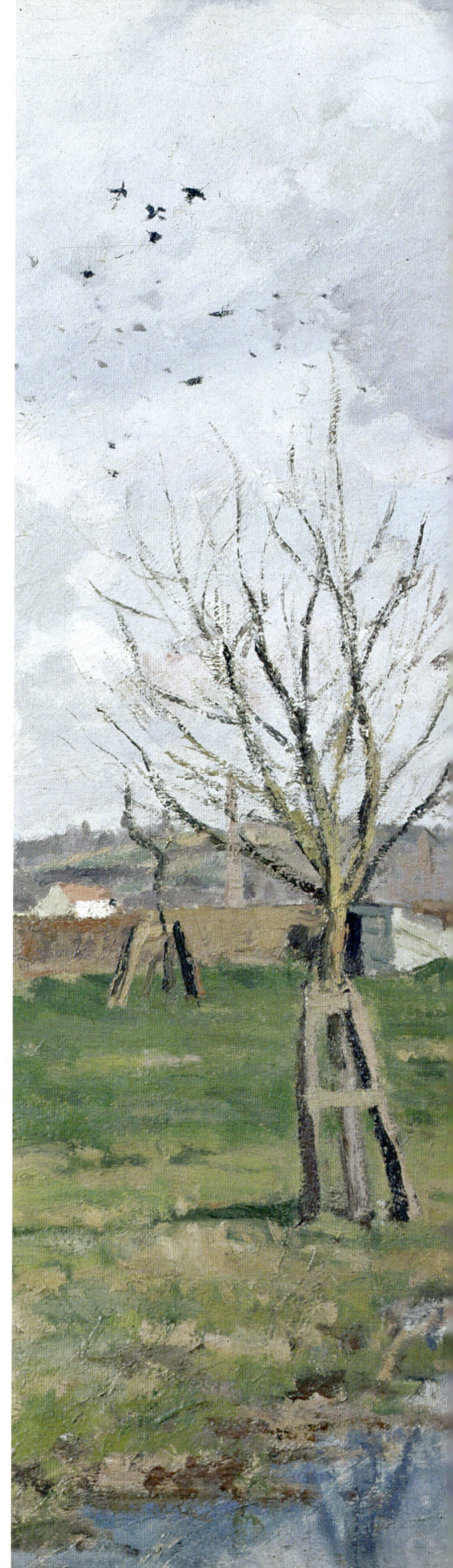

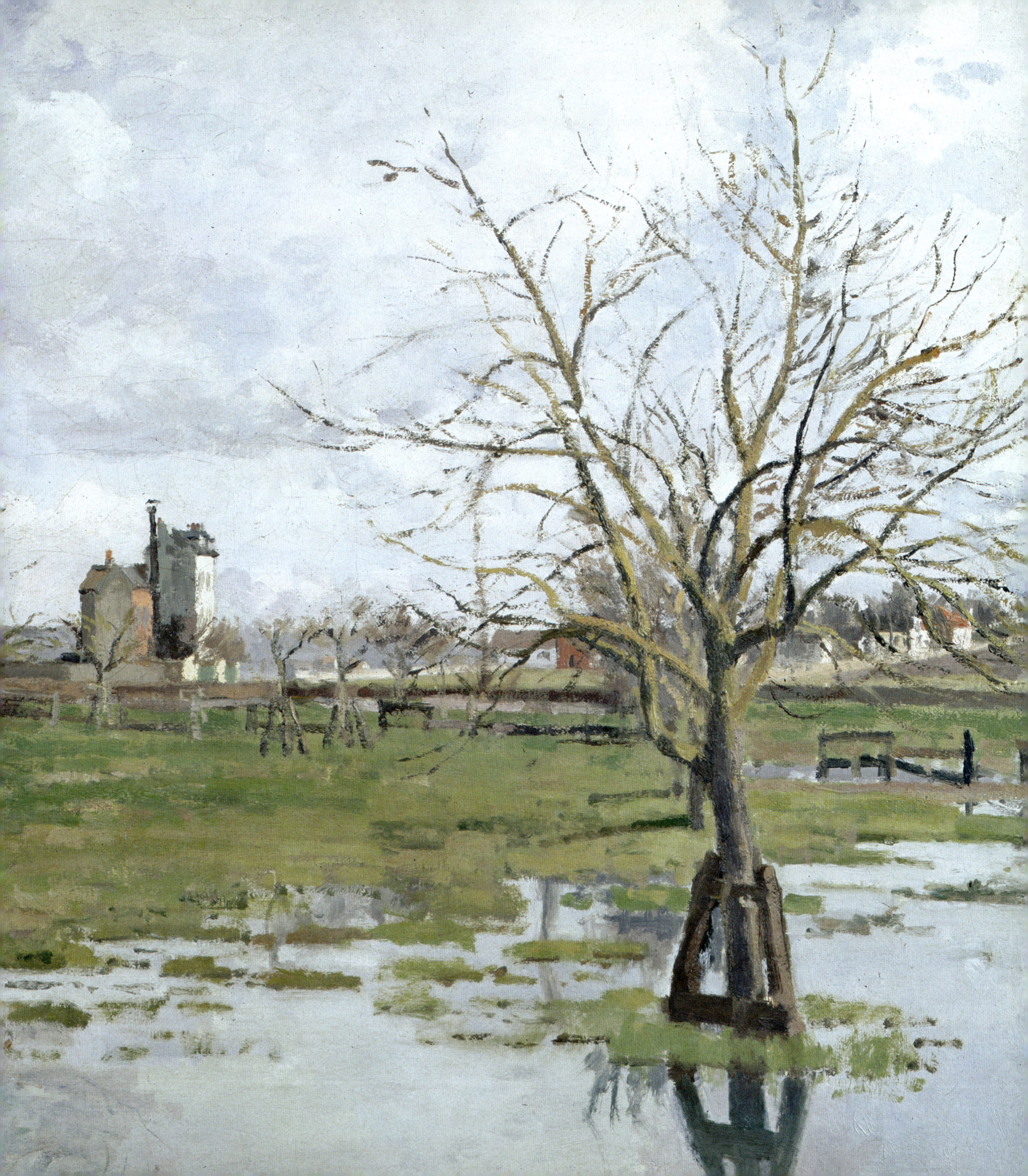

34
Rue de la Citadelle, Pontoise
Street in Pontoise, Winter
1873 (PD-RS 323)

Oil on canvas
21 ¼ × 29 in. (53.9 × 73.6 cm)
Private collection of Ann and Gordon Getty

The rue de la Citadelle was one of the locations where, one winter day in 1873, Pissarro and Paul Cézanne set up their easels together. The two artists had occasionally painted side by side starting in 1871. Cézanne and his family stayed in Pontoise in the spring of 1872, probably as Pissarro's guests, and sometime toward the end of that year or early in 1873 he settled in the neighboring village of Auvers, where he lived for another year. These two years witnessed a period of intense cooperation between the two artists. Under Pissarro's guidance, Cézanne started to observe the effects of natural light while working outdoors. He learned from Pissarro the benefits of painting in the open air, conveying the presence of light through subtle changes in color value, slowly leaving behind his early technique of painting in stark color contrasts. Pissarro, in turn, observed in Cézanne's work a different way to construct pictorial space, to situate objects, houses, and trees within it, and to acknowledge the mounting tension between depth and surface flatness. After seeing the first one-man show of Cézanne's work organized by the art dealer Ambroise Vollard in the rue Lafitte in Paris in 1891, Pissarro wrote a letter to his son Lucien reminiscing about his working relationship with the artist, "Curiously enough, in Cézanne's show at Vollard's there are certain landscapes of Auvers and Pontoise [painted in 1871–74] that are similar to mine. Naturally, we were always together! But what cannot be denied is that each of us kept the only thing that counts, the unique 'sensation.'"[1]

Rue de la Citadelle, Pontoise and Cézanne's *Snow Effect—Road of the Citadel at Pontoise* (fig. 1) exemplify common priorities as much as differing choices that motivated the two artists as they worked on the same motif. Common to both is the attention given to bringing out the geometric structure of the subject, characterized by sharp corners, sloping triangular roofs, and carefully delineated contours of buildings. These structures organize and divide the space. In *Rue de la Citadelle, Pontoise,* clear outlines of severely foreshortened houses and walls are emphasized all the more by their contrast with the softer snow. Brushstrokes of various sizes and directions represent the snow as it turns into slush on the road. Smaller, agitated touches of white pigment applied to the foliage convey the lightness of the thin layer of snow, and the fine, powdery quality of snow accumulated on roofs, especially on the roof of the house at the right, underscores the fleeting quality of this natural element. The major difference between the two paintings is that figures are included in Pissarro's version. The two men standing under the streetlight are framed by the sharp vertical lines of the garden wall on the left and the corner of the house on the right. The lamppost above them creates a frame around the figures, producing the effect of a picture within a picture.

GÇ

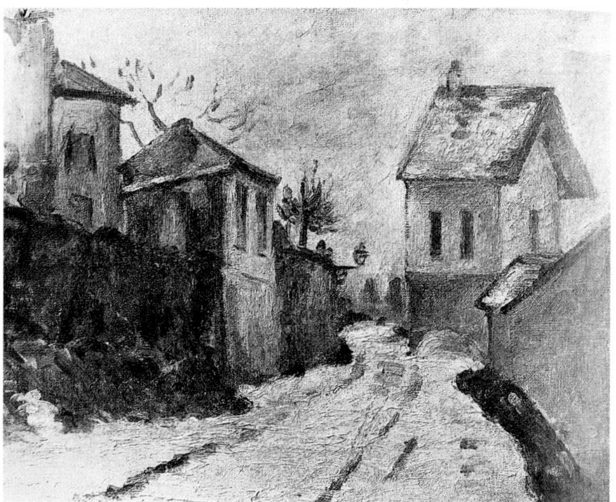

Fig. 1

1. Camille Pissarro to Lucien Pissarro, November 22, 1895, in *Letters to His Son Lucien*, ed. John Rewald (New York: Pantheon Books, 1943), 276.

Fig. 1. Paul Cézanne, *Snow Effect—Road of the Citadel at Pontoise*, c. 1873. Oil on canvas. Location unknown

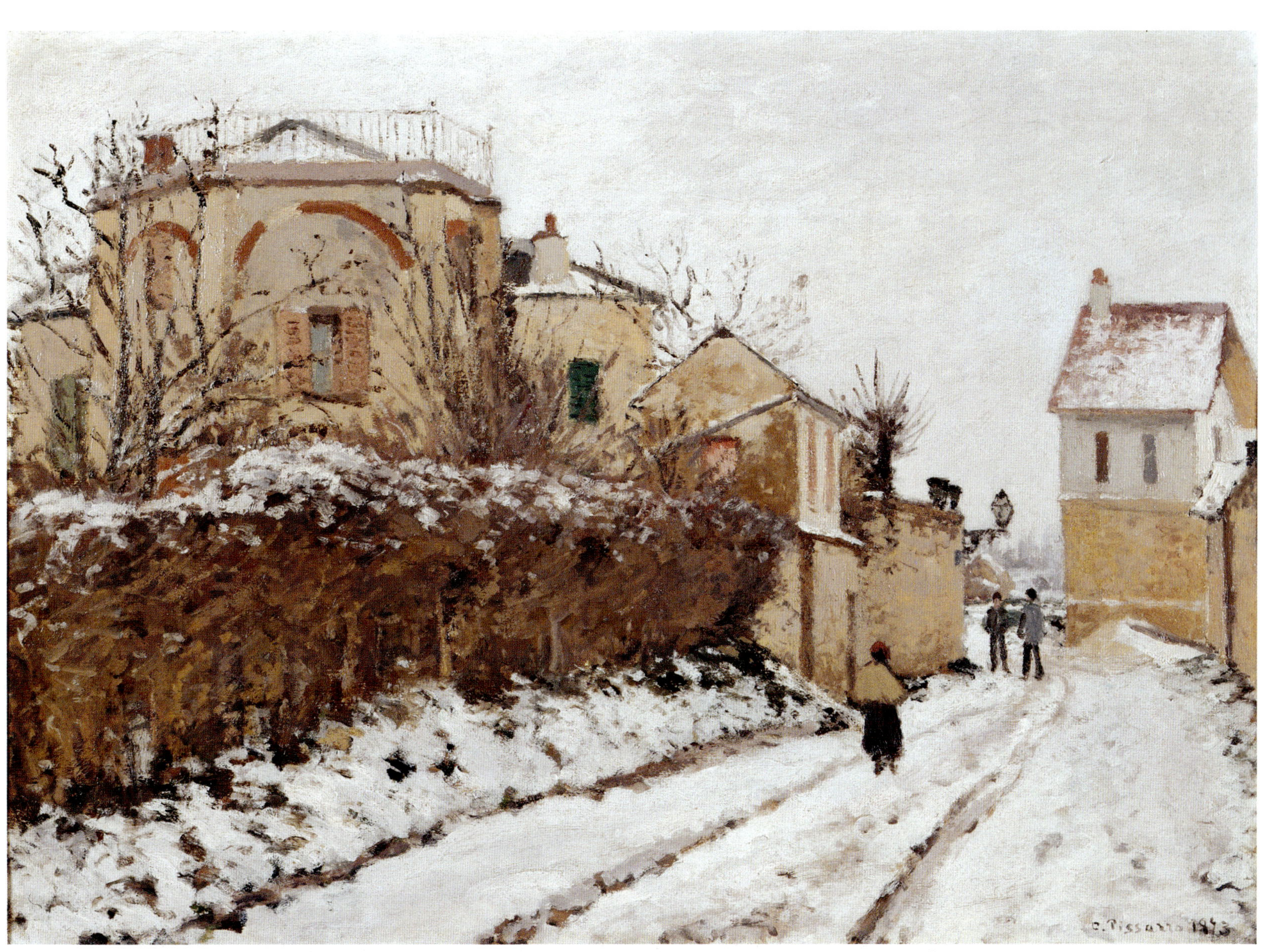

35
Rue de Gisors, Effect of Snow, Pontoise
Pontoise, the Road to Gisors in Winter
1873 (PD-RS 284)

Oil on canvas
23 ½ × 29 in. (59.7 × 73.7 cm)
Museum of Fine Arts, Boston,
Bequest of John T. Spaulding,
48.587

Until 1873 Pissarro painted only a few snow scenes that were set in a strictly urban environment. The spare palette and motif of houses receding in space on a diagonal relate this work to the large *Winter at Louveciennes* the artist had painted a year earlier as part of a series of images of the four seasons (see Rothkopf essay, fig. 12).[1] Different from the series of Louveciennes road scenes painted a few years earlier, in which the artist constructed implied spaces beyond what is visible within the pictorial field, in *Rue de Gisors, Effect of Snow, Pontoise* the basic compositional formula of a road in perspective is employed to produce the opposite effect, a feeling of constraint. Diagonals in the lower half of the composition do not lead the viewer's eye to an opening: they are blocked by buildings and figures crowding the vanishing point where these lines would meet. Compared to Pissarro's earlier scenes of roadways, the lack of a feeling for the beyond in this tightly closed street scene is compensated for by the activity within. The dynamic rhythm of the facades of the houses to the right complements the bustle of human activity on the street. Repeating yet irregular rows of windows, rising and falling rooflines, and dormers projecting and receding at uneven intervals mime the actual physical experience of walking on the steep street paved with cobblestones, sinking and rising, as embodied in the figure of the man straining to pull a handcart up the road.

Apart from its compositional dynamism, the sophisticated use of color marks this work as a high point of Pissarro's early Impressionist style. The scene is imbued with a clarity evocative of a cold yet bright and crisp winter morning. This is a result of the luminous palette, subtle tonal gradations, and lack of sharp contrast between light and dark tonal values, which has its roots in Corot's *peinture-claire* technique, in which white is added to every color to increase the picture's overall luminosity. Such compositions, exemplified by his oil studies made in the open air in the mid-1820s, were based on planes of different values. Here Pissarro breaks down Corot's broad planes of contrasting values into small, rectangular patches of color. This deployment of color in separate touches was likewise a descendant of the open-air oil sketches of the early nineteenth century. These strokes are especially prominent in the melting snow on the road and the pavement, a technique that was developed to perfection by Pissarro and Monet in the early 1870s.
GÇ

1. PD-RS 238.

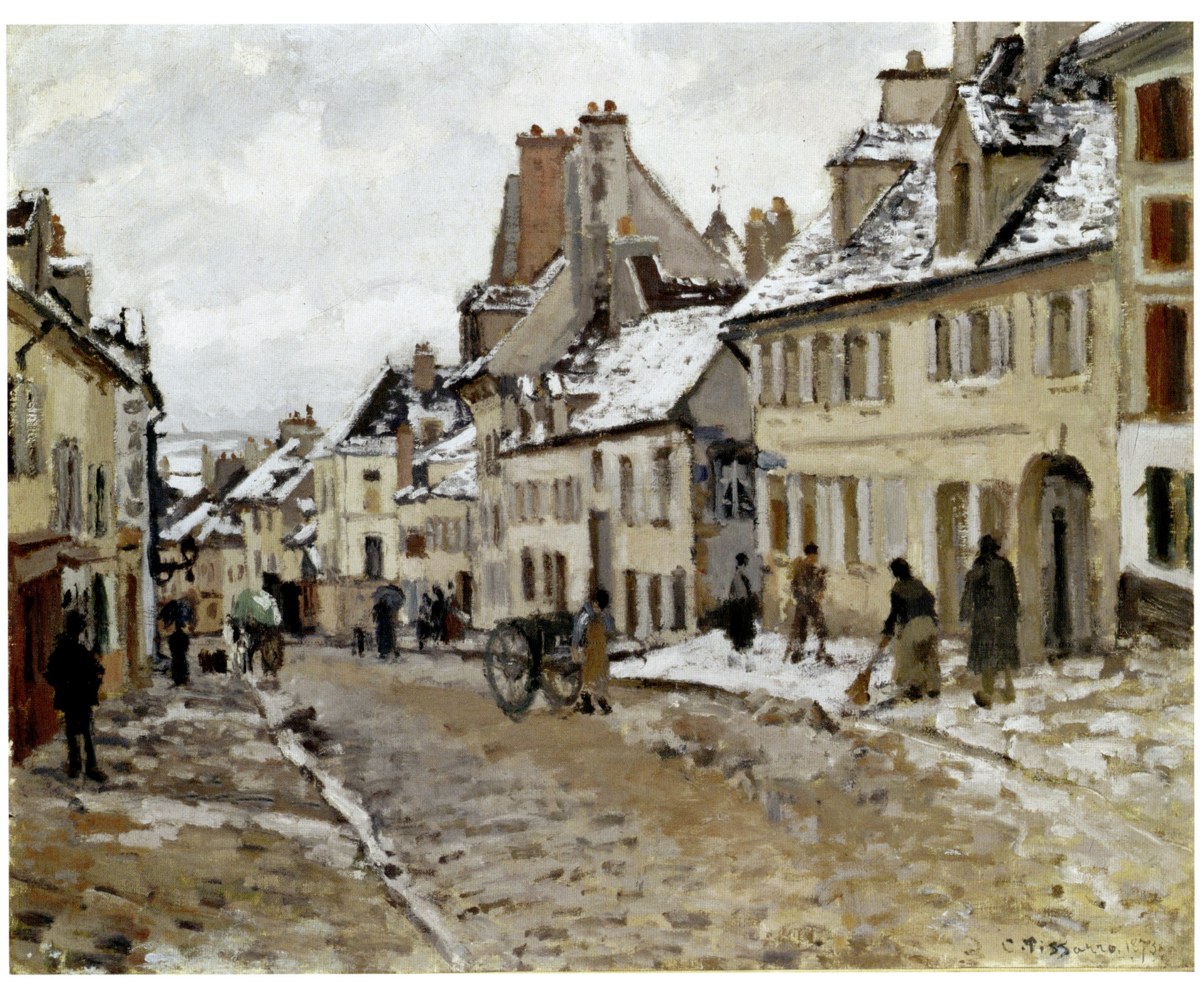
C. Pissarro. 1873

36
Factory at Saint-Ouen-l'Aumône
Factory at Pontoise
1873 (PD-RS 298)

Oil on canvas
18 × 21 ½ in. (45.7 × 54.6 cm)
James Philip Gray Collection,
Museum of Fine Arts, Springfield,
Massachusetts

1. See cats. 37 and 38 for more on the series and on the J. Châlon et Compagnie factory.
2. T. J. Clark, "The Environs of Paris," in *The Painting of Modern Life: Paris in the Art of Manet and His Followers* (Princeton, N.J.: Princeton University Press, 1999), 189.
3. Richard R. Brettell, *Pissarro and Pontoise: The Painter in a Landscape* (New Haven: Yale University Press, 1990), 78–79.
4. Camille Pissarro to Lucien Pissarro, August 19, 1898, *Letters to His Son Lucien*, ed. John Rewald (New York: Pantheon Books, 1943), 329.

Factory at Saint-Ouen-l'Aumône was painted in 1873 as part of a series of four oil paintings and one watercolor that featured the Châlon factory on the banks of the Oise near Pontoise.[1] The composition resembles that of the watercolor *Factory on the Oise at Pontoise* (cat. 38) in its narrow focus on the factory building and its immediate surroundings. However, despite this concentration, this is not a landscape where nature is dominated and suffocated by industrialization. Dense clouds of smoke declare their kinship with the dramatic sky. Where the smoke ends and the clouds begin is indiscernible. Pissarro's technique of painting impasto—in which multiple layers of paint are applied on top of each other, with each layer being allowed to dry before the next is put on—gives the final surface its dense, heavily worked appearance. This material density unites the transitory and the stable: the buildings, the river, the moving plumes of smoke, the clouds, all seem heavily anchored to the surface. The river is depicted as a strip of water, literally within the confines of a rectangular band at the very bottom of the composition. Activating the narrow, shallow space within its rectangular frame, it flows and foams. This strip of water is like a pedestal for the factory buildings. The industrial element is not a disruptive force but part of the generative process of nature.

According to the art historian T. J. Clark, the most salient characteristic of this type of industrial imagery set in the landscape, which also occurs in Monet's work in 1872–75, is an absence of the representation of labor.[2] In *Factory at Saint-Ouen-l'Aumône*, clouds of smoke coming out of chimneys seem as natural as the clouds in the sky with which they merge. Since up to that point Pissarro had made several attempts to represent agricultural labor, this absence of industrial labor is noteworthy. On the other hand, industrial motifs had been an integral part of the naturalist landscape painting tradition. As Richard Brettell argues, beginning in the seventeenth century until the end of the nineteenth, manuals of landscape painting advised painters to include such structures as windmills, watermills, *fabriques* (mills), and *usines* (factories), which embodied man's mastery over nature.[3] Windmills and watermills, intended to tame nature and make it inhabitable, frequently occur in seventeenth-century Dutch landscape paintings, a tradition Pissarro closely studied. The artist believed in the necessity of following tradition while at the same time being modern. The lack of clear reference to underlying economic and social processes in his 1873 factory series can be partially explained in terms of Pissarro's wider project, which gave priority to discovering a modern landscape according to the tenets of tradition, to "tie his medium to its time," as he would remark in a letter he wrote to Lucien from Rouen in 1898.

> [I]t must not be forgotten . . . that we have to perform, not better [the tradition of the old masters], which is impossible, but differently and following our own bent. The results will not be immediately evident. . . . For we have to approach nature sincerely, with our modern sensibilities; imitation or invention is something else again. We have today a general concept inherited from our great modern painters, hence we have a tradition of modern art, and I am for following this tradition while we inflect it in terms of our individual points of view. . . . Observe that it is a grave error to believe that all mediums of art are not closely tied to their time.[4]

GÇ

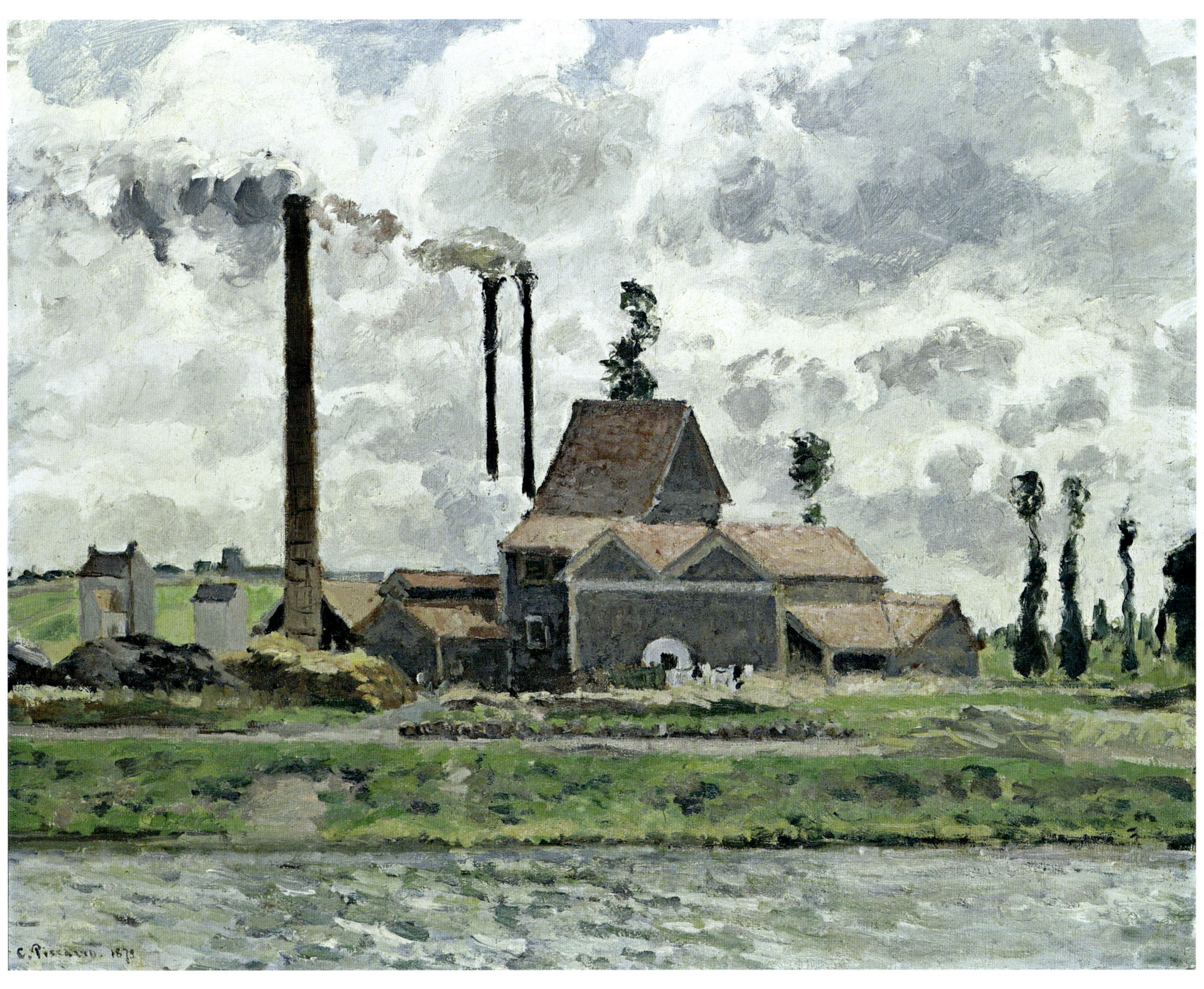

37
Factory on the Banks of the Oise, Saint-Ouen-l'Aumône

Factory at Pontoise

1873 (PD-RS 299)

38
Factory on the Oise at Pontoise

1873

37
Oil on canvas
14 15⁄16 × 21 5⁄8 in. (38 × 55 cm)
Collection, The Israel Museum, Jerusalem, Gift of the Saidye Rosner Bronfman Estate, Montreal, to the Canadian Friends of the Israel Museum, R. No. B95. 1012

38
Watercolor over graphite
7 × 9 7⁄8 in. (17.7 × 25.1 cm)
National Gallery of Art, Washington, D.C., Collection of Mr. and Mrs. Paul Mellon, 1985.64.109
Milwaukee and Memphis only

In 1873 Pissarro produced five works featuring a factory complex in Saint-Ouen-l'Aumône on the banks of the Oise River. In this series, Pissarro depicted the massive new factory as an integral part of the landscape. Different from the artist's earlier factory imagery, such as *Banks of the Oise at Saint-Ouen-l'Aumône* (cat. 8), the 1873 series features this symbol of industrialization within a decidedly rural setting. Pissarro explored the ways in which the factory complex could be depicted as situated in and interacting with nature, the smoke emanating from its chimneys merging with the clouds, its reflections cast on the water surface.

As the art historian Richard Brettell has pointed out, the large J. Châlon et Compagnie factory complex was recent, added to the environs of Pontoise after the Franco-Prussian War.[1] Its products were transported by barges that operated in a larger canal network to which the Oise was connected. As Brettell maintains, this substantial compound was a distinctly new phenomenon, differing from the smaller warehouses and factories scattered in Pontoise that merged with the landscape and the cityscape. With its gigantic smokestack dominating the surroundings, Châlon's immense factory stood on the flat plains near Pontoise, giving the town an industrial character.

The watercolor *Factory on the Oise near Pontoise* was quickly produced *en plein air*.[2] Here surfaces do not merely reflect light and produce color. The underlying motif in this

1. Richard R. Brettell, *Pissarro and Pontoise: The Painter in a Landscape* (New Haven: Yale University Press, 1990), 80–81.
2. This composition corresponds closest to *Factory at Saint-Ouen-l'Aumône, the Flood of the Oise*, 1873 (PD-RS 297), oil on canvas, private collection. Not only the composition but also the interaction between the smoke, water, reflection, and solid objects are conceived and worked out in the same way.

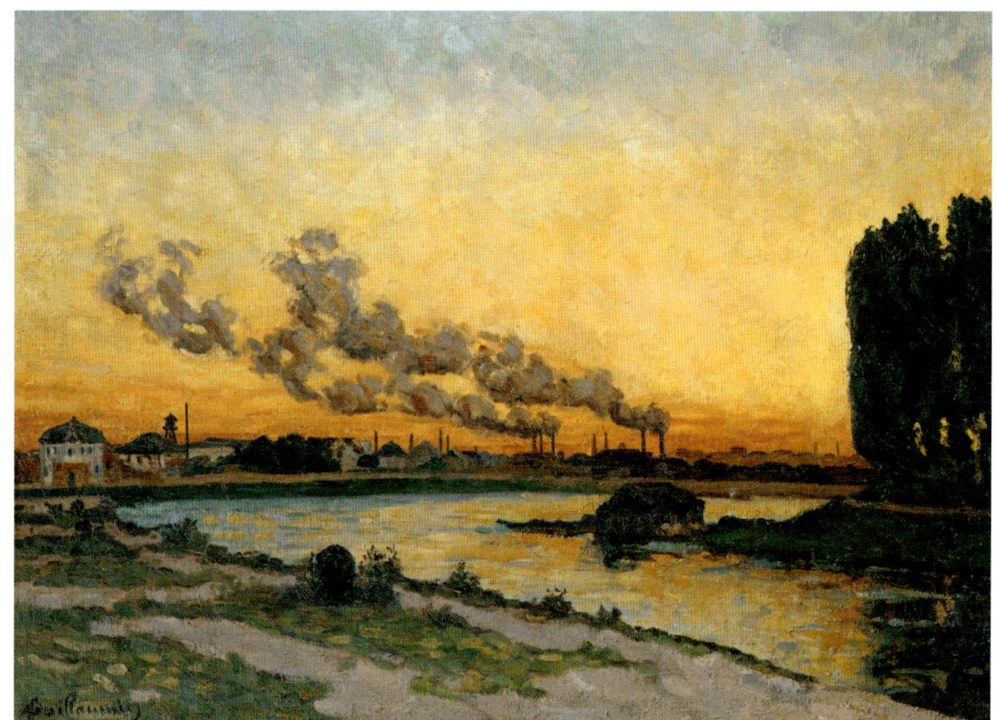

Fig. 1

Fig. 1. Armand Guillaumin, *Sunset at Ivry*, 1874. Oil on canvas. Musée d'Orsay, Paris, France

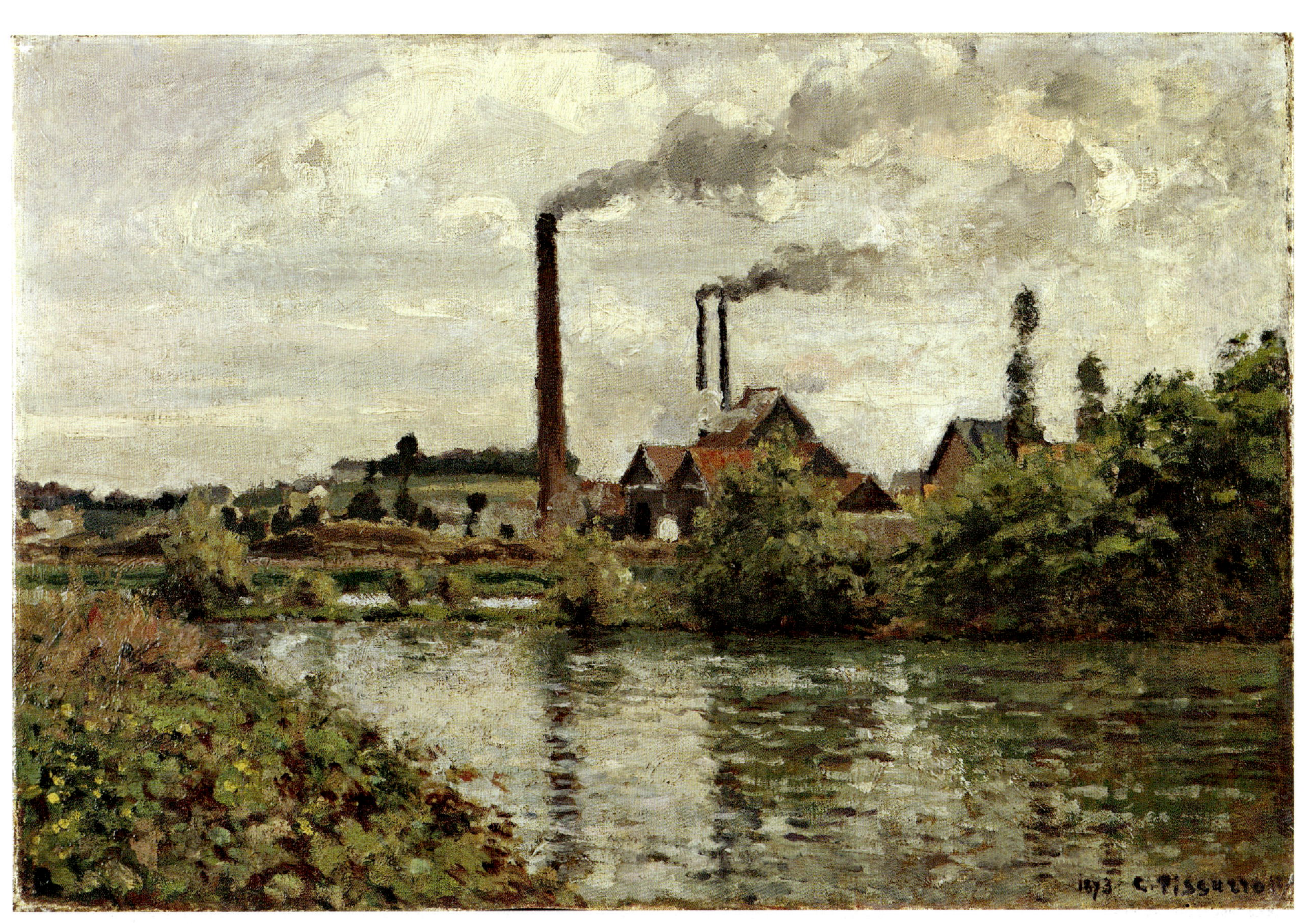
1873. C. Pissarro

3. Richard Brettell and Christopher Lloyd, *A Catalogue of the Drawings by Camille Pissarro in the Ashmolean Museum, Oxford* (Oxford: Clarendon Press, 1980), 28–33.

4. See cat. 36 for more on Pissarro's industrial imagery and the lack of representation of human labor in this series.

small composition is the contrast between the solid and the fleeting, the massive and the ephemeral. The gray and red factory building is imbued with a solid presence. In fact, everything connected to the factory has a density, a material presence, that is missing in the rest of the landscape. Huge smokestacks emit enormous amounts of dense clouds of smoke in various tones of dark gray wash. The boats in the foreground and the barren tree are thinly painted. Reflections on the water as well as the waves are merely summary touches of the brush. The artist's handling of the medium determines what is to be considered substantial and what is to be thought of as ephemeral. This watercolor might have served as the model for most of the oil paintings in this series. In all these depictions, the position of the chimneys and the identical way the smoke is swept by the wind strengthen the hypothesis that the paintings were based on this watercolor.

Pissarro introduced considerable variations to this initial idea. As the art historians Christopher Lloyd and Richard Brettell point out, this work belongs to a number of watercolors Pissarro executed between 1870 and 1873, an early period in his plein-air studies.[3] During this time Pissarro embraced the spontaneity offered by the medium and used his watercolors as preparatory studies for oil paintings. In the latter part of the decade, by contrast, the artist does not seem to have produced any watercolor sketches as the basis for paintings. The 1880s and 1890s witnessed a second period of intense exploration of the possibilities offered by this medium.

The painting *Factory on the Banks of the Oise, Saint-Ouen-l'Aumône* shows the stark geometry of the building juxtaposed against plumes of dense smoke emerging from the chimneys. Visible, discrete strokes of paint imbue the surface of the water and the reflections on it with a material quality that does not exist in the watercolor. Thick, broken brushstrokes reproduce the effect of moving water, where perfect reflections are disturbed by waves. The vantage point from which the factory is observed is somewhere across the shore. In comparison to *Factory at Saint-Ouen-l'Aumône* (cat. 36), another variant from the same series but with a narrower focus on the building, here the wider vista conveys a sense of the larger countryside in which the building is situated, where the earth is dotted with flowers and foliage, and the terrain is hilly and uneven.

Pissarro's circle of painters did not accept this imagery of a factory in harmony with nature as the only accepted model. In *Sunset at Ivry* (fig. 1), made in the same year, Armand Guillaumin (1841–1927), a member of the Impressionist group and a close friend of Pissarro whom he met at the Académie Suisse in 1861, painted a menacing silhouette of the forge at Ivry. Here, the smoke billowing from the smokestacks stains the sky rather than merging with it. In Pissarro's painting, the factory is not juxtaposed against nature. Noteworthy is the lack of human figures in this landscape; it is an image not of individual labor but one of corporate industry.[4]

GÇ

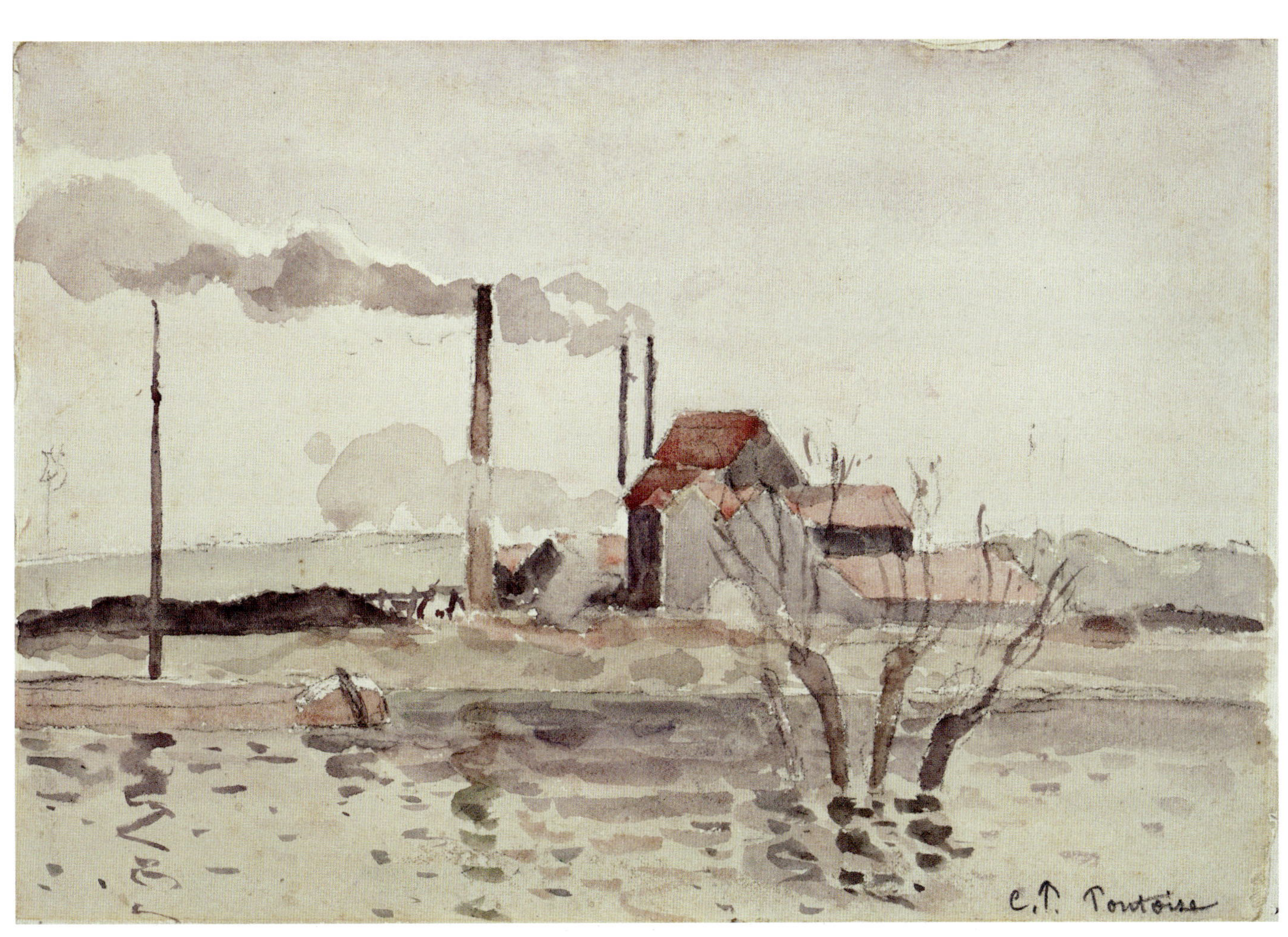
C.P. Pontoise

39
Route d'Auvers on the Banks of the Oise, Pontoise
Banks of the Oise near Pontoise
1873 (PD-RS 303)

Oil on canvas
15 × 21 ¾ in. (38.1 × 55.2 cm)
Indianapolis Museum of Art, James E. Roberts Fund, 40.252
Baltimore and Milwaukee only

As early as 1867 Pissarro began to incorporate the image of factories in his landscapes. In 1873 the artist painted a significant series of views centering on the Châlon distillery in Pontoise (cats. 36–38). Painted the same year, *Route d'Auvers on the Banks of the Oise, Pontoise* also includes an industrial building as part of a broader panorama of the environs of the town. Although the painting has no obvious central motif, a striking combination of bright colors is concentrated in the middle of the canvas: the orange-red scarf of a peasant woman, the red rooftops of the factory, and the turquoise of the water seen through the foliage by the riverbank. The viewer's gaze, following these intense spots of color, is guided toward the vanishing point of the road. The entire scene is filled with movement: a train in motion, people walking and riding, a barge floating on the river, and a broad sweep of clouds, all of them moving away from or toward the diagonal of the road. Here Pissarro has devised a powerful tool for creating spatial depth, using color contrasts, linear construction, and human figures in the creation of space.

To the right, a speeding train, running parallel to the riverbank, emits puffs of steam into the air. The white smoke, standing out against the dark blue background, is a solid mass in comparison to the cursorily drawn row of trees shaking in the wind at the left. The loose brushstrokes that define these trees are perfunctory, conveying a calculated sketchiness, which can be observed in the depiction of the sky as well. The S-shaped blue stroke in the sky above the trees does not represent a cloud, nor the wind in the sky (fig. 1). Rather, it suggests the immediate experience of the artist himself in the open air, thus imbuing a sense of spontaneity to the composition.[1] It is

1. In the 1890s, at the height of Neo-Impressionism, the art critic Félix Fénéon argued that this sketchlike technique aimed at giving the Impressionist paintings "the air of being improvised." This technique tended "to exaggerate the features of nature in order to prove that it was a unique moment which would never be seen again." Félix Fénéon, "Neo-Impressionism," in *Oeuvres plus que complètes*, ed. Joan U. Halperin (Geneva: Librairie Droz, 1970), 1:71–74, excerpted in *Art in Theory, 1815–1900: An Anthology of Changing Ideas*, ed. Charles Harrison and Paul Wood (Oxford: Blackwell Publishing, 1998), 966–69.

Fig. 1. Detail of *Route d'Auvers on the Banks of the Oise, Pontoise*

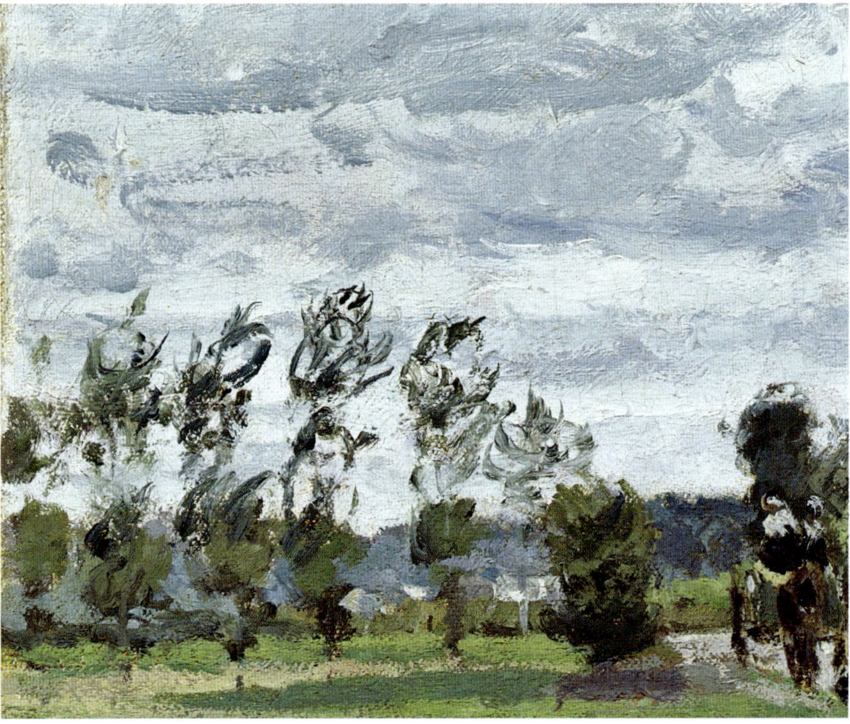

Fig. 1

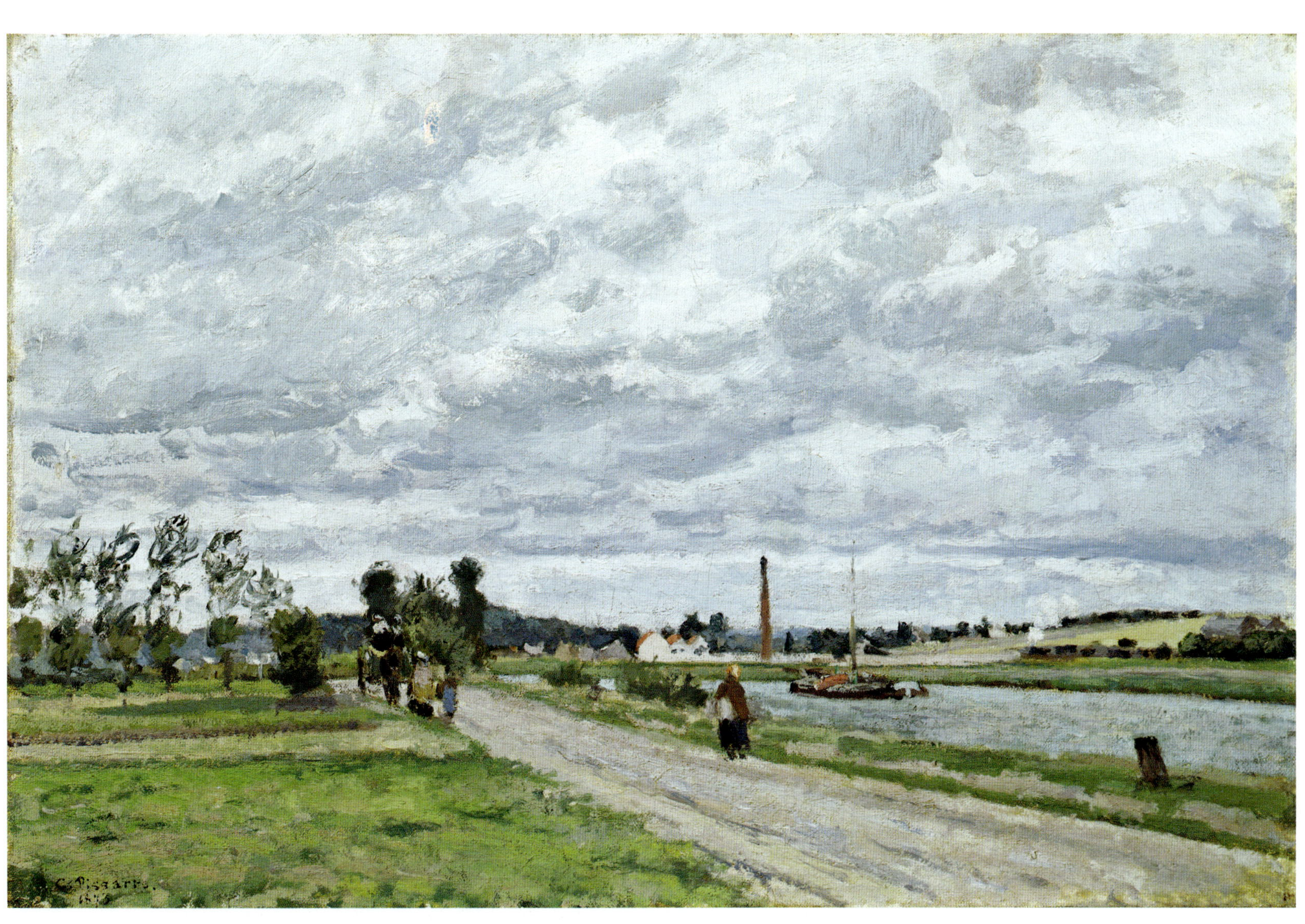

2. Théodore Duret defined this elusive translation of momentary experience into painting in relation to Claude Monet's Impressionist landscapes as follows: "He made it his rule to paint his landscapes directly in the open air. Whatever their dimensions, he completed them with the scene which he wished to represent immediately before his eyes. . . . In every scene of nature [this practice] led him to seize just that particular aspect, that fugitive notation of light or of color, under which he saw nature at the moment when he was painting it. . . . that fleeting charm, that particular envelopment of atmosphere, which he seized and notated as an ephemeral effect in the brief moment of its duration." In *Manet and the French Impressionists: Pissarro–Claude Monet–Sisley–Renoir–Berthe Morisot–Cézanne–Guillaumin*, trans. J. E. Crawford Flitch (Philadelphia: J. B. Lippincott Company; London: Grant Richards, 1910), 139.

3. Quoted in Ludovic Rodolphe Pissarro and Lionello Venturi, *Camille Pissarro: Son art, son oeuvre*, 2 vols. (Paris: P. Rosenberg, 1939), 1:28.

striking that this sketchiness is localized, since the rest of the landscape and the river are constructed solidly and meticulously with regular brushstrokes.

A few paintings from 1872 and 1873, such as *Flood at Saint-Ouen-l'Aumône* (cat. 33), include comparable notations of spontaneity, where sketchy, rapid brushstrokes reflect quick movements of the painter's hand.[2] Such brushwork, which tended to dissolve forms into agitated gestures, never completely dominated his compositions during this period. Pissarro's experiments with this style remained limited, confined to small areas on the canvas, as seen here. His attention to shape and a rigorous geometric structure established early in his career persisted. Early critics and historians of Impressionism often singled out the force of structure in Pissarro's work. The art critic Armand Silvestre argued that the fantastical eye of Monet and Sisley, especially between 1873 and 1876, required a controlling mechanism, which was provided by Pissarro's "need for a well-established compositional space."[3]

GÇ

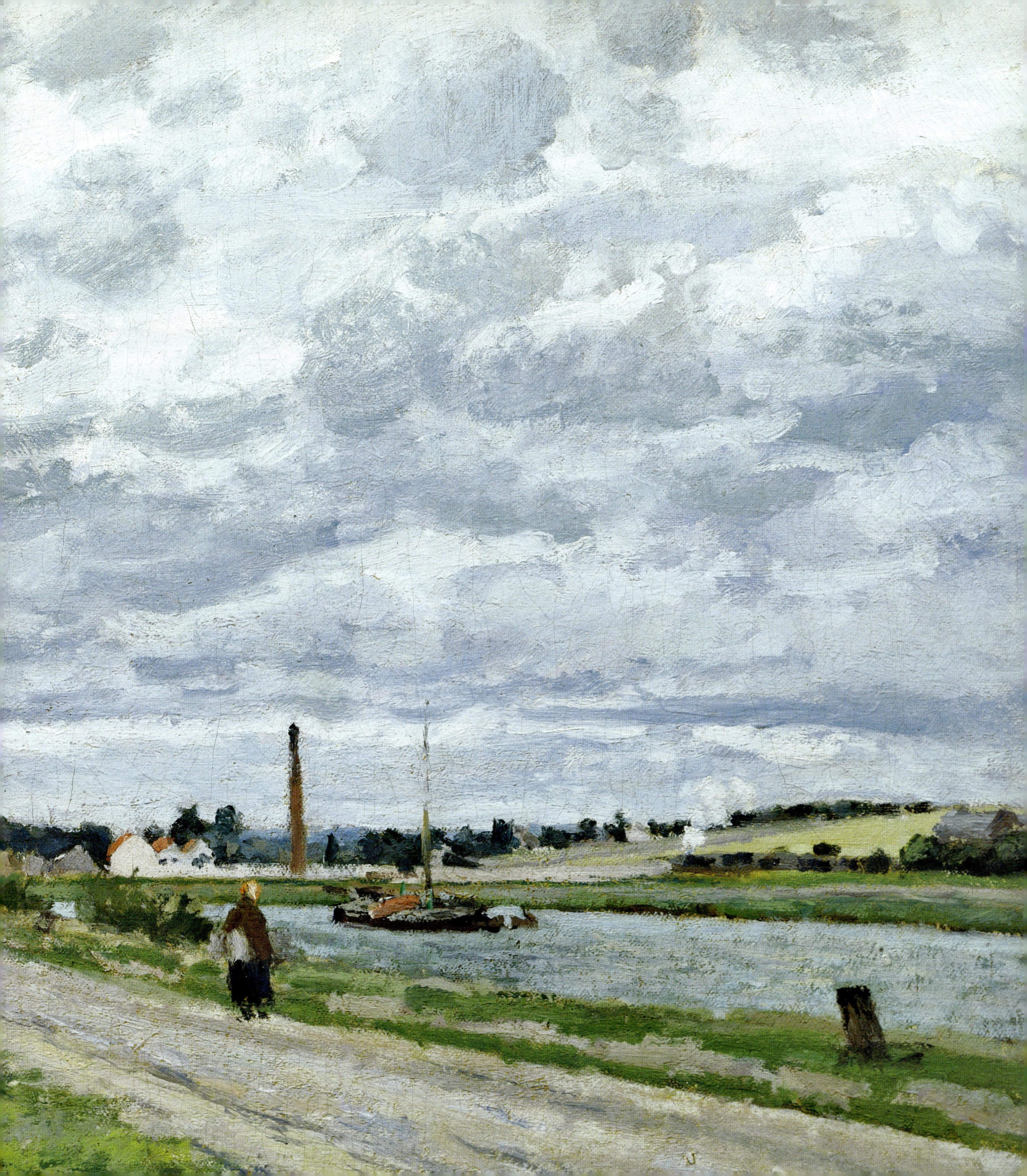

40

Landscape at Les Pâtis, Pontoise, the Harvest

1873 (PD-RS 304)

Oil on canvas
25 5/8 × 31 7/8 in. (65 × 81 cm)
Private collection
Baltimore only

1. Camille Pissarro to Octave Mirbeau, April 21, 1892, *Correspondance de Camille Pissarro*, ed. Janine Bailly-Herzberg, 5 vols. (Paris: Presses Universitaires de France, 1980–91), 3:217.

Fig. 1. Camille Pissarro, *Landscape at Les Pâtis*, 1868. (PD-RS 125). Oil on canvas. National Gallery of Art, Washington, D.C., Gift (Partial and Promised) of Mr. and Mrs. David Rockefeller, in Honor of the 50th Anniversary of the National Gallery of Art

Throughout his life, Pissarro had an affinity for the farming community. Although he was raised in a bourgeois family in St. Thomas, he always felt a strong connection with the peasants who worked the soil. Beginning in the early 1860s he regularly made his home in rural and suburban areas near Paris, painting the landscapes that surrounded him. His political interests may also have played a role in his decision to live on the outskirts of the French capital. As a philosophical anarchist who believed in the elimination of authoritarian institutions and in the benefits of self-government, he may have wanted to live a simple, quiet life, away from the extreme stratification of society in Paris. He later wrote that he did not have to be a peasant to paint an honest landscape,[1] but he seemed to have felt that he could not accurately paint peasant life without living near them.

Here Pissarro has depicted the fields surrounding Les Pâtis, a small hamlet west of Pontoise on the Voisne River which can be seen comfortably nestled in the hills in the middle ground of the composition. He first depicted this panoramic view in 1867 in a daring, large-scale composition (fig. 1), where his interest in broad areas of thick paint and bold geometric structure is evident. Six years later, he returned to the same site with a new set of interests and experiences. In *Landscape at Les Pâtis, Pontoise, the Harvest*, his increasing fascination with light and atmospheric effects has become as important as the carefully structured composition. His palette is more subtle, and his delicate, early Impressionist style allows him to provide added detail about the landscape that he depicts, highlighting the different textures in the grass, field, and trees. The foreground, a furrowed field, is depicted with countless broken brushstrokes of tan, yellow, and green that lead the viewer's eye down the slope to the fields in the center. Broader strokes in the middle ground and background are in light shades, as the artist carefully paints the view on a hot, dry summer day. The strict geometry of his earlier view of Les Pâtis has been replaced with the undulating shapes of hills and fields. Small haystacks and several figures dot the landscape, providing a human presence to the sense of calm and order in the countryside after the harvest has taken place.

This work was once owned by the well-known opera singer Jean-Baptiste Faure, an important early patron of the Impressionists who also owned *The Red House* (cat. 41) and *Effect of Snow at L'Hermitage, Pontoise* (cat. 45).

KR

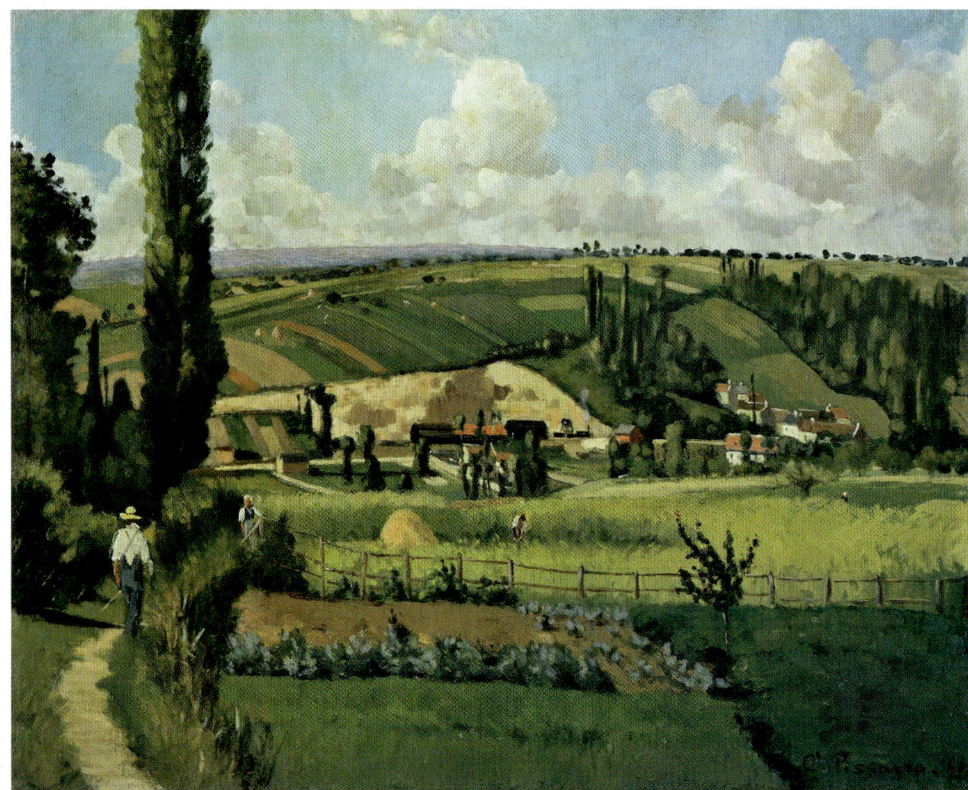

Fig. 1

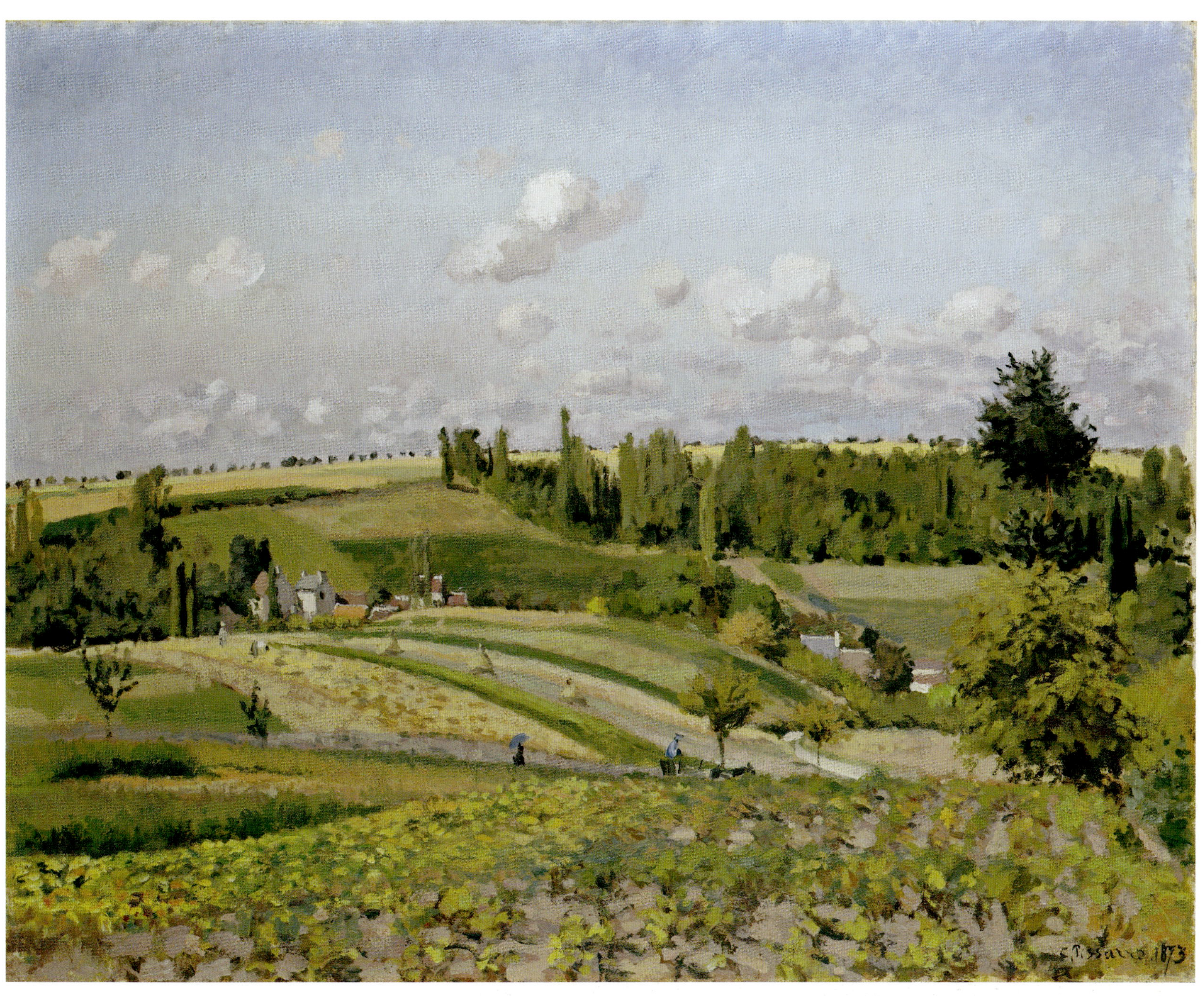

41
The Red House

1873 (PD-RS 307)

Oil on canvas
22 ¾ × 28 in. (57.8 × 71.1 cm)
Portland Art Museum, Bequest of Winslow B. Ayer, 35.22
Baltimore only

Théodore Duret, in *Les Peintres impressionistes* published in 1878, explained the Impressionists' use of bright, unbroken colors as a function of sunlight that one could easily observe while taking a walk outdoors: "If you walk along the banks of the Seine—at Asnières for example—in a single glance you will be able to see the red roof and brilliantly white fence of a cottage, the pale green of a poplar, the yellow road, and the blue river. In the summer, at noon, all the colors will seem raw, intense, impossible to tone down, or enveloped by an encompassing semitint."[1]

The Red House seems a perfect example of Duret's description, as both the front and the side of the red house placed diagonally on the left of the composition can be seen simultaneously. Sunlight hits the red and white surface of the house, making the colors shine with a brilliance that is accentuated in comparison to the muted, darker tone of the shaded side. The expansive sky and the white clouds above intensify this play of bright colors.

The main focus of the painting is the yellow and green field, dotted with white and red flowers. A row of houses and trees, fencing off the field, faces the viewer in the middle ground. This compositional scheme situates the viewer in a fiction, as if she approaches the cluster of houses from an open field, glimpsing a cropped and seemingly arbitrary snapshot. This effect is the result, however, of a careful orchestration of colors and forms; the natural and man-made are tightly intermingled, enveloping and imitating one another.

This composition is very similar to a work by Claude Monet from the same year that features a group of houses on a cloudy day.[2] While Pissarro's work is an exercise in mass and volume, Monet focuses on the dramatic light in the sky and shadows of clouds that fall on the houses.

The Red House was once in the collection of Jean-Baptiste Faure, a famous opera singer and one of the earliest supporters of the Impressionists. Faure also collected works by the Barbizon artists and Édouard Manet. In 1902 he had twenty-four paintings by Pissarro in his collection. The collector's name starts appearing in Pissarro's correspondence as a patron in 1873.[3]

GÇ

1. Excerpt from Théodore Duret's *Les Peintres impressionistes* (1878), reprinted in *Monet: A Retrospective*, ed. Charles Stuckey (New York: Hugh Lauter Levin Associates, 1985), 65.
2. Claude Monet, *Houses at Argenteuil*, 1873, oil on canvas, Nationalgalerie, Staatliche Museen zu Berlin, Berlin, Germany.
3. In a letter to Duret written on December 26, 1873, Pissarro related that he was going to Paris to show some of his paintings to Faure and to Pierre-Ferdinand Martin. Le père Martin seems to have been the first official dealer of Pissarro's work, appearing as the artist's Paris agent in the 1870 Salon catalogue. Camille Pissarro to Théodore Duret, December 26, 1873, *Correspondance de Camille Pissarro*, ed. Janine Bailly-Herzberg, 5 vols. (Paris: Presses Universitaires de France, 1980–91), 1:88–89.

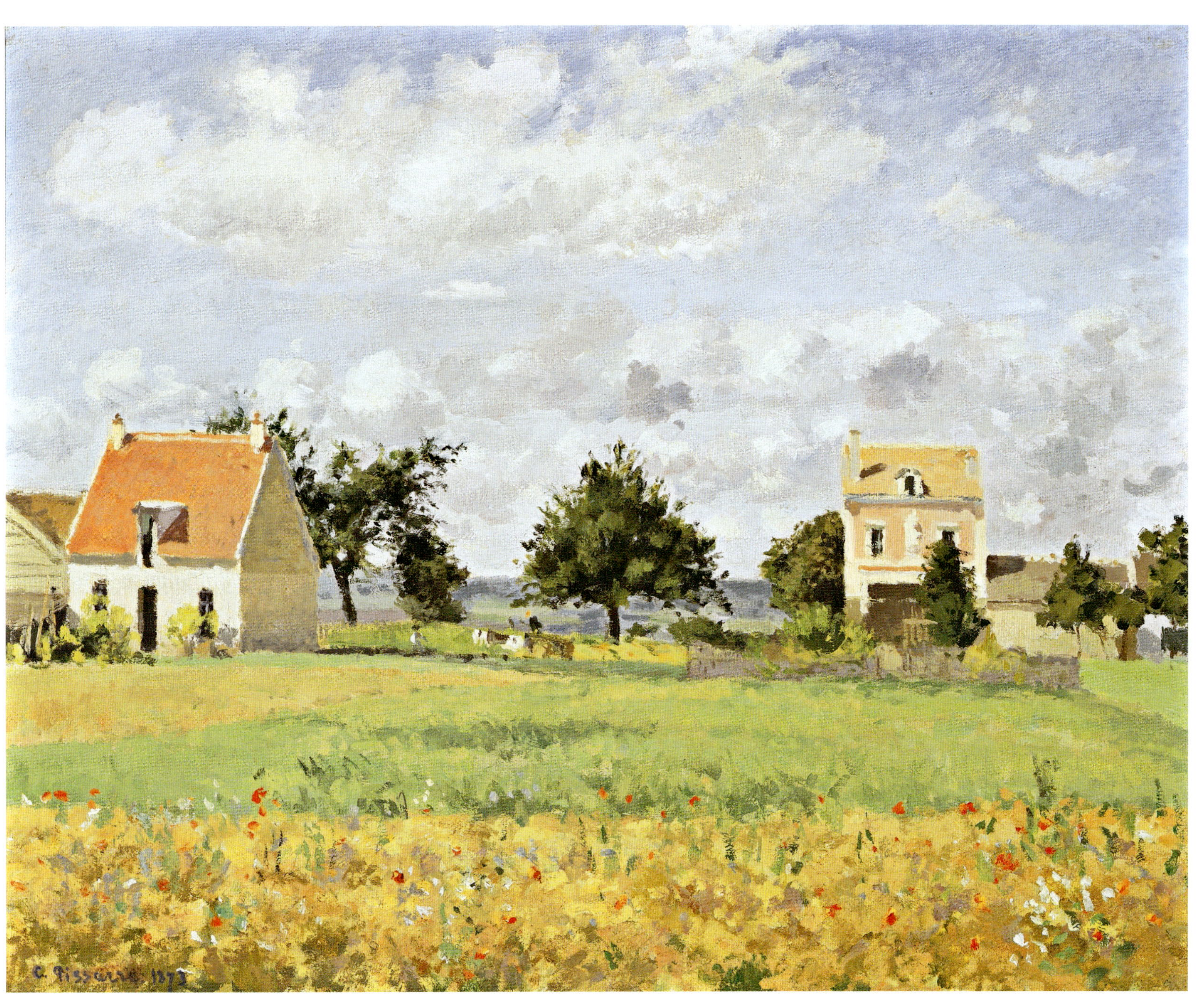
C. Pissarro. 1873

42
Chestnut Trees at Osny

c. 1873 (PD-RS 313)

Oil on canvas
25 1/2 × 31 3/4 in. (65 × 81 cm)
Collection of Jacqueline J. McMullen
Baltimore and Milwaukee only

1. Marc de Montifaud, *L'Artiste*, May 1, 1874, quoted in PD-RS 313.

This landscape, along with four others, was exhibited by Pissarro in the first Impressionist show in 1874. Unlike *Hoarfrost at Ennery* (cat. 43), which was ridiculed by several members of the press for its strange composition and rough handling, *Chestnut Trees at Osny* was mentioned in only one review of the revolutionary exhibition. The critic Marc de Montifaud seemed taken with the artist's work, despite his feeling that Pissarro's style was not yet fully defined: "The *Chestnut Trees at Osny* of Camille Pissarro, rather crude tones, but the richly rendered fields proclaim serious intentions beneath an envelope that is as yet unsophisticated."[1]

Here the artist has returned to a compositional device that first appeared in *View of Alleyn Park, West Dulwich* (cat. 23) in 1871, *répoussoir* trees on either side of the composition to frame the landscape within. This technique, frequently used by artists in the seventeenth and eighteenth century, provided Pissarro with another way to construct his work and can be considered part of his lifelong quest to experiment with both old and new ideas in his paintings. Unlike *View of Alleyn Park, West Dulwich*, however, where the artist focused on a group of houses and a train moving through the suburban landscape within the embrace of thinning foliage, here the trees are in full leaf, allowing only a glimpse into a somewhat undefined location in the distance.

The composition is divided into three bands: a field in the foreground, cultivated land in the distance that is bisected by two strong diagonal shapes that reach across almost the entire width of the painting, and the sky above. Four resplendent chestnut trees stand at the boundary between the foreground and middle ground, their abundant leaves obscuring most of the view. They dwarf a small male figure below, who bends over to carry something under his left arm as he moves through the landscape. The trees and the foreground are in shadow, but the landscape beyond is in sunlight. The construction of the composition and the use of light and shadow lead the viewer's eye to the fields in the middle ground and the small townscape that is barely visible on the rise of the hill in the far distance, details that seem unworthy of such attention amid such lush, graceful elements of nature seen in the foreground.

The field in the foreground is energetically painted with broken brushstrokes of tan, brown, and green, in a loose and free style that is typical of Pissarro's work of the early 1870s. It is similar to the thick strokes used for the leaves above, but vastly different from the wide areas of orange and ocher paint used to depict the fields in the middle distance. This is a composition that combines historic and modern elements seamlessly, and it was probably for this reason that the artist chose to include it in the first Impressionist exhibition as a statement of his best work of the time.

KR

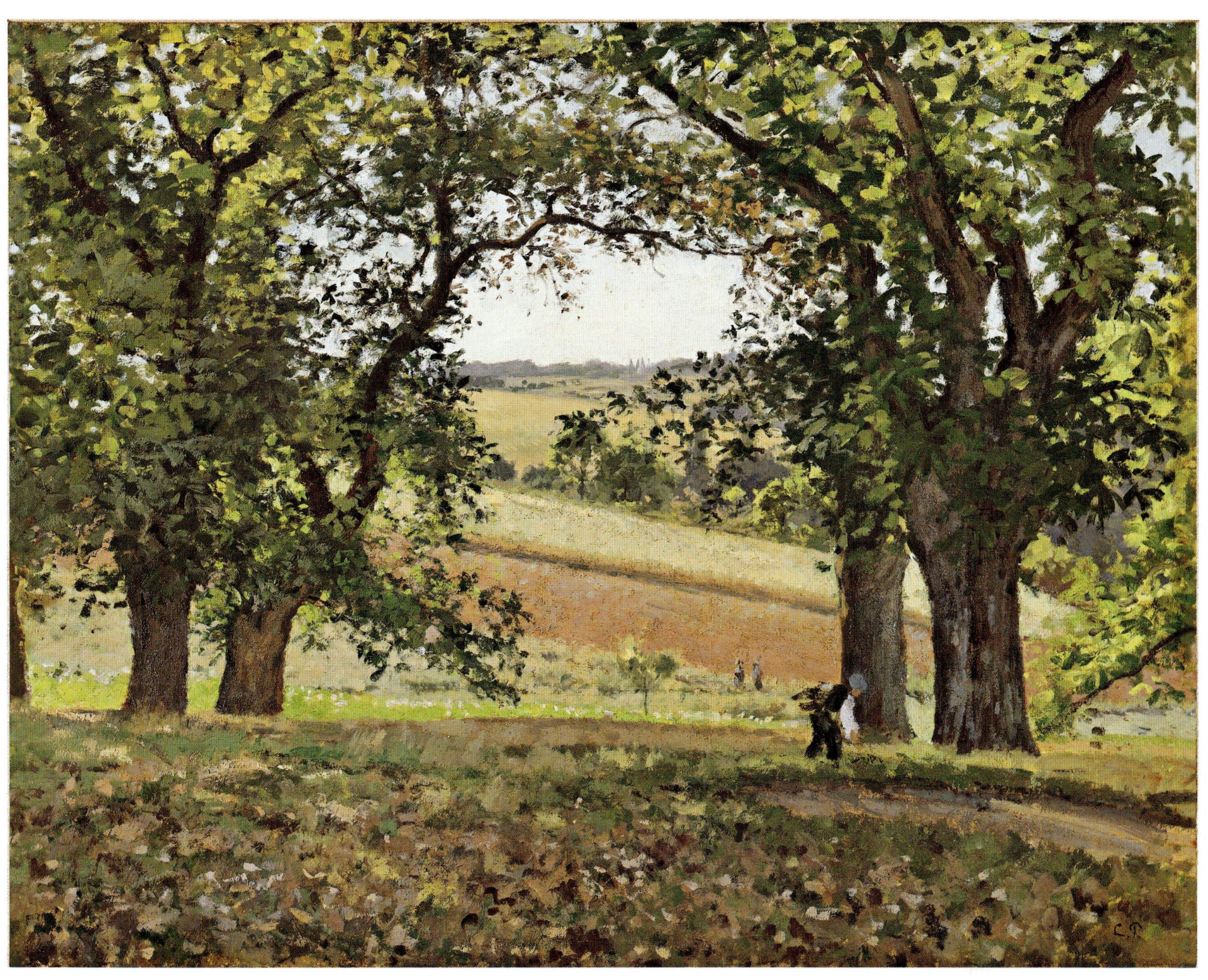

43
Hoarfrost at Ennery
Hoarfrost, the Old Road to Ennery
1873 (PD-RS 285)

Oil on canvas
25 5/8 × 36 5/8 in. (65 × 93 cm)
Musée d'Orsay, Paris, France

Painted in 1873, this is a view of the old road that ran between Pontoise and Ennery, a farming village located near Pissarro's home. A more modern version of the thoroughfare had been built by the time that the artist chose this site, making this older roadway obsolete and therefore ideal for his rural subject.[1] Pissarro produced this work after the harvest; the fields have been plowed for the following season, and haystacks dot the landscape. The furrows of the field in the foreground commingle with a remarkable set of highly colored and textured shadows cast by an equally spaced line of trees, probably poplars, which are located outside the picture plane. Jules-Antoine Castagnary, critical of the artist's decision to include these unusual shadows but supportive of the artist's work in general, remarked in his exhibition review: "Pissarro is sober and strong. His synthesizing eye embraces at a glance the whole scene. He commits the grave error of painting fields (*Gelée blanche*) with shadows cast by trees placed outside the frame. As a result the viewer is left to suppose they exist, as he cannot see them."[2]

At first glance, the road appears almost subsumed by its surroundings, barely distinguishable from the fields that border it. It cuts diagonally across the countryside, neatly dividing the composition into three parts: the path and fields to the left, the fields to the right, and the sky above. A male peasant carries a large bundle of sticks on his back as he moves up the path with the aid of a walking stick. The figure closely resembles one in a work from the following year that also depicts the outskirts of Pontoise (cat. 47). For Pissarro, this repeating character had become a symbol of the peasant worker, a member of society for whom the artist felt a great affinity. This work has often been compared to Jean-François Millet's images of peasants, although here the figure does not appear to be suffering under the burden of his existence in quite the same way nor is he the focus of the composition.[3] Instead, Pissarro concentrates on the relationship between the solitary figure and the land that surrounds him, even enveloping him in a blue shadow that marks the ground behind him. A thin layer of morning frost will quickly melt on this sunny day. This hint of the transitory quality of weather conditions is overridden by the timeless mood of the composition and its rural subject.

Louis Leroy, a critic who was unsupportive of the new painting style of Pissarro and his colleagues, was astounded at the lack of finish and sense of coarseness in the composition. In his review of the 1874 exhibition, he invented a conversation between himself and another visitor to the show:

> "Then, very quietly, with my most naïve air, I led him before the *Ploughed Field* of M. Pissarro. At the sight of this astounding landscape, the good man thought that the lenses of his spectacles were dirty. He wiped them carefully and replaced them on his nose. "By Michalon!" he cried. "What on earth is that?"
> "You see . . . a hoarfrost on deeply ploughed furrows."
> "Those furrows? That frost? But they are palette-scrapings placed uniformly on a dirty canvas. It has neither head nor tail, top nor bottom, front nor back."[4]

What Leroy saw as a dirty canvas covered in palette scrapings is in actuality one of the most experimental works of Pissarro's early career. Here he freely explored technique, texture, color, and pattern in this poetic elegy to the beauty and poignancy of the place where he lived and worked.

KR

1. See Richard Brettell et al., *A Day in the Country: Impressionism and the French Landscape* (Los Angeles: Los Angeles County Museum of Art, 1984), 248.
2. Jules-Antoine Castagnary, *Le Siècle*, April 29, 1874, quoted and translated in Charles S. Moffett et al., *The New Painting: Impressionism, 1874–1886* (San Francisco: The Fine Arts Museums of San Francisco, 1986), 138.
3. See Jean-François Millet's *Winter*, 1868–74, oil on canvas, National Museum of Wales, Cardiff, where the main figure is barely able to carry her oversized bundle of sticks.
4. Louis Leroy, *Le Charivari*, April 25, 1874, quoted and translated in *The New Painting*, 138.

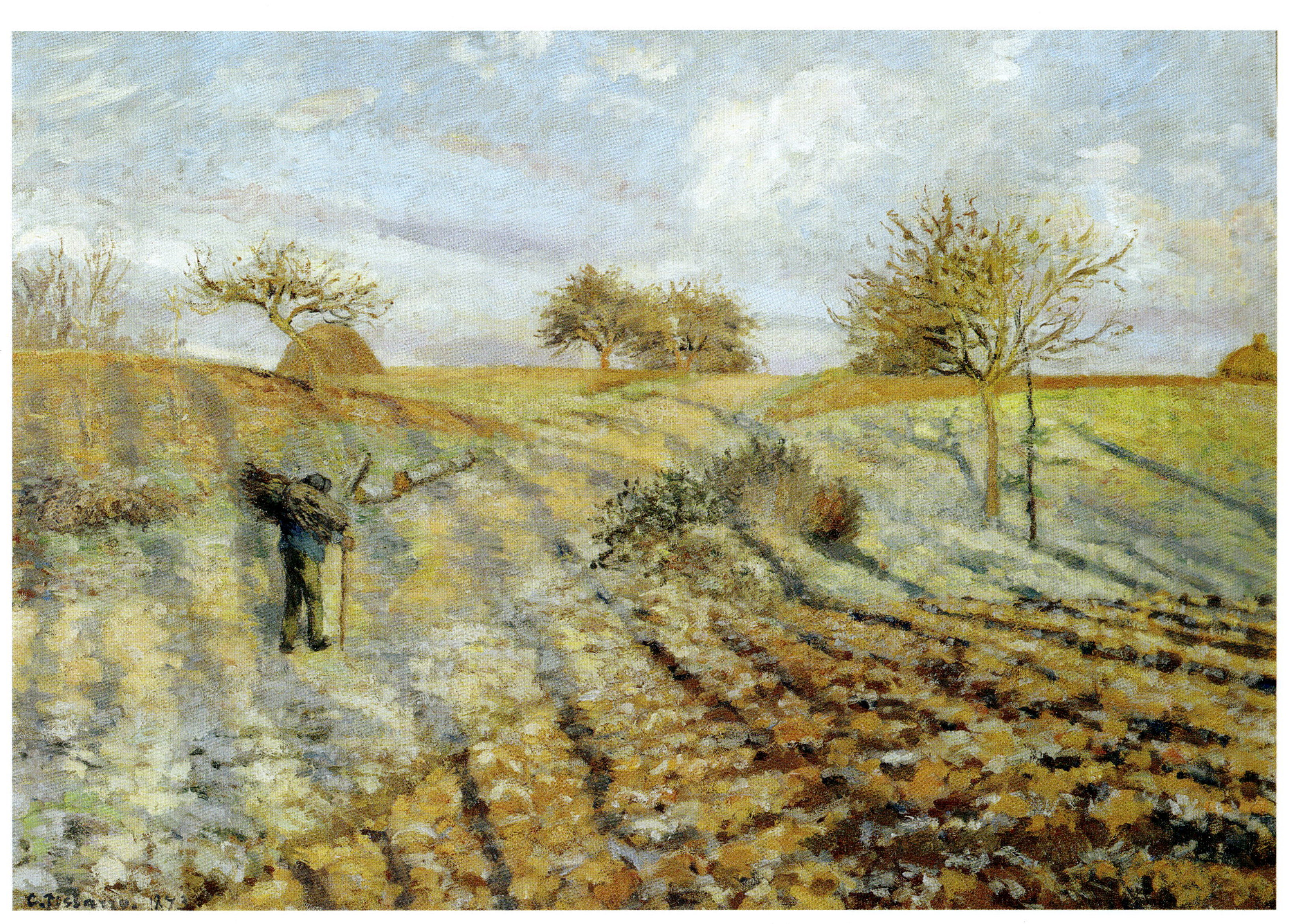

44
View of the Côte des Mathurins, Pontoise
Hill at l'Hermitage, Pontoise
1873 (PD-RS 291)

Oil on canvas
23 5/8 × 28 3/4 in. (61 × 73 cm)
Musée d'Orsay, Paris, France

This painting features a small, hunched figure treading along a precipitous street leading up a hill. The art historian Richard Brettell has identified the road as the rue de Fond de l'Hermitage in Pontoise, which was abandoned when an alternative thoroughfare, the rue de l'Hermitage, was finished in 1866.[1] The rue de Fond de l'Hermitage retained its eighteenth-century architecture and agricultural character, being forced to coexist with large mansions surrounded by pleasure gardens.[2] In *View of the Côte des Mathurins, Pontoise,* one of these mansions is depicted at the upper right.[3]

In addition to a general movement of ascent, from left to right, Pissarro includes other devices to mark a sharp recession into space: the diagonal lines of the wall, the borders of rectangular kitchen gardens, and the street all produce an effect of steepness. This incline and the difficulty of the hike are emphasized by the figure's bent left arm, which supports his back while he makes his strenuous trip. These devices encourage the viewer to see the hill as both particularly steep and spatially ambiguous: although the cottages are seen from the front, the kitchen gardens before them as well as the path on which the man is walking are depicted from a bird's-eye view. When Pissarro returned to this motif a year later in the *Effect of Snow at L'Hermitage, Pontoise* (cat. 45), he did not resort to these devices, preferring instead to depict a unified and frontal scene.

The severe foreshortening of the road, the bird's-eye view, and the stylized posture of the figure reflect the influence of Japanese prints.[4] The artist admired Japanese colored woodcuts, especially the compositions of the nineteenth-century artist Utagawa Hiroshige, for their bold perspective with sudden foreshortenings and uncommon viewpoints, flat areas of color, and sophisticated graphic language depicting a variety of atmospheric effects. In his letters to his son Lucien, he repeatedly voiced his admiration for these woodcuts and his conviction in the common vision shared by Japanese artists and the Impressionists. After seeing a Japanese woodcut exhibition at Durand-Ruel's gallery in early February 1893, he enthusiastically wrote to Lucien, "I saw Monet at the Japanese show. Damn it all, if this show does not justify us! There are grey sunsets that are the most striking instances of impressionism."[5]

GÇ

1. Richard R. Brettell, "Pissarro and Pontoise: Painter in a Landscape" (Ph.D. diss., Yale University, 1977), 181.
2. Ibid.
3. In a lithograph of the same subject, *Maison à l'Ermitage,* Pissarro excludes the mansion and focuses on the cottage, its stone wall, and the kitchen gardens outside this wall by the side of the road. See Loys Delteil, *Le Peintre-graveur illustré,* vol. 17, *Pissarro, Sisley, Renoir* (Paris: chez l'auteur, 1923), D 133.
4. See cat. 49 for more on Pissarro and Japanese art.
5. Camille Pissarro to Lucien Pissarro, February 2, 1893, in *Letters to His Son Lucien,* ed. John Rewald (New York: Pantheon Books, 1943), 206.

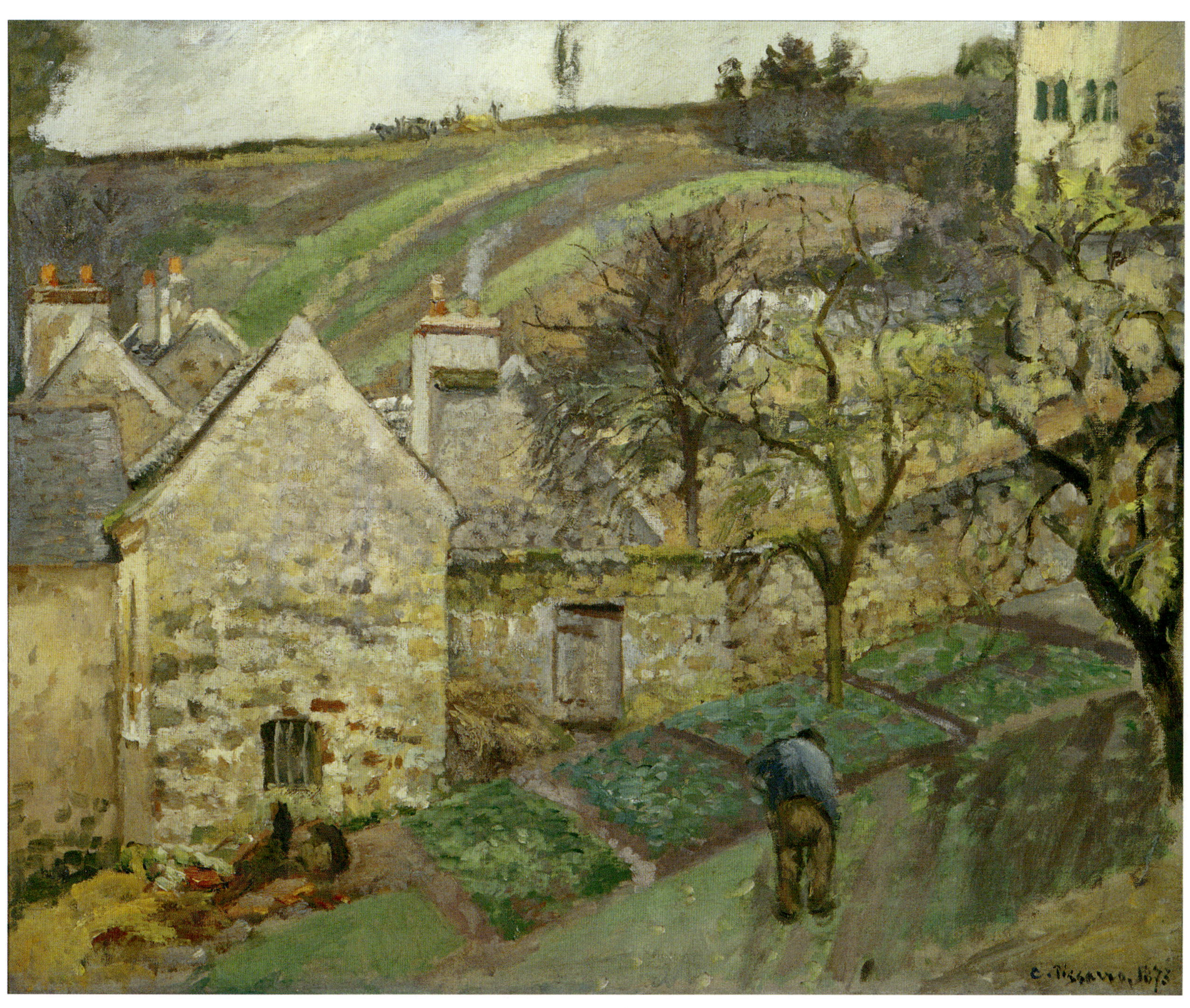
C. Pissarro. 1873

45

Effect of Snow at L'Hermitage, Pontoise

Snow at Hermitage, Pontoise

1874 (PD-RS 327)

Oil on canvas
21 ½ × 25 ¾ in. (54.5 × 65.5 cm)
Private collection

Effect of Snow at L'Hermitage, Pontoise was one of twelve works Pissarro submitted to the second Impressionist exhibition, which opened at the Galerie Durand-Ruel in Paris in April 1876. Organized by the Société anonyme des artistes, peintres, sculpteurs, graveurs, etc., of which Pissarro was one of the founding members, these exhibitions by independent artists were intended to reach the public directly, eschewing the mediation of the official Salon and the politics of its jury.[1]

Pissarro's paintings, mostly landscapes, were exhibited in the same room with Edgar Degas's seamstresses, dancers, portraits, and the idiosyncratic *Cotton Exchange at New Orleans*. Common to these seemingly different thematic interests was the hostility of their reviewers. Both artists were criticized for exhibiting incomplete, unfinished works, having no understanding of color, and of throwing general impressions on canvas or paper without filling in details. Émile Petitdidier, writing under the pseudonym Émile Blémont, announced to his readers of the republican newspaper *Le Rappel* that there was no single finished painting by Degas in the exhibition, all his entries being excellent *esquisses* (sketches). He continued, "Pissaro [*sic*] has a manner that pleases us much less." Remarking on a painting of a fog effect by Pissarro, the critic sarcastically suggested that perhaps the artist imagined that painting a tableau with a fog effect meant painting nothing except the fog.[2]

Effect of Snow at L'Hermitage, Pontoise itself did not receive any mention in the reviews. Art critics closer to the Impressionist circle wrote more favorably about Pissarro, without dwelling on the particularities of any one work. Émile Zola, in his review for *Le Messager de l'Europe* (published in St. Petersburg for the Russian audience), praised Pissarro's brushwork that was simpler and more naïve than Monet's. He defended the artist's multicolored landscapes, which he conceded might irritate the uninitiated who does not comprehend the artist's ambitions.[3] Armand Silvestre, perhaps having the fog effect painting in mind or thinking of the overall blue tonality of *Effect of Snow at l'Hermitage, Pontoise*, argued that Pissarro's blues had a charming delicacy, but he tended to envelop his paintings with them.[4]

Effect of Snow at L'Hermitage, Pontoise revisits a motif Pissarro painted a year earlier in *View of the Côte des Mathurins, Pontoise* (cat. 44). Devices such as the high viewpoint and foreshortening of only certain elements in the landscape, seen in the earlier painting, do not occur here. Instead, Pissarro approaches the same scene with an intention to unite all the elements in the landscape rather than underscoring their disjunction. A lower vantage point gives a head-on view of the cottages and the gardens. Here everything in sight is covered by a blanket of snow. The clouds cast their shadows on the earth and unify the composition in a color scheme of blue and violet. Pissarro and the other Impressionists received much negative comment in the 1870s for the way they painted light and shade. Making use of complementary colors, Pissarro and his colleagues applied a variety of purple and blue tints to depict shadows cast by objects illuminated by yellow or orange sunlight.

Although it did not receive any critical acclaim or attention in 1876, *Effect of Snow at L'Hermitage, Pontoise* was exhibited again in Pissarro's 1904 retrospective organized by Durand-Ruel in Paris.

GÇ

1. The first show was held in 1874, but a second one did not follow the subsequent year, as a public auction at the Hôtel Drouot of works by some members of the core group was a financial disaster. It was in 1876, two years after the first exhibition, that the group convened for a second time under the initiative of the collector and painter Gustave Caillebotte. The resulting exhibition was much smaller than the first one: a total number of nineteen artists exhibited 252 works.
2. Émile Blémont, "Les Impressionistes," *Le Rappel*, April 9, 1876, reprinted in Ruth Berson, *The New Painting: Impressionism, 1874–1886; Documentation*, 2 vols. (San Francisco: Fine Arts Museums of San Francisco, 1996), 1:64.
3. Émile Zola, "Deux Expositions d'art au mois de mai," *Le Messager de l'Europe*, June 1876, in ibid., 1:113.
4. Armand Silvestre, "Exposition de la rue Le Peletier," *L'Opinion nationale*, April 2, 1876, in ibid., 1:109.

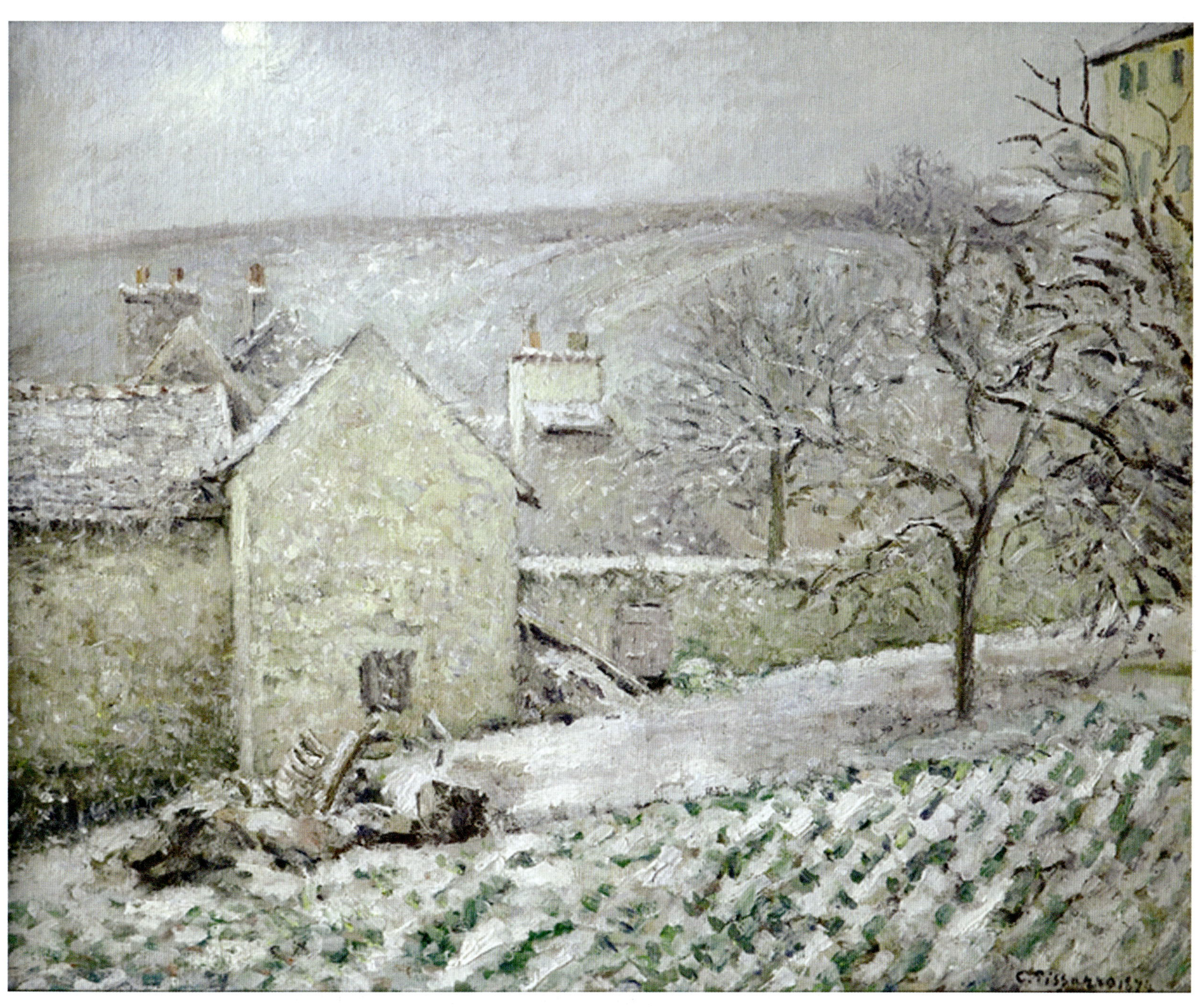

46
Peasant Woman with a Wheelbarrow, the "Rondest House," Pontoise
Landscape from Pontoise
1874 (PD-RS 337)

Oil on canvas
25 1/2 × 20 1/8 in. (65 × 51 cm)
The National Museum of Fine Arts, Stockholm
Baltimore only

Peasant Woman with a Wheelbarrow, the "Rondest House," Pontoise is one of several paintings set in the L'Hermitage hamlet of Pontoise. The most salient feature of Pissarro's treatment of L'Hermitage between 1867 and 1873 is the drastic simplification of the landscape (see cats. 44 and 45). *Côte des Jalais, Pontoise* (cat. 10), one of the earliest works by Pissarro to represent this area, sets the model for the later works by geometrizing the landscape, depicting a world of schematized, cube-like houses with pyramidal roofs and hills striped by colored rectangular bands of cultivated fields. *Peasant Woman with a Wheelbarrow, the "Rondest House," Pontoise* offers a radically different interpretation. In the foreground, the familiar cubic shapes of the architecture at L'Hermitage are partially screened by curving contours of the tree branches and the purple shadows cast by their sinuous forms. Unlike Pissarro's treatment of this subject in his 1867–68 Jalais Hill series, these houses are not large, white planes that uniformly reflect the sunlight off their white surfaces but zones of color where myriad effects of broad daylight can be observed.

Here a peasant pushes a wheelbarrow through a gate crowned by intertwined branches, a motif the artist had employed in an earlier painting, *View of Alleyn Park, West Dulwich* (cat. 23). In the later composition, however, trees do not merely frame an event that takes place in the background. Space in the foreground pushes the trees to the middle distance, somewhere between the peasant woman and the townscape at the background. This foreground space privileges the peasant who is in motion, approaching the viewer, implying that she is going to walk farther. The centrality of a single figure in the landscape foreshadows the series of large peasant paintings Pissarro would embark on in the 1880s and 1890s. This interest in the activities of peasants can also be followed in Pissarro's drawings, engravings, and lithographs from the period.[1] In earlier landscapes small-scale human figures whose bodies consist of a few brushstrokes often imitate other forms in the landscape (cat. 27); sometimes they tentatively tread on an earth that looks too two-dimensional to inhabit (cats. 43, 44, and 48); or at other times they are subordinate to a rigorously geometric structure (cat. 16). Here the figure neither emulates her surroundings nor does she merge with and disappear in the landscape.

In this painting, Pissarro uses different brushwork to produce a multilayered surface with various textural effects, such as the rough surface of a stone wall or the wet moss covering it. The handling of the brush and the opacity of the paint attract attention to the dense materiality of the surface, which is especially observable in the treatment of the solid wall to the right. In addition to his interest in surface texture, a new color scheme reflects the culmination of a period of cooperation with Paul Cézanne, an artist who shared Pissarro's vision closely during this period.[2] Most of Cézanne's paintings made in Pontoise and Auvers under Pissarro's guidance from 1872 to 1874 display a heavy reliance on contrasts of blue and yellow, as well as different shades of green. This green, blue, and yellow palette occurs in several of Pissarro's works as well, becoming salient especially in 1874 and 1875. This palette was part of a radically new pictorial language in which the two artists sought to represent, with the limited range of colored pigments available at the time, a wide array of light effects they observed in nature.[3]
GÇ

1. Pissarro's first lithographs depicting working peasant women are dated to 1874: See Loys Delteil, *Le peintre-graveur illustré*, vol. 17, *Pissarro, Sisley, Renoir* (Paris: chez l'auteur, 1923). D 134, *Women Carrying Hay*; D 136, *Haymaker*; D 137, *Woman Collecting Hay*. A peasant woman with a wheelbarrow appears in a later engraving from 1880, D 31, *Woman Emptying a Wheelbarrow*. For a drawing possibly related to the painting, see Richard Brettell and Christopher Lloyd, *A Catalogue of the Drawings by Camille Pissarro in the Ashmolean Museum, Oxford* (Oxford: Clarendon Press, 1980), 85A recto.
2. See cat. 34 for more on the relationship between Cézanne and Pissarro.
3. See Anthea Callen, *The Art of Impressionism: Painting Technique and the Making of Modernity* (New Haven: Yale University Press, 2000), 123, for more on the Impressionists' use of color contrasts as a shorthand technique to represent the myriad effects of broad daylight.

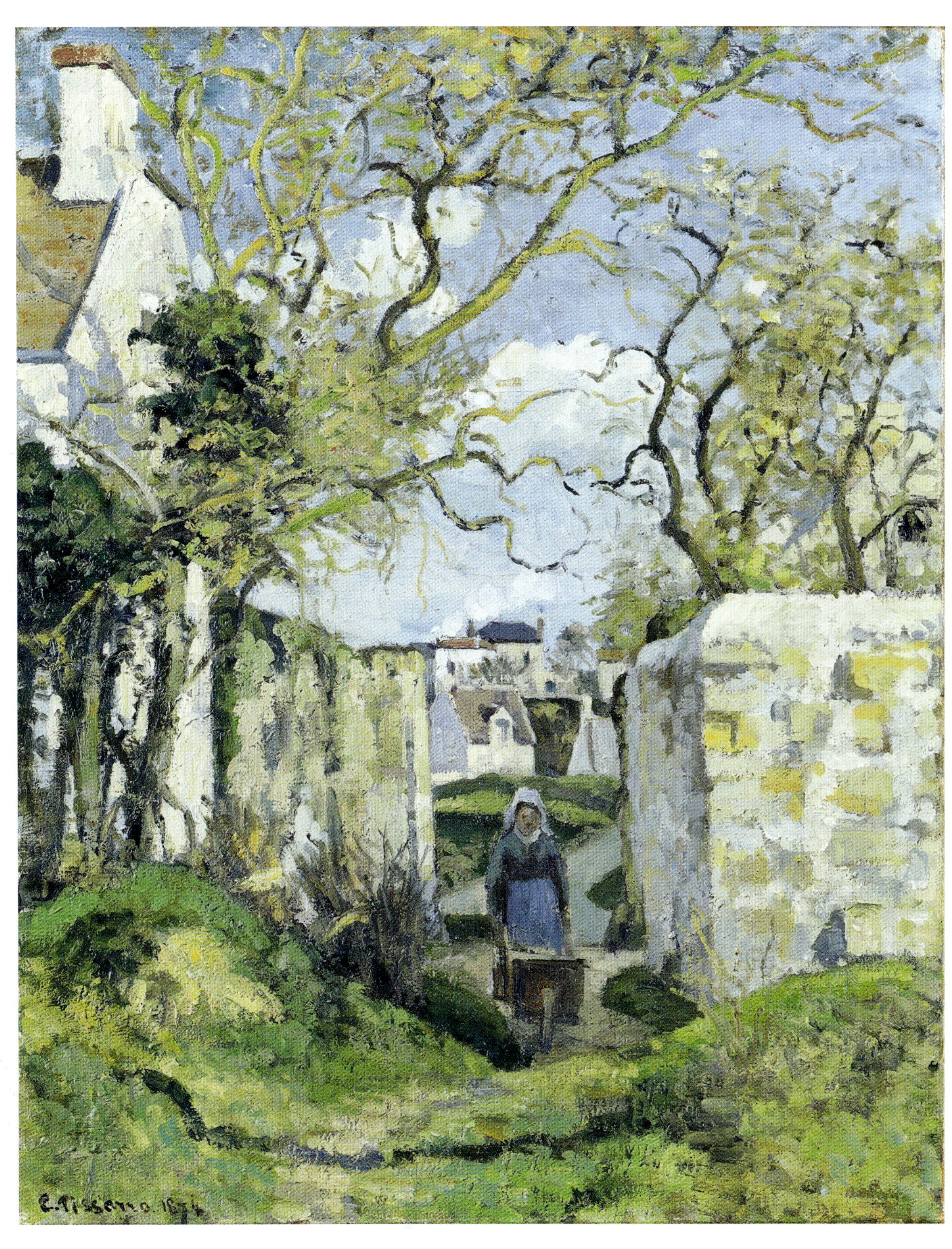

47

Rue de l'Hermitage at Pontoise

Road to Ennery near Pontoise

1874 (PD-RS 349)

Oil on canvas
21 5/8 × 36 1/4 in. (55 × 92 cm)
Musée d'Orsay, Paris, France

In October 1873 Pissarro and his family moved into a house on the rue de l'Hermitage, a peaceful lane that led from the L'Hermitage neighborhood of Pontoise into the countryside. It linked to another road that eventually led to the small village of Ennery, located almost five miles to the north. Ennery was an agricultural town, known for its grain and hayfields. Pissarro was probably attracted to this location as a subject because it was very rural and surrounded by scenic fields. When compared to a pre-Impressionist view of this area from Pissarro's first stay in Pontoise in the late 1860s (cat. 11), one can easily see how his style has changed dramatically over the course of six years. Gone are the rich, dark colors and the thick, wet brushstrokes. They have been replaced by a drier touch, smaller brushstrokes, and a vivid green palette. In addition, a reinvigorated interest in geometric structure is apparent here, evident in the fields that are neatly divided into trapezoidal and triangular forms, all carefully linked by a series of paths and borders. This concentration on geometry was presumably a result of the close working relationship between Pissarro and Paul Cézanne, who was living in nearby Auvers at this time.

Unlike his numerous street scenes of Louveciennes, London, and L'Hermitage, where the central perspectival structure quickly leads the viewer's eye down the road, here Pissarro has turned the roadway parallel to the picture plane and the horizon line. His easel is placed just below the road, so that the viewer does not have a clear entrance to the scene. Instead, the viewer is allowed a glimpse of the fleeting moment when figures on the road will encounter each other. Unlike some of Pissarro's other views of Pontoise, in which he juxtaposed members of different classes, here he celebrates rural life in its purest form. On the left side, a male figure walks with the aid of a walking stick, carrying a bundle over his shoulder. His form is reminiscent of the central figure in *Hoarfrost at Ennery* (cat. 43), signifying the peasant worker that has sacrified himself to the land as he walks with his belongings. A modest horse-drawn carriage carrying a man and woman is about to pass him, and two simply dressed female figures walk behind the carriage. All five figures are peasants or rural workers on their way to the fields or home. This work is a perfect example of the artist's interest in the tradition of farming and peasant life. The transitory nature of the imminent encounter of the figures on a road is juxtaposed with the sense of the slow movement of time and tradition in a rural, peaceful setting.

KR

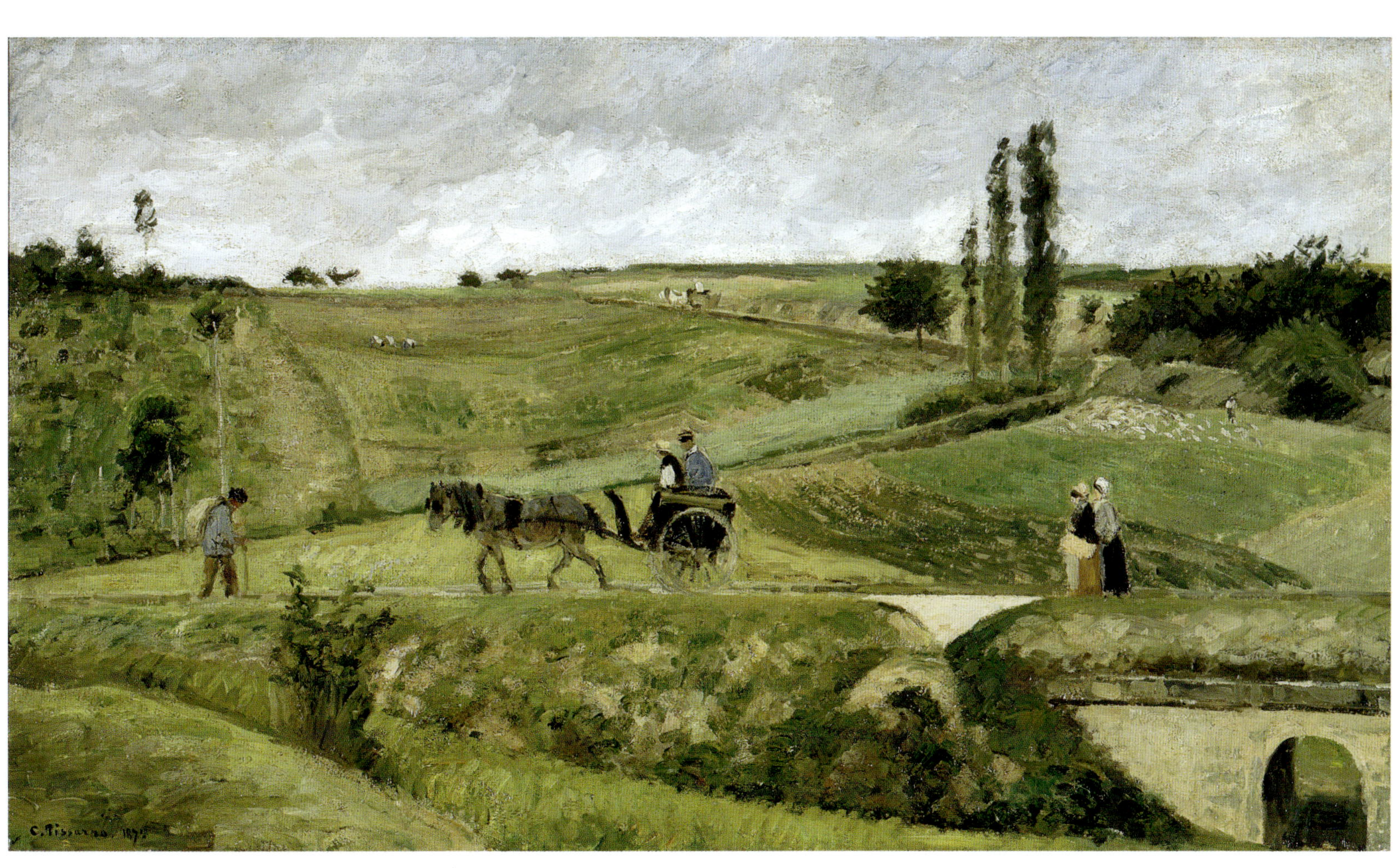
C. Pissarro

48
Landscape, Bright Sunlight, Pontoise
Sunlight on the Road, Pontoise
1874 (PD-RS 350)

Oil on canvas
20 5/8 × 32 1/8 in. (52.4 × 81.6 cm)
Museum of Fine Arts, Boston,
Juliana Cheney Edwards
Collection, 25.114

In the early 1870s Pissarro's landscapes often featured transitory and immaterial motifs such as shadows, puffs of smoke, or areas of bright light that compete with the materiality of trees, buildings, and people. Even in this context, however, the forceful presence of the triangular zone of light occupying the center of *Landscape, Bright Sunlight, Pontoise* is exceptional. In a few earlier instances, such as *The Banks of the Marne in Winter* (cat. 5) or *Place du Vieux-Cimetière, Pontoise* (cat. 31), the viewer is given a brief glimpse of the sunlight itself as it reflects off a patch of earth. In *Landscape, Bright Sunlight, Pontoise* light is given a central role. This is exemplified by the single brushstroke marking the tip of the inverted triangle of light in the foreground, which resists being part of an illusory three-dimensional world and stands there alone. It marks the tension between three-dimensional illusion and the two-dimensional flatness of the surface, which bears the marks of distinct brushstrokes that attract attention to the material qualities of the painting. Pissarro started exploring this tension between illusion and flatness, which had been implicit in his work since the mid-1860s (see cat. 8), with a renewed rigor following a period of intense experimentation with Paul Cézanne.[1]

The inclusion of the human presence would remain a constant in Pissarro's landscapes and marks one of its major differences from Cézanne's work of the same period. Here there are signs of habitation: across the river, behind a screen of trees and foliage, the orange and blue roofs of houses on the rue du Haut-de-l'Hermitage are visible.[2] A man on horseback has just passed a peasant woman walking with her child, her facial features summarily sketched with red. He appears to be waiting, with a second horse in tow. The animals are surrounded by bands of blue-gray shadow; one's first impression is that the shadows are cast by their legs. A closer look reveals that the source of these thin lines is the crowd of trees to the right. Even then, it is difficult to tell which tree casts which shadow as well as the exact place of the light source.

GÇ

1. See cat. 34 for more on the working relationship between Pissarro and Paul Cézanne.
2. See PD-RS 350 for more information on this site.

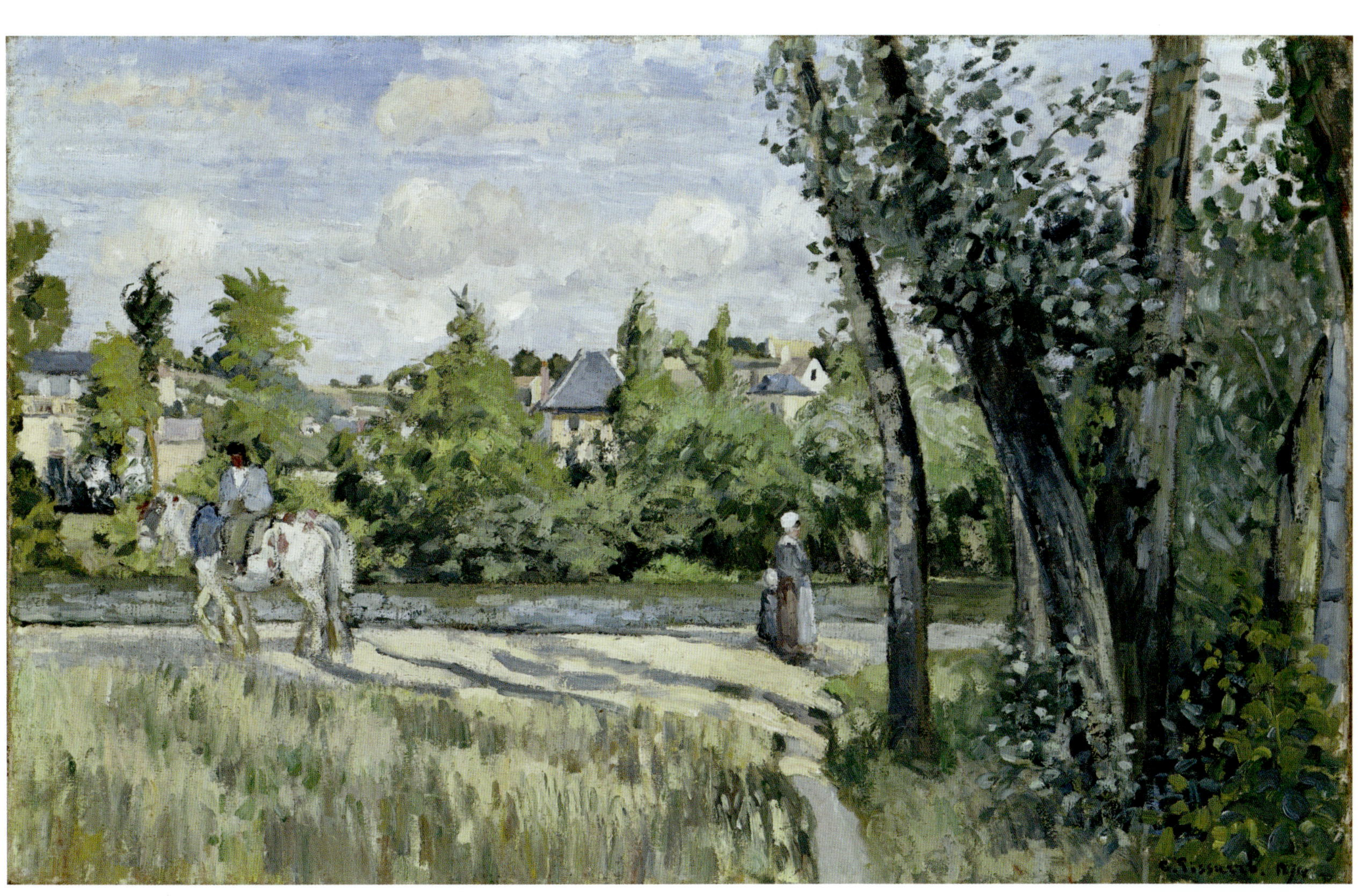

49
The Municipal Garden, Pontoise
The Public Garden at Pontoise
1874 (PD-RS 347)

Oil on canvas
23 5/8 × 28 3/4 in. (60 × 73 cm)
Lent by The Metropolitan Museum of Art, Gift of Mr. and Mrs. Arthur Murray, 1964 (64.156)
Baltimore and Milwaukee only

Themes of recreation and leisure set in urban contexts had been an important component in paintings by Monet, Sisley, and Renoir, whereas Pissarro had focused mainly on rural scenes. In *The Municipal Garden, Pontoise*, a scene of urban leisure with multiple human figures, the artist embarks on what was for him a new theme. *The Municipal Garden, Pontoise* is innovative both thematically and compositionally. Different from the majority of his paintings thus far, this work attempts to construct pictorial depth without resorting to linear perspective. This experimental approach to pictorial space reflects the artist's growing interest in the compositional tools of Japanese woodblock prints. *Dawn at Kanda Myojin Shrine* (fig. 1), a plate from Utagawa Hiroshige's famous series *One Hundred Famous Views of Edo*, first printed in Japan in 1856–58, may have provided Pissarro with a model for an alternative way of constructing space.[1]

The motif of the central pine tree in Hiroshige's print and in *The Municipal Garden, Pontoise* invites the viewer's gaze to circle around it, forcefully organizing an otherwise unmarked space. Likewise, horizontal bands of colors guide the viewer's perception of various spatial layers. Distinct from the lessons he learned from Hiroshige, Pissarro employs his own compositional tool to mark space: a subtle line of color at the lower left cuts off a roughly triangular area of blond earth from the predominant pink hue of the foreground. This line is made of tonal gradations of numerous brushstrokes and pulls the viewer's gaze from the foreground into depth, almost as far as the stone wall. This device forcefully yet very subtly suggests recession in space.

Pissarro also organizes the space through the figures, which grow increasingly small. Despite their diminutive size and lack of detail, the figures are highly expressive and delicately painted, inducing the viewer to follow them into the space they inhabit. With only a few summary brushstrokes, the artist conveys the enthusiasm of the three boys running in the background, absorbed in the game they are playing; the hesitation of the girl in blue in the foreground as she gazes at the ball in front of her, her facial features invisible yet the intensity of her gaze clearly discernible;[2] the curiosity of the toddler to the left of the tree who seems to be looking at the viewer as her mother carefully guides her; and the elegance of the women on the hilltop enjoying the view on this pleasant spring day.

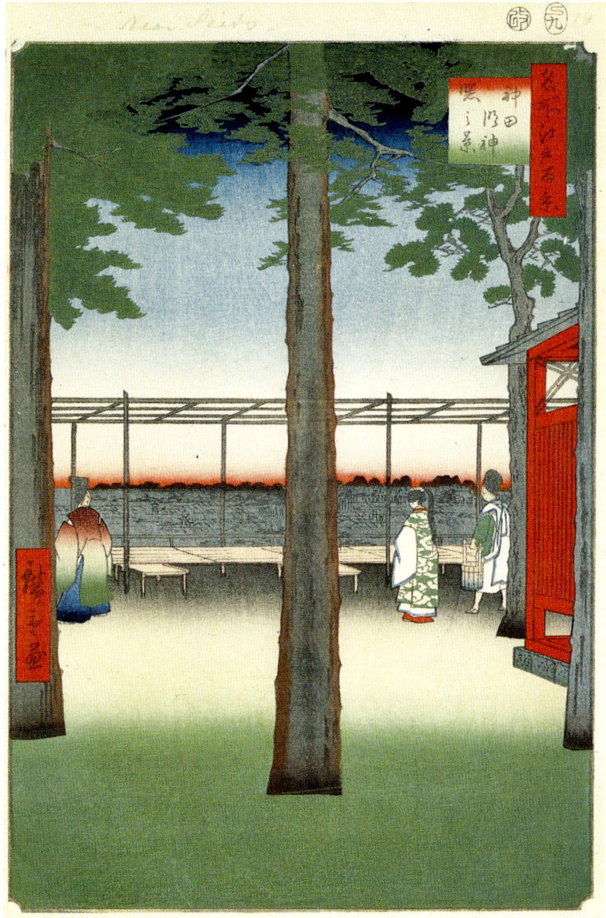
Fig. 1

1. Hiroshige's prints were known among artists in Pissarro's circle as early as 1856. The Universal Exposition held in Paris in 1867 was an important turning point in introducing French artists to Japanese art. In addition, the return of Théodore Duret, Pissarro's close friend and advisor, from a tour around the world in 1873 called the artist's attention to Japanese prints. See John Rewald, *The History of Impressionism*, 4th rev. ed. (New York: The Museum of Modern Art, 1973), 207–8.
2. Despite the cheerful mood of this painting, due to the predominance of pink as well as its theme of recreation, the girl in blue in the foreground deep in thought evokes a portrait the artist made of his daughter Jeanne Rachel, nicknamed Minette, *Portrait of Jeanne Pissarro, Called Minette*, c. 1872 (PD-RS 282), oil on canvas, Wadsworth Atheneum Museum of Art, Hartford, Connecticut, where she is also dressed in blue and standing in a similar pose. Minette died in the spring of 1874. Her death coincided with the opening of the first Impressionist exhibition.

Fig. 1. Utagawa Hiroshige, *Dawn at Kanda Myojin Shrine*, no. 10 from the series *One Hundred Famous Views of Edo*, 1857. Woodblock print. Brooklyn Museum, Gift of Anna Ferris, 30.1478.10

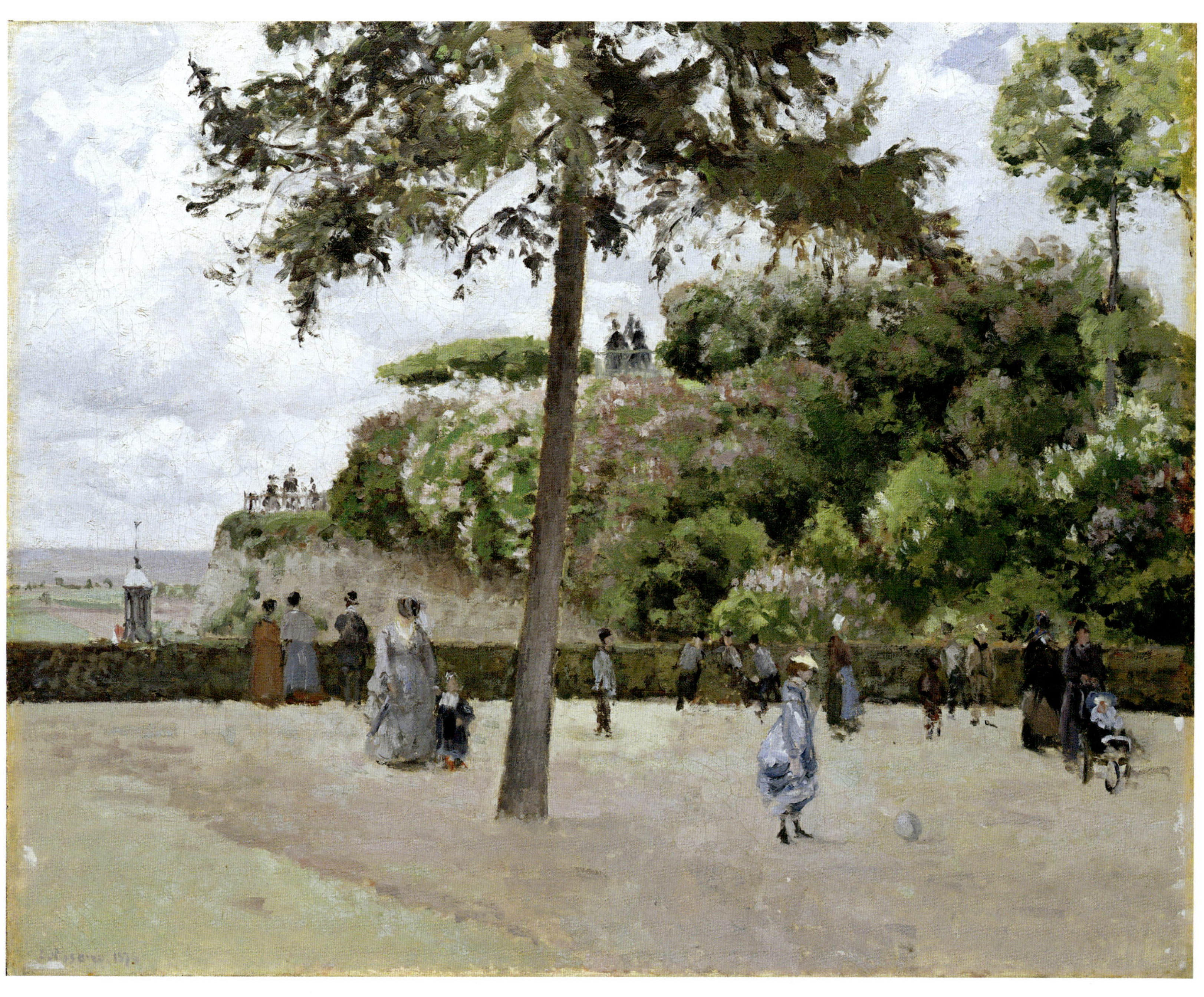

Pissarro seems to have made this painting as a pendant to the 1873 *Municipal Garden, Pontoise* (see Rothkopf essay, fig. 16), which was one of the five canvases he showed at the first Impressionist exhibition in 1874. The recreational theme with numerous figures and the predominant pink hue are common to both compositions, as are several motifs, including the girl in blue with her straw hat and the tall pine tree in the foreground. Despite these similarities, the present painting is compositionally more innovative and daring in its elimination of linear perspective. In the earlier work, the row of trees at the background to the right indicates the beginning of a shady path that leads to the depth of the woods. In the 1874 composition the artist will dispose of even this suggestion of deep space.

GÇ

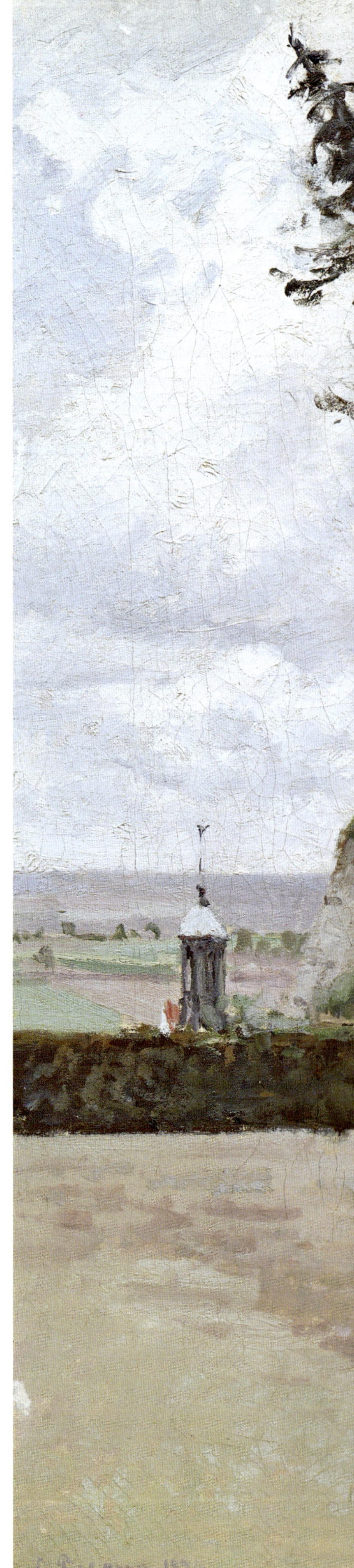

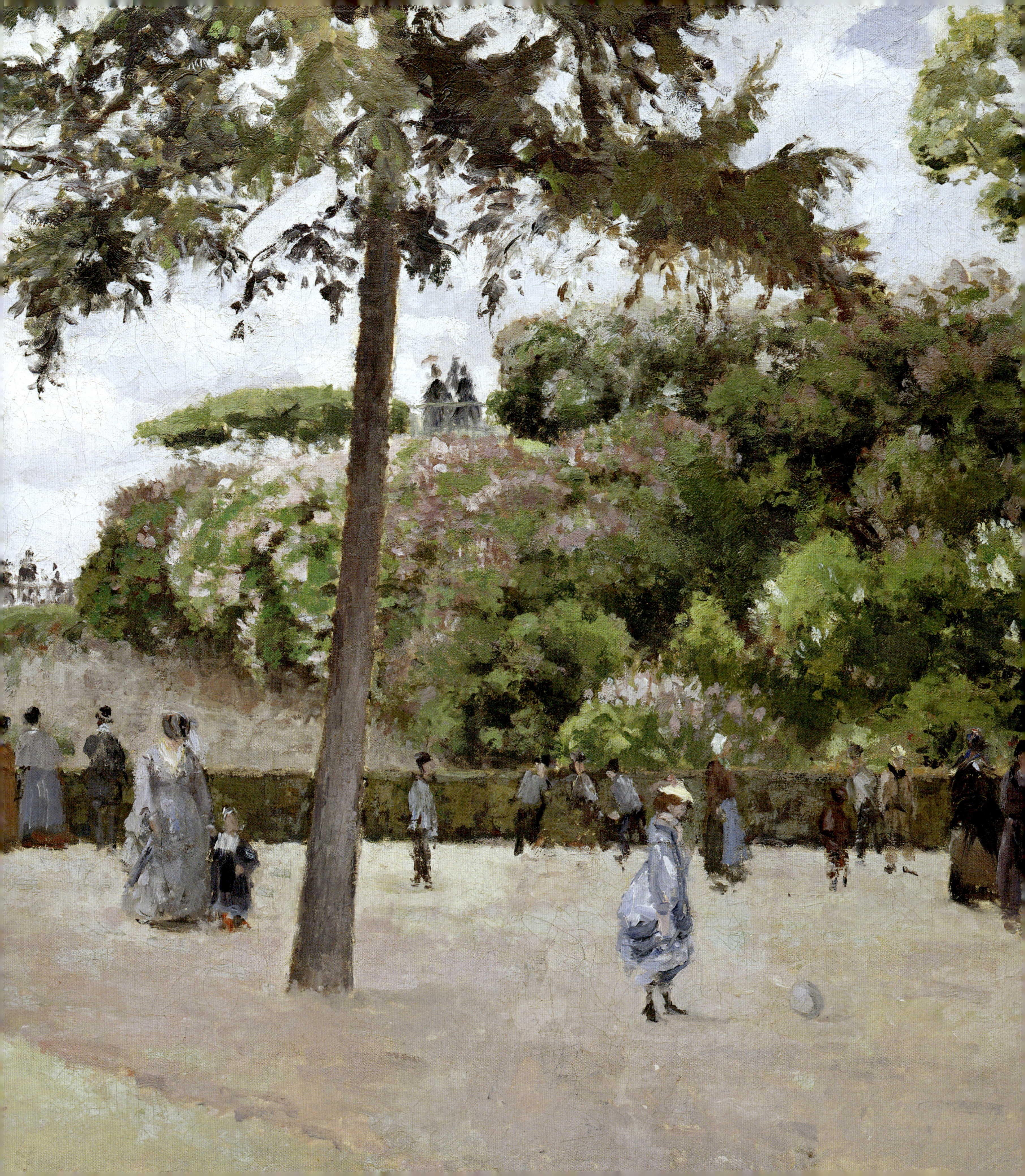

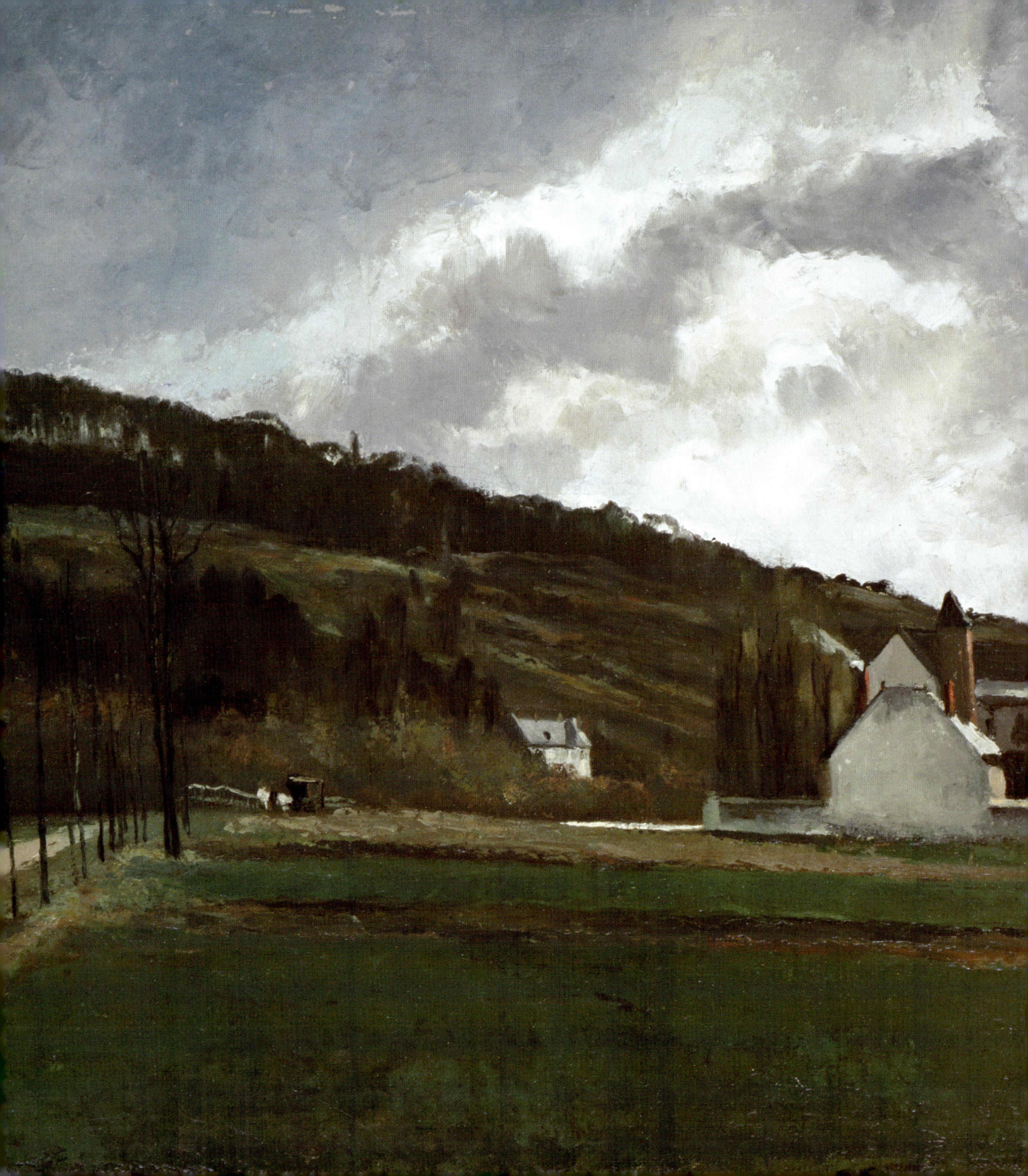

Appendixes

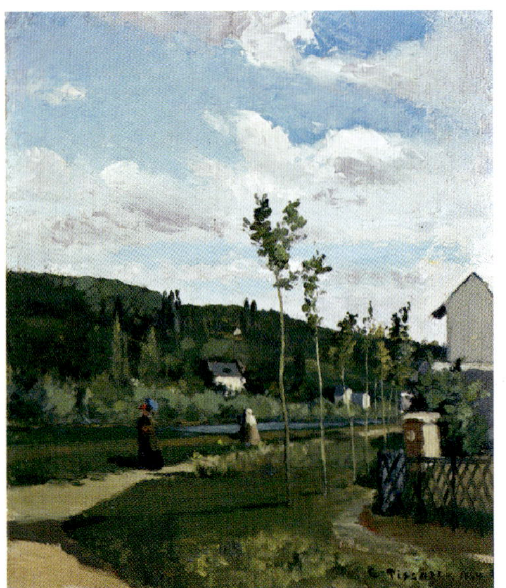

Fig. 1

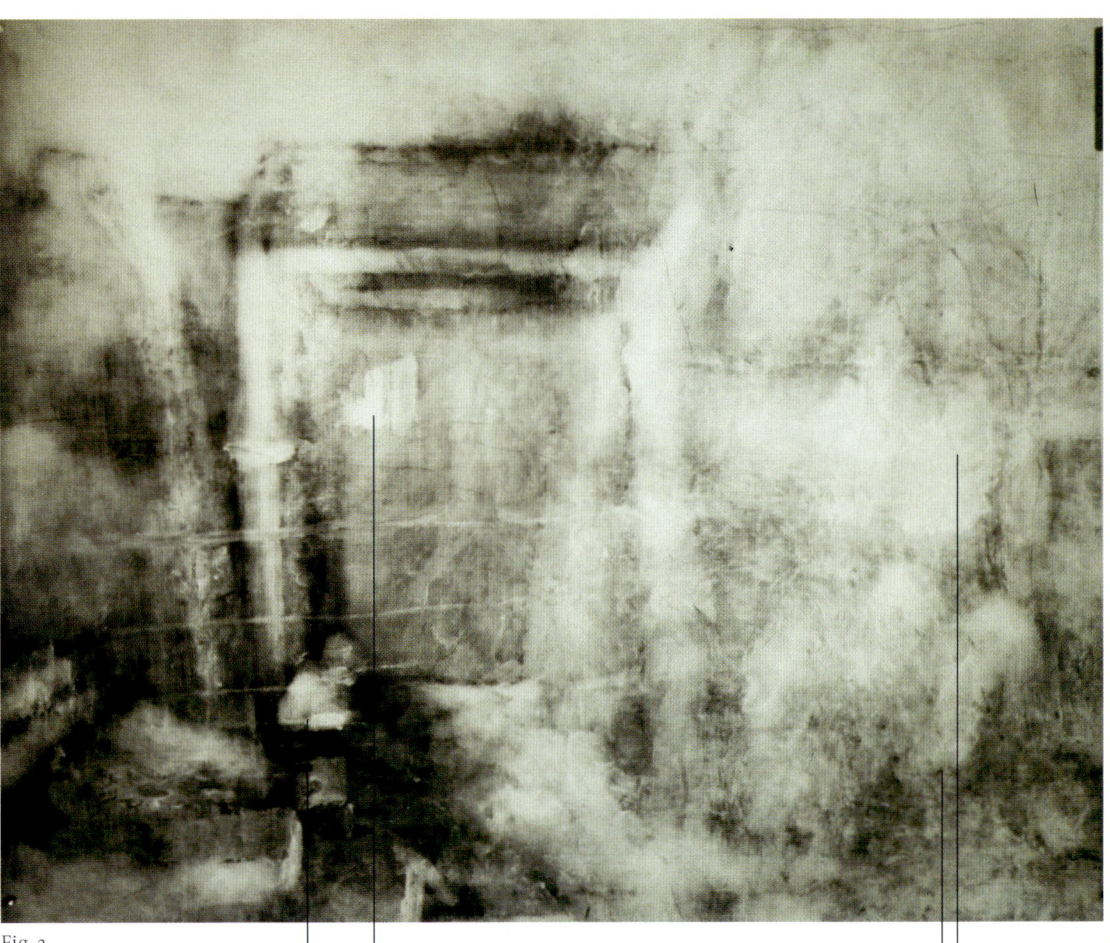

Fig. 2

Technical Notes

Mary Sebera

Fig. 1. *Strollers on a Country Road, La Varenne-Saint-Hilaire*

Fig. 2. X-radiograph of *Strollers on a Country Road, La Varenne-Saint-Hilaire*, shown in horizontal format, reveals a relatively complete painting below the visible image. It is possible to discern the figure of a woman (A) who stands in front of buildings (B). She is looking toward animals, perhaps cows (C), that stand below a large, full tree (D).

Fig. 3. Camille Pissarro, *Farmyard*, c. 1863 (PD-RS 69). Oil on canvas, 15 × 18 ½ in. (38.1 × 47.1 cm). Private collection, Chicago

Through technical analysis of four paintings produced between 1864 and 1874, the period explored in this exhibition, we learned that Pissarro made many changes while developing a particular composition. In some cases he merely adjusted the outline of a figure's arm, but at other times he made more substantial changes, such as altering horizon lines and even painting over existing motifs. Interestingly, in the 1860s the changes were largely confined to landscape features, whereas in works from the 1870s he relocated or even removed a human figure.

This technical study included examination with infrared reflectography and X-radiography;[1] many other paintings in the exhibition were inspected in their home institutions. In addition to visual examination, colleagues generously allowed me to review their object files and, in some instances, initiated analysis that has contributed to our understanding of Pissarro's early technique.

Strollers on a Country Road, La Varenne-Saint-Hilaire

1864 (cat. 3)

Although the painting presently displays an even surface (fig. 1), the pervasive crackle in the sky and the generally solid, dense feeling prompted conservators to make an X-radiograph, which clearly shows the slender poplars to the right, the path, buildings, and figures at center, and the pattern of palette knife strokes in the sky. If turned on its side, the X-radiograph (fig. 2) reveals a farmyard scene where, at left, a female figure with hands at waist level stands in front of two very large buildings, one with a chimney. She

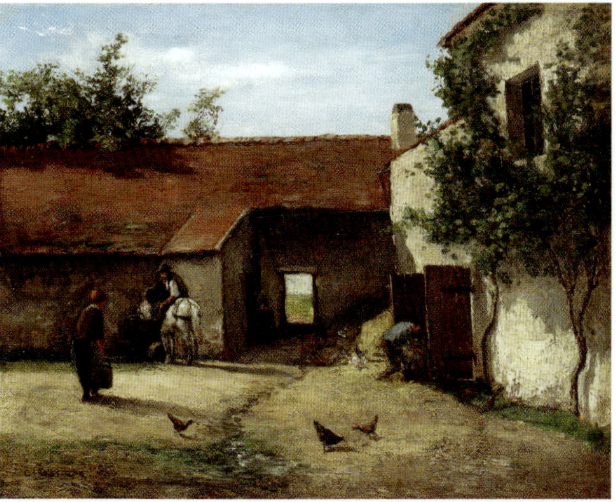

Fig. 3

is turned slightly and is presumably observing animals, perhaps cows, on the right side of the painting. Behind the animals, a tree with graceful branches can be discerned. Examination of the edges of the painting, where loss occurred in the past, confirms the supposition that the initial painting was a horizontal landscape. Considering the orientation of the underlying painting, it is likely that the traces of dark green paint present in the lower right corner are remnants of foliage in the foreground, that the dark green pigment in the upper right corner may be from the large, full tree behind the animals, and that traces of blue paint in the upper left corner originated in the sky. Indeed, by looking into cracks in the upper left corner with a stereomicroscope, it is possible to see sky blue in the layer structure. Through the fully finished visible composition, enough detail of the lower painting can be discerned to invite comparison with *Farmyard* (fig. 3), which was painted a year earlier.[2] It may be that Pissarro abandoned his initial composition, which appears fairly developed, because he decided the size of the female figure in the foreground was disproportionate relative to the building behind her. Dissatisfied with this attempt, Pissarro covered the initial composition with a lead white priming before painting the visible picture.

Banks of the Marne in Winter

1866 (cat. 5)

Banks of the Marne in Winter was Pissarro's submission to the Salon of 1866 (fig. 4). The painting is carefully organized to include a distinct foreground with fields, a middle ground featuring a broad, sloping hillside covered with leafless trees, and a wide, cold sky, all within the framework of diagonals. The thickly applied paint presents an uneven texture, which results in part from a vigorous technique but also from artist's changes.

Fig. 4. *Banks of the Marne in Winter*

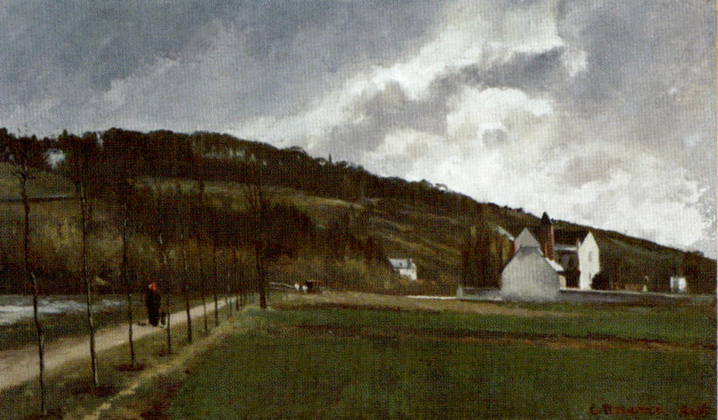

Fig. 4

Easily visible in the X-radiograph (fig. 5)[3] is a large, full tree that extends far above the hillside, occupying much of the upper left corner. Although Pissarro painted the tree with a brush and then covered it with thick paint applied with a palette knife, the presence of the tree remains as a textural irregularity. By painting out the tree and thus opening up the space, Pissarro achieved a greater sense of bleakness. He also adjusted the horizon line by covering low, rolling hills in the left middle ground with the tall wooded hillside that is now visible. It is uncertain whether these changes relate to the large, painted-out tree or to the current composition. These alterations have been made within the horizontal format of the visible image, but if the X-radiograph is rotated onto its left side, the shape of a cow can be discerned. It is not clear whether the thickly painted diagonal line under the cow forms a hill that the animal stands on, or if it is a tree in the present image that has been altered.

Fig. 5. The X-radiograph of *Banks of the Marne in Winter*, in which the artist has painted over a large, full tree (A). The original horizon line (B) is visible at left. If the X-radiograph is turned onto its left side, the shape of a cow (C) can be seen.

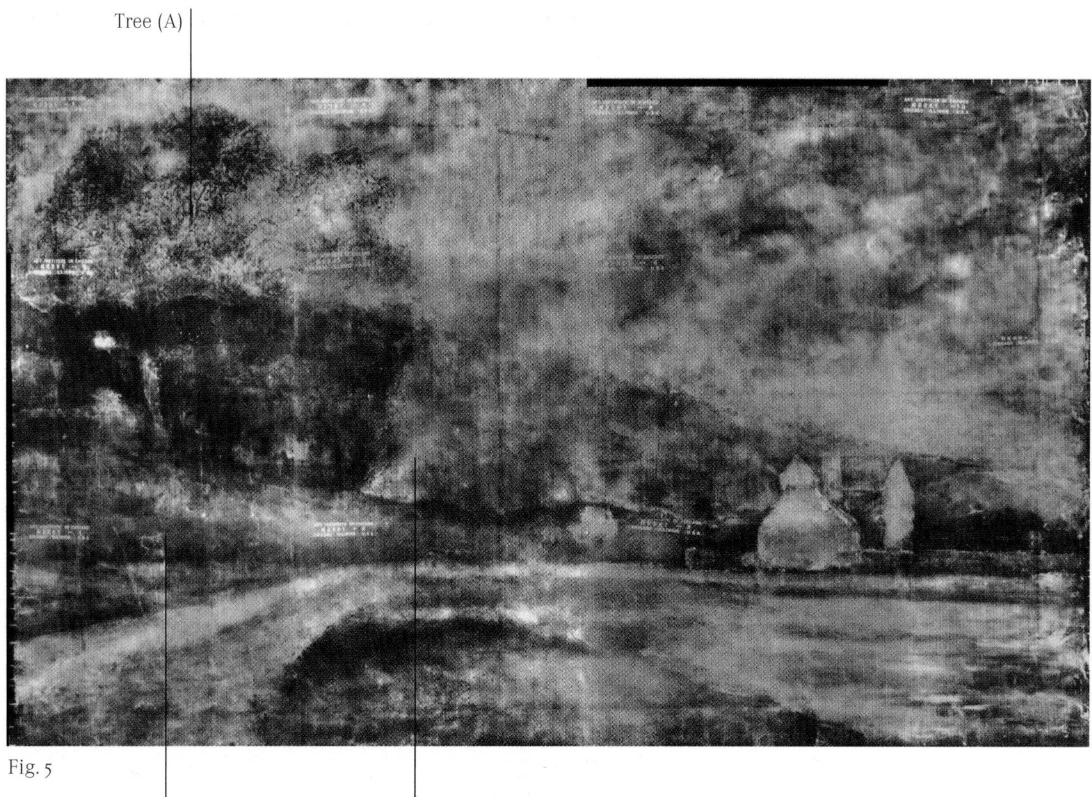

Fig. 5

L'Hermitage at Pontoise

1867

Fig. 6. Camille Pissarro, *L'Hermitage at Pontoise*, 1867 (PD-RS 119). Oil on canvas, 35 7/8 × 19 in. (91 × 50.5 cm) Wallraf-Richartz-Museum, Fond. Corboud, Cologne, Germany, WRM 3119

Note: Due to its condition, this work was unfortunately not able to be included in the present exhibition. However, conservators at the Wallraf-Richartz-Museum generously offered to X-ray and analyze the work for inclusion in this study.

This lushly painted landscape from the artist's Jalais Hill series portrays a rural scene with villagers tending vegetables in the foreground and buildings in front of cultivated hills in the middle ground. A vigorously painted sky occupies the upper horizontal half of the painting (fig. 6). Compositional similarities between this painting and *Landscape near Pontoise*, Charles-François Daubigny's depiction of the scene completed the previous year, reflect the older artist's influence.[4] It has long been known that Pissarro reused a canvas when painting *L'Hermitage at Pontoise*. Indeed, close inspection shows old damages in the paint below the exceptionally thick, opaque, upper paint layer.[5] Recent examination with infrared light does not show an underdrawing, but X-radiography revealed substantial changes. Because the painting has been lined and highly absorbent paint was used by the artist, it is difficult to identify motifs in the upper two-thirds of the composition. In the lower left quadrant of the painting, however, the X-radiograph (fig. 7) reveals a segment of a structure closely resembling the bridge of Pontoise in *The Chemin de l'Écluse and the Pontoise Bridge* painted in 1867 (fig. 8). Three vertical lines in the middle of the sky may be the outlines of chimneys or the poplar trees Pissarro frequently painted. Other changes include altering the horizon line so that it presently is a little lower and more level than its original orientation, which tapered slightly from left to right. The X-radiograph also

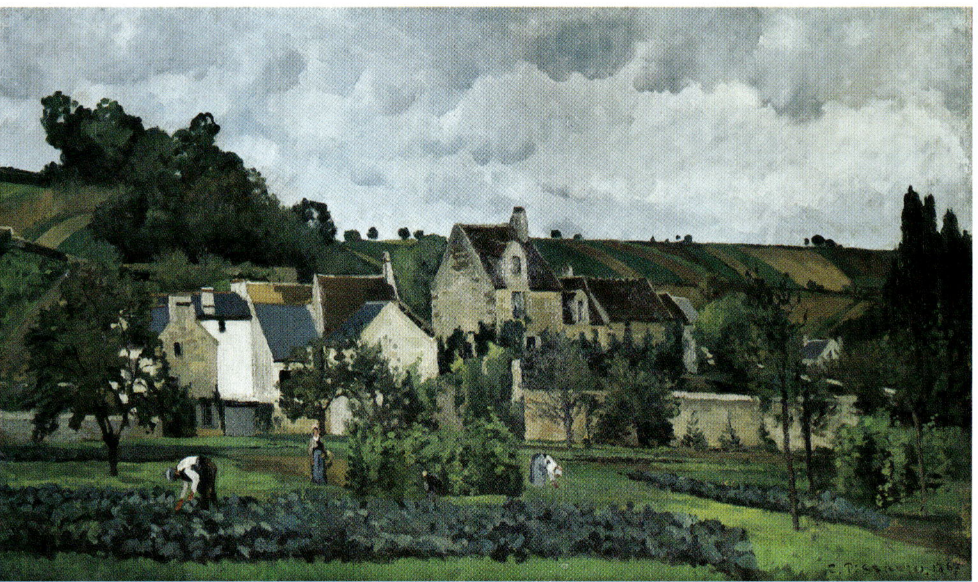

Fig. 6

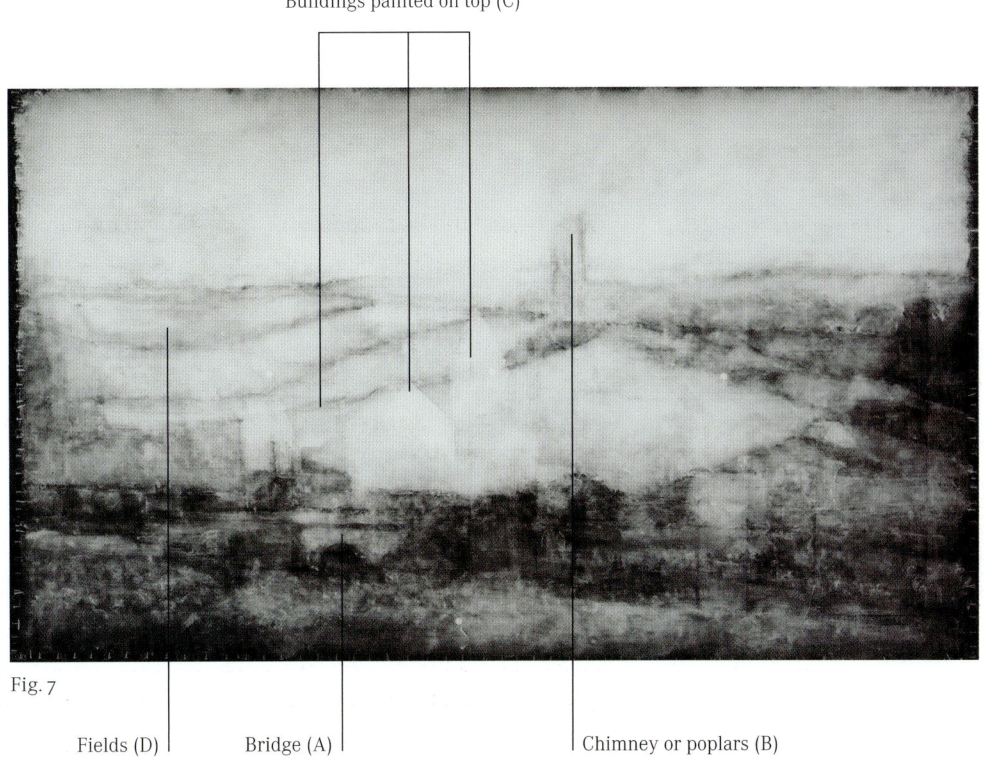

Fig. 7

Fig. 7. In the lower left quadrant of this X-radiograph of *L'Hermitage at Pontoise*, the image of a bridge (A) is clearly visible. It is very similar to the bridge in *The Chemin de L'Écluse and the Pontoise Bridge* (cat. 9), a work in which a factory is located near the center. The vertical lines (B) at the center of the X-radiograph may be chimneys of a factory, or perhaps poplar trees. The shape of the buildings in the visible image (C) are pale in comparison to what appear to be the outlines of the cultivated fields (D). This suggests that the paint used for the structures contains lead white pigment, and that they cover a greater portion of the landscape than appears in the visible image.

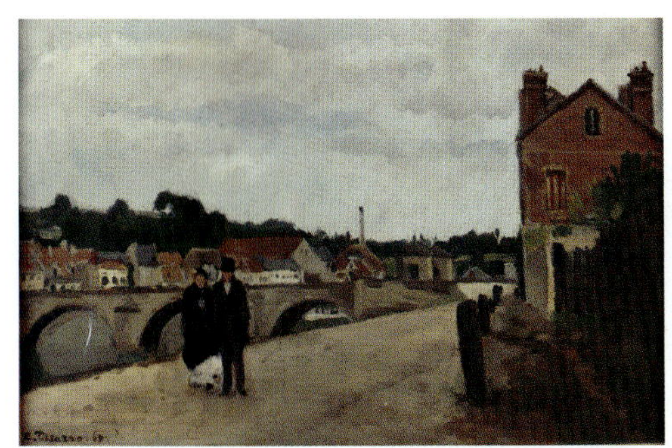

Fig. 8

Fig. 8. *The Chemin de l'Écluse and the Pontoise Bridge* (cat. 9)

suggests that Pissarro used more than one type of white paint when producing this painting. Lead being a strong absorber of X-rays, it does not permit exposure of radiographic film; consequently, areas painted with mixtures including lead tend to appear light in a radiograph. The variability of the absorbance observed in this painting suggests that in addition to lead white, Pissarro may have used commercially prepared paints that included barium or zinc. Analysis of *Strollers on a Country Road, La Varenne-Saint-Hilaire* has indicated that small quantities of barium were mixed into the lead white paint, presumably by the manufacturer, not by the artist.

The Corner of the Route de Versailles and the Chemin de l'Aqueduc, Louveciennes c. 1869 (cat. 12)

Although revisions in *The Corner of the Route de Versailles and the Chemin de l'Aqueduc, Louveciennes* are less extensive, it appears that Pissarro also modified portions of this painting during his working process. In this painting (fig. 9), which focuses on villagers and a carriage at the intersection of two roads following a snowstorm, the sky is painted with bold, energetic brushstrokes over a dark blue foundation. The X-radiograph (fig. 10) clearly shows light forms representing buildings, snowy paths, and figures. In addition, it indicates that one large, substantial tree, extending to the top edge of the canvas, was painted below the group of slender trees on the street corner at right. Its size and structure suggest placement in the middle ground of a painting; it certainly is unlike the rather slender trees Pissarro customarily painted. When viewing the painting in natural light, the position of the initial tree can be observed in the sky above the slender, visible trees. Because that area was covered with paint twice—once by the tree and once by pale blue and pink brushstrokes of the visible sky—the dark blue paint initially laid in as a foundation is completely covered and the area above the initial tree is white. Elsewhere in the X-radiograph, an ambiguous form can be seen to the left of the tree. Since the form is compromised by lead white strokes used to construct the horses in the visible image, the shape cannot be precisely identified, but it may be composed of traces of a figure looking to the left. Pissarro abandons the palette knife sometime in the mid-to-late 1860s, and, indicative of this shift in tools, *The Corner of the Route de Versailles and the Chemin de l'Aqueduc, Louveciennes* is painted entirely with the brush. Pissarro paints the sky, in particular, with well-defined, swirling brushstrokes that create a very lively, active feeling that is captured in the X-radiograph. A weave pattern of the support fabric can be seen as well. Since the painting has been lined, it is not possible

Fig. 9. *The Corner of the Route de Versailles and the Chemin de l'Aqueduc, Louveciennes*

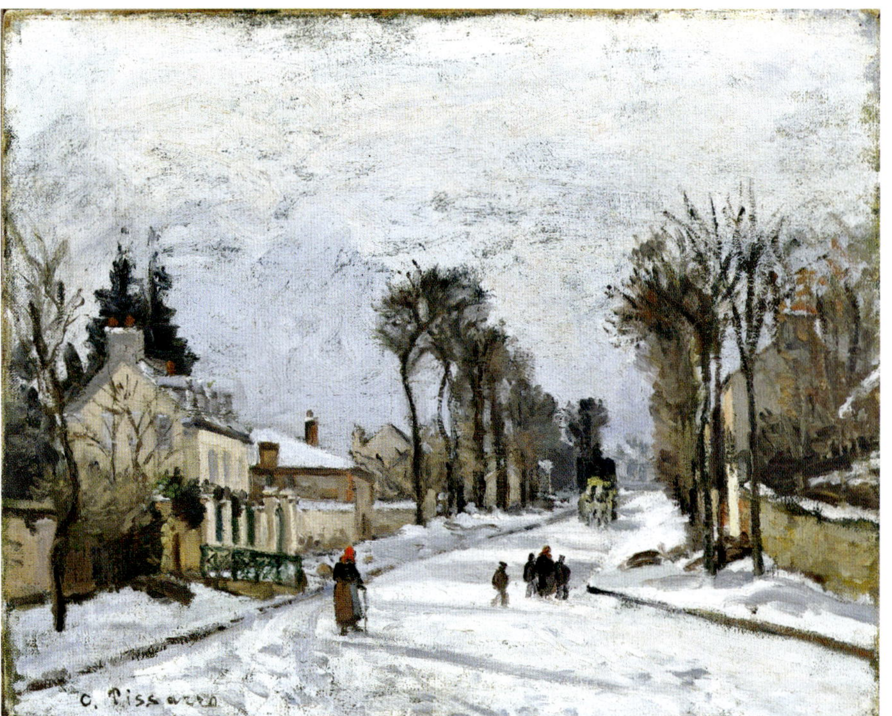

Fig. 9

Fig. 10. The X-radiograph of *The Corner of the Route de Versailles and the Chemin de l'Aqueduc, Louveciennes*, showing the substantial tree (A) and traces of a figure (B).

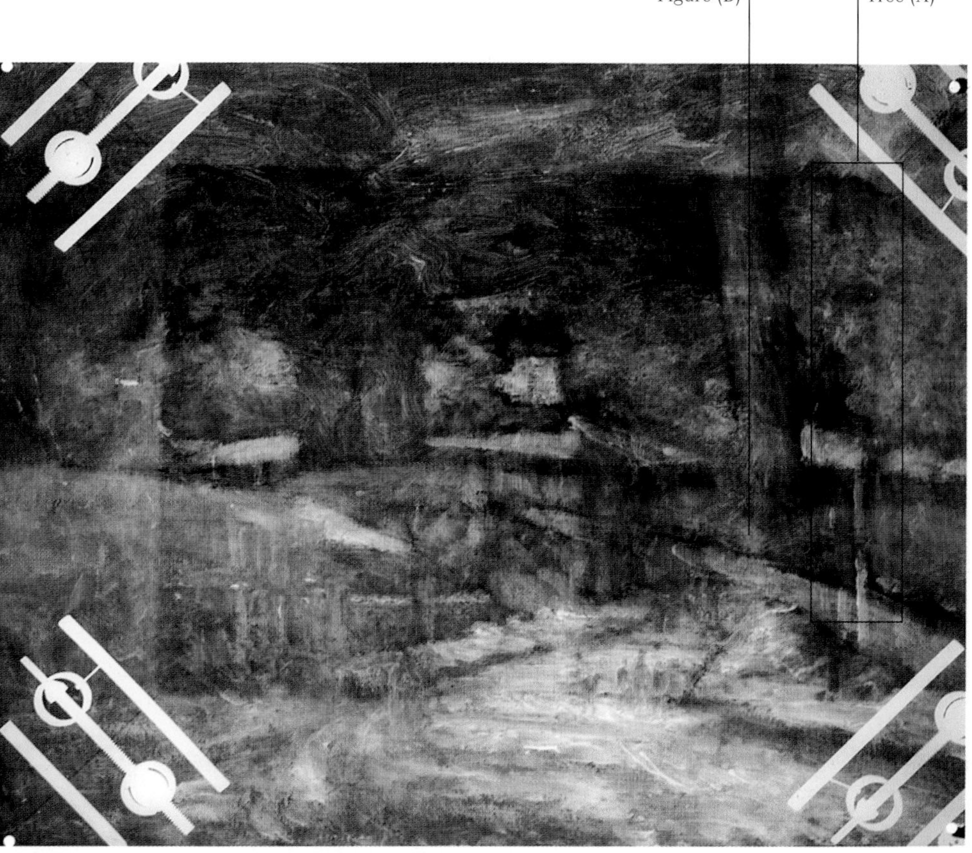

Fig. 10

to see the original fabric, but according to conservation notes,[6] it was painted on "very open weave fabric, like gauze," and a canvas maker's stamp indicates that it was manufactured by Deforge Carpentiers, a firm in Paris. It is possible that this is the *étude* canvas offered by supply catalogues of the period, which was an inferior-quality canvas meant for informal or student work. That *étude* fabric might have been used for the first atmospheric painting Pissarro produced outdoors with Monet suggests that they were experimenting or that they considered the paintings they made that day to be informal studies.[7]

Conclusion

Study of X-radiographs taken of many paintings included in this exhibition indicates that Pissarro frequently altered elements of the composition as part of his working process. In addition to these confirmed changes, a strikingly large number of conservation reports mention odd topographies that do not correspond to the visible image or paintings that display extensive cracking in their heavy paint layers. Conservation documentation regarding some of the works included in this exhibition frequently mentions attempts at X-radiography that were unsuccessful because the lead white ground layer was so thick, for example, *Banks of the Marne at Chennevières* (cat. 4), in which irregular brushwork suggests a change in the contours of the hilltop at right, and a painted underlayer can be seen through scattered losses. By contrast, a perfect correlation exists between the visible image of *Banks of the Oise at Saint-Ouen-l'Aumône* of 1867 (cat. 8) and the recently taken X-radiograph, indicating that Pissarro completed the work without making alterations. Such assurance likely results from having sketched the same scene.[8] Because he had mentally resolved compositional issues that emerged in the process of drawing, Pissarro was able to paint directly and without modifications. Perhaps, then, the changes discussed in these technical notes illustrate that, when not guided by preliminary sketches or underdrawings, Pissarro's working method resulted in an unusually large number of changes. His strained financial situation no doubt contributed to the economy of reusing an already painted canvas on several occasions.

1. All four paintings discussed here were examined with both infrared reflectography, a technique that uses light in the infrared frequency to detect underdrawings and artists' changes in the upper layers of a painting, and with X-radiography, in which the more penetrating X-rays reveal such conditions as aberrations in the fabric or panel support, adjustments to the ground layer, and concealed losses of paint as well as artists' changes.

The investigation of *Strollers on a Country Road, La Varenne-Saint-Hilaire,* in the collection of The Baltimore Museum of Art (cat. 3), was the most thorough. In addition to dispersed pigment analysis with the optical microscope, X-ray fluorescence spectrometry was performed on the paint layer by Jia-sun Tsang and colleagues at the Smithsonian Center for Materials Research and Education, and infrared microspectroscopy, also known as FTIR, was performed on select samples by Orion Analytical, Williamstown, Massachusetts. Radiography and infrared reflectography were performed at the Walters Art Museum with the assistance of Eric Gordon and the approval of Terry Drayman-Weisser.

2. The farmyard scene revealed in the X-ray is also similar to Pissarro's composition of *Village Scene, Women Chatting,* 1863 (PD-RS 70), oil on canvas, private collection.

3. The author gratefully acknowledges the assistance and technical observations of Julie Simek and Frank Zuccari at the Art Institute of Chicago.

4. Charles-François Daubigny, *Landscape near Pontoise,* 1866, oil on canvas, Kunsthalle, Bremen, 700-1955/20.

5. Anthea Callen, *Techniques of the Impressionists* (Secaucus, N.J.: Chartwell Books, 1982). Callen devotes several pages to a discussion of this painting, noting that Pissarro used a herringbone twill fabric and that the painting was executed over a previous painting. Recent X-radiography by conservators at the Wallraf-Richartz-Museum has confirmed Callen's visual observations. The author gratefully acknowledges the technical and historical observations of Iris Schaefer, Carolina V. Saint-George, and Katja Lewerentz regarding this painting.

6. Eric Gordon, Senior Conservator of Paintings at the Walters Art Museum, kindly allowed us access to its conservation object files.

7. See cat. 12 for more detail.

8. See cat. 8, fig. 1 for an illustration of the drawing.

Chronology

This chronology focuses on the years 1864–74, the period examined in this exhibition.

July 10, 1830 Camille Pissarro is born in Charlotte Amalie, capital of the Carribean Island of St. Thomas, then belonging to Denmark, since 1917 part of the U.S. Virgin Islands.

1842–47 Attends boarding school near Paris and takes his first drawing lessons. In 1847, after graduating, he returns to St. Thomas and starts working in the family business of haberdashery and the dry-goods trade.

1850 Travels with the Danish painter Fritz Melbye (1826–1896) to the Dominican Republic and Haiti in search of interesting motifs.

1852–54 Moves to Caracas, Venezuela, and sets up a studio with Melbye.

1855–57 Moves to France and briefly attends private classes given by the École des Beaux-Arts teachers François-Édouard Picot (1786–1868), Isidore Dagnan (1794–1873), and Henri Lehmann (1814–1882).
At the 1855 Paris Universal Exposition he has the chance to see works by Camille Corot (1796–1875) and Eugène Delacroix (1798–1863), as well as the Pavilion of Realism, where Gustave Courbet's (1819–1877) *The Painter's Studio—A Real Allegory* is on view.
In 1857 he meets Corot, who encourages him to paint outdoors.

1858 Pissarro sets up his studio in Paris and socializes in avant-garde artistic and political circles, meeting Courbet and the anarchist philosopher Pierre-Joseph Proudhon (1809–1865).

1859 Pissarro submits his first painting to the annual Salon, *Landscape at Montmorency* (recently identified as *Donkey in Front of a Farm, Montmorency*).

1860 Meets Claude Monet (1840–1926) at the Académie Suisse in Paris, which he attends to draw from live models. Meets the painter Ludovic Piette (1826–1877), who shares his radical political views.
Starts a liaison with his future wife, Julie Vellay (1838–1926), against his family's religious tradition and middle-class social values.

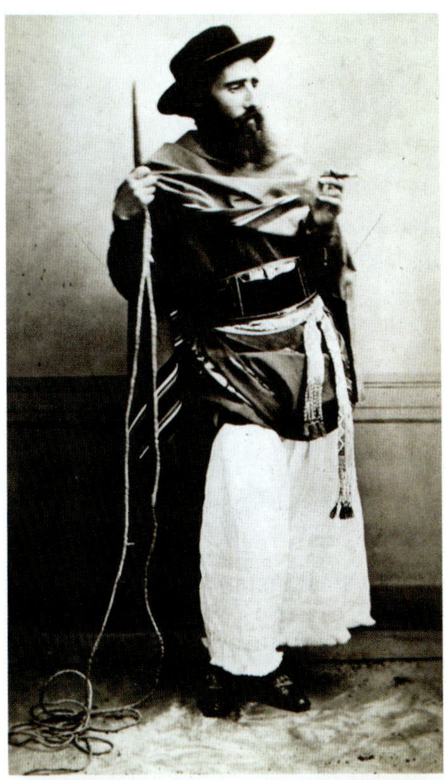

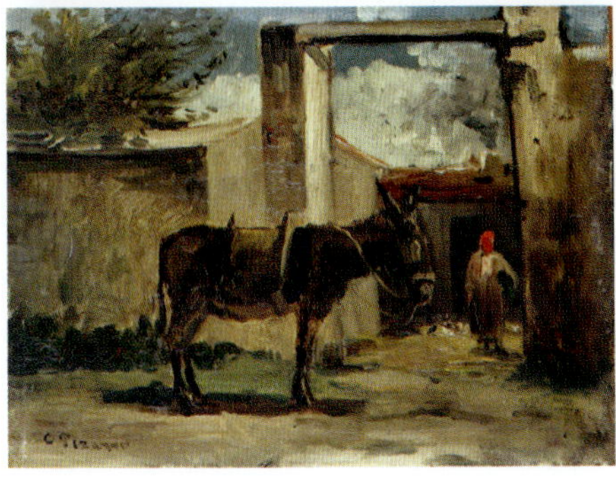

Fig. 1. *Pissarro in an Argentinian Gaucho Costume*, c. 1855. Photograph. Musée Pissarro Archives, Pontoise

Fig. 2. Camille Pissarro, *Donkey in Front of a Farm, Montmorency*, c. 1858 (PD-RS 37). Oil on canvas. Musée d'Orsay, Paris, France, R.F. 1943-38. This work was the first painting by the artist accepted into the annual Salon.

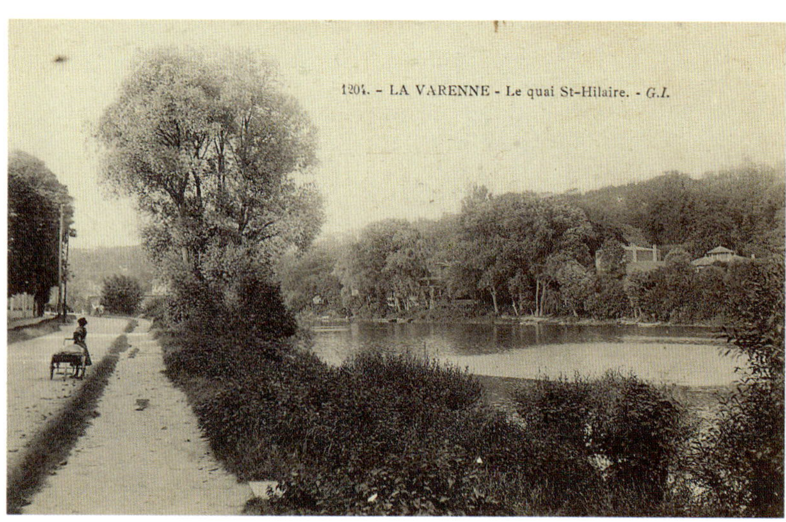

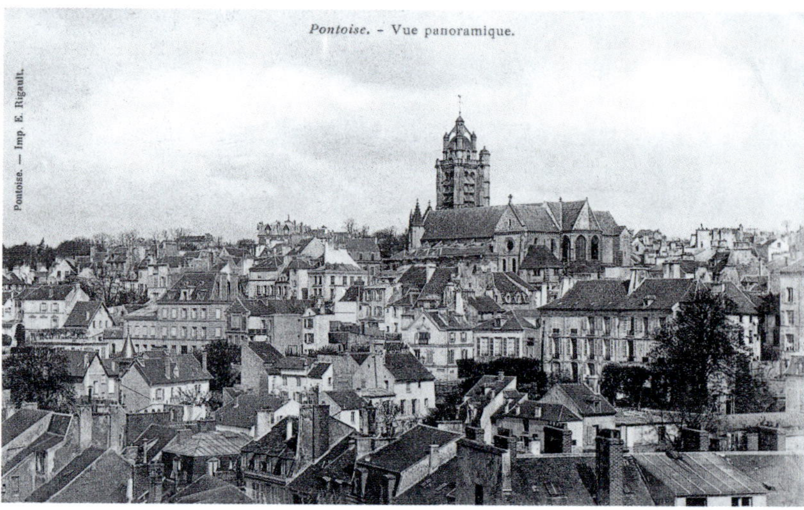

Fig. 3. *La Varenne—le quai St.-Hilaire.* Vintage postcard. Collection of Terence Maloon

Fig. 4. *Pontoise—Panoramic View.* Vintage postcard. Musée Pissarro Archives, Pontoise

1861 Registers at the Louvre as a copyist on April 16.
He meets Paul Cézanne (1839–1906) at the Académie Suisse.

1863 Moves with Julie and their son Lucien to the countryside, La Varenne-Saint-Hilaire, on the banks of the Marne River, for the summer. He paints semirural and rural motifs.
Exhibits three works at the Salon des Refusés. Édouard Manet's *Le Déjeuner sur l'herbe* causes a scandal and establishes the artist as the leader of the avant-garde. Pissarro joins the Société des Aquafortistes and produces his first prints.

1864 Exhibits two works at the official Salon, *La Route de Cachalas at La Roche-Guyon* (lost) and *Banks of the Marne.* He is described as a pupil of Corot and Anton Melbye (1818–1875) in the Salon *livret.*

1865 Exhibits *Banks of the Marne at Chennevières* (cat. 4) in the Salon of that year.
Paints with Antoine Guillemet (1843–1918) at La Roche-Guyon.
Attends the gatherings of the painters of the "new school" and the critics who defend them, such as Émile Zola (1840–1902), Louis-Edmond Duranty (1833–1880), and Philippe Burty (1830–1890), at the Café Guerbois in the Batignolles district of Paris.
Pissarro's father dies.

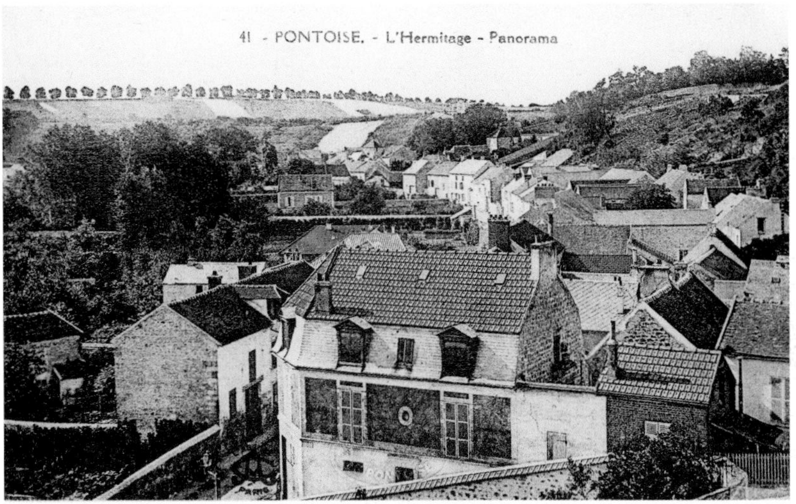

Fig. 5. *Pontoise—L'Hermitage—Panoramic View.* Vintage postcard. Musée Pissarro Archives, Pontoise

1866 Attends Thursday meetings at Zola's house in Paris. Pissarro frequently visits Frédéric Bazille's (1841–1870) studio with Monet, Pierre-Auguste Renoir (1841–1919), and Alfred Sisley (1839–1899). Meets Édouard Manet (1832–1883). Split with Corot, presumably over Pissarro's change in painting style.
The Pissarro family moves to L'Hermitage, a small hamlet located in Pontoise.
With Charles-François Daubigny's (1817–1878) mediation, one oil painting by Pissarro, *Banks of the Marne in Winter* (cat. 5), is accepted by the Salon jury. This is his first critical success at a Salon exhibition.
The art critics Zola and Jean Rousseau praise Pissarro's work for its sincerity. Cézanne's and Renoir's entries are rejected.

1867 Paints several large landscapes of the hamlet of L'Hermitage in Pontoise. Pissarro's and his friends' entries for the Salon and Paris Universal Exposition are rejected. Monet, Bazille, and their friends make plans to rent Courbet's personal exhibition space. This project will be realized in a transformed way in 1874.

1868 The Salon jury accepts two of his paintings from the Jalais Hill series (cat. 10). Favorable reviews by Zola in *L'Événement illustré* and by Odilon Redon (1840–1916) in *La Gironde.*
Participates in the Exposition Maritime Internationale at Le Havre.

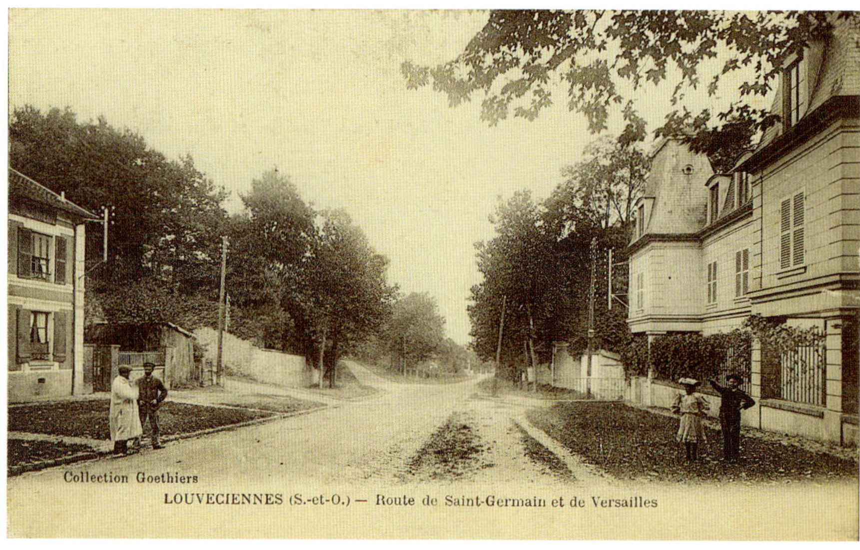

Fig. 6. *Louveciennes—Route de Saint-Germain et de Versailles.* Vintage postcard. Collection of Terence Maloon

1869 Moves to Louveciennes, a suburb of Paris. Monet and Renoir live nearby. Exhibits one landscape from the Jalais Hill series at the Salon. Paints *en plein air* with Monet, experimenting with colored shadows and the reflection of light after a heavy snowstorm.

1870 Exhibits two works at the Salon. The Franco-Prussian War is declared on July 19. The Pissarro family flees to England in December. Pissarro and Monet, who has also taken refuge in England, visit museums together and familiarize themselves with the the works of Romantic artists John Constable (1776–1837) and Joseph Mallord William Turner (1775–1851). They meet the art dealer Paul Durand-Ruel through Daubigny.

1871 Pissarro exhibits two works at Durand-Ruel's London gallery on New Bond Street. Two snow effects by Pissarro and several works by Monet are exhibited at the *First Annual International Exhibition* in London, South Kensington. Pissarro produces fourteen oil paintings during his stay in London. The French government surrenders on January 28, and the Frankfurt Peace Treaty is signed on May 10. Workers and National Guards rebel against the outcome of the war and the current French government, establishing the Paris Commune.

Fig. 7. Cézanne in the center, Pissarro standing on the right with two Cuban friends, Quinonez and Alfonso, c. 1873. Photograph. Musée Pissarro Archives, Pontoise

Fig. 8. Pissarro, c. 1873. Photograph. Musée Pissarro Archives, Pontoise

A rebellious socialist government rules Paris from March until May and is eventually suppressed by government forces.
At the end of June, Pissarro and his family return to France, to find their house in Louveciennes wrecked by German soldiers and a substantial part of Pissarro's work of the previous fifteen years destroyed.

1872 Exhibits several works at the *Third Exhibition of the Society of French Artists* (winter) and *Fourth Exhibition of the Society of French Artists* (summer) at the German Gallery in London, organized by Paul Durand-Ruel.
Durand-Ruel begins to buy Pissarro's work on a regular basis.
The family moves back to Pontoise, where the artist works closely with Cézanne, who lives in the nearby Auvers-sur-Oise until early 1874.

1873 Pissarro, Cézanne, and Armand Guillaumin (1841–1927) produce etchings at the suggestion of Dr. Paul Gachet (1828–1909), who is also an engraver working under the pseudonym Van Ryssel. Gachet establishes an etching studio at his house in Auvers.
Pissarro exhibits several paintings at *Sixth Exhibition of the Society of*

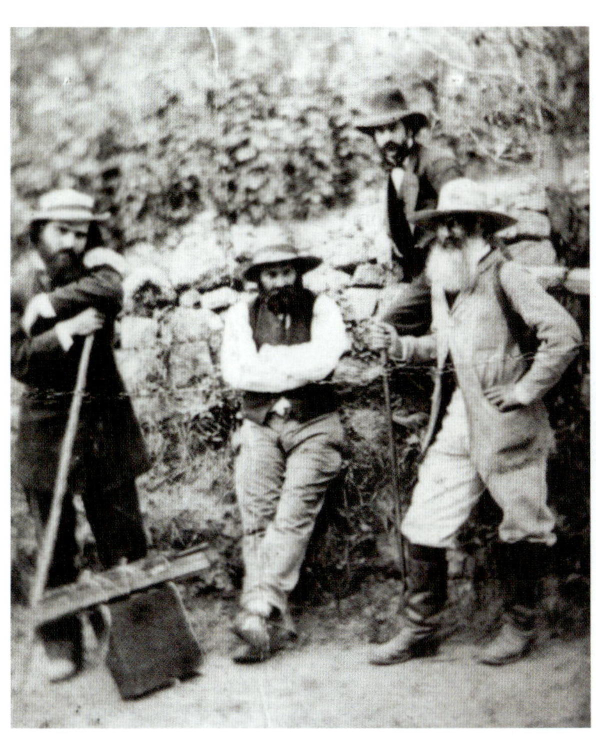

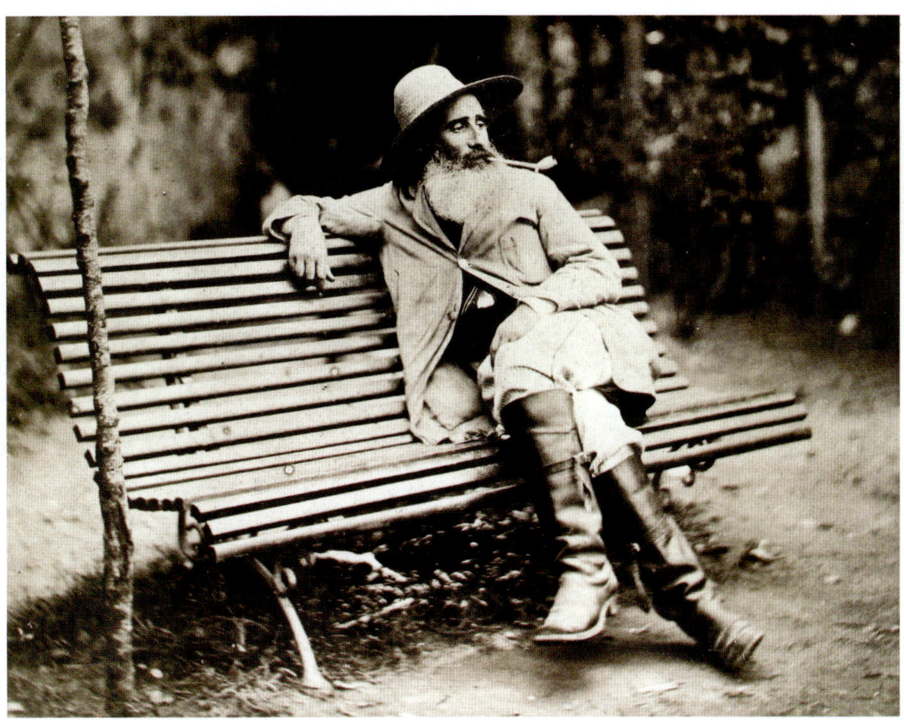

French Artists (winter) and *Seventh Exhibition of the Society of French Artists* (summer) at the German Gallery, London, organized by Durand-Ruel. Pissarro and Monet start organizing an exhibition that will become the first Impressionist exhibition.

1874 The art collection of Ernest Hoschedé is auctioned at the Hôtel Drouot, and Pissarro's works sell for record amounts.
The Société anonyme des artistes peintres, sculpteurs, graveurs etc. opens its first exhibition at the studio of the photographer Félix Nadar (1820–1910) with works by thirty-nine artists and runs between April 15 and May 15. Pissarro exhibits five landscapes (among them cats. 27, 42, and 43). Satirically named "Impressionists" by a reviewer of the exhibition, the artists adopt this label. The sale is a financial failure.
Pissarro exhibits at the Eighth and Ninth Exhibitions in Durand-Ruel's London gallery, the German Gallery.
Visits his friend Ludovic Piette at Montfoucault, where the artist completes about twenty paintings, including some of his earliest paintings of peasants.

1875–1903 Pissarro continued to paint for close to thirty more years, exploring many new themes and techniques in his pursuit of artistic expression. He died in Paris on November 13, 1903.

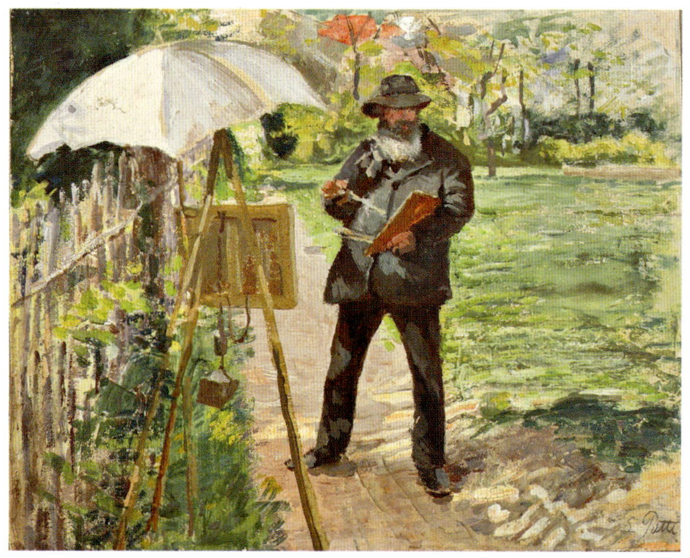

Fig. 9. Ludovic Piette, *Pissarro Painting Outside*, 1874–76. Oil on canvas. Private collection, Paris

Bibliography

Adams, Steven. *The Barbizon School and the Origins of Impressionism.* London: Phaidon Press, 1994.

Adler, Kathleen. *Camille Pissarro: A Biography.* London: B. T. Batsford, 1978.

———. *Pissarro in London.* London: National Gallery, 2003.

Art in Theory, 1815–1900: An Anthology of Changing Ideas. Edited by Charles Harrison and Paul Wood. Oxford: Blackwell Publishing, 1998.

Art in Latin America: The Modern Era, 1820–1980. Edited by Dawn Ades. New Haven: Yale University Press, 1989.

Astruc, Z. *Les 14 Stations du Salon.* Paris: Poulet-Malassis et de Broise, 1859.

Barron, Louis. *Les Environs de Paris.* Paris, 1886.

———. *Les Fleuves de Paris: La Seine.* Paris, 1889.

Baudelaire, Charles. *Oeuvres complètes.* 2 vols. Paris: Gallimard, La Pléiade, 1975–76.

Becker, Christoph. *Camille Pissarro.* Stuttgart: Staatsgalerie Stuttgart, 1999.

Benisovich, M., and J. Dallett. "Camille Pissarro and Fritz Melbye in Venezuela." *Apollo* 84 (July 1966): 44–47.

Berson, Ruth, ed. *The New Painting: Impressionism, 1874–1886; Documentation.* 2 vols. San Francisco: Fine Arts Museums of San Francisco, 1996.

Boime, Albert. *The Academy and French Painting in the Nineteenth Century.* London: Phaidon, 1971.

Bomford, David, et al. *Art in the Making: Impressionism.* London: National Gallery, 1990.

Boulton, Alfredo. *Camille Pissarro en Venezuela.* Caracas: Editorial Arte, 1966.

Brettell, Richard R. "Pissarro and Pontoise: Painter in a Landscape." Ph.D. diss., Yale University, 1977.

———. *Pissarro and Pontoise: The Painter in a Landscape.* New Haven: Yale University Press, 1990.

———. *Impression: Painting Quickly in France, 1860–1890.* New Haven: Yale University Press, 2000.

Brettell, Richard R., and Christopher Lloyd. *A Catalogue of the Drawings by Camille Pissarro at the Ashmolean Museum, Oxford.* Oxford: Oxford University Press, 1980.

Brettell, Richard R., and Joachim Pissarro. *The Impressionist and the City: Pissarro's Series Paintings.* New Haven: Yale University Press, 1992.

Brettell, Richard R., and Karen Zubowski. *Camille Pissarro in the Caribbean, 1850–1855: Drawings from the Collection at Olana.* St. Thomas: Lilienfeld House; New York: The Jewish Museum, 1996.

Brettell, Richard R., et al. *A Day in the Country: Impressionism and the French Landscape.* Los Angeles: Los Angeles County Museum of Art, 1984.

Callen, Anthea. *The Art of Impressionism: Painting Technique and the Making of Modernity.* New Haven: Yale University Press, 2000.

Camille Pissarro. Ferrara: Ferrara arte, 1998.

Camille Pissarro, 1830–1903. London: Arts Council of Great Britain, 1980.

Campbell, Christopher. "Pissarro and the Palette Knife: Two Pictures from 1867." *Apollo* 136 (November 1992): 311–14.

Castagnary, Jules-Antoine. *Salons (1857–1870).*

2 vols. Paris: Charpentier-Fasqeulle, 1892.

Champa, Kermit Swiler. *Studies in Early Impressionism.* New Haven: Yale University Press, 1973.

———. *The Rise of Landscape Painting in France: Corot to Monet.* Manchester, N.H.: The Currier Gallery of Art, 1991.

Clark, T. J. *The Painting of Modern Life: Paris in the Art of Manet and His Followers.* Princeton, N.J.: Princeton University Press, 1999.

Conversations avec Cézanne. Edited by P. Michael Doran. Angers: Collection Macula, 1968. English edition with the same title was published by the University of California Press in 2001.

Delteil, Loys. *Le peintre-graveur illustré.* Vol. 17, *Pissarro, Renoir, Sisley.* Paris: chez l'auteur, 1923.

DeLue, Rachael Ziady. "Pissarro, Landscape, Vision, and Tradition." *Art Bulletin* 80 (December 1998): 718–36.

Dewhurst, Wynford. *Impressionist Painting: Its Genesis and Development.* London: George Newnes, 1904.

The Diary of George A. Lucas: An American Agent in Paris, 1857–1909. Edited by Lillian M. Randall. 2 vols. Princeton, N.J.: Princeton University Press, 1979.

Eves, C. W. *The West Indies.* London: Sampson Low & Co., 1889.

Fénéon, Félix. *Oeuvres plus que complètes.* Edited by Joan U. Halperin. Geneva: Librairie Droz, 1970.

Frankiss, Charles C. "Camille Pissarro, Théodore Duret and Jules Berthel in London in 1871." *Burlington Magazine* 146 (2004): 470–72.

Herbert, Robert L. *Impressionism: Art, Leisure, and Parisian Society.* New Haven: Yale University Press, 1988.

House, John. "New Material on Monet and Pissarro in London in 1870–1." *Burlington Magazine* 120, no. 907 (1978): 636–39, 641–42.

von Humboldt, Alexander. *Personal Narrative of Travels to the Equinoctial Regions of the New Continent during the Years 1799–1804. . . .* Translated by M. Williams. Vol. 3. London: Longman, Hurst, Rees, Orme and Brown, John Murray, H. Colburn, 1818.

Impressionism in Perspective. Edited by Barbara Ehrlich White. Englewood Cliffs, N.J.: Prentice-Hall, 1978.

Isaacson, Joel. "Constable, Duranty, Mallarmé, Impressionism, Plein Air, and Forgetting." *Art Bulletin* 76, no. 3 (1994): 427–50.

Joets, J. "Camille Pissarro et la période inconnue de St-Thomas et de Caracas." *L'Amour de l'Art* 27 (1947): 91–97.

Kunstler, C. "La Maison d'Eragny," *ABC, Magazine Artistique et Littéraire* 5 (March 1929): 79–83.

Lloyd, Christopher. "Camille Pissarro and Hans Holbein the Younger." *Burlington Magazine* 117, no. 872 (November 1975): 722–26.

———. *Camille Pissarro.* New York: Rizzoli International Publications, 1981.

———. *Retrospective Camille Pissarro.* Tokyo: Art Life Limited, 1984.

———. "Camille Pissarro and the Caribbean." *Horizontes: Revista de la Universidad Catolica de Puerto Rico, Ponce* 28, no. 56 (1985): 23.

———. "The Market Scenes of Camille Pissarro." *Art Bulletin of Victoria, Melbourne,* no. 25 (1985): 17–32.

———. "Reflections on La Roche-Guyon and the Impressionists." *Gazette des Beaux-Arts* (1985): 37–44.

———, ed. *Studies on Camille Pissarro.* London: Routledge and Kegan Paul, 1986.

———. "'Paul Cézanne, Pupil of Pissarro': An Artistic Friendship." *Apollo* 136 (November 1992): 284.

Manet and the French Impressionists: Pissarro–Claude Monet–Sisley–Renoir–Berthe Morisot–Cézanne–Guillaumin. Translated by J. E. Crawford Flitch. Philadelphia: J. B. Lippincott Company; London: Grant Richards, 1910.

Memoirs of Madame Vigée-Lebrun. Translated by Lionel Strachey. London: Grant Richards, 1904.

Moffett, Charles S., et al. *The New Painting: Impressionism, 1874–1886.* San Francisco: The Fine Arts Museums of San Francisco, 1986.

———. *Impressionists on the Seine: A Celebration of Renoir's "Luncheon of the Boating Party."* Washington, D.C.: The Phillips Collection, 1996.

———. *Impressionists in Winter: Effets de Neige.* Washington, D.C.: The Phillips Collection, 1998.

Monet: A Retrospective. Edited by Charles Stuckey. New York: Hugh Lauter Levin Associates, 1985.

Perrucchi-Petri, U. "War Cézanne Impressionist? Die Begegnung zwischen Cézanne und Pissarro." *Du* 35 (September 1975): 50–65.

Piette, Ludovic. *Mon cher Pissarro: Lettres de Ludovic Piette à Camille.* Edited by Janine Bailly-Herzberg. Paris: Éditions du Valhermeil et Association les Amis de Camille Pissarro, 1985.

Pissarro in England: A Loan Exhibition of Works by Camille Pissarro (1830–1903) Drawn from Public and Private Collections in England and Scotland in Aid of the Save the Children Fund, and Children and Youth Aliyah. London: Marlborough Fine Art, 1968.

Pissarro in Venezuela: Works in Venezuelan Collections of Camille Pissarro's Venezuelan "Oeuvre" (1852–1854). Caracas: Editorial Arte, 1997.

Pissarro, Camille. *Correspondance de Camille Pissarro.* Edited by Janine Bailly-Herzberg. 5 vols. Paris: Presses Universitaires de France, 1980–91.

———. *Camille Pissarro: Letters to His Son Lucien.* Edited by John Rewald. New York: Pantheon Books, 1943.

Pissarro, Joachim. *Camille Pissarro.* New York: Harry N. Abrams, 1993.

———. *Pioneering Modern Painting: Cézanne and Pissarro, 1865–1885.* New York: The Museum of Modern Art, 2005.

Pissarro, Joachim, and Claire Durand-Ruel Snollaerts. *Pissarro: Critical Catalogue of Paintings.* 3 vols. Paris: Wildenstein Institute Publications, 2005.

Pissarro, Joachim, and Stephanie Rachum. *Camille Pissarro: Impressionist Innovator.* Jerusalem: The Israel Museum, 1994.

Pissarro, Ludovic Rodolphe. *Camille Pissarro.* Paris: P. Rosenberg, 1939.

Pissarro, Ludovic Rodolphe, and Lionello Venturi. *Camille Pissarro: Son art, son oeuvre.* 2 vols. Paris: P. Rosenberg, 1939.

Ravenel, J. "Salon de 1865." *L'Époque* 1 (June 15, 1865).

Reed, Nicholas. *Camille Pissarro at the Crystal Palace.* 2nd rev. ed. London: Lilburne Press, 1995.

Reff, Theodore. "Pissarro's Portrait of Cézanne." *Burlington Magazine* 109, no. 776 (1967): 626–31, 633.

Reid, Martin. "Camille Pissarro: Three Paintings of London of 1871; What Do They Represent?" *Burlington Magazine* 119, no. 889 (1977): 251–61.

———. "The Pissarro Family in the Norwood Area of London, 1870–1: Where Did They Live?" In *Studies on Camille Pissarro,* edited by Christopher Lloyd, 55–64. London: Routledge and Kegan Paul, 1986.

Rewald, John. "L'Oeuvre de jeunesse de Camille Pissarro." *L'Amour de l'Art* 17 (April 1936): 141–45.

———. "Camille Pissarro: His Work and Influence." *Burlington Magazine for Connoisseurs* 72, no. 423 (1938): 280, 284–86, 288–91.

———. *Cézanne, sa vie, son amitié pour Zola.* Paris: Albin Michel, 1939.

———. "Camille Pissarro in the West Indies." *Gazette des Beaux-Arts,* 6th ser., 22 (October 1942): 57–60.

———. *The History of Impressionism.* 4th rev. ed. New York: The Museum of Modern Art, 1973.

———. *Camille Pissarro.* New York: Harry N. Abrams, 1963.

———. *Camille Pissarro in Venezuela.* New York: Hammer Galleries, 1964.

———. *The Paintings of Paul Cézanne: A Catalogue Raisonné.* 2 vols. New York: Harry N. Abrams, 1996.

Rousseau, Jean. "Le Salon de 1866, IV." *L'Univers Illustré* 9 (July 1866): 447.

Röver, Anne. *Camille Pissarro: Radierungen, Lithographien, Monotypien aus deutschen und österreichischen Sammlungen; Ausstellung des Kupferstichkabinetts, Kunsthalle Bremen.* Bremen: Die Kunsthalle, 1990.

Saint-Simon at Versailles: Selected and Translated from the Memoirs of M. le Duc de Saint-Simon. Edited and translated by Lucy Norton. London: Hamish Hamilton, 1958.

Shikes, Ralph E., and Paula Harper. *Pissarro: His Life and Work.* New York: Horizon Press, 1980.

Stevens, MaryAnne. *Alfred Sisley.* London: Royal Academy of Arts, 1992.

Thomson, Richard. *Camille Pissarro: Impressionism, Landscape, and Rural Labour.* Birmingham, Eng.: South Bank Centre, 1990.

Tinterow, Gary, and Henri Loyrette. *Origins of Impressionism.* New York: The Metropolitan Museum of Art, 1994.

Tinterow, Gary, Michael Pantazzi, and Vincent Pomarède. *Corot.* New York: The Metropolitan Museum of Art, 1996.

Trollope, Anthony. *The West Indies and the Spanish Main.* London: Chapman and Hall, 1859.

Wildenstein, Daniel. *Claude Monet. Biographie et catalogue raisonné.* 4 vols. Paris: Taschen/Wildenstein Institute, 1996.

Zola, Émile. *Écrits sur l'art.* Edited by Jean-Pierre Leduc-Adine. Paris: Gallimard, collection Tel, 1991.

———. *Le Bon Combat de Courbet aux impressionnistes.* Edited by J.-P. Bouillon. Paris: Hermann, 1974.

———. *Salons.* Edited by F. W. J. Hemmings and R. J. Neiss. Paris: Minard, 1959.

Photographic Credits

 Additional photography credits are as follows:

Musée des Beaux-Arts d'Arras, photo: Thériez, p. 106
Photography © The Art Institute of Chicago, pp. 33, 83, 109
Bildarchiv Preussischer Kulturbesitz / Art Resource, NY, photo: Jörg P. Anders, p. 49
© Sterling and Francine Clark Art Institute, Williamstown, Massachusetts, p. 103
Photo: Dan Dennehy, p. 111
Photo: Ali Elai, p. 141
© The J. Paul Getty Museum, p. 113
The Baltimore Museum of Art, photo: Mitro Hood, pp. 77, 79, 192
Photo © The Israel Museum, Jerusalem / Max Richardson, p. 161
Copyright © 2005 by Kimbell Art Museum, Fort Worth, Texas, p. 127
Courtesy Galerie Koller AG, Zurich, p. 86
Erich Lessing / Art Resource, NY, pp. 72, 160
Photograph Howard Matthew Korn, p. 149
Robert Lifson, p. 179
Photograph © 1982 The Metropolitan Museum of Art, p. 148
Photograph © 1990 The Metropolitan Museum of Art, p. 44
Photograph © 1997 The Metropolitan Museum of Art, p. 93
Photograph © 2001 The Metropolitan Museum of Art, p. 187
Museum of Art, Rhode Island School of Design, photo: Del Bogart, p. 124
Photograph © 2006 Museum of Fine Arts, Boston, pp. 132, 157, 184
© National Gallery, London, pp. 55, 57, 117, 120
© 2005 Board of Trustees, National Gallery of Art, Washington, pp. 105, 139, 163
© 2006 Board of Trustees, National Gallery of Art, Washington, pp. 22, 168
Réunion des Musées Nationaux / Art Resource, NY, photo: Arnaudet, p. 116
Réunion des Musées Nationaux / Art Resource, NY, photo: Hervé Lewandowski, pp. 175, 177, 183, 201
© Sotheby's, private collection, France, p. 126
© Tel Aviv Museum of Art, pp. 87, 91
© Wallraf-Richartz-Museum, Cologne, Rheinisches Bildarchiv, pp. 52, 196
Photograph Courtesy of Wildenstein & Co., New York, p. 88

Index